THE WORLD IN FLAMES

THE SHORTER WRITINGS OF FRANCIS PARKER YOCKEY

The Centennial Edition of Francis Parker Yockey's Works

Greg Johnson, General Editor

Volume One:

IMPERIUM

THE PHILOSOPHY OF HISTORY AND POLITICS

Edited by Greg Johnson

Volume Two:

THE ENEMY OF EUROPE

Edited and Translated by Thomas Francis

Volume Three:

THE WORLD IN FLAMES

THE SHORTER WRITINGS OF

FRANCIS PARKER YOCKEY

Edited by Kerry Bolton and John Morgan

THE WORLD IN FLAMES

THE SHORTER WRITINGS OF FRANCIS PARKER YOCKEY

Edited by
KERRY BOLTON
&
JOHN MORGAN

Centennial Edition Publishing
2020

Cover image: Thomas Cole, *Destruction*, 1836,
from *The Course of Empire* cycle

Cover design by
Kevin I. Slaughter

Limited Hardcover ISBN: 978-1-940933-22-1
Standard Hardcover ISBN: 978-1-940933-23-8
Paperback ISBN: 978-1-940933-24-5
E-book ISBN: 978-1-940933-25-2

Compliments
of
Ulick Varange

Autograph courtesy of Tim Turner

The Centennial Edition is
Dedicated to Willis and Elisabeth Carto
For their work in preserving and propagating
Yockey's legacy.

—Greg Johnson, General Editor

Contents

APPENDICES

INTRODUCTION

KERRY BOLTON

This volume attests to the increasing interest by new generations in the Euro-American thinker, Francis Parker Yockey. It is the first volume to be issued of the three-volume Centennial Edition of the Works of Francis Parker Yockey, published in honor of the 100th anniversary of Yockey's birth on September 18, 1917. The volumes to follow are *Imperium,* Yockey's *magnum opus,* and *The Enemy of Europe,* a geopolitical study written by Yockey particularly for the leadership of the burgeoning post-war Socialist Reich Party in Germany, which the Allied occupation authorities could only stop by jail and prohibition.

This volume, *The World in Flames,* is named after Yockey's final essay. This title was actually suggested by Yockey's American colleague, H. Keith Thompson. Yockey's original title, "An Estimate of the World Situation," remains the subtitle of the essay. It was published posthumously by Thompson and distributed by Yockey's mentor Frederick Weiss, a German First World War veteran whose Spenglerian outlook is hardly distinguishable from Yockey's. The essay was reissued a decade later by Douglas T. Kaye as part of a collection entitled *Yockey: Four Essays,* which also included Yockey's first published political article, "The Tragedy of Youth." This was carried by *Social Justice,* the mass circulation Depression-era newspaper of Father Charles Coughlin, the famous "radio priest," who posed a serious threat to the war-mongering Roosevelt administration.

Also in the collection was "What is Behind the Hanging of the Eleven Jews in Prague?," issued by Yockey in 1952 as an analysis of the purging of Zionists from the Czech Communist Party. Yockey saw this as a definitive break by the Soviet bloc with Jewish influences, at a time when the "Right" dogmatically insisted that Soviet-bloc Communism remained under Jewish domination, and any appearances to the contrary were a cunning plan. This analysis by Yockey resulted in his condemnation by Jew-fixated types such as Arnold Leese and The Britons Society. However, despite their efforts to smear Yockey, his ideas were gaining attention within the Right. Most notable in the United States was the relatively large nationalist newspaper, *Common Sense*. Yockey was also well-received among the best thinkers of the European Right, such as Maurice Bardèche in France and General J. F. C. Fuller in Britain. The third essay, "The Destiny of America," was published in 1955, and finally "The World in Flames," issued in 1961, was given to Douglas Kaye by Fred Weiss' widow.

Kaye was among those most notable for having kept Yockey's ideas alive, and during the 1970s published a particularly lively Yockeyan journal, *TRUD*, the name intended to suggest the approaching march of newborn legions. *TRUD* was a project of both depth and satire, and among its pages was a serialization of Yockey's *The Enemy of Europe*.

While it is well-known that Willis Carto and Noontide Press kept *Imperium* in print, Yockey's ideas were also perpetuated by the National Renaissance Party, *Common Sense*, and *TRUD*. The National Youth Alliance, a Rightist answer to the Establishment/CIA-initiated "New Left," initially directed by Yockeyan zealot Lou Byers, carried the message to campuses and confronted the Left. Yockey would have been delighted by the NYA and by *TRUD*.

Other important Yockey essays were collected by the American, Keith Stimely, in his research for a Yockey biography that was never completed due to Stimely's untimely death. However, the essays, which this writer republished in very limited circulation in 1998 in a photocopied document entitled *Varange: The Life and Thoughts of Francis Parker Yockey*, are reproduced herein: "Life as an Art," "Two Reflections," "Twentieth Century Metaphysics," "Thoughts Upon Waking," "Culture," and "Thoughts Personal and Superpersonal." These essays show the cogent development of Yockey's thought while still in his student days, during which he was already noted in Rightist circles as a speaker with leadership potential.

Of particular importance is the essay "Philosophy of Constitutional Law," written while Yockey was a student at Georgetown University's School of Foreign Service in 1937. This is the earliest known example of Yockey's work and shows that the premises of his ideas were already established as a 19-year-old. This essay was obtained from H. Keith Thompson by Linton Hall and is likely being published in this volume for the first time.

Other material unlikely to have been published previously include Yockey's correspondence with the Canadian Rightist leader Adrien Arcand, and other items sought out on hunches from archives and personal collections. The outcome is a unique anthology that will hopefully contribute much to Yockey studies, tracing the development of Yockey's thinking from his days as a university student of notable brilliance to his tragic death in an American jail cell.

My thanks go to Linton Hall, Douglas Kaye, and the late H. Keith Thompson; my appreciation to the pioneering work of the late Keith Stimely and the valuable corpus of memories imparted to him by Yockey's British colleague, Anthony John Gannon (unfortunately, neither of whom I knew); to Elisabeth Carto, the widow of Willis Carto, for making available from her husband's papers a number of previously unknown documents by and about Yockey; to the editorial work by John Morgan; and to Dr. Greg Johnson of Counter-Currents Publishing, for the idea and for making this volume possible.

EDITORIAL NOTE

JOHN MORGAN

This book has been a long time in the making, primarily due to the unusual nature of the source materials that went into it. Francis Parker Yockey spent most of his adult life as both a thought criminal and as a man hunted by his own government, constantly on the move and without any place to call home for more than brief periods of time. As a result, apart from *Imperium* and a handful of shorter essays that were handed down and published by admirers in later years, most of Yockey's writings are either lost, exist only in fragments, survive only in other languages, were never published and thus only remain as typewritten manuscripts, or else appeared in obscure, long-forgotten publications that can only be found in private collections or in the deepest recesses of a handful of research libraries.

In a case of supreme historical irony, many of Yockey's texts still exist solely because of the diligence of the institution that expended a great deal of effort in tracking him as a subversive, and which ultimately brought about his arrest and untimely demise: namely, the Federal Bureau of Investigation. The sole copies that we have of many of Yockey's essays and letters exist only in the FBI's investigative records, and were brought to light by researchers who obtained them through Freedom of Information Act requests (many of these files have since been put online). Perhaps the FBI has unintentionally earned itself a small measure of redemption for this service to future scholars.

This volume contains every text of Yockey's that is known by the editors to be extant, apart from *Imperium* and *The Enemy of Europe,* which will be reprinted in future volumes of this set. In some cases, the texts themselves have not survived, but fragments and summaries in the FBI reports do—we have included these for the sake of completeness, for want of the originals. For the inclusion of several of the others, we must extend our thanks to the generosity of a number of people with private collections who have asked to remain nameless, as well as to library staff at institutions across America who helped us. One person I can thank by name is Tim Turner of Biffer Books, who helped us to locate a complete copy of "1848–1948: Years of Decision," given that the original copy we had to work with had been partially eaten by rats. We also have Mr. Turner to thank for Yockey's signature, under his pen name of Ulick Varange, which adorns the frontispiece of this book; it was handwritten in H. Keith Thompson's personal copy of *Imperium*, which was in Mr. Turner's possession. We also thank Elisabeth Carto, the widow of Yockey's hardworking supporter Willis A. Carto, who provided us with copies of several texts which were previously unknown to us.

Others to whom we are grateful are David Yorkshire, who helped with the deciphering of the handwritten note in German that Yockey appended to the Translator's Preface to *Der Feind Europas*, as well as help with its translation into English. We must also thank Thomas Francis, who was the translator of Yockey's *The Enemy of Europe* back into English from German given that the original manuscript has been lost, who here kindly provided us with a translation of "America's Two Ways of Waging War," a lost Yockey essay which was translated into German in abbreviated form in the Argentinian-German expatriate journal *Der Weg* and to which a supporter called our attention. There are also a number of people who have asked to remain anonymous who helped me and Kerry Bolton with questions that arose while we were researching these texts and preparing the introductions, references, and annotations.

Our biggest thanks, however, must be extended to Douglas T. Kaye, who very generously provided us with the only known, complete copy of Yockey's 1959 essay on China, which was long thought lost. Mr. Kaye, who has been active in promoting the ideas of the True Right for many decades, describes the circumstances under which the manuscript was discovered in his Introduction to the essay. Although copies of the manuscript had been privately circulated many years ago, this is the first time that the essay is being formally published in its entirety anywhere.

Given that Yockey texts continued to be discovered even while we were in the process of preparing this book, it seems certain that yet more of them will surface in the years to come. Perhaps we will discover more of Yockey's own essays; if nothing else, there surely must at least be copies of the remaining *Frontfighter* issues out there somewhere, waiting to be found. As such, this anthology should be seen as a work-in-progress. Rest assured that when more texts become available, we will issue a revised and expanded edition. If any reader is in possession of Yockey texts that are not included in this volume and is willing to share them, or else knows where such texts can be found, please contact Greg Johnson at editor@counter-currents.com. It will be a great service to Rightists around the world, both now and in the future, if you can help to complete the record of Yockey's achievements.

In closing, I must convey how privileged I was to be given the opportunity to help bring some of Yockey's forgotten words back into print. Francis Parker Yockey was a great inspiration and guide to me when I was first becoming acquainted with the ideas of the True Right and formulating my own philosophical orientation, and remains one of the True Right's greatest American expositors; as such, I humbly hope that my labors have been worthy of his legacy and will help to convey his genius to future readers, and perhaps pass some inspiration on to them as well. I also felt very fortunate to be able to collaborate with Dr. Kerry Bolton, who has likewise been an important influence on me, and who has dedicated his life to elevating the standard of Rightist discourse and propagating the currents of Yockey's thought to new readers. It is an honor to stand in such illustrious company.

Yockey's texts have been reproduced here exactly as they have survived, although I corrected the occasional typos, spelling, or grammatical errors. In some cases, small parts of the text in the extant copies are no longer legible; I have noted these. The layout of the texts has also been retained as closely as possible to the originals, although words and phrases that appeared in all capitals, in bold, or which was underlined has usually been converted to italics, with some exceptions (particularly in the cases of those texts which were published under Yockey's supervision, such as *The Proclamation of London*); in some texts it seemed that Yockey deliberately used bold and italics for different purposes. All of the footnotes in this volume were added by the editors, and were not part of the original texts. The introductions to the texts, except where otherwise indicated, were written by Dr. Bolton, although I occasionally revised or expanded upon them.

I also wish to thank Kevin Slaughter, James O'Meara, and Scott Weisswald for their help in bringing this book to press.

PHILOSOPHY OF CONSTITUTIONAL LAW

1937

EDITORS' NOTE

"Philosophy of Constitutional Law" is a student paper written by Yockey while at the Georgetown University School of Foreign Service in 1937.[1] It is evident that at 19, Yockey had already been thoroughly imbued with Oswald Spengler's thinking. Yockey seems to have met a mentor of like mind in Walter Jaeger, Professor of Law in the Department of International Relations at Georgetown.[2] The essay is the earliest so far available from Yockey, the next being his "Tragedy of Youth," published in 1939. It is therefore of special interest, especially given that the primary themes of Yockey's thought were already developed while a teenager, and the seminal influence is that of Spengler.

Here Yockey applies Spengler's morphology of the organic cycles of Culture to analyze "constitutional law" from an "organic" perspective as part of a historical process, applying this method to nations as the political units within a Culture. Hence, from the Spenglerian viewpoint of the epoch in which he lived, Yockey could see a decisive world conflict approaching, what Spengler called the "conflict between Money and Blood," represented by the democratic and the fascist powers, respectively. However, the democracies were of historical necessity obliged to take on the mantle of absolutist, authoritarian politics in the epochal struggle for world mastery: We might say that the period of the Second World War was that of a historical juncture in which the era of absolute politics overlapped the nineteenth century era of democracy-plutocracy; hence Money could only win against Blood by assuming the outward expressions evoked by

---

[1] Kevin Coogan, *Dreamer of the Day* (New York: Autonomedia, 1999), p. 82.

[2] Ibid., p. 64.

the era of Absolute Politics while retaining its old slogans of "liberty, equality, fraternity." Behind the sloganeering, however, the post-war aftermath, with Money victorious, assumed a form of brutality more in keeping with the Old Testament than with traditional Western legal jurisprudence, or its ethos, as evidenced by the Nuremberg lynch-party and the Morgenthau Plan.

This situation continues to pertain to the present, with American global foreign and military policies following the same formula as that developed during the Second World War. Here there is the legal façade of "international law," and the Nuremberg-derived laws on "genocide" and "human rights," for the purposes of extending the hegemony of Money with "legal" sanction to hunt down and eliminate any military or political leaders—Slobodan Milošević, Saddam Hussein, Muammar Gaddafi—who stand in the way.

Philosophy of Constitutional Law

I. Philosophy of the General Idea of Law

It will be my endeavor here to present a picture of constitutional law in its origin and its significance, past and future, that will be to a certain extent novel in that it will be a picture having in it nothing *a priori* judged to be true. I avoid a critical attitude because all critical activity rests upon a method, and the possibility of obtaining this method itself by criticism is only apparent. Hence, I use the non-critical method of examining the relevant phenomenon from the historical viewpoint, which recognizes only the physiognomy of the living and that which has lived, and which treats truth (i.e., theories, doctrines, systems, in other words, the *anti-historical*) merely as facts, and not as quantities of a separate order. To this method similarities in terminology do not *per se* indicate similar inward ideas or experiences.[3]

The notion of law itself must first be examined. The generic

---

[3] In the margin next to this paragraph, Yockey wrote, "If facts are separated from truth, what is a doctrine or system?"

kinds of law have been classified in numerous ways; that of Blackstone,[4] as I remember it, listed the laws of inanimate matter, the laws of nature which are rules imposed by God on men discoverable by reason, the revealed or divine law which is part of the law of nature expounded by God alone, and finally, municipal laws, including in that term international law, Constitutional law, common law, statute law, equity, etc. All of these contain the common element that they are rules of action dictated by some superior being. Without stopping to consider the justification of covering such diverse ideas with one term, it will be my task to show the origin and significance of the last type of law—law made by men for men, and with a human sanction.

What, then, is this kind of law? Is it more closely related to politics or to ethics? Is it transferable and eternally valid? Does each separate law represent the decision of a political power problem? Is it an outgrowth of an economic system? These questions and others suggest the nature of our problem, and also show the one source where may be found the components of an historically accurate picture of law: men.

Men make law, and thus the law always contains something that its author willed to express. To understand the *raison d'être* of a law requires far more data than the mere statement of the law, because what is self-evident, hence unexplained in the law outweighs by far the actual written content. The kind of law is dependent directly and completely on the kind of lawgiver, and therewith on the society in which he has matured—whether primitive or cultured, whether feudal or cosmopolitan, aristocratically or democratically ordered, industrial or agricultural, whether Russian, Western, Chinese, Indian, Egyptian, or Classical. A nation is as much a legal unit as it is a political or economic unit. In the law of a people its world-outlook finds pure and clear expression (there are outstanding excep-

---

[4] Sir William Blackstone (1723–1780) was an English jurist best known for his *Commentaries on the Laws of England,* which were a summary of the entirety of English law which was highly influential on the development of future Anglophone law.

tions, but in these cases the alienness of the law dominated the legal picture, and eventually the law was either spiritually transformed [Roman law by the Arabian Culture], or became the object of a violent political abrogation [Roman law by Germany in 1935]).

Everywhere and always has the law been the result of duties, whether the unwritten law of the Vikings or the megalopolitan law of Rome A.D. 100, is meant. Who owes the duties, to whom they are owed, their relative stringency, their administerers—these are all a reflection of the nation, the culture, and the stage of development. A historical outlook on law perceives that the law does not order a life—it is the expression of the will-to-order of that life which precedes and forms the law. The development of law follows closely the spiritual, political, and economic growth of a people. If the development of the law were a thing unto itself all law of all times and places would be homogeneous at least in tendency. But the fact emerges that there is no legal sense in men divorced from the rest of his being.

Because there is no such legal instinct it is a grave error to suppose that a law contemplates all things evenly, or that it is not influenced by political and economic interests at all. The imagining of this state of things lies at the basis of the thought of scholars who think that the imagining of political possibilities is a political activity. But a law is not born of an abstraction, but of life. The law itself contains in abstract form the legal world-picture of its authors. Every law is established by a minority—the minority that represents the rest in world history. The duty conception of the higher natures is merely a potentiality in the great mass of any social organization. The idea of law merely enjoins upon all this duty conception—it makes explicit, actualizes, what is possible. It cannot create a nation out of a given mass—it can only embody in a living mandate and secure by sanction that which already exists, is being brought to existence, or which resides as permanent possibility in a superpersonal soul. It cannot even stifle these living actualities: it can march and grow with them, or it can stay behind; a law born of life is a tool (English common law)—a law of purely archeological significance imposed on a people by a trick of fate (Roman law on Germany after the discovery of the Pandects[5] in 1050) is a burden.

Every law corresponds to a duty. *A duty*—to individuals, to family, to the state—*is a law* insofar as one does not receive it, but gives it. A sovereign is he whose duties are subject to the sanction of nothing outside of himself. The duties of all others are to their superiors only, to the source of the sanction thereof. An obligation to inferiors is only the fulfilling of a duty to superiors. In feudal times the nobility was sovereign (in the legal sense, not the spiritual). The rise of the idea of the Nation-State set up a new sovereign—the State. From 1300 to 1800 the State, first in its aristocratic, later in it absolute form, is the sovereign. All legal duties have the sanction of the State during this period, but there are no limitations or commands set upon the State. (I take it to be superfluous to state that international "law" is purely and throughout comity and can in no sense be called "law" in the sense in which we speak of the public and private law of a nation.)

II. Historical Provenance of the Constitution-Idea

During the period of the maturity of the absolute state arises a phenomenon of which the last development succeeds in dethroning the high sovereignty of the State. The phenomenon is urban rationalism and its last development is the generic idea of "democracy." The same type of mind that has busied itself with discovering the natural law for more than a century now sought out the "natural" government; the "natural" sovereign. From the middle of the eighteenth century the idea gestates, and in 1789 it is triumphantly born into the world of actuality. Here is the background of the idea of the Constitution. As the natural law is timeless and eternally true, so the form of government must be eternal, and it is committed to writing so that there may be no doubt about it. Justice is to be secured once and for all; the

[5] The Pandects, or the Digest, was a compendium on all Roman law up to that time that was ordered compiled by the Emperor Justinian I in the sixth century.

"rights of man" are to be inviolate; not men but eternally valid concepts are to rule; these are all ordained by the Constitution. The old order is swept away and the millennium begins.

Legally the Constitution idea means that the state sovereignty is replaced by the sovereignty of the people, at least theoretically. The Constitution is their pronouncement (again theoretically). Thus it has the force of law, and constitutional law thus becomes one of the legal disciplines.

The present attempt is, of course, only a flying attempt of the possibilities here. The main thing that stands out is that just as the idea of the Constitution means the coming to expression of an entirely new feeling in Western mankind about domestic politics, so constitutional law, conceptually speaking, represents a law of a different order and significance from anything called "law" before. The State was hitherto supreme in fact and in common acknowledgement but now the law theoretically steps out as the supreme ordering force among men. Formerly law has had the sanction of the State; now the State has the sanction of the law (supposedly).

But here as always we cannot see into law without understanding life. We have seen the high possibilities that stood before constitutional law. Now the Constitution and Democracy are coeval; historically speaking they are almost identical. They both originated in abstract thought and not in experience, hence their actualization should have remodeled the sphere of internal politics completely. But the ideas were not actualized by the first who committed them to paper—they were actualized by born leaders, true master-natures for whom (consciously or unconsciously) the people is[6] only an object and an ideal but a means. Authors of constitutions, because they were working on their schemes and this in spite of their painstaking care in the direction of prevision and calculation.[7]

---

[6] Presumably, Yockey actually means "is not" here.

[7] This sentence is clearly unfinished. In the margin next to this paragraph, Yockey wrote, ". . . with concepts and not with facts, have never had any idea of the practical working . . ."

III. Nature of the Actualized Constitution-Idea & the Historical Problem Presented Therein

The actual effect of a constitution did not depend at all on its wording. Insofar as the constitution is the basis of the State at [illegible] it is the practice of the living constitution that mattered, and this practice did not begin in any case with the adoption of the constitution. It developed itself out of the experience of Time, the situation, and above all, the race-properties of the nation. If this *natural* growth of the body politic has been sure and powerful, it maintains the State in the form of itself, and the letter of the written constitution has no influence—it does not even have to be explained away (i.e., "interpreted") in case it contradicts the actuality. What do the constitutional powers of a person or a class matter when that person or class is the government? What was the *defined* relation, constitutionally or otherwise, of Cecil Rhodes[8] to the government of Great Britain? And remember too, that the nobility which directed Roman politics during the period of the three Punic Wars[9] had, from the point of view of constitutional law, no existence whatever.

But these examples are not the exception, but the rule—especially in democratic conditions. And here emerges the possibility of *a morphology of the constitution*. Inevitably such a morphology must have a national basis, since the soul of the nation, as expressed in its ruling class, is the basis of the actual policy. It is this ruling class, in all States and everywhere, that represents the nation in world history, and even within that the actual group holding the power (more often than not against the spirit of the Constitution) consists of a handful of skillful (ergo conscienceless) politicians.

Statecraft is an art, and like all of the higher arts, it is accessible only to the few. It is the art of the *possible*, not of the conceivable. Thus the heights of this art belong to those who have a su-

---

[8] Cecil Rhodes (1853–1902) was the founder of the British colony of Rhodesia in the 1890s.

[9] The Punic Wars were a series of conflicts between the Roman Republic and the Carthaginian Empire in the third to second centuries BC, which led to the eventual destruction of the latter.

perior eye for the things of reality. To a statesman, for instance, the extension of a franchise is of small importance compared with the technique, Spartan or Roman, German or American, of operating the votes. How the English Constitution reads is of little import compared with the fact that it is managed by a small stratum of high families. Charles Merriam[10] says, "The truth is that a constitution does not consist of words alone but of public attitudes and habits" (*The Written Constitution and the Unwritten Attitude*, p. 11, published by Richard Smith, New York, 1931). Alexander Hamilton has this same general truth in mind when he says (83rd Federalist Paper), "Free institutions rely in the last instance on the general genius of the government. Particular provisions, although not altogether useless, have far less efficacy than are commonly ascribed to them."[11] As the great Burke[12] wrote (*Correspondence*, pp. 332, 335), "The principles that guide us in public and private, which as they are not of our devising but molded into the nature and essence of things, will endure with the Sun and Moon, long very long after Whig and Tory, Stuart and Brunswick, and all such miserable Bubbles and playthings of the Hour are vanished from existence, and from memory." In an historical treatment of constitutional law, therefore, as it determines the workings of a government, one should not expect to find the Constitution as the historically prior element before national pulse and tradition, but rather as either an expression of that pulse (English Constitution) or else as an ineffectual and even hindering form (Prussian Constitution of 1850).

---

[10] Charles Merriam (1874–1953) was a Professor of Political Science at the University of Chicago, a progressive, and an advisor to several American presidents, including Franklin Delano Roosevelt.

[11] The actual passage reads, "The truth is that the general GENIUS of a government is all that can be substantially relied upon for permanent effects. Particular provisions, though not altogether useless, have far less virtue and efficacy than are commonly ascribed to them . . ."

[12] Edmund Burke (1730–1797) was an Irish statesman and political philosopher who is considered to have laid down the principles of modern Anglo-Saxon conservatism.

IV. Falsity of All Classifications of Constitutional Law

A long accepted classification of constitutions is that of Lord Bryce[13] which recognized the written type and the unwritten type and then went on to equate them respectively with the rigid type and the flexible type. In this classification the British Constitution was described as being an example of the unwritten, flexible type and the United States Constitution as an example of the written, rigid type. This is a thoroughly superficial analysis, worthy of the dogmatic materialism which is native to the English soul. It is refuted by all the pertinent facts of history. Leaving for the moment the historical accuracy of the division into "written" and "unwritten" let us look at the facts concerning the amendment of Lord Bryce's "rigid" and "flexible" constitutions. The British Constitution (which is under this classification preeminently flexible) was amended in the course of a century only for various extensions of the suffrage, subordination of the House of Lords, and the altered imperial status of the dominions (by the Westminster Stat.).[14] In the same period the United States Constitution was amended seven times and has since been amended twice. Obviously Lord Bryce here confused the difficulty of the amending process with the political flexibility of the constitution. The French Constitution of 1871 can be amended as easily as a statute can be passed, yet it was not altered from 1884 to 1926. The German Constitution of 1871 was legally simple of amendment, yet it was very infrequently amended.

Another classification of constitutions (Ernst Freund in *Encyclopedia of Social Sciences,* article on Constitutional Law) makes three different divisions: first, the unwritten type, exemplified by the English; second, the Continental type, written, not enforced judicially; third, the American Constitution, written and judicially enforced. This merely takes legalistic appearance again as indicative of the actual rank and force of a constitution. It gets

---

[13] James Bryce (1838–1922) was a British jurist and ambassador to the United States who favored good relations between Britain, Germany, and the US. He was also influential upon causing the US to be seen as a specifically Anglo-Saxon country.

[14] The Statute of Westminster, passed in 1931, granted legislative independence to the various dominions of the British Empire.

nowhere near to affording a glimpse at these realities which are responsible for two utterly unlike physiognomies presented by two States with very similar written constitutions.

The uniform confusion prevailing about this subject can only now be cleared up. None of the writers so far have actually been free enough from legalism and abstract theory to see the real *components* of the *historical* picture of which constitutional law is a part. John Burgess,[15] for instance, says (*Political Science and Comparative Constitutional Law*, 1890, p. 73), "Looked at from one standpoint all states are constitutional; and from another, none." I take this to mean that no State has ever functioned on a day-to-day basis without any experienced principles as the groundwork of its policy, and in the second place that *no* State (in Rudolf Kjellén's[16] understanding of that word) has ever been contained in form or restrained in action by a written constitution. Thus what he says is undoubtedly correct, but has he said anything illuminating or definitive about the historical rank of the constitution-idea and its relationship to the State? Does his dictum throw any light on the weakness and short life of the Weimar Constitution of Germany in 1919? Does it hint at the real significance of the broad constitutional conflict now going on in the United States? A. V. Dicey, an eminent English writer on constitutional law, thus discloses his confusion (*Law of the Constitution*, 1927, p. 21): "Is it possible that so-called 'constitutional law' is in reality a cross between history and custom which does not properly deserve the name of law at all, and certainly does not belong to the province of a professor called upon to teach nothing but the true indubitable law of England? Can it be that a dark saying of De

---

[15] John Burgess (1844–1931) was a Professor at Columbia University and was one of the first to forge political science as a discipline. Despite having been a veteran of the Union army during the Civil War, he believed that blacks were inherently inferior to whites.

[16] Rudolf Kjellén (1864–1922) was a Swedish political scientist who also served in the Swedish Parliament. He is best remembered for having coined the term "geopolitics" and for establishing some of the foundations of later geopolitical theory. In his writings on the concept of the state, he argued that the state goes beyond its legal and political framework to encompass society as well.

Tocqueville's, 'the English constitution has no real existence,' contains the truth of the whole matter?"

The English Constitution affords as good a place as any other to point out the essence of the whole matter. In the first place it is a very grave error to speak of the British Constitution as a constitution in the same sense as the French constitutions of 1799 to 1870, or the American Constitution, or the Constitution of Tanna Tuya. Merely to qualify it as unwritten and to suppose that this is the decisive distinction between it and the Continental constitutions is about as shallow as even English thought can be. As a matter of fact, most of the British Constitution is written. The other platitude which differentiates this Constitution as being the product of evolution while the others were the product of revolution misses the mark completely, for actually the British Constitution is the product of many revolutions. Nor is the touchstone the fact that the British Constitution is the result of history, for history has left its imprint on the written constitutions of the Continent and the American Constitution.

What the English understand by the word "constitution" is the exact opposite of what the same word conveys on the Continent—*to the Englishman his Constitution represents the organic link which binds the living past to the present*—It is the focus of national tradition and national feeling. On the Continent, however, *constitutionalism is the focal point of all anti-traditionary forces, the break with the past, and the quintessence of all nationalistic efforts to destroy the State.* In England there has been no constitutional conflict in the Continental sense—the Constitution was altered when the security of the traditionary inner political system demanded it. On the Continent there was always a group that wanted to alter the constitution—and, note well, not toward consolidating the State power but to destroy it. In England it was exactly the traditionary forces—Church, society, Navy—for whom the Constitution was the most self-evident, but on the Continent the forces of tradition—Army, State, and aristocracy—who were anti-constitutional in feeling but usually did not possess the power to make the constitution subservient to them had to put up with the constitutions as fetters, and (after 1848) it may be added as defenses against the absolute rule of the proletariat. The British

Constitution is preserved history and affirmation of tradition—the Continental type of constitution is the denial of history (as springing from rationalism) and negation of tradition.

Only because it may offer the key to a historical understanding of the American Constitution, we shall glance briefly at the reason for this proposition. In England and the Empire alone were the gentry victorious in the seventeenth-century Fronde.[17] The *Declaration of Rights*, 1689,[18] put an end to the State in England. Since then England has known only aristocratic class regimes (up until 1916, that is). The English analogy to the State-idea is the term "society," expressing the fact that the nation was not under the care of a State, but of a class. In western Europe one owed the same duties to the State that one owed in England to "society." The word "state" itself died out, and "society" was substituted therefore. In the revolutionary period which set in, in full force, at the end of the eighteenth century, the formation of the "Third Estate"[19] on the Continent was directed against *State* authority. In England there was no absolute government, and furthermore, there was a vigorous reigning plutocracy which successfully coped with the first great revolutionary flood. During the nineteenth century, England was unable to maintain her Constitution unimpaired because of a series of prudent measures of the nobility which drew the bourgeoisie into cooperation with it, but under its guidance, thus maintaining the tradition in spite of the complete transformation of the basis of power. Thus, no matter which party was in power, the nation remained in form for outward politics. In Prussia the situation

[17] The Fronde was a series of civil wars in France between 1648 and 1653 in which the nobility and the commoners rebelled against the authority of King Louis XIV but were defeated. Here, Yockey is using the term in a more general sense to include the English Civil War as well.

[18] The *Declaration of Rights* was drafted by Parliament to limit the power of the monarchy and make it answerable to them following the overthrow of King James II in the Glorious Revolution of 1688 and was accepted by William and Mary upon their coronation in 1689.

[19] In France, the Third Estate consisted of the peasants and the bourgeoisie.

was the opposite. There, the nation was maintained in form as a State because *no* party was able to rule. If Bismarck had had to depend on the Reichstag, there would have been no German Empire. In Western Europe a monarchy was, in the nineteenth century, a denial of party, of the spirit of party. But the spirit of party was inseparable from the rationalistic idea of a written constitution, hence the idea of a "constitutional monarchy" is a contradiction in itself and meant either a government in the spirit of party—France and Italy, or a government by the Right, the denial of party—Austria-Hungary and the Hohenzollern Empire.

V. MORPHOLOGY OF CONSTITUTIONS; ACTUAL SOURCE OF CONSTITUTIONAL LAW

We all know what is meant when the practice of government is spoken of. Now if we call this the living constitution, it is apparent that every nation has its own distinctive living constitution, the expression of the national soul. The memory of this national soul is what we call tradition. A nation with a sure tradition is one that can surmount historical crises unfalteringly. It is in the national soul, preserved in tradition and expressed anew at every epoch, that we must look for the source of the living constitution—that constitution that exists (in any Western nation) for nine hundred years before the brief interlude of rationalistic written constitutions and will continue, after their inevitable demise, to the end of Western history. The British-codified Constitution owes its powerful symbolic force precisely to the fact that it is nothing but the preservation of the *living constitution* in my sense of the word. The Prussian Constitution of 1850 and *a fortiori* the Weimar Constitution of 1919 were outright denials of the Prussian soul, the Prussian *living constitution,* and so each one in turn created so much inner friction in the conduct of government that the available political energy was consumed in internal politics and a Caprivi[20] and a Bethmann,[21] with 1914 as

[20] Leo Graf von Caprivi (1831–1899) was the Chancellor of the German Empire from 1890 until 1894.

[21] Theobald Theodor Friedrich Alfred von Bethmann-Hollweg

a result, were the outcome of the progressive weakening of Prussia-Germany by these alien, rationalistic, written "forms of government." How is the living constitution recognized? First of all, it cannot *be learned,* not in the systematic sense in which one can learn the written constitutions of nations. As Nietzsche says somewhere, "Only that which has no history is capable of being defined,"[22] and nations are, above all, the pure expression of super-personal historical becoming. A nation is not the creator of a culture, but is itself a grand creation of a Culture. The way to penetrate the soul of a nation is to live oneself into all the expressions of that soul, political, technical, and economic, no less than artistic, religious, and philosophical. To do this requires the physiognomic tact of the born statesman, the judge of men. To the methods of Benjamin Kidd[23] and Darwin such an effort is equally impossible. At the basis of every nation is an *idea*—in the Goethian sense of that word. But that idea is a spiritual, and not as Darwinian materialism thinks, a biological reality. Hence the dominant spirituality of the Culture at a given time (which is another way of saying the life-stage of the Culture, whether youth, maturity, or old age)[24] determines what constitutes a nation. (Thus, for instance, the present "International of Nationalism,"[25] no matter how the actual movement eventuates, contains germs of the future, which will develop and realize themselves regardless of any intellectual movement.) In Scholastic times already, the flair of the physiognomist could recognize from its *style, its soul,* a work of literature, a face, a painting, a bottle, a philosophy, as French, as Italian, as Spanish, although there was

---

(1856–1921) was the Chancellor of the German Empire from 1909 until 1917.

[22] Nietzsche writes this in *On the Genealogy of Morals,* second essay, section 13.

[23] Benjamin Kidd (1858–1916) was a British sociologist who attempted to apply the Darwinian theory of evolution to societies, and believed that religion was the crucial factor in their development.

[24] The influence of Oswald Spengler, in terms of the organic "age" cycles of a Culture, is here apparent.

[25] A reference to the sundry varieties of "fascism" that had arisen throughout the world.

yet no French State, no Italian State, nor any Spanish State. In the Revolutionary period beginning c. 1750, the separate nations of the West, now in the form of absolute Nation-States, each experienced the first crisis inwardly and solved it in its own distinct, distinguishable way. It is from the eighteenth-century tradition of these Nation-States that what I have called the *living constitutions* of the nineteenth-century Western nations derive. *This* is the source to which we must look to discover the living secret of the inward history of nations. Here will be found the answer to the internal history of France and Great Britain in the nineteenth century, the death of Spain, the late arising of the Prussian nation (last of Western nations), and no less the answer to the partitioning of the Austro-Hungarian Empire, the Bolshevist revolution in Russia, and the late attainment of Italian unity. A nation has no system, but a Physiognomy, hence penetration of the expressions of the national soul offer the only method towards comprehending the inward possibilities of the nation.

Now, the secret of the historical rank of the constitution-idea, and constitutional law therewith, lies in the fact that while the idea is a superpersonal, cultural force, clothed with necessity, *it is in origin and development an intellectual force*, and thereby it is historically bound to the brief period of cultural history in which intellect is supreme.

We have seen that the constitution-idea was actualized differently in England and Prussia, and in both of these differently from France. We have seen that there was in England no constitutional conflict in the Continental sense and why this was so. But in Prussia, in France, the living constitution was often in fundamental conflict with the written constitution. Contrary to what Lord Bryce thought, we have seen that the actual basis of flexibility or rigidity of a written constitution is pragmatic and not legalistic. Then, what is the basis of the rigidity of the living constitution? Just this—*the practice of the living constitution is as unchanging as the national tradition is sure and unfaltering*. Another historical relationship makes itself clear—whether the written constitution or the living constitution is supreme depends on whether the national tradition is weak or sure and strong, or what amounts to the same thing, whether intellect or blood is the ruling force. For, be it said, though this is still the age of intellect, as was the nineteenth century, it is only in the other world—the world of books, of truths, of ideals—that intellect is unconditionally supreme; in politics it can only cause discord, it can only say no to tradition—only in this way can it ever be said to be the ruling force. Thus in Prussia and Austria the written constitutions were never very important at first in the presence of the older political traditions, and constitutional law occupied a back place in the list of legal disciplines. After 1848 it is a different story, and from 1919 till 1933 Germany appeared internally as a French state.[26] The French tradition was too weak, the nation too used up to weather the rationalistic flood, and the 1789 revolution, as a result of the weakness of French absolutism, occasioned by the social degeneration of the aristocracy, swept away the State. Of course there was nothing to replace it—*a Republic is merely the continuation of the dynastic idea without the dynastic tradition and the dynastic means*—and so the big accomplishment of the French Revolution was to remove France from the political combinations of Europe for ten years and to assure the establishment of a military dictatorship at every critical juncture (1800, 1851, 1871, 1918). Try as they will, even the most idealistic revolutionaries have never been able to set up an ideal government of any description whatsoever; in France the destruction of the State merely turned the nation over to money. The real sovereignty in France has resided in the Bourse since Thermidor.[27] The serfs were freed from the pressure of feudal taxation (paid in kind), and simultaneously turned over to the vastly greater pressure of Money and the City.

With constitutional law as with all other kinds of man-made law, the spirit of the law is always the spirit of a minority. In feudal times the law differed from manor to manor, and the no-

---

[26] That is to say, the German political democratic system was "French" rather than German in inspiration.

[27] The Bourse is the Paris stock exchange. Thermidor was the eleventh month in the French revolutionary calendar, and on 9 Thermidor (July 27, 1794), Maximilien Robespierre and his Committee of Public Safety were arrested and executed, ushering in an era of greater stability following the chaos of the Terror.

ble's law was entirely a *private,* customary law—*honor* was its criterion and its sole norm. With the first stirrings of the State-idea this private law is in sharp conflict with the new idea that events must be viewed as well from a *public* law aspect. The conflict, however, like the later one in which the law of the towns strives to make itself the law of the rest against the law of the First Estate,[28] is a conflict of Life, and not of law. No legal principle will induce men to take up arms, but the internal history of Western nations shows that a class will fight to the end to impose *its* law on the whole. A law conflict is a power conflict, and it can only be settled in the way in which political power conflicts can be settled, i.e., by the sword. I will name two instances which show this clearly, both concealing the will-to-power of two functions by an ideal conflict of two conceptually opposed legal systems. First there is the attempt of the absolutist Stuarts to introduce Pandect law into England (as it is the law of a culture at a stage demanding unlimited central power, codified by Justinian). And who opposed it? Sir Edward Coke,[29] member of the class whose power it would destroy, a politically-minded judge, and personal enemy of the King and his attorney-general. Coke had a long history of political opposition to the centralization of power in the monarch. Secondly, there is the "Reception" of Roman law in Germany (actually the Justinian Digests as they had been worked over by Bartolus).[30] Who called it in? Who opposed it? The hard-pressed Imperial with its absolutist supporters fostered its gradual replacement of the customary Germanic law during the fifteenth and eighteenth centuries. The Emperor Maximilian[31] in 1496 constituted his *Kammergerichtsordung* on

---

[28] In France, the First Estate was the clergy.

[29] Sir Edward Coke (1552–1634) was an English jurist who had been appointed Attorney General by Queen Elizabeth. Later in life, under both James I and Charles I, as a Member of Parliament Coke worked to establish the rights of Parliament to limit the powers of the monarchy.

[30] Bartolus de Saxoferrato (1313–1357) was an Italian jurist who was regarded as the greatest authority on Roman law during the Renaissance.

[31] Maximilian I (1459–1519) was Holy Roman Emperor from 1493

the highly centralized model developed in Italy from centralized Roman Empire criteria, and decreed that at least half of the judges constituting it must be trained in the Roman law. The First Estate opposed it, but the Imperial cities and other independent cities were more against the nobles than they were against the Emperor. This triumph of Roman law in Germany represents the triumph of the host of petty princes with their territorial rights over the feudal rights of their inferiors, so that in the seventeenth and eighteenth centuries the German rulers, e.g., the King of Württemberg, the Duke of Prussia, the King of Bavaria, stood in an absolute relation (the French relation) to their subjects, and in a feudal relation (the English relation, approximately) to the Emperor. But through it all, Roman law was a *possession* of the logic-chopping scholars and jurists and a *weapon* of, first the Emperor, and later the petty princes.

With this we reach some of the deepest historical relationships between law, state, and the internal constitution of living States. It is always a minority that represents a nation in world-history at any given time, and the law of the nation is the law of the minority. The law of the minority contains implicitly a politico-economic tendency dependent on the circumstances of the minority, but withal it is a distinctive expression of the national soul, for he who is custodian of a nation in history becomes necessarily part of the nation and imbued with the national pulse, and thus cannot act publicly as an individual, but only as part of a super-personal organism.

The constitution idea is an expression of a minority, and the conflicts it engenders are conflicts of two minorities. These are class conflicts just as surely as the struggle between Emperor and First Estate, King and Parliament (seventeenth and eighteenth century), are class conflicts. The class which wins gives the law to the rest. Every law is established by a few in the name of the generality. (For an impassioned presentation of one instance

---

until 1519. The *Reichskammergericht*, or Imperial Chamber Court, was founded in 1495, and was empowered to make legal judgements in all except criminal cases, or in areas where the political leadership was exempted.

of this, see John Galsworthy's ironical little essay "Justice" in the volume *Satires*.) As Anatole France said, "Our law in majestic equality forbids the rich no less than the poor to steal bread and to beg in the streets."[32] However, make no mistake here, I most emphatically do not mean to imply that class law in this sense has any similarity to the materialistic stupidities of the valiant class-warriors of the gutter. Economic distinctions rarely by themselves determine a law, and even insofar as they are a factor at all they only have weight within a definite historical period—in our case beginning c. 1820. To resume—the constitution idea is historically bound up with rationalism and its political concomitant democracy and thus is radically revolutionary. Where it succeeds it puts the nation out of condition and spells defeat on the battlefield. Only in one possible way can it be actualized without disaster, and then it is merely, in Schiller's phrase, being trained towards non-fulfillment.[33] This is the meaning of English "democracy," where the change from aristocracy to democracy meant a change only in terminology, and not in methods of internal politics. Just as the establishment of Dracon's legislative code[34] is a class political act, so is the establishment of the Spanish Constitution of 1931, only, opposite classes in each case. In Western Europe *new constitutions* were symbols of political victories; in the United States *new interpretations* of the same Constitution. The answer to the question "Which is the ruling class?" is also the answer to the question "Who gives the law?"

With the end of the period of absolute states the various ideal structures conceived in the minds of scholars are set up as governments, losing their identity in the process. The one main idea the pedants had was to pen such a document as would forever

---

[32] Anatole France (1844–1924) was a French novelist. This quotation is taken verbatim from the English translation of Oswald Spengler, *The Decline of the West* (London: George Allen & Unwin, 1971), vol. II, p. 64, where it is cited by Spengler in the context of stating that law is produced by a class for the generality.

[33] Friedrich Schiller (1759–1805) as cited by Oswald Spengler, *The Hour of Decision* (New York: Alfred A. Knopf, 1934), pp. 180–81.

[34] Dracon (seventh century BC) was the first known lawgiver of Athens.

make "tyranny" impossible. Now, it was supposed that the "people" would never tyrannize over themselves, ergo they must govern. But since this is inconceivable as well as impossible (for the pedants have never admitted the latter as a barrier) this plan gave way to the totally different idea of "representative government." It was still supposed to be the "rule of the People," but even in the rarefied atmosphere of the mind the two concepts are poles apart. All over the world the ideologues gave themselves up to the most fantastic Utopian dreams; it was generally thought that essentially the world had changed, that we stood at the beginning of a new era which had no historical precedent. So it was the "representative government" dream that actualized itself. It did not take long for English politicians of eminence to lay down the rule (by 1700) that ". . . on 'Change one deals in votes as well as stocks, and the price of a vote is as well-known as the price of an acre of land'" (J. Hatschek, *Englische Verfassungsgeschichte*, p. 588). The *actual* counterpart of the concept "representative government" is Party government. Party government, when in sole control, means the alternating dictatorship of the Party leaders instead of the hereditary rule of the crown. Pelham, the successor of Walpole, paid to members of the Commons through his secretary £500 to £800 at the end of each session according to the value of the services rendered by each recipient to the government—i.e., the Whig Party. The party agent Dodington described his activities in these words: "I never attended a debate if I could help it, and I never missed a division that I could take part in. I heard many arguments that convinced me, but never one that influenced my vote."[35]

VI. Philosophy of the Constitutional Law of the United States

Thus the metamorphosis of the idea of "Democracy." Its twin concept, the constitution idea, did not remain static, either. The federal Constitution of the United States is clearly and definitely

---

[35] The previous four sentences are taken verbatim from the English translation of Spengler, *The Decline of the West*, vol. II, p. 403, footnote 8.

one of delegated powers as respects the Federal Government, yet in 1791 already arose the doctrine of "implied powers" which was sanctioned by Congress. It did not arise as a matter of theory, but as a legal basis for a *political* act which would have been illegal if the actual wording of the written document were taken as a source of power. A piece of paper cannot visit its wrath upon one who disobeys its solemn injunctions, hence Hamilton established his unconstitutional system, without any of the usual sanctions that overtake the lawbreaker. In 1801, with the Alien and Sedition Acts, constitutional law received, in effect, a Federalist interpretation, and note well, a *legislative* interpretation. The Supreme Court at this time was the weakest branch of the government. Madison's motion in the Constitution (Notes for August 15, 1787): ". . . that all acts before they become laws should be submitted both to the Executive and Supreme Judiciary Departments, [and] that if either of these should object 2/3 of each House, if both should object, 3/4 of each House, should be necessary to overrule the objections and give to the acts the force of law." Which would have given the court a veto coordinate with the veto power of the President, and was voted down in the Convention, yet years later we find the Congress discussing its power in terms of judicial decisions. Thus Senator Lodge:[36] "The right of Congress to abrogate a treaty directly or indirectly by statute is unquestioned and has been sustained by the Supreme Court" (*Congressional Record*, Vol. lxi, 1921, Part 1, p. 386). What is the historical explanation for this transformation?

John Marshall was appointed Chief Justice of the United States a few weeks before Thomas Jefferson was inaugurated as President. He was a Federalist and a man of strong race and dominating personality. Before his accession, the Justices used to

---

[36] Henry Cabot Lodge (1850–1924) was a Senator for Massachusetts from 1893 to 1924, and was Chairman of the Senate Foreign Relations Committee from 1919 until 1924, during which time he successfully prevented America's entry into the League of Nations because of his objection to the fact that member states would be required to cease military aggression if ordered to do so by the League.

read their opinions verbatim, after the prevailing English custom, but beginning with the term of December 1801, the Chief Justice became almost the sole mouthpiece of the Court. In the succession of cases *Marbury v. Madison, Cohens v. Virginia, M'Culloch v. Maryland,* and *Gibbons v. Ogden,* Marshall made a Federalist constitution out of the document which he interpreted. It is Marshall's merit that he kept the Federalist voice important in the government for thirty-five years after the Federalists had lost control of the executive and the legislative. It was a fatality for the United States that the Federalist tradition became effective in the judiciary instead of in the executive. Every single event of our history would have been changed thereby. But let us be dispossessed once and for all of any legal or ideal views of the origin of judicial review in the United States. It was a *political, personal,* and *class* act, and its great significance has been political. To show the historical value of one idealistic view, listen to John W. Burgess (*Political Science and Comparative Constitutional Law,* 1890, Vol. II, p. 365). "It is then the consciousness of the American people that law must rest upon justice and reason, that the constitution is a more ultimate formulation of the fundamental principles of justice and reason than mere legislative acts, and that the judiciary is a better interpreter of those fundamental principles than the legislature." But was John Marshall thinking of "justice and reason," or was he thinking of the founding of a national state when he set forth his system of constitutional law? Was Marshall a theoretician, philosopher, and idealist, or was he a practical man, far-seeing, historically acute? Was it his aim to be legalistically consistent? "The judicial authority can have no right to question the validity of a law, unless such a jurisdiction is expressly given by the constitution." Thus John Marshall in his argument before the Supreme Court as attorney in the case of *Ware v. Hilton.* It is historically wrong, but legalistically correct to characterize Marshall's establishment of judicial review as a usurpation. Every constitution belongs to someone, and he holds it until someone takes it away from him. It is not usurpation, but Life. Just as the personality of Hamilton was decisive for the political party of Federalism, so was that of Marshall decisive for what we may call the spiritual tradition of

Federalism, meaning by that the tacit feeling, always effective among at least a few men throughout our whole history and today experiencing a powerful spiritual implementing, that we are one nation, one historical unit, and hence should be represented in history by one state instead of being shut out from history by the provincial policies of a federation. The defeat of the Federalists was not the defeat of one party by another: it was the defeat of the incipient American state-idea by the spirit of Party. It was the defeat of Blood by Money, of politics by economics.[37]

And with its defeat the whole American nation was changed: and a new ruling class meant a new constitutional law. Insofar as the old law was susceptible of use by the new ruling class, it was kept, but new interpretations filled out the gaps. The principle of judicial review was a political weapon which the succeeding courts maintained. It was not used, however, during the years 1803–1857. During these years, the center of gravity of the nation shifted from politics to economic activity. It was during these years that the word politics began to acquire an aura of chicanery, and now was developed the idea that the government exists to promote the economic activity of its citizens, that any governmental function which does not strictly subserve this is mischievous. During these years, too, matured two systems within the United States: a patriarchal, aristocratic society with an economic basis of agriculture and a technical basis of muscle-energy, and a plutocratic society based on manufacturing and commerce with a technical basis of coal-energy.[38] It was the former that spoke in Chief Justice Taney in the Dred Scott Decision.[39] It was the last time that Blood spoke; since then our con-

---

[37] The symbolic allusion here is quintessentially Spenglerian: "A power can only be overthrown by another power, not by a principle, and no power that can confront money is left but this one. Money is overthrown and abolished only by blood." Spengler, *The Decline of the West*, vol. II, p. 507.

[38] For a view of the South as a society in the tradition of the Cavalier, against the plutocrat and the Puritan, see K. R. Bolton, "Was the Confederacy a Tool of International Finance?," *Counter-Currents*, October 21, 22, *&* 23, 2010.

[39] *Dred Scott v. Sandford*, on which the Supreme Court ruled in

stitutional law has been the law of Money. (It is perhaps not remiss to point out here that Taney was brought up in the Federalist tradition and was an ardent nationalist; he had no intention of making an economic decision in favor of the South or against the North, but was merely trying to settle the *political* aspect of slavery.)

With 1865 Money stepped forth as lord of the land. He who would be master must have money. The labor leader realized this as quickly as the industrialist, but he was not in such a good position for getting control of enough of it, and had to be content with gnashing his teeth, fomenting strikes and riots, and learning ways to get more money. There being no class trained in statesmanship, the economic leaders, financial, industrial, and commercial, were the only ones left to rule, and Presidents of this period derive their significance from their relation to the economic leaders. The Presidents appointed the Supreme Court Justices, and the appointments had to be satisfactory to the real rulers. Their constitutional law also was satisfactory.

Presently, the offensive came from below, from the labor leaders, the agrarian leaders, and the intellectuals. They could elect Congressmen, hence there begins around 1880 a stream of legislation designed to transfer power from the economic leaders to the economic led . . . *A labor union is a trust just as much as is a holding company*; it is the talents of their respective leaders that determine the different fields of their respective operations. But they could not elect (i.e., did not have enough money to) the President; the industrialists alone could do that, so the use of John Marshall's splendid weapon forged in *Marbury v. Madison* kept pace with the anti-industrialist legislation (little did John Marshall think his system of constitutional law would ever be the bulwark of a grasping plutocracy). Another example of the irony that has always selected the builders of States and leaders of nations for its special target; "Congress has not the power . . ." is an expression of the political power of a class; whether they

---

1857, determined that Negroes could not be considered American citizens if they were the descendants of slaves, regardless of whether they were enslaved or free themselves.

subjugate politics to economics has nothing to do with it. (This, I think, is what Max Lerner had in mind when he said [quoted from the *Yale Law Journal* in Woodward's *New American History*, p. 302] that Marshall's decisions "were to be the strategic link between constitutionalism and capitalism."[40] But I am not sure—this conceptual jargon is vague, at best.)

From 1787 to 1870 the Court vetoed three acts of Congress. Since then it has vetoed sixty-seven, more than half of them since 1920. Thus the invocation of judicial review has increased exactly in proportion as the Leftist fury has taken legislative shape. May I say once more, at the risk of boring, that constitutional law in the United States has not primarily a legalistic, or even a legal, significance. To prevent the several states from dethroning the economic leaders, the Court said they (the states) could not control interstate commerce (and every big industry was in interstate commerce), and to prevent the legislation of Congress from so doing, it invoked "due process" and "just compensation," phrases which do not have in an individual case any legal significance, but which were *legal tools* serving the end of preserving absolute economic freedom for the industrialists. It is a waste of time to do as Morris Ernst,[41] member of our powerful lawyer intellectual caste, did in *The Ultimate Power* when he struts cleverly over page after page subsequent to showing that the Supreme Court was inconsistent or invoked "due process" to distinguish the indistinguishable. But it is typical of the intellectual to believe in the power of words, and as a corollary to think that you have destroyed a man when you have shown him inconsistent. Only when the Court was deciding common law cases did it have genuine legal significance; but for the last fifty years it has been what used to be called in Europe a public law (or administrative law) court.

---

[40] Max Lerner (1902–1992) was a Jewish journalist who supported the New Deal and various other social justice and anti-racist causes. Late in life, though, he became a supporter of Ronald Reagan.

[41] Morris Ernst (1888–1976) was a Jewish lawyer who was co-founder of the National Civil Liberties Bureau in 1917, which became the American Civil Liberties Union (ACLU) in 1920.

VII. Historical Philosophy of the Unique Judicial Character of the Constitutional Law of the United States

How came it that this direction of politics into judicial forms was possible in the United States? Not, as Dicey thought, because judicial scrutiny of legislation is a necessary concomitant of a written constitution. The only reason John Marshall's innovation was able to stand was that it had a long tradition of paramount law, evolved in the colonies, behind it (the colonials believed in paramount law because the executive in some colonies was a royal governor, while the judges were native born; *thus paramount law was their law*). The political struggle within the royal colonies thus created a traditionary bias toward legalism. This was greatly in evidence at the Constitutional Convention when men (mostly lawyers) talked hours about the separation of powers, the securing of justice, the prevention of "tyranny" (compare the present-day use of the word "fascism"), the perpetual maintenance of "the rights of man"; all this, of course, to be done by strictly *legal* means. Not a word went into the Constitution that did not pass under the *legal* microscope. One man alone in the Convention knew that the real powers in history are the very opposite of any planned scheme of lawyers, and Alexander Hamilton left the Convention early, making plans later to capture the Constitution, rendering it his in the usage, let the words read as they would. The finality of legislative interpretation of the Constitution has express recognition in the Prussian Constitution of 1850 and the Swiss Constitution of 1874, but subsequently constitutions of these states and the numerous constitutions of France did not all include such a provision, yet legislative interpretation was nevertheless regarded as final. Here alone does constitutional law have a judicial character.

The establishment of judicial politics in the form of legalistic prestidigitation was not, of course, inevitable, even in the lawyer-ridden early United States. In the long run, judicial review breaks down the central State-power, and a Federalist government would not have permitted it. But once the legalistic idea of politics was grafted on to the national character (the soul of the American people was created in the War of Secession; at any time before that could an entirely different national tradition have been formed) it remained and it remains today, as we have seen in the popular reaction to President Roosevelt's plan to enlarge the court. In fact it cannot be ignored as a political factor, and it was this national legalistic feeling about politics that brought about the Great Executive Silence on the Supreme Court plan.

The mutual interdependence between the executive and the Supreme Court, with its constitutional law on the one side and the economic leaders on the other, has been so close that the disruption of the relation became immediately manifest upon the swinging into action of the "New Deal." Just as Marshall was the Federalist rear guard *vis-à-vis* the Jefferson Revolution, so the pre-Black Supreme Court[42] was the economic system's political support in the face of the Roosevelt Revolution; the first opposition was a political one, while in the second case it was purely economic. No case like Marbury's came before the pre-Black Court, however, in that case the administration won the judgement, but the Supreme Court and its adherents won the historical decision. The analogy, however, is purely functional and not morphological.

The dominant spirit in nineteenth-century America, as we have already observed, was the spirit of economic activity. Were this fact not so, judicial review would not have been able to establish itself. Owing to this, political controversies, when they arose, were settled by economic means, and thus did not find their way to the high tribunal. But they could not have been thus settled if they had been of any magnitude—and the fact is that, except slavery, *there were no greatly controverted political issues in nineteenth-century America* (to avoid a possible misunderstanding, let me say that to the organic, historical method which I am using here, the question of secession is another aspect of the question of slavery, and as regards the War of Secession they are inseparable historically: political feeling ran high—yes—but

[42] Hugo Black (1886–1971) sat on the Supreme Court from 1937 until 1971, and is remembered for his liberalism, despite having joined the Ku Klux Klan to advance his political career.

why did this particular political question come up at just this time, and between just these opposing groups?). As it was, the question of slavery was the one question of serious political possibilities that did come before the Supreme Court (the Dred Scott case), and the Court's decision thereon around the immediate opposition of the executive branch. The possible ultimate adverse effect on the power of the Court was averted by the War, after which harmony was re-established between the Court and the executive which persisted right down to 1933. True, at times there were petty differences between the two branches (over court decisions having purely economic significance, like that of *Hepburn v. Griswold,* the upshot of which was that Grant proved once and for all that constitutional law also is the law of the rulers as regards the nation, and the law of the majority as regards the constituency of the Supreme Bench), but historically they have no rank *vis-à-vis* the really important contemporary decisions of the lords of the trusts.

One other thing must be taken into account in understanding the successful establishment of this utterly unique situation. Very early, under Marshall, who had a keen feeling for the limits of political situations, the Court set for itself certain canons of judicial restraint according to which it refused to consider political questions, such as the constitutionality of treaties, the type of government within a state of the Union, the motivation of legislation, etc. Had it not observed these restraints, it could not have assumed successfully the judicial veto.

Once established, however, judicial scrutiny of legislation dominates constitutional law as a branch of jurisprudence. In America, a treatise on constitutional law has been merely an analysis of judicial decisions. The professional and academic study of constitutional law has been the study of case law. It is the nature of judicial review that it confers political significance on the judiciary whether or not it desires it. It would thus be a misunderstanding to interpret any of my remarks on the philosophy of constitutional law in the United States as implying political intent on the part of every judge when he declares the law of the Constitution. In some cases, the political and economic effect of the decision has been inextricably intertwined with the unconscious motivation of the legal ratiocination of the decision, but generally the decisions have contained a minimum of the personal. The real motivation in any individual decision has been one in which class (i.e., political and economic), legal, and personal aspects have been inseparable. Certain judges indeed have not welcomed the extra-legal position which the habit of judicial scrutiny has conferred on the Bench. Thus, in the case of *Eakin v. Raub* (12 S. & R. 330, 348, 1825) ". . . the constitution, then, contains no practical rules for the administration of *distributive justice*, with which alone the judiciary has to do; these being furnished in acts of ordinary legislation . . ." said Chief Justice Gibson of Pennsylvania. (In 1845 he recanted this unlegalistic opinion.)

The politico-legal weapon of judicial review has had its own destiny apart from the other intellectual weapons, such as "due process of law," "impairment of contract," "just compensation," "equal protection of the laws," "inherent limits of the taxing power," etc. When the nation passed finally under the complete and undisputed control of a plutocracy (1865)[43] the legal means of politics, as well as every other, passed into their exclusive possession. It served them well against the several States; three hundred times between 1870 and the Millennium (1933)[44] it struck down unfavorable legislation of the several State legislatures. It served them no less well against the Federal legislature (see above), and when the executive took over the legislative function (1933 again), it continued in their service. At that time, it was the sole effective political defense the industrialists possessed; and herein lies the fate of that defense: it was purely negative, it could only say "No," and victory has always ultimately lain with the attack. In 1870, the executive had shown that it could defeat the Supreme Court. The difference between

---

[43] That is, with the victory of the Union over the Confederacy.

[44] The year of Franklin Roosevelt's assumption to the Presidency, which to Yockey was an epochal event. In this essay, he has already referred to it as the "Roosevelt Revolution," and was also to term it the "American Revolution of 1933," in *Imperium* (Sausalito, Cal.: Noontide Press, 1969), p. 527.

that situation and that in 1937 is that Grant was fighting *one decision* and with Money behind him, where Roosevelt II fought the *whole trend* of constitutional law as it has actualized itself since the War of Secession. We all know the outcome, and here I wish to anticipate the historians of the future and declare that *judicial review* as a politico-legal fact *began in 1803, and after undergoing many vicissitudes, many changes of master, finally came to an inglorious end in 1927.* It will never again be used. It arose at one historical epoch (that of 1800), it was transformed at another (1861–1865), and ended at another (1935–1937). Consciously or unconsciously, it served the best tendency in the nation existing at any one time: first, the Federalists, next, the industrialists (remember there was no question of high politics then, it was either the Lords of Industry or the Knights of Labor), and finally, as between proletarianism and the political rule of the economic leaders in their own interest, it served the latter. Like the whole of constitutional law, it was indissolubly wedded to parliamentarianism, and in the face of powerful extra-parliamentary forces, it suddenly became no longer efficacious.

VIII. Conclusion: Future of our Constitution & Constitutional Law

It remains only to say a few words as to the future of constitutional law. Parliamentarianism is like a game; two must play at it; a Party is a unit of *opposition*, even when it is in power; one party implies another, and thus there is no such thing as a one-party government. The essence of parliamentarianism is that both sides are willing to preserve the form even where it contradicts the advantage. Party means bourgeoisie, just as surely as Estate meant nobility. Even as the only tactical unit of internal politics in 1500 was the Estate, so the only one in the nineteenth century was the Party. Thus even Marxism, the negation of the bourgeoisie, with its program of civil war, constituted itself as a Party in the nineteenth century, because the real source of power was the bourgeoisie. Even the nobility of Western Europe set itself up as a Party after Metternich.[45]

---

[45] Prince Klemens von Metternich (1773–1859) was the Foreign

The World War marked the inevitable decline of the bourgeoisie and its peculiar political institution. Since then, Western nations have known either proletarian governments, national governments, or military dictatorships, the latter being frankly temporary and provisional.[46] *In Rome, the course of events was from Patricians and Plebeians, through Optimates and Populares,*[47] *to Pompeians and Caesarians.* We now stand at the epoch leading to the last period. (Even now, his followers refer to Roosevelt as "Our Leader.")[48] Constitutional law was a *finely balanced instrument* in the Rome of 140 BC, but in 104 it suddenly became a phrase, when Marius [word missing] himself with Imperium.[49]

Minister of the Austrian Empire who established the Concert of Europe in the aftermath of the Napoleonic Wars, which was intended to stabilize international relations between the European monarchies, as well as suppress revolutionary movements across Europe. At the Congress of Vienna in 1815, he was instrumental in establishing the new map of Europe and the balance of power between the Great Powers which was to last, more or less intact, until the First World War. He was forced to resign during the Revolution of 1848.

[46] An allusion to Fascism and National Socialism, which Yockey always regarded as transitional, as did Spengler: "The prefiguration of Caesarism will soon become clearer, more conscious and unconcealed. The masks will fall completely from the age of the parliamentary interlude. All attempts to gather up the content of the future into parties will be forgotten. The Fascist formations of this decade will pass into new, unforeseeable forms, and even present-day nationalism will disappear." Oswald Spengler, *The Hour of Decision*, p. 230.

[47] In first century BC Rome, the Optimates were the part of the nobility that opposed the plebeian Populares.

[48] The epoch of the revival of Caesars replacing democracy, as the triumph of instinctual forces ("Blood") against "Money" (Spengler, *The Decline of the West*, vol. II, pp. 506–507).

[49] Gaius Marius (157–86 BC) was a Consul of the Roman Republic, which was the highest political office, with two Consuls serving jointly per term. Consuls were elected for one-year terms, and by law, no man could stand in a Consul election twice within ten years. Marius, however, was elected Consul again for the year 104, even though he had already served in 106, and went on to serve four more consecutive terms thereafter, which was unprecedented and shows that by this time the Republic was willing to overlook the law.

When a group drops its Party garb and organizes itself for extra-parliamentary political activity, it is suicide for the opposing group to carry on the game of majorities and rules. This is the significance of the arising in Western Europe of *followings of individuals* instead of the historically dead party formations.

In Italy and Germany, inwardly the strongest of the world-powers, no one any longer mentions constitutional law; it is no longer a legal discipline, nor is it even taught in the law academies. In France, always two steps away from another Reign of Terror, no one pretends that constitutional law will afford any more precedents or impose any limitations on the coming annihilation-conflict. And so far, no one has raised the cry of "unconstitutional" in the face of the establishment of the Corporate State in England, after the Italian model.

Anti-constitutional feeling in the United States comes at present from the Left, as does most of the extra-parliamentary activity. This administration has stepped beyond the bounds, not of this or that decision, but of the whole idea of imposing legal limitations on internal political activity. There is as yet no focus of resistance to the bolshevisation of the nation. May I step once more into the role of vaticinator and say that *any effective resistance to it must of necessity be extra-legal and extra-constitutional. An unconstitutional attack demands an unconstitutional defense,* and in the struggle the Constitution, even though it be a slogan for one side or the other, will be quietly interred in the vault of History.

In Germany after 1919, the same conflict between judiciary and administration occurred as occurred here from 1933 to 1937. Later, the viewpoint of the judiciary triumphed (1933), but no one thought of restoring to the judges the prerogative of refusing to give effect to laws, as they did under the Weimar Republic, which was the German form of proletarian dictatorship.

Where one wrestler is confining himself to the Roman style, and the other is wrestling "catch-as-catch-can," the tactical superiority of unscrupulousness of method is demonstrated clearly. The question quickly becomes "When will the first man throw off his suicidal restraint?," and, looking at the cheering example of the quickly-formed "Vigilantes" in the proletarian uprising of last winter,[50] the answer happily appears to be "Not long." But be under no debilitating illusions: although the slogan of the Vigilantes is "Law and Order," it will soon cease to mean the old law, the old order. My last word on the Law of The Constitution thus is:

Requiescat in pace

---

[50] The "Vigilantes" were formed as a strikebreaking organization in Detroit. It is apparent that in such a group Yockey saw the embryonic possibilities of an "American Fascism"—in Spenglerian terms, an American "Caesarism"—emerging that would be far more profound than as a mere strikebreaking force, and that would establish its ideology on the streets. The "American Caesar" that did emerge, through the contingencies of wartime emergency, was Franklin Roosevelt, taking on the form of what might more aptly be called an "Anti-Caesar" in the era of Absolute Politics, as did the other wartime "democratic" politicians, to forestall the epoch of Caesarism predicted by Spengler. Hence the democracies adopted authoritarian measures as a necessity of the times; an example of the Yockeyan dialectic of "polarities" described in Yockey's essay "Twentieth-Century Metaphysics."

BIBLIOGRAPHY

The following books were made use of, either to gain certain specific facts, or to quote as typically in error:

Burgess, John William, *Political Science and Comparative Constitutional Law* (Boston: Ginn & Co., 1890)

Chadman, Charles E., *Constitutional Law, Federal and State* (Chicago: Frederick J. Drake & Co., 1899)

Composite Authorship, [blank] *and State in Neuen Deutschland,* 1925[51]

Dicey, A. V., *Introduction to the Study of the Law of the Constitution* (London: MacMillan, 1927)

Ernst, Morris, *The Ultimate Power* (Garden City, N.Y.: Doubleday, Doran & Co., 1937)

Hatschek, Julius, *Deutsches und Preussisches Staatsrecht* (Berlin: Stilke, 1922)

Hatschek, Julius, *Englische Verfassungsgeschichte bis zum Regierungsantritte der Königin Victoria* (Munich: Oldenbourg, 1913)

Jennings, William Ivor, *Cabinet Government* (New York: MacMillan, 1936)

Long, Joseph R., *Cases on Constitutional Law* (Rochester, N.Y.: Lawyers Co-Op Publishing Co., 1936)

McConaughy, John, *Who Rules America?* (New York: Longmans, Green & Co., 1934)

---

[51] The editors have been unable to identify this work, so it has been reproduced as Yockey had it.

Merriam, Charles Edward, *The Written Constitution and the Unwritten Attitude* (New York: R. R. Smith, 1931)

Renouvin, Pierre, *The Forms of War Government in France* (New Haven, Conn.: Yale University Press, 1927)

Sohm, Rudolf, *Institutionen* (Leipzig: Duncker & Humblot, 1898)

Taylor, Hannis, *Origin and Growth of the English Constitution*, 2 vols. (Boston: Houghton Mifflin, 1896, 1898)

Woodward, William E., *A New American History* (New York: Literary Guild, 1937)

I also read the various contributions which are cited, and was amazed, although not surprised, at the incredible acts of faith of which the rationalistic head is capable. The best collection is *Select Constitutions of the World*, published by the Irish Stationery Office in 1922. Of interest too is *Select Documents and Constitutions of France, 1791–1871*.

THE TRAGEDY OF YOUTH

1939

EDITORS' NOTE

"The Tragedy of Youth," in Father Coughlin's magazine *Social Justice,* seems to have been the first *published* essay by Yockey. Even by this time, his ideas were well-formed, and the fundamentals did not change. The article addresses the moral decay imposed on young Americans by a corrupt system and the forces that were pushing them to war. Yockey wrote that youth is the primary target of the forces of subversion, and that it is from youth that resistance must come. He stated that "alien" influences, through their control of entertainment and the press, pour out a constant stream of propaganda aimed at "complete spiritual power over the minds of young Americans."[1] This took the form of "exhibitionist dancing," "a perverted and insane pictorial art," and "jungle music," which are the norm for American adolescence. For the more serious, thinking youth, they have been targeted by internationalist, class war propaganda. There has been "spiritual regimentation" of the young in Leftist-controlled academia "by the preachers of Roosevelt-Leftism."

Yockey here identified himself as a "Christian nationalist," with a keen analytical mind in seeing the broad picture of events. He had declared himself in favor of Italy and Germany. Interestingly, he recognized the crucial role of debt-finance in enslaving a nation. The question of debt and the international bankers was the *raison d'être* of Father Coughlin's National Union for Social Justice. Coughlin, once he realized that Roosevelt had no intention of throwing out the "money changers," and was rather in league with them, established the National Union to campaign for state credit and the elimination of usury. It was pure Catholic social doctrine and part of the Church's traditional

---

[1] Francis Parker Yockey, "The Tragedy of Youth," *Social Justice,* August 21, 1939, p. 7.

role in condemning usury.[2] However, the Church hierarchy was persuaded by Roosevelt to shut Coughlin down, while in April 1942 *Social Justice* was charged under the violation of the Espionage Act and was barred from the mails. Being an obedient servant of the Church, Coughlin returned to the obscurity of his parish, and so one of the most dynamic forces in American history was silenced.

Yockey showed that he was acutely aware of the cultural degeneration being fostered by Hollywood and New York and that youth were succumbing to the cycle of decadence in art, dancing, and "jungle music," which had become the "spiritual norm." Yockey returned to these issues in *Imperium* in 1948 and *The Proclamation of London* in 1949, where he explained them as symptoms of Culture-distortion. Given today's situation, and the manner by which youth, now worldwide, are still targeted by the "Culture-distorters," immeasurably empowered via "social media," "The Tragedy of Youth" is surely one of Yockey's most prescient and relevant essays for our own day.

THE TRAGEDY OF YOUTH

Their Generation, Now Unemployed, Must Fight the War Then Become Slaves in Red State That Follows

---

[2] Point 6 of the 16-point NUSJ program stated, "Abolition of private banking, and institution of a central government bank." Point 7 demanded control over the value of money by the central government. The Federal Reserve Bank, like other central banks that were being formed around the world, gave the appearance of being a state bank, but such banks are run by international financiers. The Federal Reserve Bank was based on the blueprint of Paul Warburg, a scion of the Warburg banking dynasty. Germany, Italy, and Japan broke free of the international financial system and operated on state credit and barter. While the Axis states flourished in the midst of a world depression, Roosevelt's acclaimed New Deal, which tried to ape the success of the Italian corporatist economy, got nowhere, and the United States only achieved recovery through war production. See K. R. Bolton, *The Banking Swindle* (London: Black House Publishing, 2013).

Observations about the pitfalls of youth, by oldsters like Gov. Dickinson of Michigan, do not always stress the degree to which youth is the *deliberate victim of planned demoralization*, nor do they have the viewpoint of youth. Youngsters, on the other hand, do not see with the wisdom of their elders. In Mr. Yockey, however, we have both the viewpoint of youth and, what's more, the vision to perceive how his generation is made the scapegoat.—THE EDITOR.[3]

No section of the American populace has been more completely deceived by the forces interested in keeping the truth from the people than America's youth. Youth stands to suffer most from the present regime of America's enemies in control of America. Therefore, *it is from youth that the Leftist dictatorship might some day have the most to fear.*

The alien-minded minority in control of the cinema, the radio, and the newspaper and magazine press has poured out a constant stream of propaganda with the intent of gaining complete spiritual power over the minds of young Americans emerging into maturity. With what success the attempt has met everyone knows who has talked on their own level to representative American youths from the ages of 19 to 27. One and all their world-views have been cut out for them in New York, Hollywood, and Washington.

Appalling numbers of youth have been led into a cynical ultra-sophisticated attitude which regards drinking as a badge of social aptitude, which makes a fetish of sport, and professes eroticism as a way of life. A perverted and insane pictorial art, lewd exhibitionistic dancing, and jungle music form the spiritual norm of this sector of America's youth.

Books, Magazines Carry Propaganda

For those serious-minded youths, who are genuinely interested in the tremendous problems now facing us, another insidious attack has been devised. Books have been written, plays have been staged, and an unending train of lecturers have mounted

[3] In the original text.

the platform—all to convey to these thinking youths the same message of class war and international hatred.

Magazines have been founded for none other than propaganda purposes—*vide Life, Look, Click, Esquire, Ken, Coronet*—and have been made up in such a way as to prove attractive to the young readers.

The result of this campaign to destroy Christian Americanism among the youth is that *every periodical, 95 percent of the books, and all the lecturers are Leftist.* Leftist ideas are a part of the very atmosphere which American youth breathes. The young person whose reasoning powers have come to full development within the past seven years has never even come in contact with a conservative, Christian view of life. His professors are in the main Leftists, those who are not are afraid to speak out for fear of their jobs. Most of the parents do not realize the spiritual regimentation of their children because they themselves have been indoctrinated along with them. Those parents who do think otherwise are considered "old-fashioned," and proponents of the "horse-and-buggy days" by the preachers of Roosevelt Leftism.

YOUTH VICTIMS OF RED DEMORALIZATION

The tragedy of this conscription of American youth under the banners of atheism, class-war, and social degeneration is just this: *that the continuance of the economic and spiritual distress of the youth is an integral part of the revolutionary program of the same Communist forces which have seduced and indoctrinated them.*

According to Communist leaders, the revolutionary struggle in the United States is in the stage of the "Popular Front," with Mr. Roosevelt as the leader *pro tempore.* The aim of a "Popular Front" government can best be set forth in the words of Maurice Thorez,[4] French Communist leader:

---

[4] Maurice Thorez (1900–1964) was the leader of the French Communist Party from 1930 until his death. Strongly supported and controlled by Stalin, and a strict Stalinist himself, he served in the Chamber of Deputies for many years and nearly brought about a Communist revolution in France in 1948. The quotation comes from a speech by Thorez that was delivered to the Eighth Congress of the French Communist Party that was held in Villeurbanne in 1936. The

> It will be a government which will give the working-class and the Communist Party all possibilities for agitation, propaganda, organization, and action, a government which will make it possible to prepare for the complete seizure of power by the working-class (i.e., by their self-chosen leaders), in brief, *a government which will be a prelude for the armed insurrection for the dictatorship of the proletariat.* . . . For the Communists, the Popular Front is not a tactic of expediency. Still less is it an election move. It is an element of their fundamental policy, and application of the principles of Marx and Lenin . . . (From his speech at Villeurbanne, January, 1936.)

PROSPERITY FATAL TO COMMUNIST HOPES

Now it is easy to see that this program, however successful to date in America, cannot be fulfilled if our nation is prosperous and if the population is engaged in productive, decently paid labor. Both the "Popular Front" which we now endure and its successor, *the blood-bath Communist dictatorship,* are based on national conditions of widespread economic distress and unemployment such as we now have.

The tactic that is being employed to bring about the necessary crisis for the "complete seizure of power" is that of producing a financial collapse by profligate and insensate government expenditures on everything and anything. It does not matter whether the projects are needed or not, all that matters is that the money gets spent, and spent in such a way as to make the greatest number possible dependent on the Government, thus to break their spirits and render them fertile ground for planting class hatred, and prepare them for enrollment in the Left Army, an army which now includes labor unions, WPA workers,[5] those on relief, organized Negroes, the teachers and professors, and

---

translated text was published in the pamphlet *The Unity of the French Nation* (New York: Workers Library Publishers, 1936), p. 53.

[5] The Works Progress Administration was an agency created by the New Deal in 1935 to create jobs for millions of American workers during the Great Depression by employing them in public works projects.

the greater part of the youth.

The tragedy for youth lies in this, that every condition for the success of the Communist scheme is created at the expense of youth, and every tactic employed in actualizing it makes the position of youth more desperate and more nearly hopeless.

Revolutionists Do Not Want Improvement

First, there is the ghastly extent of unemployment among the youth. Hundreds of thousands of young Americans up to the age of 27 have never had any other employment than Government relief work. When will they realize that the alien-minded minority in control of our country *does not want this condition with its revolutionary possibilities removed?*

Second, the burden that the ever-growing national debt imposes is almost solely a burden on the youth. No matter how this debt is liquidated, by confiscatory inflation, or by being paid off, dollar for dollar, it will be paid at the cost of liberty and happiness of present-day American youth. If all the private and corporate wealth of the nation is confiscated to pay off the debt, what economic force will be left in the country that can run a country and employ the idle millions? And such a collapse is just the crisis out of which a Red dictatorship will fasten on America. If the other alternative is adopted, it will mean that the youth of the present will be slaves during their whole life, working, not for their own wants and happiness, but in order to pay $2 out of every $3 they earn to the Government. The national standard of living in this case would not be pleasant to contemplate.

Third, the individual future of almost every American youth has been jeopardized. Not one of those same young men now in universities and professional schools who spend their conversation in deciding "how to stop Hitler" knows where or whether he can start his career.

Where is there research or construction to take up all the young engineers, business to take up accountants and stenographers?

How many families can now afford to have a doctor every time they need one?

Or to litigate their legal claims?

Where is there a future for those trained in commerce?

Youth Always Fights the Nation's Wars

Lastly, American youth by the millions will be conscripted into armies to be sent to Asia and Europe to fight the battle of world Communism, *unless a powerful Christian nationalism arises to cast out the alien-thinking minority in Washington.* A war will give our "liberal" Government a chance to avenge wrongs done it by those foreign governments which have liquidated class war within their nations, and to defeat by a repressive war-dictatorship the incipient movement among the people against radicalism and in favor of a Christian nationalistic government.

Those to return from the battlefields where world Communism would send them to a Communist America would perhaps wish they were in the war cemeteries of Western Europe with their buddies.

With this prospect—with the assurance of Communist leaders that the Popular Front is not only to defeat Fascism, but also to bring about Communist dictatorship—with the mask torn off the Leftist trend of many in high posts of control in the Federal Government—no longer controlled by Americans—is American youth to wait supinely, absorbed in picture magazines, for the butchers to start their blood bath here?

Youth of America—*Awake*! It's *your* problem and *your* task. You are the special victim if they win.

LIFE AS AN ART

1940

EDITORS' NOTE

This essay was written in December 1940 in South Bend, Indiana, while Yockey was a law student at Notre Dame University, having enrolled in September 1940.[1] Yockey had already been actively involved with the Right, in particular as a writer and speaker for Father Charles Coughlin's movement and the Silver Shirt Legion.

"Life as an Art" already encapsulates all of the major premises of Yockey's philosophy, including his vision of "Western Empire," explicated in detail in 1948 in *Imperium*.

In this essay, two seminal influences are dominant: Spengler and Nietzsche. The latter's concept of the "higher man" forms the basis of Yockey's rejection of equality in favor of a resurgence of hierarchy, the concept of the will-to-power, and an overriding self-discipline. He applies these Nietzschean concepts to the concept of the "mission," which emerges as an involuntary compulsion welling up from whatever set of complexes form the "higher man," an inner imperative to follow a life's path that is no more to be subjected to rationalizing, intellectualizing, and analyses than the instinctual impulsion of a bird of prey to act on his nature.

The "art" of the life of higher man is not aesthetic, as in prior centuries, but is of a martial nature. When Yockey states that the Western Civilization has exhausted its aesthetic possibilities, and that its art must now focus on other tasks, he is drawing directly from Spengler. Spengler foresaw the emergence of Caesars, after the overthrow of the rule of Money in the epochal crisis of the Western Civilization, having triumphed in a battle of wills: Money versus Blood.[2] By "Blood" is here meant the instinctual-

---

[1] Coogan, *Dreamer of the Day*, p. 103.

[2] Spengler, *The Decline of the West*, vol. II, p. 507.

intuitive in contrast to the artificial; the mentality of the counting-house that dominates the decadent epoch of a Civilization.

The task that Yockey gave these Spenglerian Caesars or Nietzschean "higher men" was to create a new Empire of the West that would fulfill the West's creative possibilities in a new direction. As Yockey mentions, a preview of these possibilities was that of Napoleonic Europe, an era ushered in by a "higher man," a new Caesar, who not only negated the doctrines of the French Revolution by imposing a return to authority and hierarchy, but also sought to shape a unified Europe.

Looking to analogous historical examples outside of Western Civilization, one might also compare Yockey's image of the future State with that of Sparta, where luxury was eschewed and culture was martial rather than aesthetic. National Socialist Germany had sought to regenerate Western aesthetics and could do no better—or worse—than to recreate the best of both the monumental Classical and Gothic traditions, and here one sees the possibilities of an aesthetic blossoming within the context of the Yockeyan martial state, regardless of the sneers of modernist art critics.[3]

However, as if to prove the contention of Yockey and Spengler that the West had fulfilled its aesthetic possibilities insofar as great *new* art forms would not be forthcoming, it is notable that this artistic flowering in Germany was derivative of the Classical and the Gothic rather than creating a new aesthetic. Fascist Italy tried to synthesize the traditional with the modern in creating an Italian Fascist aesthetic, their new innovation being Futurism,[4] which aimed to reflect the new epoch as being one of technics, steel, and motion.

However, Yockey's conception of the Western Empire as one of martial ethos, where the soldier-statesman regards the High Culture of the West as passé in terms of the imperial tasks

---

[3] See Frederic Spotts, *Hitler and the Power of Aesthetics* (New York: Abrams, 2002); and Jonathan Petropoulos, *The Faustian Bargain: The Art World in Nazi Germany* (London: Penguin Books, 2000).

[4] Günter Berghaus, *Futurism & Politics: Between Anarchist Rebellion and Fascist Reaction, 1909–1944* (Oxford: Berghahn Books, 1996).

ahead, is again Spenglerian. His passages on this in "Life as an Art" very closely parallel Spengler. Spengler had written, for example:

> And herein, I think, all the philosophers of the newest age are open to a serious criticism. What they do not possess is real understanding in actual life. Not one of them has intervened effectively, either in higher politics, in the development of modern technics, in matters of communication, in economics, or in any other *big* actuality, with a single act or a single compelling idea.[5]

And the final sentence of *The Decline of the West* states what Yockey expresses in his essay, that the "mission" of the "higher man" is not something that is realized by intellectual processes, but something that is already within, that instinctively impels the "higher man"—Spengler's new "Caesar"—to act in accordance with historical necessity: "And a task that historic necessity has set will be accomplished with the individual or against him."[6]

LIFE AS AN ART

Written, December 1940, in South Bend, Indiana

Life has been said to be an art, the greatest of the arts. But it is immaterial to the vast impersonal directedness which we attempt to conjure under the name of Destiny whether we regard life as an art, a task, a burden, or whether we trouble to objectify it at all. Destiny's purpose (thus human-like to personify not only all other things *discerned*, but even Destiny which is only *felt*) is merely that the form impressed be unfolded. It is sublimely unconcerned with its divine counterpart, the Soul of Man, which tortures and frustrates itself—on the individual plane—with first one and then another picture of Life. Always the living tries to

[5] Oswald Spengler, *The Decline of the West*, vol. I, p. 42.
[6] Ibid., vol. II, p. 507.

regard Life, and never is Life other than it is by reason thereof.

Even the superpersonal, endowed with the Destiny that is the hallmark of the living, taking up into itself the lives of generations and nations, evinces complete indifference toward the outcome of the problems it poses. History, with its many volumes and its one page, carries this message to the man of comprehension. It is well enough for man to invent an ethic which will obtain for its brief period and over its brief territory: the inward force of life—Destiny—will make sure that this temporary ethic will in no case interfere with the necessity of Life's course of happening. If we wished, we might speak of an *ethic of Life*, for it is surely one of the privileges of man, securely imprisoned by Life, that he can contradict himself in a harmless way.

Confer comprehension on the unfolding rosebud—does it matter to its process of actualization that the rosebud knows its destiny? Will it become any the less a full-blown rose that it remembers the content and significance of its unfolding? In the same way proceeds the actualization of the chthonic-divine creature called man. Even such an inorganic thinker as Schopenhauer saw that one could never change his character.

Out of a hovering chiaroscuro of metaphysics and ethics emerge two great actualities of Life. We must live, and we must regard Life. It is probably not Life which makes these demands, but it is not for us to understand, but only to see the necessary and to do it. The setting sun, which each day marks the end of another recapitulation of the life of this man, that man, the sum of men, the world and the universe of stars, is the best background for the probing after explanations, and the man in whom the pulse of life beats strongly will confine his questioning to the evening twilight. Life permits us to ask questions as the arc is about to close on itself, when the entirety of one set of possibilities—whether those of one day, or those of one's life—have been realized, but woe will betide him who mistakes high noon for sunset!

We must regard life—that is, entirely unawares Life demands of its rare products, the men of comprehension, to set off whose rarity the others exist at all, that they conduct their conscious acts on the basis of a *picture* of Life. In some cases the process of finding the correct picture occupies the whole life course of a man. This is the philosopher. But Life is not a background for philosophers—philosophers can only discern the problems. Men of action bring the solutions—and the solutions are the deeds themselves. The course of *superpersonal* happening is just as inevitable as the expression of its possibilities by the unfolding rosebud.

Within the men of action, deepest phenomenon of becoming, occurs *the free will in the service of the destined.* Freedom and necessity—to men this must remain a contradiction that they are free to do the necessary.

The question here is: what picture of Life is most suitable for the man of action?

It would be absurd to attempt to place my selection of such a picture on any other basis than that of taste—taste being in the last resort the true basis of even the most highly rationalized and mechanized philosophies.

Higher men and lower men—the few called to rule and the masses born in order that the higher men may actualize a grander destiny—differ in spirituality so much that they cannot be comprehended otherwise than as two different species. In all reverence it can be said that the lower men rely on God, and the higher men on themselves. This basic natural hierarchy is the fundament upon which rests all practical philosophy of human nature. It must therefore be definitively set forth.

There are two species of men—as different in spirituality as lions and lambs. Their whole manner of experiencing life, of nourishing themselves in the struggle of life, of fighting the battle of life, of solving inwardly the problem which life presents, the resulting pictures of life—all are totally different.

In each case the method of higher men is the inversion of the method that the lower men pursue. Lower men live in continual fear, and this fear, metaphysical and physical, dominates their whole life-outlook. Their world must be freed of chaos, and, in a High Culture, the primeval beginnings in a great religious awakening and a patriarchal organization of society testify both to the individual and the superpersonal fear of the tremendous inanimate world, the world of upheavals and catastrophes, of dim, mysterious, unaccountable non-ego. Every subsequent development in the social and religious aspects of a High Culture conceal this same fear and its concomitant desire to be free from fear by conjuring the world-around. The development of religion through the supremacy of philosophy to the final degeneration in free science is the story of the seeking by lower men for inward security—for protection in their weaknesses against the unknown. Correspondingly society from its patriarchal origin through the complexities attendant on the growth of cities and the money organization of life down to the present demand for "social security" has always been premised at any one moment on the need of the weak—the lower men—for external and internal security.

The higher men, however, unable to attain in the herd-like comfort of lower men, filled inwardly with a rushing [illegibile] which must find expression, find their significance and their temporary satisfaction in grand creativeness—literary, musical, philosophic, religious, technical, or greater than all these, the creativeness of deeds. Higher men themselves are the servants of culture in that the style of their creativeness is fixed for them in advance by the accident of their birth which places them in this or that cultural epoch. Thus great technical achievements, acknowledged by the age as supreme, there were not in Gothic times. No more is the greatness in the arts of form today, hence no higher men, but only weaklings and jealous inferiors are uncreatively at work in these arts today. In the age when Western philosophy was at its peak of grandeur, one is not surprised to find one of the most perfect higher men as the philosopher, Goethe. But regardless of the cultural stage, high politics is always appropriate, and so for the past thousand years of the Western Culture, there has been a continuous succession of higher men in the supreme field of high politics. From Frederick II, Rainald von Dassel, and Barbarossa, through Wallenstein, Oxenstierna, Richelieu, Pitt the Younger, Napoleon, Metternich, Bismarck, Hitler, politics has chosen from the higher men, regardless of the drain that other fields of high creativeness made on the precious blood of the Western nations. Politics, by usurping the pages of the volumes of history, has shown thereby its commanding position in human cultural creativeness. One and all, from Richard Plantagenet to Mussolini, from Torquemada to Spengler, higher men have each had the same deep, unspoken feeling of *the mission*. The smaller men, filled perforce with venomous jealousy of anything so forceful and carefree, so sure of itself, have always described this feeling of the higher natures as vanity, and the consequent reverence that higher men feel for themselves as egomania.

This it is that distinguishes the higher natures—they have reverence for themselves; their own souls contain to them something precious which must be brought to fulfillment, for the higher natures have some of the attributes of superpersonal souls. Like history in its fulfillment laying waste human resources, denying and frustrating human wishes, reaching deep into private life to chasten souls with tragedy, the higher men deny and subordinate their own emotions, sacrifice their private lives, and all because *there is something more important to them than all this: the mission*. In the conduct of his Life, the higher man does not employ reason any more than History itself employs reason. There is no **reason** for the cycle of the generations, for the universal life cycle of birth, growth, fulfillment, decline, and death, for the human life span of 70 years, the Culture's of 1000 years, the nation's of 300. Instinct is the sure guide of the higher man, and unconscious decision is his surest method of accomplishment. Herein, in this all-demanding sense of a mission, is the explanation of Napoleon's rejection of Désirée Clary, Goethe's flight from Friederike.[7] The choice of a mate, if any, is also decided by the inward voice.

This is a strange selfishness [illegible] his desires. Father, mother, wife, and brother have their claims on such men, but something higher has a prior claim. *The higher man does not belong*

---

[7] While still a Brigadier General in the French army, Napoleon was briefly engaged to Désirée Clary in 1795, but broke it off after only a few months to marry Joséphine de Beauharnais. She later married Charles XIV John of Sweden, becoming Queen of Sweden and Norway. At the age of 20, Goethe fell in love with Friederike Brion, but ended it after less than a year. She never married.

to himself, but to his time and his mission. Egomania!—say rather demi-divinity!

It was an American who said, "I shun father and mother and wife and brother when my genius calls me."[8] This sentence describes every higher man. His genius—genius means *creative force*, or, using the word honorifically instead of descriptively, it means *great creative force*—is his hallmark, it makes him what he becomes, it gives him what he acquires of this world's goods, whether palaces like those from which Napoleon could choose, the peasant cottage on the barren globe, like Burns,[9] or the death-garret of Chatterton.[10] It deprives him of all contentment, peace, and happiness until the mission is accomplished. But creative force—this will remain forever incomprehensible to those, far more than 99% of humanity—who cannot see deeply into the soul of Culture-man—**is at bottom artistic**. In the deeps the will-to-power merges with the aesthetic instinct. In the brief moment of satisfaction which follows the completion of a work—a novel, a building, a suspension bridge, a symphony, a victorious battle—the soul of a higher man feels an intense and profound aesthetic satisfaction in the form of self-reverence and a feeling of union with the essence of Being. For a moment the abysmal mystery is dissolved, and the man becomes a god. But the swirling chaos which demands form returns with its tireless whip, and only death can end the ceaseless dictation of the inner voice.

How ludicrous it is that in the present time—and the present is so swiftly becoming the past—extreme development of the faculty of intelligence is called genius! Correspondingly it seems

---

[8] Footnote in original: Emerson, one of the four higher men to arise in America outside the realm of technics, the others being Hamilton, Franklin, and Poe. (The quotation comes from Emerson's essay "Self-Reliance.")

[9] Robert Burns (1759–1796) is regarded as the national poet of Scotland. Being poor and earning little from his poems, he attempted to make a living (rather unsuccessfully) as a farmer.

[10] Thomas Chatterton (1752–1770) was an English poet and political writer who committed suicide at the age of 17 because he could not make enough money from writing. His tragic death inspired some of the Romantics.

that the value of a man is measured by **how much he has!** Smile with me. A test has even been devised whereby men move wooden blocks into patterns and skilled "psychologists" can then pick out the "geniuses." "Genius" is a number. Idiocy is a number. Controversy as to whether one can by taking thought change his number. The apotheosis of asininity! This nowadays calls itself "science." One gains a glimpse into the human soul by studying the salivation of dogs. The brave free science of the Baroque, so sure of itself, so eager and confident, is mocked by this silly stuff, its waste product. The last thing added to science's stock of objects is the human soul, or "mind" as they say. The soul turns on itself methods created by itself. These methods were first devised to subjugate natural phenomena and were found to be appropriate. How surprising that the soul was found by these methods to be just another natural phenomenon! Life is a complex physico-chemical reaction!

This is a conscious age. It knows whither it is going. In any other age it had not been necessary to base one's life-outlook on one's prevision as to the future. But the present form of our world-knowledge leaves no doubt that the Western soul has in this field closed its cycle of development, and that the future field of development of this soul is not in religion, philosophy, art, and science, but in the field of technical, economic, and political activity. **The Western soul has become finally extroverted.** It has entered the last stage. Old religions, old systems, are now mere forms, mere recesses in which the uncreative and the fearful may take refuge. The religion that is appropriate for this age is already clearly outlined. And with it goes an ethic as rigid as that of St. Ignatius.

Our religion can be put into one word: skepsis.[11] And ethic into one: discipline. Of course all creeds exist in all ages, in one form or another. But at different times, different creeds are uppermost—that is, they are those of the significant men. In the Crusades, the significant man was a Gothic Christian. In the eighteenth and nineteenth centuries he was an atheist. And now he is a skeptic—not in the older sense meaning one who does

---

[11] The definite singular form of skepticism.

not accept the Christian religion, but in the sense that he doubts not of this or that tenet, but that he doubts the ability of mere intellect to understand anything. He is not a subjectivist, he is not atheist, positivist, nor pragmatist—these are all systems, explanations, and he has no explanations, he builds no systems. He builds instead roads, colonies, empires, deeds. It is immediately apparent that such an attitude toward life is not possible to a metaphysician or an ethician. And the significant men of the future will number among them no men of thought, no logicians, no abstract thinkers. The great men of the Crusades conquered in the name of Christendom, the great scientists from Roger Bacon to Max Planck conquered in the name of intensified knowledge; the thinkers, from Aquinas to Kant strove each to reduce the totality of things to their intellects in the name of Truth. But now the tide of old Gothic Christianity has subsided, pure knowledge has been dissolved into technics, and the quest after Truth no longer attracts the great minds. Napoleon heralded the man of the future, Nietzsche described his nature, Spengler has announced his imminent arrival.

Our future, having been shown, unveils for us the secret of the present. If there is one contest whose result can be foretold with strictness, it is the struggle of the Past against the Future. Victory in these days, as in all previous days will go to him whose spirituality is consonant with the living Idea of the times.

Skepsis and Discipline! Just as the skepsis of the coming age is a new and deeper skepsis, so is the discipline. It is the discipline of self, first of all. The ideal of self-discipline will be realized of course only by the higher man, just as in Gothic times, the ones to realize the dominant idea of the time were the saints, the higher men, the bearer of the mission of those days. But the idea of self-discipline nevertheless is dominant, and it will attract with irresistible power the leading men of the coming time. But the discipline will only start with the self, it will continue into the field of training of the young, the organization of the economic life, the form of the State. Above all, it will bring back the eternal idea of political organization, the monarch—call him dictator or president, he will return, and the hereditary idea is too strong in our Western blood not to break out once our rationalism is finally buried. Education, law, technics, armies, and fleets, all will be governed by discipline, all will be at the service of the State.

They will be in the service of the State rather than the service of the Church, rationalism, "humanity," universal equality, the proletariat, or something else, simply because the new idea is completely externalized. It has no religion, no art, no Golden Age of literature, no Utopia, to bring forth. It contains the germs of no Renaissance, no Flemish school of painting, no Spanish drama, no German metaphysics, no English economic imperialism, no French chauvinism and militarism. *It will be the complete actualization of the Idea of Power.* In his Cultural biography, Western man has pursued at successive times eternal salvation, Truth, beauty, knowledge, and has even sought to enthrone Reason. There is left for him the externalized pursuits of technics, the military art, political imperialism, and State organization. The same intensity that developed the arts of oil painting and the fugue, that wrested from Nature her secrets, that proclaimed the universal rule of Liberty and Equality will now turn to write the history of the planet in terms of Western Empire.

The inquiry has been answered: **the picture of life most suitable for the man of action is that life is an artistic task to be performed in the service of the will-to-power.** There is no such thing as the man of action, as dissociated from the conditions which time, place, and culture impose, therefore I have spoken of Western man, the most important type of man in the world today. His metaphysic of skepsis is the only one appropriate to an externalized era. His ethic of discipline is the one least divergent from the true nature of higher man as a type. Such an ethic is an ethic of fact as distinguished from that advocated in the Sermon on the Mount, which is completely at variance with fact in every word. It is the ethic of the battlefield, not the confessional. Its remedy for a private wrong is the dueling ground, not the court-room. It understands government as the twin processes of commands and obedience. Its understanding of society is the ordered ranking of men according to their worth and significance. Its understanding of marriage is a spiritual life-long union, not an intellectual childless companionship.

I am aware that there are those who oppose the full blooming of the twentieth century. The plaintive cries of these world-improvers will be drowned out by the tramp of marching feet. The slogan of equality, the watchword of the inferior, will disappear, and no one will even remember it. Life produced rationalism, and Life has tired of it.

Finis

TWENTIETH-CENTURY METAPHYSICS

CA. 1945–1948

EDITORS' NOTE

These aphorisms can be dated to the period between late 1945 and 1948, from the reference Yockey makes to the Nuremberg Trial (which began in November 1945) and the number of themes mentioned here that were developed further in *Imperium* (1948), such as those on Marxism, Freudianism, and Darwinism. It should also be noted that Yockey refers to part of the *nom-de-plume* he used for writing *Imperium*: Varange.

XXTH CENTURY METAPHYSICS

My philosophy—and incidentally also, that of the Spirit of the Age: the **true** is that which *I feel;* the **good** is that which *I want;* the **beautiful** is that which *pleases me*.

❖ ❖ ❖

There are five planes of becoming: the cosmic, the plant, the animal, the human, the High Cultural.

As to the first, no one can be inwardly sure whether it is *living* or not. No definition of life can be constructed which will exclude all cosmic phenomena. The distinction between Being and Becoming, like all other distinctions, vanishes upon the deepest passive observation.

In passing from one plane to the other, there are no frontiers; all of the planes overlap the adjoining planes in the succession; each subsequent plane retains the characteristics of the preceding planes to a greater or less degree. The presenting of these five planes in this ordering conveys no "evolutionary" idea, in the Darwinian sense, but is a purely anthropomorphic ordering, based on the increasing complexity, refinement, elaboration, and multifariousness of the phenomena on each plane—**as they appear to human observation.**

All of the planes affect all the other planes, but there is nothing to be gained by trying to work out a symbolic algebra here.

No one can be inwardly sure about the comparative distance from any one plane to the next. At first glance, the greatest step appears to be that from the cosmic to the plant—but are you **sure**? The measuring stick is lacking.

The "human race" is mostly not human—i.e., not only numerically does the animal element predominate, but in a given sample of large numbers, the animal plane predominates. Examples: obviously outside the Western Culture-area the animal plane dominates the human component in the "human race." Let him who does not yet know this visit China, India, Africa, Islam. But in Europe itself, in any great city, for example, the greater part of the population is governed by animal needs and ideals, this **in fact**, but not in theory. In America, this is true also in theory.

Each phase of life has its prime characteristic, and on each plane, each species of life has its special characteristic; among animals, the eagle's **eye** distinguishes him, the dog's **nose**, the horse's **fleet foot**. What, however, is human? What is it that human beings have that no animal whatever has, no other form of life whatever? **Mind** is the prime characteristic of the human, but mind at its highest potential exists in vanishingly few members of the "human race."

Life and Death are not opposites, not polarized—Life and *matter* are the poles. Death is only through poetic derivation the opposite of life—in death, the living become *matter*, the principle of life, spirit, departs. The process of this occurring is called death, or in other words, Death is the last performance of Life.

❖ ❖ ❖

Life and spirit are identical.

❖ ❖ ❖

Superiority is an attempt; mediocrity is an accomplished fact.

❖ ❖ ❖

Philosophy in the XXth Century no longer has the obligation to present a *system*, but a *picture*.

Why is philosophy necessary at all in the XXth century, the Age of Absolute Politics? Because even we children of machinery and statistics still have our proto-human *metaphysical sense*—we must fill in the background of our minds, however roughly, however superficially. For most men, this is no problem: the parents transmit their metaphysical notions to the children, and—the child is father to the man. How many men create their own world-outlook, independently of family and immediate environment? Quite factually, with no wish to exaggerate, I estimate one in each million in culture-populations, far less among savages, fellaheen, and barbarians.

❖ ❖ ❖

Freud is a fairly truthful picture of the usual man; so is Marx; so is Darwin. The common denominator of these three vile systems is the *equality* idea. All three of these systems are, in their unconscious origins, revolts against superiority, aristocracy, culture. Darwinism says: "You see, with all your pride, you are only an ape." Marx says: "All you superior ones are merely richer, and thieves at that, and we shall now expropriate you, and you shall be our servants." Freud said: "Even your proudest accomplishments are nothing but your sexual impulse."

❖ ❖ ❖

The three vile systems have absolutely no validity applied to superior men, higher men, creative men. **But it was against these that the three systems were directed.** With Darwin, it was purely intellectual, but with Marx and Freud hatred and jealousy are the motive forces, and all the ponderous verbiage merely decks out their "inferiority complexes," the smoldering resentment of inferiority. How Marx and Freud would have enjoyed the Nürnberg trial!

From the beginning, Marxism and Freudianism were *polemical* systems, never "scientific" systems. They aimed, as did all those who used these vile doctrines, at *levelling*.

It is the easiest thing in the world for a beginning student of logic to destroy the vile systems scholastically; e.g., Marxism: if everything is economic, if religion, poetry, heroism, philosophy, warfare, are all economics, this does not obliterate the actual, living differences between these things. Poetry is still not warfare, even if both are economic. So, what has been done other than to change names, to transpose words? Freudianism: if, as the Freudians say, Mozart's music represents the attempt by Mozart to return to his mother's womb, and Napoleon's battles represent the same thing, even if they are all sex, there is still a morphology of music and a morphology of war, and harmony and composition cannot be better taught or understood by bringing in embryology. Furthermore, if everything is sex, then sex is everything, therefore with an equal logic it can be said that Mozart in his mother's womb is writing music, that Napoleon is fighting battles there.

Both Marx and Freud wanted to describe that to which they were unequal in terms of something they did understand. What is the imperative of Marx: get rich at the expense of the rich. Marx understood greed, therefore he made the whole world and its history into a sticky mass of greed. Freud's system makes it obvious he was a monster of unspiritualized lust. If he had been gifted for love or erotic, Vienna would have had a Jewish Casanova. But love and erotic are both unknown to him. His lust is dark and animalistic, and dominated his nature utterly. Because it was coupled with impossibility of satisfaction, owing to his lack of money, position, and personal charm, it was utterly frustrated, and, like the cripple who makes himself into a master chess-player, Freud smeared his unsatisfied lust over the whole world, and said, "Look at this dirt, this filth—this is what you all are, even when you think you are so refined and spiritual."

To Marx, the world is a huge money-bag; to Freud it is a dung-heap; to Darwin a zoo.

How different was the world of the author of *Theologia Germanica*![1] For him the world was an endless striving, a constant tension between the soul's loneliness in the grey infinite and the soul's warmth in the feeling of the Perfect, God. For him, the essential was the relationship of man to God, and that of man to man is so plainly a mere reflection of the first that he barely mentions it. And what was the path of salvation to this man? Surely the most intense and dynamic religious imperative ever formulated: *das Lassen der Ichheit*,[2] the abandonment of the very principle of Individuality and mystical union with God. This to be attained however, not like an Indian, by sitting still and refusing to live, but in the midst of active life.

All theories and proofs of the soul's immortality beg the question. The question "what comes after Death?" already contains in the words "comes after" the idea of Life. Life is Time; the phrase "comes after" is also Time.

It is a simple impossibility for the Principle of Individuality to assume or conceive its own termination. Every one of us believes

---

[1] The *Theologia Germanica* is an anonymously-written mystical text from the fourteenth century which was first published by Martin Luther.

[2] "To abandon selfness." Spengler references this doctrine in *The Decline of the West*, Vol. II, p. 292.

instinctively in his own immortality, just as every atheist instinctively believes in God—all he does is to bring a change upon names, and God becomes Nature, or something similar. But to assert in the XXth century that either God or immortality can be logically proved is stupidity; this is for the common people and for those minds which have remained stuck in the XVIIth century. To prove God, or soul-immortality is to insult them, doubly, for every such proof shows a weakening of the *instinctive* belief. Reason **kills** instinct.

The bitterest of all things is frustration. It is the denial of Life by Life. It is a victory of the outside over the inside, the victory of Accident over Destiny.

There are degrees of frustration. Defeat is no frustration, provided one has been able to exert his powers to the utmost, to use himself up. Who can say Napoleon, or Hitler, were frustrated? The worst frustration—ask me, I know it—is **lack of opportunity**.

1848–1948:
YEARS OF DECISION

1948

EDITORS' NOTE

The first issue of *Union*, the newspaper of Sir Oswald Mosley's new post-war Union Movement, appeared in February 1948 and featured articles by Guy Chesham[1] and Yockey, who worked together in the European liaison section of the movement. Yockey wrote that the "old" must inexorably make way for the "new," despite resistance, according to the organic laws of history. The past era was that of "democracy," "materialism," and plutocracy. No conservative reaction could prevent it. The new epoch would be one of the resurgence of authority, of which Fascism and National Socialism had been provisional forms. The military defeat of these provisional forms by the old forces of democracy and money would be no more enduring than the defeat of Napoleon by the forces of conservatism in the previous epoch. "History has its own logic," and the old cannot forever hold back the new. Democracy was the Idea of the "Spirit of the Age" from the nineteenth century, but the Resurgence of Authority would be the Idea for the new *Zeitgeist*.

Yockey proclaimed that 1848, the year of *The Communist Manifesto* and democratic-bourgeois revolutions throughout Europe, was superseded by 1948, when *Imperium* appeared and the European Liberation Front was born as the vanguard of the new *Zeitgeist*. At that moment, Yockey had hoped that Mosley and the Union Movement would fill that historical necessity, and thus concludes this piece with a eulogy to Mosley's heroic struggle.

No material force, not Communism or International Finance, nor their puppet governments, could withstand the imperative

---

[1] "G. C.," "What Price Western Union?," *Union*, No. 1, February 14, 1948.

of the Age, "the mystical force of its Destiny." Alluding to Spengler's theme, Yockey asked, "Is a mighty Civilization to be strangled in this fashion? Is the Blood of the Western Civilization to be turned into Money?"

Here we see a major theme of Yockey's as-yet-unpublished *Imperium* manuscript. Like Karl Marx explaining the historical inevitability of Communism, Yockey drew on Hegel to show the historical inevitability of the Western Empire. As we know, there were "Right-wing" Hegelians and "Left-wing" Hegelians, Marx being among the most prominent of the latter. Yockey listed Hegel as one of the philosophers to develop an "organic" theory of history, along with Goethe, Spengler, Carlyle, Nietzsche, *et al.* "The Destiny-Idea is the central motive of organic thinking," Yockey wrote in *Imperium.*[2] To Marx's "dialectical materialism" as a "scientific" analysis of history, Yockey countered with what the German Idealists called the *Zeitgeist*, or "spirit of the age." To the Hegelian dialectic, Yockey added Spengler's historical morphology and the "Heroic Vitalism" of Thomas Carlyle, to show that the historical dialectic is unfolded not by proletarian masses impelled by their stomachs, but by heroic individuals with a sense of destiny. The instrument of that destiny Yockey hoped would be Mosley and the Union Movement.

1848–1948: YEARS OF DECISION

Everyone is familiar with the events of 1848. It was the year of the victory of the Democracy Idea everywhere in Europe.

That victory however, did not come suddenly in this decisive form. Nor was it the first success of the Idea of Democracy. The Napoleonic Wars were the expression of this same spirit, and the Vienna Congress of 1815 at the end of those wars was the absolute denial of this spirit, as well as the symbol of its complete defeat.

But—History has its own logic, and only on the surface could

---

[2] Yockey, *Imperium*, pp. 13–16.

Metternich and the Fürstenbund[3] prevail. In the historical depths, the Idea of Democracy—the real ruler of men's minds in that Age—continued to live and grow. It rose in 1830, and was repressed. Its positive force compelled all men's souls. Opposition to it was a mere negative, for this Idea was the creative force of the Age.

It is not surprising that men resisted this Idea, for the New is always established only over the blind and sterile opposition of the Old. For two great reasons, the forces of the Old Idea fight the New Idea. First: the leading minds do not become the servants of the Old Order, for these minds are claimed by the New Idea, the Idea of the Future. Thus the Old Order simply does not understand the Spirit of the Age. Second: this Old Order has material interests in the perpetuation of the existing forms of organization, which by their existence work for its purposes.

Nevertheless—the Old Idea always goes down before the New Idea, and 1848 is a symbol of this invariable organic law.

1948 sees also the struggle between the Old and the New. In one respect, it resembles 1848—it is the struggle of the supernational Spirit of the Age against the forces of sterile Conservatism and Reaction.

In every other respect it is the contrary of 1848, for the Spirit of our Age is no longer that of Democracy and Materialism, but that of the Resurgence of Authority in every sphere of Life. Regardless of what it meant in 1848, in our day Democracy means the rule of finance-capitalism through the technique of party-corruption.

Just as no force within the Western Civilization could stand against the Democracy-Idea in 1848, so today, no inner Western force can oppose the further organic development of the West and the Resurgence of Authority.

It is today a stark and gruesome fact that non-Western forces

---

[3] The Fürstenbund was an alliance of Protestant princes in the Holy Roman Empire established by Frederick the Great in 1785 in order to prevent the Catholic Habsburgs from gaining possession of Bavaria. It dissolved after the outbreak of the French Revolution and the death of the then Habsburg monarch, Joseph II.

alone are frustrating the natural development of our Civilization, by starving and looting the peoples of the West. They base themselves in Communism and International Finance. These forces perpetuate the Balkanization of the West, and they direct their puppet governments in Europe.

The victims of this gigantic process are not alone the Peoples of Europe, but all who fall beneath Communist or Financial rule.

Is this to continue? Is a mighty Civilization to be strangled in this fashion? Is the Blood of the Western Civilization to be turned into Money?

The Spirit of the Age says: NO! This Spirit claims the best men of the Western Civilization all over the world, and imbues them with the mission of the Resurgence of Authority, and the destruction of that finance-capitalism which today covers up its operations of Death and Chaos with the outworn catchword of Democracy.

It bestows upon them the mystical force of its Destiny, a force which no mere material preponderance, and no mountains of lying propaganda, can overcome.

Against Money, we pit the Spirit of Heroism; against their compulsion-propaganda, our Discipline; against their cynicism, our Faith; against the reactionary rule of their unclean parties, our Leader on the path to the Future, Oswald Mosley.[4]

F. P. Y.

[4] "F. P. Y.," "1848–1948 Years of Decision," *Union*, No. 1.

ITALO-ENGLISH CONVENTION

1949

EDITORS' NOTE

One of the earliest outreaches by the European Liberation Front (ELF) to Europe was in Italy. *Imperium* had received immediate interest from elements of the Italian Social Movement (MSI). In 1949, shortly after the founding of the ELF, Yockey was in Italy. He met with N. Neri, a pseudonym for someone apparently well-connected in the MSI who was heading the European League. An "Italo-English Convention" was signed, uniting the ELF and the League with the intention of moving the Front's headquarters to Rome.

It seems from this joint statement that Yockey was willing for Neri to assume leadership of the ELF. Neri must have been an individual of significance within the neo-Fascist milieu. What happened to these plans is not known. However, Yockey was back in Italy in 1951, organizing the foreign delegates to an international convention called by a Fascist aid society, the Movimento Italiano Femminile Fede e Famiglia.[1] This had been founded by Monsignor Mattei Silveri and Princess Maria Pignatelli di Cerchiara di Calabria on October 28, 1946, the anniversary of the Fascist March on Rome. The Princess was a war heroine who had organized female guerrillas for the Salò Republic.

That Yockey lacked narcissism is indicated by his willingness to turn the leadership of the ELF over to others for the sake of the "Idea," again offering this opportunity a few years later to the American "anti-Semite," Gerald L. K. Smith.[2] The idea of coordinating "mass movements" in a worldwide "Fascist struggle"

---

[1] The Italian Women's Movement of Faith and Family (MIF).

[2] Gerald L. K. Smith (1898–1976), a minister in the Disciples of Christ church, founded the racialist Christian Nationalist Crusade in St. Louis in 1944, and the isolationist America First party in 1943.

seems unrealistic, yet in 1949 this was not the case. The Italian Social Movement had been formed in 1946, mainly by veterans of the Italian Social Republic (Salò Republic). Giorgio Almirante, a former high official in the Salò Ministry of Culture who later endorsed *Imperium*, led the MSI for decades. During the 1948 elections, the MSI gained six seats in the Chamber of Deputies.[3] In Germany, the Socialist Reich Party (SRP), formed in October 1949, soon had a membership of ten thousand and gained eleven percent of the vote in Lower Saxony in 1951.[4] Again, *Imperium* was well received by the SRP leadership.

The statement is instructive as to Yockey's practical aims for the ELF.

ITALO-ENGLISH CONVENTION[5]

I

From today, the European League assumes the name European Liberation Front. The Direction of the European Liberation Front is assumed by the Direction of the European League. The Headquarters of the ELF is established in the city of Rome. U. Varange and N. Neri mutually pledge themselves to realise at once the integration of the two organisms.

II

The ELF operates on the European plane, creating and co-ordinating mass-movements. Europe is understood to comprise the area from the Urals to the Atlantic, from the Mediterranean to the Arctic.

III

The ELF considers itself in all things the weapon of the Fascist struggle.

---

[3] Roger Eatwell, *Fascism: A History* (London: Vintage Books, 1996), p. 198.

[4] Ibid., p. 220.

[5] "Italo-English Convention," Rome, 1949, Archives Canada, MG30-D91, finding no. 1293, vol. 4, file no. 1.

IV

The strategical objective is the integral realisation of Fascism in Europe and in the world. The tactical objective is the liberation of Europe from military, political, economic subjugation by extra-European forces, from Jewry, Masonry, Liberalism, Bolshevism, Capitalism, Parliamentarism, and Individualism.

V

In view of the possibility of orienting world-opinion by means of a manifesto expressing the beliefs of the elite which fights against all manifestations of materialism, and which, simultaneously, answers modern problems, social, political, and economic, individual and collective, therefore, such a manifesto must be elaborated in collaboration with the elite of the Fascist movements, and must be discussed and approved by an international convention to be held in 1950.

VI

The present ITALO-ENGLISH CONVENTION, stipulated in Rome on 21 November, 1949, in the Italian language, in two copies, was signed by U. Varange for the ELF, and by N. Neri for the EL.

for the
European Liberation Front
U. Varange (signed)

for the
European League
N. Neri (signed)

YOCKEY TO ARCAND ON THE ITALO-ENGLISH CONVENTION

That Yockey's hopes were high for the alliance between the ELF and the Italian neo-Fascists is indicated by a letter he wrote to the Canadian fascist leader, Adrien Arcand.[6] Yockey referred to the Italian component as representing the MSI and "all other fascist groups in Italy," although the MSI had "not yet" changed

---

[6] Letter from Yockey to Arcand, December 29, 1949, Arcand collection, Archives Canada, MG30-D91, finding no. 1293, vol. 1, file no. 1.

their name to the European Liberation Front. Apparently, at least among an influential faction, the Front was regarded as the secret coordination and directing center of an "international fascist organization." There were elements within the MSI who participated in subsequent attempts to form a "fascist international." These included the convention held in Malmö, Sweden in 1951 which led to the formation of the European Social Movement, whose four-man directorate included MSI leader Augusto de Marsanich; and the 1962 Venice conference organized by Sir Oswald Mosley to create a National Party of Europe. The Yockey-Neri statement seems to have been the first such attempt.

Westropa Press
Proprietor: Anthony Gannon
Temple Bar 5039
[illegible]
December 29

My dear Mr. Arcand,

The enclosure is a result of my visit to Rome. Neri is of course a pseudonym, necessary under the circumstances. The Italian part of the convention represents the MSI and all other fascist groups in Italy. The state of organization is not yet very high there, but nevertheless now, for the first time, we have an international fascist organization. It is but a beginning. They are not yet going to change the name of the MSI to Liberation Front, preferring for the present to conceive the Front as the super-organization over all fascist parties and movements.

There are also secret clauses, not reproduced here, which deal with the setting up of a clandestine organization to be behind the Front.

In England the public movement is called the Liberation Front, and will always keep this name. We hope to begin public meetings in the spring, but it is all conditioned on money, since we are all so miserably poor. We need very little, but some we must have.

The Proclamation is to be done in English, Italian, and

French. The German edition will be held up a while, and an edition in Spanish is hardly possible considering the strong anti-fascist attitude of the regime there.

As soon as the English version is out, you will receive a copy for your personal use, and you can then let us know how many you want in French and English for your organizational use.

I am enclosing a new circular we are sending out for *Imperium*. If you have a list of addresses of people who may buy it, we would be happy to have them, or else to send you circulars which you may distribute.

In my nine months traveling over the continent, nearly all of the well-known fascists I met knew of you, and all spoke highly of you. You will also be interested to hear that among true fascists there is no variation in policy; all agree that the enemy is America-Jewry. Washington Bolshevism is everywhere recognized as more dangerous than Moscow Bolshevism, although there is no suggestion of any compromise with Moscow. The idea is that no fascist will fight for America under any circumstances.

Please receive my best wishes in all that you undertake in 1950, and be assured of my high esteem and that of my comrades.

Front Heil!
Varange[7]

---

[7] Yockey has handwritten beneath this, "You may write us: 54 Saddlewood Av., Manchester, 19."

THE PROCLAMATION OF LONDON
OF THE EUROPEAN LIBERATION FRONT

1949

EDITORS' NOTE

This is the Right's answer to *The Communist Manifesto* of the "Culture-distorter," providing a synopsis of all the key ideas in Yockey's *magnum opus, Imperium*. Published in 1949, a year after *Imperium,* under the imprint of Westropa Press, London, *The Proclamation* comprised 32 pages, had a deep red cover, and bore the Front's symbol: a black sword, in a white circle, on a red background. At the back of *The Proclamation* the aims of the Front are distilled further in twelve points. *The Proclamation* was reprinted, presumably around 1971, by Douglas T. Kaye of Nordland Press, who was also the publisher of Yockey's *Four Essays,* and who had been on the team of the Yockeyan journal, *TRUD*.

The following text, however, is based on the original 1949 printing. We have retained Yockey's use of capitalized words and bold type.

THE PROCLAMATION OF LONDON

Contents

1. Class-War
2. The Emergence of the Jew
3. Social Degeneration

B. The Destruction of the Political Unity of Europe.

C. The Destruction of Europe's World Empire.

Section III.
The Mission of the Liberation Front.

INTRODUCTION

Throughout all Europe there is stirring today a great superpersonal Idea, the Idea of the Imperium of Europe, the permanent and perfect union of the peoples and nations of Europe. This Idea embodies in itself the entire content of the future, for unless this Idea is fulfilled, there will be no European future.

Those who regard this Idea, which is expressed at this moment in the Liberation Front, as a danger to them, wish to destroy it at all costs. Its enemies are, first, the anti-European forces without the Western Civilization who, at this moment of history, dominate the entire world, and second, their subservient lackeys within the Western Civilization, the reactionary party-politicians, together with the self-interested forces they represent. Both are united in their blind hatred of this young and vital Idea, which is irresistibly releasing forces which threaten to engulf these old powers of reaction, finance-capitalism, class-war, and Bolshevism.

This is addressed to the entire Western Civilization: to the colonies planted all over the world, and to the heart and soul of the West, the Mother-soil and Father-Culture of Europe. It is Europe that is the focus of the historical force of the world. The profundity and strength of this soul and body dominate even those extra-European forces which have just concluded a temporarily victorious war against Europe, and who are now engaging in preparations for war against one another, in which each hopes to push its crude and formless lust for negative conquest even to the mastery of the world. In the plans of their masters of today, the true American people and the Russian people figure only as expendable material. In these two populations, there are wide and deep strata which inwardly belong to the Western Civilization, and who look to the sacred soil of Europe as to their origin, their inspiration, and their spiritual home. To these also, this proclamation is addressed.

By gigantic war, by terror, and by manifold persecution, the party-politicians and their extra-European masters have sought and seek to stifle this mighty Idea. They have sought in vain to deprive it of voice, and of all means of self-expression, through the written word or the spoken.

They themselves thus testify that the Liberation Front is already a power in Europe. Against the organic Imperative of the Front, they seek to enlist all the forces of the past. They create thus a spiritual disjunction which compels all men to take their place on the one side or the other.

It has become necessary that those who are in the service of this Idea should proclaim to the Western Civilization the spiritual foundations and significance of the Liberation Front, and of the Imperium of Europe for which the Front will clear the way, for this Front is the sole creative force of our times.

Therefore the representative adherents of the Front, from all the former nations of Europe, have gathered together in London for the purpose of documenting their outlook, their aim, and their position in the world. This Proclamation is published in the original in the German, English, Spanish, Italian, French, and Flemish languages.

I.
THE HISTORICAL FOUNDATIONS OF THE LIBERATION FRONT

1. THE UNITY OF THE WESTERN CULTURE

From the beginning, the Western Culture has been a spiritual unit. This basic, universally formative **fact** is in the sharpest contrast to the shallow and ignorant outlook of those who pretend that the unity of the West is a new idea, a technical thing which can only be brought about on a limited and conditional basis.

From its very birth-cry in the Crusades, the Western Culture had one State, with the Emperor at its head, one Church and religion, Gothic Christianity, with an authoritarian Pope, one race, one nation, and one people, which felt itself, and was recognized by all outer forces, to be distinct and unitary. There was a universal style, Gothic, which inspired and informed all art from the crafts to the cathedrals. There was one ethical code for the Culture-bearing stratum, Western chivalry, founded on a purely Western feeling of honor. There was a universal language, Latin, and a universal law, Roman law. Even in the very adoption of older, non-Western things, the West was unitary. It made such things into an expression of its proper soul, and it universalized them.

More important than anything else, this Culture felt itself to be a power-unit as against all outer forces, whether barbarians like the Slavs, Turks, and Mongols, or civilized like the Moors, Jews, and Saracens. Embryonic national differences existed even then within the West, but these differences were not felt as contrasts, and could not possibly become at that time the focus of a struggle for power. A Western knight was fighting equally for his Fatherland whether in battle against the Slav or the Turk on the Eastern Marshes of Germany, against the Moor in Spain, Italy, or Sicily, or against the Saracen in the Levant. The outer forces recognized as well this inner unity of the West. To Islam, all Westerners whatever were lumped together as Franks, *giaours*.[1]

This higher Cultural unity embraced within its rich possibilities the several Nation-Ideas which were to actualize so much of Western history, for it is obviously a part of the divine plan that a High Culture create as phases of its own unfolding, not only higher aesthetic units, schools of music, painting, and lyric, higher religious and philosophical units, schools of mysticism and theology, higher bodies of nature-knowledge, schools of technics and scientific research, but also higher power-units within itself, Emperor versus papacy, Estates versus Emperor

[1] *Giaour* was a derogatory slur used for infidels in the Ottoman Empire.

and Pope, Fronde versus King, Nation versus Nation. In Gothic times, the intra-Cultural power struggle between Emperor and Pope was always strictly subordinated, by the universal conscience, to the outer tension with the non-member of the Culture, the barbarian and heathen. The Nations existed then, but not as power-units, not as **political** organisms. The members of the nations felt themselves to be different from one another, but the differences were in no case determining of the whole orientation to life. A Slavic, Turkish, or Moorish attack on Europe was met by forces drawn from all parts of Europe.

The first political expression of Europe was in the Crusades, in which Europe was a power-unit, acting against the outer world in unitary self-assertion of its new-born soul. Alongside of this form of politics there arose the tension, which endured for three centuries within the Culture, of the twin factions of Emperor and Pope. And then from the middle of the 13th century began the revolt of the great barons and bishops against the absolute power of Emperor and Pope. This was a step further away from the prime Cultural unity, but it in no way affected the great essential idea of unity of the West *vis-à-vis* any extra-Cultural force. Thus, during this period, the Pope decreed that the crossbow was a barbarous weapon and forbade its use against members of Western Christendom, but expressly sanctioned its use against barbarians and heathens.

The increasing political differentiation within the Culture was simply the organic process of fulfilling the manifold possibilities of the soul of the Western Culture. The entire process was organically necessary, and thus divinely necessary, for the soul of a High Culture is a direct emanation of the Godhead. The development continued with the breaking of the religious unity of the West, in Renaissance, Reformation, and Counter-Reformation. These phenomena, religious in origin, show us the true meaning of the political: whenever any superpersonal movement or idea rises to the intensity at which it involves the question of life or death, it therewith becomes **political**, regardless of its origin in a non-political sphere. From that moment, the contestants are States, political organisms, regardless of how they describe themselves, and the way of conducting the organism is the political way: dividing the world into friend and enemy; seeking after power, and not after truth; pursuing alliance, war, and negotiation, and not conversion and salvation. This is the lesson of the Reformation-centuries as it had been of the centuries of the Papal-Imperial conflict.

Accompanying the breakdown of religious unity, which transformed itself into a political struggle, was the rise of the dynastic State, and the beginning of large-scale intra-Cultural wars among Western States. Again, the disunifying process within the Culture was **limited**. The intra-European wars which took place were conditioned entirely by the great fact, felt and understood by all, that the European States belonged to the same Cultural world. Thus these wars never proceeded to the political annihilation of the opponent. They were prosecuted only to the point where the limited issue which had occasioned the war could become the object of negotiations which could satisfy both contestants.

The handing over of a strip of territory, or the recognition of an inheritance—such were the limited issues of these intra-Cultural wars. The scale of these dynastic wars gradually increased, until the dynastic form of politics was itself finished, towards the close of the 18th century, when a new form of intra-Cultural power-struggle emerged.

But during the centuries of dynastic politics, with its limited wars, and its consequent preservation of Cultural unity, the other type of politics, with its other form of war, went on between Western political units and outer forces: absolute politics. These wars were unconditioned by the fact of mutual membership in a High Culture, and the presence of a common code of honor, for the barbarian and the heathen did not share the feeling of Western chivalrous obligations. The Hussite Wars, 1420–1436, show the nature of warfare between a Culture-people and a barbarian people. For 16 years, the Hussite armies flooded over large areas of Germany, burning, ravaging, killing, and destroying. This nihilistic Slavic outburst was totally unconnected with any constructive war-aim and was thus merely an early expression of what is now called Bolshevism, the spirit of negation and destruction, wherever it manifests itself, which aims at the utter annihilation of everything Western. During the centuries of Gothic and Baroque, it was primarily Germany and Spain which protected the body of the West and saved it from the barbarian horrors which had been its fate if the outer forces had prevailed.

2. The Age of Materialism

During the centuries of its growth and unfolding, the Western Culture increased in power and maturity. The inner aspects of life steadily receded before the external aspects, until by the end of the XVIIIth century, the West stood before its deepest crisis up to that time. Since the issue was great, fundamental, and intense, it immediately became a matter of life and death, that is to say, political. The great crisis took political shape in the French Revolution. As ever, when an idea rises to **political** intensity, it absorbs everything else within it, and focuses all human attention and effort on to the power-struggle. The Revolution, however, was not French alone, but European.

This total revolution marked the victory of democracy over aristocracy, parliamentarism over the State, mass over quality, Reason over Faith, equality-ideals over organic hierarchy, of Money over Blood, of Liberalism, pluralism, free capitalism, and criticism over the organic forces of Tradition, State, and Authority, in one word, of Civilization over Culture. Rationalism and materialism were the common denominators of all the new ideas which rose in revolt against the old order of thought, State, economy, society, war, and politics. Metaphysics was to be a matter of weighing and measuring; government was to be a matter of counting noses; economy was to be entirely reduced to money-trading; the structure of society was to be a reflex of money; international relations of war and politics were to be the apotheosis of national egoism, with utter disregard of the great, inclusive, Cultural unity, of which the nations are mere separate manifestations.

Even today, after more than a century of undermining, the traditional connections of the Culture-bearing stratum of Europe are unimpaired and reach straight back to the self-evident pride and mastery of our Gothic youth. And this connection is not weaker, but stronger with time, for the direction of our spiritual development has changed, and a second great world-transformation has occurred in the life of the West.

We are now in the midst of the second great turning-point of the maturity of Culture. The noise and shouting of democracy and materialism have died away; liberalism has become a foul tyranny masking an evil and anonymous dictature of money; the parliaments talk now only to themselves, and it no longer matters what they say; the critics have dissolved themselves in their own acid, and cannot believe now in either their methods or their results; rapacious capitalism has eaten up its own foundations; finance has converted the nations into huge spider-webs of debt in which all Western mankind is trapped; above all, fanatical chauvinism has destroyed all the former Fatherlands and delivered them to the occupation of extra-European forces of barbarism and Culture-distortion.

All of this is the legacy of the Age of Materialism. The servants of that Age continue to apply its outmoded and sterile methods to the living tasks of the present. But even as their dead and rigid hands grip the reins of power, the revolt continues. They cannot build a wall against Destiny; they cannot order History and Time to stop in their tracks. The assertion of liberal-capitalistic-democratic-parliamentarism that it has a timeless and eternal right to rule is an organic lie. The methods of the materialistic Age, its antiquated ideologies and cadaverous sterility, cannot even survive except as an instrument of extra-European forces, unfeeling to the inner force of European destiny.

Even as the cadaver of Materialism tries to divert the life-blood of the new and vital forces into its hardened arteries, it sinks deeper into the clammy rigidity of Death. Against this corpse rises now the upthrust of the Resurgence of Authority, the highest embodiment of the old, eternally young and manly virtues of Discipline, Responsibility, Duty, Loyalty, and Faith. In the face of the chaos of individualistic-liberal-capitalism, it flings its demand for a superpersonal ethical-socialist Order. Over the equality-ideals of democracy and the chaos of national and international pluralism rises now the imperative of Hierarchy and Imperium. Displacing suicidal petty-stateism is the Idea of the monolithic Culture-State-Nation-Race-People of Europe as the prelude to the greatest task of all: the expression of the absolute Western will to unlimited political Imperialism.

The ultimate outcome of this gigantic struggle is known to us, for we have seen before this struggle of the Past to retard the Future. From 1800 to 1850, the reactionary adherents of the negative alliance against democracy allied themselves with the ideas and methods of the Past in order to prevent the Future. But it was the democrats of that time who represented the true idea of the times, and history does not go backward. The Holy Alliance[2] had to fail, regardless of the material power at its disposal, for armies and cannon cannot fight against an Idea.

Within a mere century, the democrats, equalitarians, liberals, critics, ideologues, and parliamentarians have become the most radical opponent of the Spirit of the Age, for this Age is no longer that of Money, Democracy, and Equality, but that of Authority, Discipline, and Faith.

No more than the Liberal-democrats could be permanently suppressed in 1850[3] can they suppress us in 1950. Even as the liberal-democratic tyrants bring their economic pressure, they have a bad conscience. They show it further in their vacillation between senseless cruelty and clumsy bribery, in their childish propaganda and their vain cajolery. But to the bearers of a superpersonal mission, no yielding is possible, either to terror or to compromise, for this mission emanates directly from the ultimate reality of God. To the materialistic-liberal-Communist-democrats, the inner enemy of Europe, we present only one, unalterable demand: they must vanish from the face of History.

Against this inner enemy and the spirit he embodies, we now

---

[2] The Holy Alliance was a coalition of Austria, Prussia, and Russia which was signed in Vienna in 1815. Originally it was intended to defend Christian values in Europe, but, as it was used by Austrian Prince Metternich, it became a force to counter the influence of the French Revolution and opposed both democracy and secularism. Eventually, all the European states of the time signed onto it, except for Great Britain, the Ottoman Empire, and the Vatican. It is generally regarded to have ceased functioning after the death of Czar Alexander I in 1825.

[3] With the suppression of the revolutions of 1848.

document our charges before all Europe.

In three realms, materialistic-communistic-liberal-democracy has injured the body and thwarted the Destiny of Europe: (1) within the European nations, (2) in the relations among the nations of Europe, and (3) in the relations of Europe to the rest of the world.

II.
The Chaos of the Present

A. The Undermining of the Nations

1. Class War

In its first phase, the great revolution of nationalism and Materialism turned itself against the two poles of the Cultural life, the forces of Authority in the spiritual life and the political-social life. Encyclopedism, Jacobinism, Freemasonry, and Republicanism are some of its early forms. They fought all signs of rank, and against anything which had grown organically through the centuries. The spirit of this revolt permeated the ruling strata in some countries, particularly in France, and it was this weakness above that made the Revolution and the Terror of 1793 possible. The *canaille*[4] never breaks loose until the ruling elements permit it; this was equally true in 1789 as in 1944, with the American conquest of Europe.

The worship of Reason applied to State and Society developed the test of quantity as the sole measure of legitimacy. Not rank, talent, genius, or ability, but number alone mattered to the materialists. The source of power, according to the doctrinaire democrats, was in the broadest, most undifferentiated mass of the population, and not in the spiritually differentiated strata born with the mission of accomplishing the life-task of the Nation and actualizing the national Idea.

Blindly, the democratic ideologues continued with their work of levelling and destroying. In the century 1850–1950 they actually succeeded in undermining the State and society. What suc-

---

[4] The rabble.

ceeded the old order? Nothing that the democrats of the early period had sought. The new center of gravity of Life was in economics, and the dominating economic rivalry was between the industrial-capitalist and the financier. All the idealism and all the sacrifice of the equalitarians had only succeeded in wiping out an organic aristocracy and substituting for it a sordid and vulgar plutocracy. Within all countries, there now began the next form of class-war, the war between economic groups instead of between social groups. The differences engendered by quality and tradition had been undermined, and the economic materialism now supplied the cadre of forms of the struggle.

By speculation and manipulations on the exchange, the finance-capitalist attacked the productive forms of property so that they might all be working for him, the unseen and unknown master, controlling the economic life of continents through his universal network of debts and interest. The exigencies of the struggle forced the industrialists to squeeze every possible source of profit tighter, and thus to increase the already cruel oppression of the laborers and their families.

The ruling code of honor was now that of the cut-throat, and the economic life of the nations was a vile scramble for profit. Into this scramble there now entered new contestants. First was the proletariat, which now allied itself with the finance-capitalist in the attack on the industrialist from above and below. The proletarian conscript was fitted out by his self-chosen non-proletarian leaders with a doctrine, organization, and tactics. The doctrine was that the entire history of the world was nothing but a continual class struggle, with money as its sole end and aim. The fact that this repulsive and grotesque outlook could even be formulated is itself the only commentary necessary on the kind of world Liberalism creates. The organization-form was the trade-union, and the tactic was the strike. All three, the doctrine, the organization, and the tactic, are entirely economic, purely materialistic and capitalistic. Although they proclaimed themselves against capitalism, they thought in its cadre, shared its aim, and fought with its weapons.

Instead of manipulating the supply of goods, like the industrialist, or the supply of money, like the finance-capitalist, they manipulated the supply of labor. The labor-leader now became the third member of the snarling capitalist trinity.

2. THE EMERGENCE OF THE JEW

More important than these domestic contestants was a new element, the Culture-alien. His entrance into Western affairs was a direct result of the victory of Rationalism and Materialism. Since only quantity mattered, then obviously the quality of a man was indifferent. The fact that he came from a different Culture, that therefore he felt himself to be a member of a different race, people, nation, State, religion, society—these meant nothing to the doctrinaire liberals. They spoke fervently of "humanity" and wished to embrace it, little thinking that outside of the Western Culture there was no reciprocal feeling, but only sullen envy, indifference, or resentment. The liberal ideology prevailed, and from that moment the Rothschilds, Ricardos, Marxs, Lasalles, Bebels, Dreyfuses, Guggenheims, Loebs, Trotskys, Staviskys, Kruegers, Baruchs, Frankfurters, and Blums entered into the public life of the West.

The Culture-State-Nation-Religion-Race-People of the Jew is a product of a Culture which was already completed and rigidified by the time of our Gothic period. At the time when we were just emerging from the primitive, these Culture-aliens dispersed themselves throughout Europe. Money-thinking, regarded as evil by the West, was the forte of the Jew. Interest-taking was forbidden to Westerners by their religion, and the Jew was not slow to seize the usury-monopoly that this conferred on him.

In the Culture of which the Jew was a product, a nation was a unit of belief, entirely independent of the notion of territory, of Fatherland. Strewn over all Europe, the Jew naturally regarded all Westerners as alien. There was no place in the Western world of Gothic Christianity, chivalry, piety, and simple agricultural economy for this landless and uprooted stranger with his Torah and Talmud, his money and his cynicism, his dualistic ethics, one for his own kind, and another for the *goyim*. The Jew created his own ghetto as a symbol of his complete inner isolation from his environment. The general feeling of the religious Gothic Age was that the Jew was the creation of the Devil, who appointed him to drive his trade of usury.

Between the members of the Western Culture and this element which lived in and on the body of the West, but in no way shared in or contributed to its development, there arose mutual hatred and oppression. Crusaders massacred entire Jewish communities on their way to the Levant and returning. Protests against usury produced plunder and burning of the Jews. Popes and Scholastic philosophers denounced the Jew. All Western kings, at one time or another, drove out the entire Jewish population of their kingdoms. Jews were hanged *en masse* as reprisal for their usury and counterfeiting. Any possibility of assimilation of the parasite by the host that may have been present was forever rendered impossible by the infinitely deep resentment and revenge-imperative that developed in the Culture-State-Nation-Race-People of the Jew.

Between him and his Western host-surroundings there was no inner connection. He looked upon all Western developments with an even eye, the eye of the calculating spectator who seeks solely his own advantage. Shylock is the symbol of the Jew in the Western Culture, the usurer counting his coins and accumulating his resentment. For almost a thousand years the Jew drank his gall and bided his time, and then at last his opportunity emerged. With the coming of materialism, capitalism, democracy, and liberalism, a great wave of excitement went through the Jewish world. The Jew had seen the potentialities of these things and had fostered their growth in every way. The Illuminati and all of its Freemasonic offspring were infiltrated by the Jew and made into instruments of his revenge-politics. To the Jew the great attraction of all of these Western movements was that they were quantitative, and thus all tended to break down the exclusiveness of the West, which had kept him out of its power-struggles and confined in his ghetto, dreaming of his revenge for centuries of persecution. Henceforth, he was generously accorded the same spiritual status as Westerners in their own Culture, and the same civic status as Westerners in their own Nation-States. He kept his own exclusiveness of course, and his own public life, for the New Year's Resolutions of Liberalism—humanitarianism, brotherly love, "tolerance," and the like—

were one-sided. They were a phase of our development and could not be echoed in the Jewish organism, which had long since passed beyond all development, like the Chinese, Hindus, and Moslems.

In finance, in trade, in society, in education, in letters, in diplomacy, the Jew now forged steadily ahead, a closed organism inside an open one. While Westerners applied the test of **ability**, the Jew chose his associates and subordinates on the basis of their membership in his Culture-State-Nation-Race, or in one of his secret societies which extended horizontally through the Western nations.

By 1858 the Jew was able effectively to demonstrate his ability to direct the power of Western States into his channels, in the Mortara affair.[5] During the entire XIXth century, the Jew intervened constantly in the internal and external affairs of all the European Nation-States. Within each country he sought to impose the policy which would give the Jew at last the complete mastery over the Western Civilization. Thus in England, he was an Imperialist and Free-Trader, in Germany and Austria he was a liberal and social-democrat, in France he was a liberal or communist.

During the latter part of the XIXth century, the Jew embarked upon an invasion of America, when the word went through the

---

[5] In 1851, Edgardo Levi Mortara was born to Jewish parents in Bologna, which was then one of the Papal Legations and governed by the Vatican. In 1857, a rumor reached the authorities that one of the family's servants had secretly baptized Edgardo out of mercy when he had been seriously ill, which would make him a Catholic in the eyes of the Church. When questioned, the servant confirmed that this was true, and in 1858 the Church seized the child in order to bring him up as a Catholic under the personal care of Pope Pius IX. The Mortara family used legal means to try to get the child back, and the conflict achieved notoriety across Europe and North America, dividing opinion between Vatican supporters and critics. The court ruled in favor of the Church, and Edgardo was later trained and ordained as a priest, although the matter continued to negatively impact public opinion. Some historians believe that it influenced the end of the Papal States' authority in the Second Italian War of Independence.

Jewish Culture-State-Nation-Race that opportunities were as great there and resistance was less, because of the absence of high traditions. In Europe, it has been impossible for the Jew to annihilate Tradition, which constantly opposed its silent and strong barrier, but in America, because of its colonial origins, there had never been creativeness and exclusiveness, and there were no barriers to the Jew. America was more thoroughly disintegrated by rationalism, materialism, liberalism, and democracy than any European land, because a colony has not, and cannot have, the spiritual profundity and continuity of the Mother-soil of the Culture. As a result, the success of the Jew has been greatest in America, and in the year 1933, the entire continent of America passed into the control of the Jewish Culture-State-Nation-Race-People.

The presence of a Culture-alien generates spiritual, political, economic, and social phenomena of a kind which could never arise from domestic elements and happenings. These phenomena are manifestations of Culture-disease and of necessity arise when human groups are in contact which do not share the same Culture. When one of the groups belongs to the Culture, and the other does not—the case of the negroes in the Boer colony, or the negroes and Indians in Brazil—the relationship is simply **Culture-parasitism**. The disease-condition displaces Culture-members and has a slowly sterilizing effect on the Culture-body.

More aggravated is the condition when the Culture-alien intervenes in the pubic and spiritual affairs of the host, for then he must of his own inner necessity distort the life of the host, warping and frustrating its proper tendencies to make them serviceable to his alien needs. The Jew is the only Culture-alien who at present exercises this **Culture-distortion** on the life of the Western Civilization.

The domestic disease-elements within the Culture which wish to retain the outmoded ideas and methods of the Past and to fight against the creative spirit which is actualizing a Cultural mission are the forces of **Culture-retardation**. These have been brought into the service of the Culture-distorter. Actually these elements simply desire to lead, but are themselves incapable of leadership, and therefore devote their lives to opposition, to great formative Ideas, creative spiritual currents, and leaders of vision and genius. They are the churchills, the spaaks, the gaulles,[6] the rejects of higher history who offer themselves to the forces of negation and destruction. The most critical form of the disease of Culture-retardation is the condition in which it seeks to prevent the realization of the Idea of the Future even at the shame of allying with outer forces, the degradation of becoming their vassal, and the risk of destroying the entire Culture. Before showing the effect of the disease-elements on the external relations of the Culture, their internal effects must be summarized.

3. Social Degeneration

The forces of rationalism, materialism, atheism, Jacobinism, democracy, and liberalism became ever more radical in their demands during their century. Their most intransigent product was communism. The leading values of communism are identical with those of liberal democracy: communism also preaches the economic meaning of life, the supremacy of the individual, the sublimity of "happiness," the doctrine of heaven-on-earth, the superiority of the lowest type of man, materialism, criticism, atheism, intellectualism, hatred of authority, race suicide, feminism, and pacifism. The sole difference between liberal-democracy and communism in practice was that communism was an intensification of those beliefs to the point where they became **political**. Liberalism was anti-political, and hoped to conquer with drooling sentiments, but communism was filled with an intense hatred which demanded expression in class-war.

All aspects of social decay were permeated by the Culture-distorter, who well realized their value in his program for ascendancy. At the same time that he spread and advocated all of these forms of social decay for the white nations, he carefully strove to keep his own Culture-State-Nation-Race-People free from them. It was an invariable characteristic of the tactics of the Jew that he, himself the bearer of Culture-disease, instinctively

---

[6] It was Yockey's habit not to capitalize the names of those whom he held in contempt among the political class. "Spaak" is probably Belgian socialist politician Paul-Henri Spaak (1899–1972).

allied himself with all forms, theories, doctrines, and practices of decadence in every sphere of life.

The degradation of the social life did not merely happen, it was planned, deliberately fostered and spread, and the systematic undermining of the entire life of the West continues today.

The instruments of this assault are the weapons of propaganda: press, radio, cinema, stage, education. These weapons are controlled at this moment in Europe almost entirely by the forces of Culture-disease and social degeneration. The chief fount of the propaganda is the cinema, and from his capital of Hollywood, the Jew spews out an endless series of perverted films to debase and degenerate the youth of Europe, as he has so largely succeeded in doing with the youth of America. Concomitantly he inspires a vicious literature of journalism, novels, and dramas which preach the same message of destruction of healthy individual instincts, of normal familial and sexual life, of disintegration of the social organism into a heap of wandering, colliding, grains of human sand.

The message of Hollywood is the total significance of the isolated individual, stateless and rootless, outside of society and family, whose life is simply the pursuit of money and erotic pleasure. It is not the normal and healthy love of man and wife bound together by many children that Hollywood preaches, but a diseased erotic-for-its-own-sake, the sexual love of two grains of human sand, superficial and impermanent. Before this highest of all Hollywood's values, everything else must stand aside: marriage, honor, duty, patriotism, sternness, dedication of self to a higher aim. This ghastly distortion of the sexual life has created the erotomania which obsesses its millions of victims in America, and which has now been brought to the Mother-soil of Europe by the American invasion.

Not only the individuals are the victims of this technic of degeneration, but the family and the race are dissolved wherever it touches. Divorce replaces marriage, abortion replaces birth, the home acquires a purely commercial *raison d'être*, the family becomes the battleground of individual strife for personal advantage. The erotic-as-its-own-end deliberately reduces the numbers of the race, even as it also disintegrates the higher organism into sand. As a part of the technic, woman is made into a feminist, an unhappy derailed creature who would contest with man in his own domain and seek to lose all the attributes of her polarity which assure her destiny of its unfolding and guarantee her the natural dignity which is hers. The end of the process is seen in those wide strata in America which have been completely Hollywoodized. Hollywood-feminism has created a woman who is no longer a woman but cannot be a man, and a man who is devirilized into an indeterminate thing. The name given to this process is the "setting free" of woman, and it is done in the name of "happiness," the magic word of the liberal-communist-democratic doctrine. It accompanies the spreading of inverted Puritanism, which seeks to spread erotomania by surrounding the sexual life with an aura of attractive evil.

From the standpoint of the race, the result of this technic of degeneration is the attenuating, and finally the dying out, of racial instincts. The disintegrated victims, shorn of their organic connections with the great superpersonal content of Life, become unfruitful, lose their will-to-power, and soon lack the ability to believe in or to follow anything onward and upward. They become cynical, give up all inner discipline, seek a life of ease and pleasure, and sneer at all seriousness and honor. All intense feelings depart, for they might involve risk and sacrifice. Love of Fatherland gives way to money-madness and erotomania.

The complete mediocrity that results is shown by the disintegrated and unhappy Americans who were conscripted and thrown onto Europe in the Second World War. Utterly lacking as they were in any desire to fight or to accomplish even the destruction which was expected of them, nevertheless they allowed themselves to be sent abroad and killed rather than defend themselves and their Fatherland against the plans of the alien regime in Washington.

This condition of degeneration, so widespread in America, with its colonial lack of resistance to Culture-disease, and so threatening to Europe under the present American domination, has not arisen by accident. A century ago, the liberal-communist-democrat Karl Marx and his coterie formulated as their program the destruction of the family, of marriage, and of the Fatherland. They declared a horizontal war against the Western Civilization, affirming their aim of disintegrating all social, cultural, and political forms. America **is** their program in process of actualization, and its example shows Europe what the liberal-communist-democratic regime of Culture-distortion is preparing for it during the coming generations.

But let there be no mistake: there is nothing inevitable about this Culture-disease. As long as the Culture-organism retains its traditions, its racial instincts, its will-to-power, and its natural exclusiveness and resistance to everything culturally alien, this result cannot be. The example of Quebec is proof.[7] There, healthy instincts of resistance to Culture-disease made it impossible for the Washington regime to conscript the population of an entire third of Canada in its war of revenge, hatred, and destruction against the Father-Culture and Mother-soil of Europe. The mass-heroism of the entire Quebec regiment which laid down its arms and refused as a unit when ordered to participate in the hostile invasion of the sacred soil of Europe is an inspiring proof of the prevalence and high potential, even in the colonies,

[7] The Canadian government's attempt to introduce conscription in Quebec in the First World War was met with fierce resistance and even led to severe rioting, as the Québécois did not feel that they owed loyalty to either Britain or France and did not want to serve in units with Anglophone troops with whom they couldn't communicate. This situation resurfaced in the Second World War, and in 1944 the Canadian government again attempted to introduce conscription given its military's high casualty rates. Maurice Duplessis had just been re-elected as Premier of Quebec, largely because he had pledged to stop an alleged plan by International Jewry to resettle a hundred thousand Jewish refugees in Quebec, and he also opposed Canada's participation in the war. The crisis reached its peak when word that troops who were stationed on Canada's coasts in order to defend against possible Japanese or German attacks would be redeployed to Europe, and in November 1944, when soldiers in Terrace, British Columbia heard of this plan, they mutinied, refusing to obey orders from officers and even seizing weapons. By the end of the month, however, the mutiny had petered out. Ultimately, a small number of conscripts were called up after political negotiations, but many deserted and few ever saw combat.

of the invincible Western tradition of cultural purity and exclusiveness. Similarly, in the Boer colony, strong resistance was continually opposed to the war of the extra-European forces against the Western Culture.[8] Even in America itself, the main focus of the efforts of the Culture-distorter, and the base of his greatest power, the main body of the people held aloof from the War, in the attitude castigated by the alien regime as "isolationist." Far from being isolated, the inner soul of the true American people is connected indivisibly by the strongest possible tie, the mystical cord binding the Mother-Organism to its colony, and it was precisely because of this connecting bond that the true American instinct shrank from the hateful war against Europe. It sought isolation only from the foul treason against Europe which was hatched and directed in Washington.

This great fact demonstrates to Europe and to History that America is not lost, and from this moment the Liberation Front exists also in America. The war for the Liberation of the Western Civilization embraces the colonies as well, since it is a horizontal war, like the Culture-diseases against which it is fighting. Attempts to split the West into separate units, economic, political, military, racial, are purely artificial in this age. The vertical battle of all against all belongs to the dead capitalist-nationalistic past, and its resurrection now is simply a technic of the inner enemy, an attempt to strangle the future with the dead clutch of the past. The Liberation Front, both on the Mother-soil and in the colonies, turns its back on the old vertical struggles, and opposes the Washington regime within America as totally as it opposes the puppet administrations it maintains in Europe. Within the Western Civilization itself, there are no more **real** vertical differences; the only **real** struggle of this kind in the world is the revolt of the outer world against the supremacy of the European race.

In the sphere of national economy, Culture-disease pursued during the materialistic age the same program of destruction which the liberal-communist-democratic Marx had enunciated

---

[8] In South Africa, popular resistance against the country's participation in the war meant that conscription was never introduced there.

for it. Communist-democratic literature demanded crushing income and inheritance taxes in order to destroy the industrialists and transfer the wealth to the finance-capitalist, whose wealth is invisible, and cannot be found or taxed. In a century-long battle the forces of disease almost completely succeeded in destroying any propertied groups with Western traditions whose ascendancy itself represented a barrier to degeneration and conquest by Culture-distortion. They brought in the device of huge anonymous financial structures, called holding companies, they made the currency of nations a function of their banks, and enforced the principle of constant flux on the national economy, in order to create the possibility of financial coups.

The corrosion of Culture-disease affected not only the forms of society and economy, but those of government as well. Where once the State had stood, speaking authoritatively for all, the focus of respect and the source of order, they introduced the chaos of ideologies, each claiming to have the formula for millennium, the secret of building the Old-Testament promised land, in each case purely materialistic and economic. They did not speak of a World-Idea, of the Western mission in the world, of the construction of the Imperium of the West, but of trade, distribution, and the exchange. The soul of Western man was to them a function of imports and exports, of shipping and book-keeping, of possessing and non-possessing, of rivalry between classes. The World-Mission of the West they understood as the securing of markets and raw materials overseas.

Where Authority had stood, clothed with dignity, they now brought in gabbling parliaments, wherein the gabble became ever more meaningless, and the sham ever more patent. For these deputies are mere things, replaceable units describable only mathematically, in aggregates. Among them there is not, and cannot be, a strong individuality, for a man, a whole and entire man, does not sell himself like these parliamentary whores.

To replace the authoritative principle of public responsibility, Culture-disease has brought in the anonymous irresponsibility of the decision of the amorphous majority, which can never again be found after it has committed its treason to Europe. To complete the destruction, the lying fraud of so-called elections tries to re-convince the European peoples every few months that somehow they govern themselves. Between the lies that the candidates offer the populace, and the commitments they make to their real masters, there is not the slightest connection. The programs submitted to the electorate are compounded out of old liberal-communist-democratic ideological material, long-since historically dead. To these creatures without honor, character, or even bare understanding, the future is to be simply an extension of the past. To talk of new organization is to talk about a bigger and better parliament, of a league of nations with a gigantic parliament, bringing possibilities of higher prices for greater lies. Only the scale is to be raised. Even in England, the birthplace of the parliamentary idea, and the only place where it even had dignity and value, the idea is completely dead. With a sound instinct, the population dubs the local parliament the "gas-house." Everywhere in Europe, the populations show what they think of this putrescent fraud by insulating themselves from it: they close their ears against the programs and the lies, they hate the ideologies, they boycott the elections, they despise from their souls the entire Old-Testament Tower of Babel which today has the temerity to call itself government, and to ask for the confidence of the peoples.

This is the world that the inner enemy, the liberal-communist-democrat, has created, working with, and often under the very direction of the Culture-alien, the State-Nation-People-Race-Society of the Jew. With their disease of Culture-retardation, with which they would strangle the future of Europe, they have reinforced the diseases of Culture-parasitism and Culture-distortion which are the gift of the Jew to Europe.

They have brought in materialism, atheism, class-war, weak happiness-ideals, race-suicide, social-atomism, racial promiscuity, decadence in the arts, erotomania, disintegration of the family, private and public dishonor, slatternly feminism, economic fluctuation and catastrophe, civil war in the family of Europe, planned degeneration of the youth through vile films and literature, and through neurotic doctrines in education. They have sought to rot Europe, to attenuate its racial instincts, to devirilize it, to deprive it of honor, heroism, and manliness, of the sense of its World-Mission, of its sense of Cultural unity, even of its chivalrous military code. They have sought to paralyze the will of Europe and destroy its will-to-power by bringing in the ethical syphilis of Hollywood to poison the sacred soil of Europe.

This we lay to their charge. Those things are facts, and nothing in the future can ever eradicate the knowledge that they have been done and attempted by the inner enemy. Nor is this the full extent of the destruction wrought by the hatred, negation, and revenge of the enemies of Europe. This is the devastation **within** the peoples of Europe. It remains to document their effects in the sphere of the mutual relations of the nations of Europe, and lastly, in the sphere of the relations of Europe to the outer world.

B. The Destruction of the Political Unity of Europe

During the dynastic period of Western history, although intra-European wars were of large-scale and long duration, they were limited into their aim, and the exploitation of victory was strictly conditioned. They were not national wars, but dynastic wars. Power was the stake, but only power within the prevailing forms of chivalrous ethics, comity, and Cultural unity. This unity was known as the Concert of Europe, and the very name itself reflects the deep sense of unity throughout the European family.

With the coming of the Age of Materialism, and the assault on all the traditions of the West by the forces of liberalism, Jacobinism, democracy, money, and rationalism, the dynastic concept of the Nation-idea slowly broke down and was replaced by the linguistic concept of the nation. The mystical-authoritative symbol of the ruling house had been the ultimate expression of the Nation-Idea for centuries, but now a new age demanded a new form of the nation-concept to reflect the materialistic outlook of the XIXth century. Materialism thus created the linguistic test of nationality.

The increasing expansive tendency of the Western organism had resulted in a vast increase of the Western population, the reflection of its more extensive life-task. From this arose huge economic systems, stronger States than any that had previously existed, larger-scale wars, and constant increase of the power-content of the struggle.

The literary concept of the Nation-Idea isolated the nations from one another and accentuated their national feelings *vis-à-vis* one another. Out of this arose the distorted patriotism called chauvinism, or jingoism. It invaded the universities, the world of letters, the cabinets, and the political parties. It concentrated all of its hopes, feelings, ideals, and understanding on to the nations, and in its last stage, it finally attained to the ridiculous idea that nations are the creators of culture, that, thus, there were as many Cultures in Europe as there were nations. Since it had been the feeling of Culture unity which had bound Europe together, and had kept its internal politics and wars limited and chivalrous, this insane form of nationalism was striking at the very basis of the unity of Europe. If, in a war between two European States, each one regarded itself as a Culture, then the opponent was a **total** enemy, and the struggle was an **absolute** one. This new concept of war and politics governed the minds of the materialistic democrats and liberals, who now welcomed the jingoist into their republic of destruction. The jingoists reinterpreted the entire past in terms of the XIXth century nations. They spoke of these nations as though they had always existed and were mechanically and causally necessary to the existence of the world, as if they were the sole units of higher history, and as if the future, as well the past, belonged to these historical building blocks.

But once more, the materialistic assault was not entirely successful. Tradition did not break down completely, because it is the very core, the wrapping of the soul of the Western Culture. Thus, after the Franco-Prussian War, late in the XIXth century, Bismarck saw to the safety and honorable treatment of the defeated French Emperor, and the treaty of peace was in the XVIIIth century chivalrous style. The vertical nationalism of materialistic jingoism did not succeed in destroying entirely the feeling of Cultural unity, and the proof is in the Western reaction to the Chinese Boxer Rebellion in 1900.[9] As one, the European

---

[9] The Boxer Rebellion was an uprising against Western imperialism in China that began in 1899. After Westerners, foreign legations,

nations joined, together with the American colony, in sending a joint expeditionary force to represent and protect Europe as a unit, under the command of the German Field-Marshal Waldersee.

The struggle between Tradition and vertical nationalism continued and finally reached its highest intensity with the caesura of the First World War. But suddenly, with the end of that war, there was a new world in existence. Europe, in that powerful tremor, had entered upon a new phase of its existence. The break was just as profound as that of the Revolution of 1789, the other great turning-point in recent European history. The old notions of materialism, nations, society, history, politics, State, war, culture, education, ethics, science, were all swept away. In their place was a new, complete, organic view of life. Its relation to the old materialist-rationalist-democratic-communist view is most easily understood, not as true to false, but as the Future to the Past. The old materialistic, disintegratory, atomistic, liberal-parliamentary view of the world had simply died a natural death. This is the only way historical Ideas can be overcome, the organic way, by complete fulfillment and death. The First World War itself was a creation—the last independent creation—of that old outlook; it was the highest expression of vertical nationalism and the Age of Materialism.

Out of the death of the Age of Materialism came the new values. First, in the realm of economics, the favorite preserve of the liberal-communist-democratic gentry, the old ethical principle of capitalism yielded to the new principle of ethical socialism. Instead of the cut-throat code of every man for himself, and the concept of life as a ruthless Darwinian competition to get rich, there arose the new code of each man for all, the feeling that the State is the custodian of the destiny, and thus, of the power, of all within it, that the aim of Life is not to get rich, but to actualize one's self and one's possibilities within the higher organism. In-

---

and Chinese Christians began to be attacked, Austria-Hungary, France, Germany, Great Britain, Italy, Japan, Russia, and the United States all contributed troops to a joint expeditionary force which crushed the Rebellion.

stead of the supremacy of economics and individualism, the subordination of economics and the integration of the individual into the superpersonal life. The good conscience and theoretical foundations of *laissez-faire* vanished.

In the spiritual realm, atheist materialism slowly began to recede from its heights and to yield to a renewal of true religious feelings. In philosophy, sensualism gave way to the historical method, and the organism of the Western Culture throbbed anew with the rediscovery of its unitary destiny and its mighty Imperialist mission in the world.

In the sphere of Society, opposing the chaos of atomism, feminism, disintegration of home and family, race-suicide, and universal decadence, arose the idea of race-ascendancy, fertility, the preservation and integration of society, the return to social health.

The idea of the State resumed its pristine sway in the realm of politics, and parliamentarism, with its chaotic train of election, programs, utopias, and corruption, took its place among the archaic things. The attempt to use legalism to deprive the European organism of life was overthrown, and the European will-to-power increased. The political life intensified, pacifism disappeared, European man oriented himself to the coming absolute wars for the survival of Europe, and against the outer forces.

After more than a century of constant disintegration, division, and disunification, of a constant crisis arising from the autopathic Culture-disease of rationalist-materialism, the Culture came back once more to health and soundness, to Authority and Faith. The provisional form of the restoration of Europe to health and unification of Europe was gradually assimilated by the countries of Europe, one after the other.

In the First World War, the Rationalism and Materialism of the XVIIIth and XIXth centuries had won a pseudo-victory over the Resurgence of Faith, Authority, and Imperialism, which are the spirituality of the XXth and XXIst centuries. The Culture-retarding elements which exploited this victory strove to perpetuate the old ways and ideas. With their capitalist-parliamentary league of nations they accentuated the pluralism of the States of Europe, just as they continued within each State to accentuate social-economic pluralism. The difference now was that these States were not true political units, but merely remnants which had to unite if the organism of Europe were even barely to survive. The attempt in this situation to perpetuate petty-stateism and vertical nationalism was treason to Europe and to every petty-State within Europe as well. But treason is the profession of Culture-disease elements; their only acquaintance with Europe's grand Imperialist mission in the world is as with an enemy. When they see something great arising, they resolve in their crooked and envious souls to thwart it and to tear it down.

Thus it is that they resolved to destroy the European Resurgence of Authority, with its reborn Faith, and its high task of uniting the European organism for its World-Mission. When in 1936 the four leading powers of Europe signed a pact forever renouncing war among themselves, and thus affirming their European unity, the Future of Europe seemed forever guaranteed.

But in the outer world, hostile developments towards Europe far transcended the efforts of the inner-disease elements, the liberal-communist-democrats. For in America in 1933, the Culture-State-Nation-Race-People of the Jew had seized the total power, and the entire resources of America were at his disposal in his mission of hatred, revenge, and destruction of the Western Civilization, and in particular of its heart and soul, the European organism. By poisonous propaganda, by bribes on an unprecedented scale, by the purchase of whole governments and parliaments, by financial manipulations with European currencies, and by economic pressure, the Culture-distorting regime of Washington split Europe into two halves and began to prepare a World War against Europe. The instrument of this preparation in America was the monster Roosevelt, who made of his life a study in infamy, and whose name is synonymous with the pinnacle of Jewish power in the world. The Jew and his Roosevelt accomplished what no inner force in Europe ever could have attained, the creation of an unnatural and inorganic war of destruction and terror against Europe, which at long last succeeded in its negative aim. The re-union of the European organism is temporarily frustrated, the Resurgence of Authority is temporarily halted, the power of every one of the former States of Europe is reduced to nil, the power of the European organism in the outer world is gone, the prestige of Europe is overshadowed by extra-European powers.

This is the new Europe, the creation of Liberal-communist democracy, the Europe of rationalist-materialism, of proletarian-Marxist-finance-capitalism, of class-war and vertical nationalism pushed to their limits. From the one direction comes the Jew, dragging in his train his nervous unhappy American victims, with their self-appointed task of "educating" Europe; from the other direction, at the invitation of and with the assistance of the Washington regime, comes the barbarian flood of the Moscow Red Army into the heart of Europe.

Where yesterday the Resurgence of Faith and Authority had stood up to open the way into the European Future, where the will-to-power, to order and achievement, to plenty and to beauty, had gone calmly ahead with its work, today the hysterical legalism of excited Jews and dead liberals enforces a grisly and monstrous terror against the peoples of Europe. Replacing the one will to unity and power, there are now a multitude of parliamentary bourses, where every day the soul of Europe is bought and sold, and where the economic existence of European humanity is treated as an entry in the ledger of the American foreign ministry. The triumphant disease-elements have destroyed the stability and the order of the economy of Europe and have brought in universal poverty to replace the security and plenty which are Europe's right. With their disintegration, cut-throat capitalism, petty stateism, senseless competition, and canonized selfishness, they have created want and insecurity, hunger, malnutrition, unemployment, despair, and suicide. When they hang the chain of economic dependence on America around our necks, they expect a song of gratitude from the peoples of Europe, who have known independence and grandeur, but who have never known slavery.

This also we lay to their charge. The disease-elements of liberal-communist-democracy, the inner enemy of Europe, have sought to destroy permanently, and have temporarily brought low, the Cultural unity of Europe, which served to unite all the peoples through the superior Cultural bond, holding them, even in war with one another, to chivalrous usages, mutual self-respect, and political restraint. They have done it, and they cannot explain it away, for these results have flowed of necessity from their inverted outlook and their dishonorable methods.

Nor is this yet all: with its social degeneration of more than a century, with its undermining of the Cultural unity of Europe by intensifying the petty-stateism, chauvinism, and vertical nationalism, the coalition of Jewish Culture-distortion and liberal-communist-democratic Culture-retardation has accomplished automatically a third result, namely in the political relationship of Europe to the rest of the world.

C. The Destruction of Europe's World-Empire

In 1900 the affairs of 9/10ths of the surface of the earth were ordered directly from European capitals. This was the World-Empire of Europe. This empire was the basis of the power, the security, the prosperity, yes, the very existence of Europe's peoples. In reality this Empire was simply and solely **European**, and its superficial organization as a collection of empires—French, English, German—was only **apparent**. But the internal tension created by petty-stateism was generating a centrifugal tendency within the European Empire, and extra-European forces were exploiting this tendency. In particular, a revolt was spreading among the colored races. The only way the great World-Empire could maintain its world-strength was by firmer integration in order to uphold its mastery and reverse the diffusion of power.

The final proof of the organic unity of this World-Empire was the fact that no single European Nation-State could injure the power of another European Nation-State without at the same time injuring itself in an equal or greater measure. But this ruling organic fact was ignored, and the tragedy of the First World War, the creation of the Culture-retarders, the chauvinists, jingoists, and vertical nationalists, was the price Europe paid for the presence of Culture-disease. Any colored or extra-European troops whatever that fought in this war were fighting against all Europe. Any extra-European fleets that participated were fighting the sea-power of Europe.

The demonstration of these organic facts was the new situation created by the war. The English fleet, the chief upholder of European power on the seas of the world was defeated by the extra-European sea power of Japan and America. The new arbiters of the destinies of the earth-ball were the extra-European forces, Japan, America, and Russia.

Before the First World War, Russia had figured as a Western State. Its ruling strata, its ruling outlook, were Western. The tension which existed between the Western elements of Russia and the Asiatic will-to-destruction underneath was however strained to the breaking point by the First World War, and the Asiatic elements, in conjunction with and assisted by the Culture-State-Nation-Race-People-Society of the Jew all over the world, gained the upper hand and re-oriented Russia against Europe. From then onward, and also today, 1950, Russia figures as one of the leaders of the colored revolt against the European race. But European possibilities still exist within Russia, because in certain strata of the population adherence to the great organism of the Western Culture is an instinct, an Idea, and no material force can ever wipe it out, even though it may be temporarily repressed and driven under.

The First World War showed, to those who did not know the difference, the mutual independence of military and political victory. Thus, although Russia was defeated in the field, it emerged from the war with increased power and voice in the affairs of the world. Japan, which took no military part in the war, was a leading political victor. Although England was supposedly victorious in the fight, it lost its power in the Pacific to Japan and America, its power in the Western Hemisphere to America, its naval hegemony to Japan and America, and its world-prestige to the colored revolt against the European race. The European-English Raj in India was completely undermined by the war, and the successful Indian Mutiny in 1947 stems directly from the First World War.

But the Culture-retarders had not finished their work. They had found a Europe which controlled 9/10ths of the surface of the planet. With their suicidal war, they had reduced the empire to the point where it controlled 2/10ths of the world, but their destructive potentialities and instincts were not yet exhausted.

They formulated a league of nations to strangle Europe and to admit the entire world into the direction of Europe's internal affairs; they asserted their system of degeneration, destruction, and death was the **legal** system, and that it could never be changed. Law does not exist to express and to serve life, no, these liberal-communist-democrats said that **Life** exists in order to serve the **Law**. This Old-Testament legalism determined to forever prevent Europe from rising again out of the general defeat of the First World War and from reconquering the world-domain which belongs to it by virtue of its strength of will, its organizatory ability, its necessity of self-expression, its irrepressible instinct, its Destiny, and its Faith. Here, as always, the various forms of Culture-disease showed their natural affinity. The Culture-distorting Jewish State-Nation-Race supplemented the efforts of the Culture-retarders to hold Europe down and back, to strangle it economically, and to force the dispersion of the European populations over the earth as despairing poverty-stricken, futureless emigrants.

All the disease-elements united in the negation and hatred of the great European Resurgence of Authority. The conquest of the savage negro landscape of Abyssinia by the European race[10] was diabolically represented as a "crime" by the Jewish-democratic-liberal-communist disease. While the soul of Europe throbbed with renewed hope and vigor at this manifestation of its old eternally-young re-assertion of its will and its Destiny, the disease-elements embarked on the preparation of a treacherous and dishonorable war forever to destroy the European World-Empire, the European homeland, the soul of Europe, and the high Destiny of Europe.

They sought to open the war in European Spain in 1936. Russian Bolshevism sent agents and arms, Hollywood-American Bolshevism sent military and financial assistance, Jewish Bolshevism sent leaders and organizers. The liberal-communist-democratic gang all over the Western world, the inner enemy of the West, waxed enthusiastic, and from their ranks flowed a

---

[10] Yockey is referring to the conquest and colonization of Abyssinia, or Ethiopia, by Fascist Italy during the 1930s.

stream of conscripts on their mission of destruction. But Europe reacted as a unit and frustrated the Bolshevik-trinity of the outer enemies.

The next attempt was on the European frontier of Bohemia in 1938. Again, the four leading units of Europe mutually joined to prevent the destruction of the Empire and organism of Europe. Therefore, the next assault was more carefully prepared and preceded by a thorough organization of the Culture-retarding elements for the supreme treason of creating a Second World War in the form of a senseless struggle within the European organism. All the world knew that such a war, if prolonged, could only ruin the European Empire and every people and province of Europe. Even the traitors knew it in part of their souls, but a traitor is willfully blind. Treason is nothing but incapacity when it becomes resolute. If it had not been clear to them before the war, it was made clear during the war. The Architect of the War, the crypto-Culture-distorter Roosevelt, expressly stated his two war-aims to his churchills as the destruction of the German State and the English Empire, the two halves of the body of Europe, the foundation and the edifice of the European Empire.

This was their Second World War. It was made possible only by the treason of the inner enemy, the liberal-communist-democrat. No force within the Western Culture could even think of opposing successfully the powerful wave of Destiny sweeping through Europe, the Resurgence of Authority and the will-to-Imperium. But in their crooked, dark, and jealous hatred of greatness and grandeur, the liberal-communist-democrats, the class-warriors and finance-capitalists, the materialists and parliamentarians, called in the outer forces, the Bolshevisms of Washington, Moscow, and Tel-Aviv, and invited them to do the destruction to which they were not equal. Chauvinism and jingoism were merely techniques, and they could not inspirit any Europeans. The burden of the fighting was borne by the extra-European forces, for European troops simply were not equal spiritually to a contest against the organism of Europe.

The very tactics of the war were in the pattern of negation and hatred. The extra-European forces, led by the Culture-distorter, evolved the principle that the purpose of warfare is to destroy the civilian population of the arbitrarily-chosen enemy. The industrial life of Europe was unimpaired, the armies were intact, but the American-Jew and the Jewish-American continued their war against homes and families, while the forces of Asiatic Russia carried on the real, the military war. The warfare of revenge and hatred from the air was a deterrent to the military victory of the American-Jewish synthesis, but that did not matter, for their mission was not political **victory**, but total **destruction**, destruction of the Culture-People-Race-Society of Europe. Thus, the military assistance to Russia was not on a political basis, but was given recklessly, without any thought to the future, because the Washington-Tel-Aviv alliance was not even thinking of increasing its own power or of building a world-empire for itself, but simply, solely, and only, of destroying the Empire, the organism, and the Destiny of Europe. Consequently, American-Jewry negotiated a generous peace with Japan, which recognized the victory of the Japanese mission in the Orient, and in the occupation of Japan, a policy of friendship, benevolence, and reconstruction was put into effect. Their exploitation of victory was in the same twisted and crooked pattern as their own souls. Their great compulsion is the inversion of every truth and the perversion of all higher life.

At the beginning of their efforts to create the Second World War in the form which they gave to it, they found a Europe which was master of its own territory and ruler of 1/5th of the world. At the end of their war, they were able to survey the Europe of their own creation. Europe stripped of its World-Empire and occupied by extra-European forces, economically dependent on them as a slave upon his master.

In this Europe of liberal-democracy, the enemies of Europe proceeded to exploit their victory. Drunk with their power they began to kill *en masse* those who had opposed them and who had devoted their lives to furthering the Destiny of Europe. Even in murder, they could not be straight: they had to find Old-Testament reasons, legalistic rituals, to mask their murders. They invented, and sought to engraft onto the Culture of Europe, the device of the scaffold-trial. They reveled, they gloated, they prolonged their greatest Mosaic trial of all for a year. They sought to humiliate their victims in life by every imaginable meanness, and in death they thought to deprive their victims of historical rank by the hateful and stupid trick of distributing their ashes over the landscape. They tore into shreds the chivalrous traditions of treatment of war-prisoners and twisted the Geneva Convention out of shape by asserting it gave them power to hang any soldier as a criminal who had opposed the victory of the American-Jewish-liberal-democratic forces. The more they widen their Mosaic ritual of trial-killing, the more transparent it is to Europe that it is two worlds which are here in front of one another, and that this conflict cannot be settled in an Old-Testament courtroom, but will grow and continue, deepen and intensify, until the Culture-alien is expelled totally and finally from the sacred soil of the West.

Their terror includes every land of Europe, despite their pretense that it is isolated. The trick of showing a smiling face to part of Europe and concentrating the hostility onto another part of Europe deceives no one. As long as the Culture-retarders who administer Europe remain docile, accept American food rations, service American investments, and receive American garrisons, the Washington regime will smile. But Europe has seen the other face of the American-Jew and the Jewish-American, devoid alike of sympathy, wisdom, and policy, cruel, sneering, and stupidly arrogant. This attempt to divide Europe might perhaps succeed if the feeling of comradeship were absent from European populations. But a thousand years of Cultural unity, of the same experiences in every realm, of the same sufferings, even at one another's hands, has united the Europeans indissolubly. They know it now more than ever before, for they have learnt it anew under the Jewish-American lash.

Lastly, we lay to the charge of the inner enemy that he has destroyed the World-Empire of Europe with his vertical nationalism and petty-stateism, and by his vassalage to the Bolshevism of Washington, Moscow, and the Culture-State-Nation-Race-People of the Jew. He has thus destroyed the power of every European State and has turned over the soil of Europe to outer enemies.

III.
THE MISSION OF THE LIBERATION FRONT

Europe knows the identity of the inner enemy and that for which he is responsible. It knows that he is the worst enemy of Europe, because he masquerades as a European, but Europe has outer enemies toward whom also it must adopt a definitive position.

The outer enemies are the Bolshevik regime of Moscow, the Jewish-American Bolshevik regime of Washington, and the Culture-State-Nation-Race of the Jew, which has now created a new center of intrigue for itself in Tel-Aviv, a secondary New York.

The outer enemies are today the arbiters of Europe. They have set up their alternative to the natural, destined Europe of Authority and Faith: Europe as a source of booty for extra-European forces; Europe as a reservoir of man-power for the disposition of the American generalate; Europe as a loan-market for the New York financier; Europe as a beggar-colony watching for crumbs from the table of rich America; Europe as a historical sight for visiting colonials, a place where once there were great happenings; Europe as a museum, a mausoleum; Europe as a moribund collection of petty-states and squabbling peoples; Europe as an economic mad-house where every tiny unit is against every other; Europe as a backward population waiting for re-education by the American world-clown and the sadistic Jew; Europe, as a laboratory for gigantic social experiments by Moscow and for the genocide experimentation of New York and Tel-Aviv; Europe as a Black Mass of scaffold-trials, backward-looking persecution, treason, terror, despair, and suicide.

And a mere fifty years ago, Europe was a proud independent organism, sure of itself and master of the world. The sacred soil of the Western Culture is now occupied by the Mongols, Turkestani, and Kirghizians of Asia, by the Negroes of America, the Senegalese of Africa, the Jews from the pavements of the world. This is democratic Europe, liberal Europe.

But these conditions are only external, material. The **soul** of Europe cannot be occupied, ruled, or dominated by Culture-aliens. Only a materialist could think that the possession of the tangible appurtenances of power guarantees the eternal continuance of power. If that had been so, a few castes and States would have always ruled the world, from its beginning. But, in the ultimate test, power is the reflection of inner qualities, and these qualities are not possessed by any of the outer enemies of Europe. Their transitory empires are built on sand, because underlying them there is no superpersonal soul, no World-Mission, no World-Idea, no Destiny. Even in our short lives we have seen empires come and go, and the temporary power-agglomerations of Moscow and Washington will go the same way.

The outer enemies of Europe are doomed just as the inner enemy is. Time is against the inner enemy, because History cannot go backward, even if for a short time backward-looking dotards may try to force History to share the death-rattle with them.

And so with these crude and heterogeneous things that the Moscow barbarian and the Washington Jew like to think are empires. They will vanish like the morning mist under the bright rays of History. The Future belongs only to those who have the Inner Imperative to actualize a World-Idea latent in them, and there is only one source of this Imperative. It cannot be invented artificially, it must be organic, and no man or men can make it. It derives from the basic cosmic-spiritual origin of the universe, itself, derives from God.

Thus, the Liberation Front now states to Europe its two great tasks: (1) the complete expulsion of everything alien from the soul and from the soil of Europe, the cleansing of the European soul of the dross of XIXth century materialism and rationalism with its money-worship, liberal-democracy, social degeneration, parliamentarism, class-war, feminism, vertical nationalism, finance-capitalism, petty-stateism, chauvinism, the Bolshevism of Moscow and Washington, the ethical syphilis of Hollywood, and the spiritual leprosy of New York; (2) the construction of the Imperium of Europe and the actualizing of the divinely-emanated European will to unlimited political Imperialism.

Replacing the Culture-disease of extra-Europeans and traitors are the pristine ethical values of Europe: Authority, Faith, Discipline, Duty, Order, Hierarchy, Fertility, Will-to-Power.

This Proclamation is thus a Declaration of War.

In this War, the Liberation Front speaks for Europe, it represents Europe, it is the custodian of Europe's Destiny. It is thus clothed with the mantle of superpersonal invincibility that is the attribute of the European organism. No massacres, and no scaffold-trials, no terror or persecution can touch this force; the cannon and bayonets of Washington cannot harm it, but in the end it will dissolve them. It will drive the Jewish-American forces into the seas, it will throw the Asiatic armies of Moscow back into the remoteness of Asia.

In this struggle, all the former peoples, races, and nations of Europe coalesce, for in the beginning the war is solely a horizontal one:

Race now means, in Europe, the quality of having honor and pride;

People means the we-feeling of all Europeans;

Nation now means the organism of Europe itself.

English, German, French, Italian, Spanish—these are now mere place-names and linguistic variations. Like all of the other rich products of our great Culture, they will continue, but they are no longer political terms. Local cultures in Europe may be as diversified as they wish, and they will enjoy a perfect autonomy in the European Imperium, now that the oppression of vertical nationalism is dead. Anyone who seeks to perpetuate petty-stateism or old-fashioned nationalism is the inner enemy of Europe. He is playing the game of the extra-European forces; he is dividing Europe and committing treason.

Treason now has only one meaning to Europe: it means serving any other force than Europe. There is only one treason now, treason to Europe. The nations are dead, for Europe is born.

The Liberation Front does not allow Europe to be distracted by the situation of the moment, in which the two crude Bolshevisms of Washington and Moscow are preparing a Third World War. In these preparations, the Culture-retarders, the inner enemies, the liberal-communist-democrats are again at their posts:

with one voice the churchills, the spaaks, the lies,[11] the gaulles, croak that Washington is going to save Europe from Moscow, or that Moscow is going to take Europe from Washington. There is nothing to substantiate this propaganda. The **fact** is that only American intervention in the Second World War prevented Europe from completely destroying Bolshevik Russia as a political unit. The present Russian Empire is thus the creation of America. Never in the 500 years of Russian history has Russia been able to make its way unaided into Europe. It invaded Prussia against the great Frederick only when aided by France, Austria, and Sweden. It invaded France in 1814 and 1815 only when assisted by England, Austria, and Prussia. It invaded Europe in 1945 only by the help of America. Russia is only a threat to a divided Europe; a united Europe can destroy the power of Russia at the moment of its choosing. It is a crass lie to say that Europe cannot defend itself against Russia. Do they think it is possible for Europe to forget the knowledge that it has just purchased with the blood of millions of its sons? Do they believe that Europe can forget that the Jewish-American regime, and it alone, brought the Red Armies into the heart of Europe? Is it possible that they think that Europe can forget that the inner enemy with his liberal-communist-democracy led Europe into this abyss? Europe remembers, and it knows the liberal-democrat as the creature of the abyss, the spirit of negation who seeks an ever-lower abyss. He destroyed a World-Empire, and now he asks for the confidence of Europe for a new crusade.

Washington's program is to conscript the Europeans—what it cynically calls the "man-power" of Europe—and thus to spare the jitterbugs of North America the losses of arduous campaigns against Russia. Abysmal stupidity motivates this wish-thought. Do they really think that Europeans will accomplish military wonders fighting against one enemy of Europe on behalf of another? Do they think an American-Jewish High Command inspires the feelings necessary in a European officer-corps to elicit

---

[11] Trygve Lie (1896–1968) was a Norwegian politician from the Labor Party who had given shelter to Leon Trotsky after he was expelled from the Soviet Union.

its heroic instincts?

No, Europe is no more interested in this projected war than in a struggle between two negro tribes in the Sudan.

The European struggle is the fight for the liberation of our sacred soil and our Western soul. It is a horizontal struggle, against all enemies of Europe, inner enemies and extra-European forces, whoever they are. Before Europe can fight a vertical war, it must be constituted as the Imperium of Europe, the organic Culture-State-Nation-Race-People of the West. And when Europe makes war then, it will be against the political enemy of its own choosing, and at the time of its choosing. In these decisions, Jew, Moscow, and Washington will figure not at all. The propaganda of the American-Jew and the Jewish-American deceives no one. With their talk of a struggle between "East" and "West" they hope to entice the marginal minds of Europe into co-operation with them. But to us, the West is a word containing a divinely-emanated Mission, a sacred word, and it does not refer to America, to Russia, or to the Jew, but solely to the sacred soil of Europe and to the European organism.

All extra-European forces on European soil are enemies to precisely the same extent and in exactly the same degree. Europe will never fight for any extra-European force; Europe will never enter into any relationship in which it is not master; the outcome of wars between extra-European forces is a matter of indifference to the future of Europe.

The crude-power structures of Washington and Moscow have no Past, and therefore no Future. They are without Tradition, without a World-Mission, without a Nation-Idea, without a Destiny, without organic unity, without a State, and without Imperial possibilities. Both of these formless things are mere pale caricatures of the one, true, World-Mission, which inheres in Europe alone. This Mission does not arise from human will but is a direct emanation of God.

In this great struggle for the Liberation of Europe, every European of race, honor, and pride belongs with us, regardless of his provenance. The only Europeans outside of our ranks are the Culture-traitors, the disease of our Age. The Liberation Front itself is the provisional form of the European nation, and it will endure until the permanent form of the European Imperium is established.

In the mission of the Liberation of Europe, the exact date of final accomplishment is secondary to us, precisely because we know that our victory is already determined.

With every decade, every year, that goes by the European will to the perfect union and full flowering which are its Destiny becomes stronger. Our will is unbroken, our resolution stronger than ever a European resolution before us. With massive calmness we enter upon this greatest of all tasks to which ever European men have dedicated themselves.

Against the bayonets and cannon of the extra-European forces we oppose a will harder than their steel, which will wrench their weapons and their power from their grasp. With contempt we will grind the inner enemy into the dirt.

A millennium of European history, of joy and sacrifice, of heroism and nobility, impel us to our task. To the blood that has flowed on the sacred soil of Europe we shall add the blood of our enemies. We shall continue until Europe is freed from its enemies and the European banner floats over its own soil from Galway to Memelland and from North Cape to Gibraltar.

Europe Awake!

The Liberation Front

Fights for nothing less than the following:—

1. Liberation of Britain and of Europe from the regime of the inner-Traitor and the outer-Enemy.
2. Integration of liberated Britain into one sovereign European People-Nation State.
3. Immediate expulsion of all Jews and other parasitic aliens from the Soil of Europe.
4. Establishment of the Organic State.
5. Cleansing of the Soul of Europe from the ethical syphilis of Hollywood and the Marxist Bolshevism of Moscow.
6. Recognition of the fundamental significance of the Family and

Motherhood, and the real protection of the spiritual and material welfare of both.

7. Recognition of the Youth as the Vanguard of Tomorrow, and thus its systematic training, without exception, including the provision of educational facilities to each youth according to his ability, regardless of his social and economic status.
8. Affirmation of the Duty to Work and the abolition of all unearned income.
9. Immediate ending of the suicidal Export-War and the smashing of the Tyranny of interest.
10. Abolition of Poverty.
11. Intensive development of the soil of the Homeland and the Colonies overseas, along with the rationalization of Industry, to secure the existence of the People and raise its standard of life.
12. Since the LIBERATION FRONT is the only force within Britain which is an integral part of the EUROPEAN LIBERATION FRONT, therefore, the LIBERATION FRONT is opposed to all other parties within Britain.

YOUR PLACE IS IN THE FRONT!

MARCH WITH US!

Westropa Press, BCM/Westropa Press, London, W.C.1.

CORRESPONDENCE WITH ADRIEN ARCAND

1949-50

EDITORS' NOTE

Yockey sought out potential leaders for a post-war Western revival while Europe was still in ruins and the leadership and cultural strata were being exterminated. Yockey was vehemently slandered and belittled by the philosophically bereft, such as Gerald L. K. Smith in the United States and Arnold Leese in Britain, who could not go beyond an anti-Semitic fixation. Yockey did, however, find an enthusiastic response among the surviving and persecuted frontfighter veterans of defeated Europe. *Imperium* was met with acclaim by the German émigré group around Dr. Johann von Leers and *Der Weg* in Argentina; British Major-General, Thelemite, and tank expert General J. F. C. Fuller; Maurice Bardèche, a survivor of the wartime French fascist intelligentsia; and Girogio Almirante of the Italian Social Movement. Also notable was the endorsement and comradeship Yockey received from the Canadian fascist Adrien Arcand (1899–1967), who had been contacted early on by Yockey's primary English colleague, Anthony John Gannon.

Arcand had been a journalist of note in Quebec but had been removed from *La Press* by its publisher for attempting to organize a trade union. In 1929 he had been hired by the writer and publisher Joseph Menard, who aimed to establish a nationalist movement in Quebec. Arcand was given editorship of *Le Goglu*, which was both nationalist and anti-capitalist. Menard founded two other journals in 1930, the Sunday *Miroir* and *Le Chameau*.[1]

Around these a movement formed, the Ordre Patriotique des Goglus, which had a fascist orientation, like the fascist "leagues"

[1] Lita-Rose Betcherman, *The Swastika and the Maple Leaf* (Ontario: Fitzhenry & Whiteside Ltd., 1975), p. 5.

that had been forming in France since the 1920s.[2] The Ordre reached fifty thousand members and held strong interest for Montreal's twenty-two thousand Italians.[3] By 1932, Arcand was writing supportively of Hitler as a fighter against international Jewish banking.[4]

Arcand was a devout Catholic who saw the struggle as being between Jewish materialism—whether Communist or capitalist—and the teachings of Christ. It was a widespread attitude among Catholics throughout the world and incorporated Catholic social doctrine as the means of fighting the materialist hydra. In the United States, Father Charles Coughlin translated this into a mass movement, the National Union for Social Justice, which had a militant wing, the Christian Front.

In 1934, with support from the Quebecois Catholic associations, the National Social Christian Party was formed under Arcand's leadership. This had a corporatist program, reflecting the Catholic social doctrine of the Papal encyclicals that urged an alternative to the equally godless materialistic doctrines of Marxism and free-trade capitalism. The Church sought a restoration of the guilds of the Medieval era. This "corporatist" doctrine of the Church, while predating fascism, and assuming various forms as reflected in, for example, widespread Catholic support for Social Credit, also provided an impetus for fascist movements that had a corporatist policy.

Although Arcand did focus on the Jewish issue, this was not to the detriment of developing a coherent and detailed ideology called "National Corporatism." In 1936, Arcand was an important figure supporting the conservative party in Quebec, Union Nationale, and he edited *L'Illustration Nouvelle*, a daily tabloid supporting the party.[5] The party's leader, Maurice Duplessis, became Premier that year, indicating that Arcand was not a marginal figure.[6]

---

[2] Ibid., p. 6.
[3] Ibid., p. 7.
[4] Ibid., pp. 20–21.
[5] Ibid., p. 85.
[6] Ibid., p. 86.

In 1938, at a congress of several thousand in Kingston, Ontario, the main nationalist parties merged under Arcand's leadership, taking the name the National Unity Party (NUP).[7] Despite war-mongering against Germany which was already underway in 1938, Anglophone Canadians generally supported either diplomacy or non-intervention, while Francophone Canadians were solidly against Canadian involvement in a war.[8] It was a phenomenon that Yockey was to remark upon in *The Proclamation of London* as a sign of Culture-health among Quebecois. Although the government ordered the NUP disbanded in September 1939, when Canada entered the war, hundreds of members in Quebec continued to meet in church halls thanks to the efforts of a priest, while smaller meetings were held privately in other parts of the country.[9] Prompted by the internment of Sir Oswald Mosley and around eight hundred members of the British Union of Fascists, plus several hundred others, in Britain under emergency defense regulations, in March 1940 Arcand and his aides were also detained. Arcand was not released until July 1945.

In reduced circumstances, living in the little town of Lanorai, Quebec, Arcand continued to receive support from his old friend, Premier Duplessis, who provided him with translating and editing work.[10] Despite his post-war hardships, Arcand ran in the federal elections in 1949 as a NUP candidate in Richelieu-Verchères, coming in second with 29% (5590 votes).[11] In 1953 in Berthier-Maskinongé-Delanaudière he also came in second with 39.75% (7496 votes) as a "Nationalist."[12] The NUP continued into the 1970s, briefly surviving Arcand, who died in 1967.

Arcand's admiration for Yockey as a person and as a philosopher was deeply felt and enduring. The Italian artist Edigio Boschi (famous for his paintings on pin-heads), a Fascist, and

---

[7] Ibid., p. 119.

[8] Ibid., p. 128.

[9] Ibid., p. 145.

[10] Ibid., p. 146.

[11] Canadian Parliament, "History of Federal Ridings since 1869," www.parl.gc.ca/About/Parliament/FederalRidingsHistory/hfer.asp?Include=Y&Language=E&rid=608&Search=Det.

[12] Ibid., Berthier-Maskinongé-delanaudière, 1953.

Yockey stayed with Arcand for several days at Lanorai. Through John Gannon, Arcand was among the first of the European Liberation Front's overseas contacts. Already having read *Imperium*, it seems that Arcand had been sent a draft of *The Proclamation of London* in 1949 and had an influence on it. Gannon wrote to Arcand, thanking him for his "helpful and constructive criticism" of *The Proclamation*, and adopted his suggestions.[13]

Arcand wrote to H. Keith Thompson, Yockey's American colleague, after being informed of Yockey's death in 1960: "The news gave me quite a shock, though I knew that our friend had to be careful at all times. He was precious—or dangerous!—for his brains, and his opus was a real masterpiece . . ."[14] Several weeks later, Arcand wrote of what an honor it had been that Yockey had stayed at his home in Lanorai for "a whole week." Arcand wrote later of first meeting Yockey with Boschi at the Windsor Hotel in Montreal. He alluded to how they were aware that Yockey was under surveillance from the FBI and Canadian Intelligence. Arcand had been tipped off by the desk clerk, an Arcand supporter, that a tape recorder had been installed in the adjoining room, "so we had the fun of our lives in giving the FBI and Canadian Intelligence improvised messages in most loud talk about the Zionists being masters of our mutual governments, FBI, RCMP and what not."[15]

It is unfortunate that, in regard to the following correspondence from Yockey to Arcand, the latter's replies are not available. Much of the correspondence concerns Yockey's dealings with the American Right, particularly as it gravitated around the comparatively wealthy Gerald L. K. Smith. Yockey sought out Smith as one of the notables of the pre-war Right, as he did in Britain with Sir Oswald Mosley, in Germany with Major General Otto Remer, in France with Maurice Bardèche, and many others. Smith had been the organizer of the "Share the Wealth" movement of Huey P. Long, Governor and Senator of Louisiana, whose impending challenge to the presidency of Franklin D.

---

[13] Letter from Gannon to Arcand, December 12, 1949.

[14] Arcand to H. Keith Thompson, June 30, 1960.

[15] Arcand to Thompson, July 16, 1961.

Roosevelt was perhaps the motive for his assassination at the State Capitol in 1935. Smith, trained as a preacher, was a fiery speaker who, like Father Coughlin, could attract a large and zealous following. He was also comparatively well-connected, having known Henry Ford, Senior, and after the war, despite his notoriety as an "anti-Semite," gained the confidence of senators John Rankin and Jack Tenney. Smith founded an educational association, the Christian Nationalist Crusade, which endured until his death in 1976, and the short-lived Christian Nationalist Party.

This was the milieu with which Yockey got in contact, and in 1950 he spoke at Smith's three-day annual convention in Los Angeles, where he received enthusiastic applause, although he was treated pettily by Smith.

Having failed to enlist Sir Oswald Mosley as the apostle of his doctrine of Western "imperialism," for reasons more complicated than his dealings with Smith, the result was that about ten percent of Union Movement members broke away to form the European Liberation Front. Returning to the United States, Yockey proposed himself to Smith as the leader of a worldwide movement for Western imperialism. However, Smith was ideologically shallow and saw no reason to extend his actions beyond publishing and lobbying for a banal "American patriotism."

Another problematic figure that Yockey encountered was Ernest Elmhurst, a German First World War veteran and apparently a rumor-monger. Elmhurst had been active among the Coughlinites and the German-American Bund. His main claim to fame had been the writing of *The World Hoax*, a book on Jewish involvement in Communism which was published by William Dudley Pelley of the Silver Legion in 1938.

While Yockey had failed to win over Mosley to act as the front man for his doctrine, the acrimony actually came from the British Hitlerites and anti-Semites around Arnold Leese, while Mosley retained a little-known high regard for Yockey throughout his life, which he expressed to correspondents such as Ivor Benson, a former information adviser to the Rhodesian government, and himself an enthusiast for *Imperium*. Leese was obsessed with Jews and did not develop a doctrine for his pre-war Imperial Fascist League (IFL) beyond anti-Semitism. Leese regarded Mosley's fascism as "kosher fascism," because Mosley had developed a cogent doctrine that did not rely on Jew-baiting, and he suggested that the Mosley name derived from "Moses Levy." For someone who tested the racial purity of applicants to the IFL with calipers, Leese and others of the type regarded Yockey's Spenglerian ideas on the race of the spirit as akin to Communism.

This chapter includes all of the known extant correspondence between Yockey and Arcand apart from the former's letter dated December 29, 1949, which is reproduced in Chapter 6, "The Italo-English Convention."

Correspondence with Adrien Arcand

November 21, 1949, Roxana, Illinois

Cher Monsieur:

Your letter came, and I was indeed happy to hear from you again. I have no idea what can have happened to your previous letter to me. I, like you, do not leave letters unanswered. This makes us rarer people in this period, for a great many people for whom one has a right to expect a high ethical standard do not recognize any obligations whatever to answer letters.

You may be perfectly certain that I shall not in any way use the information that Smith slandered me in that particularly vicious fashion.

I agree with all of the observations in your letter—the fact that our Idea need not be impatient, that it needs an unassailable philosophical foundation, that members of the Right should be amalgamated, and that the book should be spread.

I respect as do you the *code du gentilhomme*,[16] but I must also insist that Duty and Discipline supersede it. I do not see any other alternative, since we are not living in 1750, but in the Age of Absolute Politics. The *code du gentilhomme* only survives among

[16] "The code of the gentleman."

individuals—as a great, general ordering of life, it is dead, unfortunately so, but nevertheless dead. I am sure you will agree with me.

As to Leese and Smith, and the answer of the Front to Leese's public attack, I can only say that both these individuals attacked the Front first, not in a superficial way, but as being an organization subservient to Jew and Bolshevism. Surely you cannot expect us to let such slander pass. Please note that we do not accuse these people of being knowing agents of the Jew, although inevitably by their divisionist tactics they are serving Jewish policy, but unwittingly. Furthermore, from my experience in English circles, I consider that all materialists, including the vertical racists,[17] are and must be, hostile to us. Thus, for instance, English racists are opposed to Ethical Socialism, and believe in Ethical Capitalism. They favored National Socialist Germany mainly for the reason that it was anti-Jewish. This is not the reason that I was won to the Prussian Idea—I am not first an anti-Semite, but am anti-Semitic only because they are frustrating our Western Destiny, but they are not the only group, and **not the most powerful group** doing that. Our worst enemy is the inner enemy, the liberal-capitalist-democrat, for it is he that alone enables the Jew to enjoy his present power.

Furthermore, these two characters, Leese and Smith, have mainly nineteenth-century outlooks. Leese, for instance, is not anti-churchill; he is a British imperialist, a firm believer in the English monarchy. Smith is an anti-Catholic bigot of the variety that is bred only in the Baptist Church—at luncheon he assured me that the Pope is Antichrist. He said this knowing that I do not belong to any organized religion. To a Catholic he would have talked completely differently, of course.[18] I have small tol-

[17] "Vertical race" means race defined by physiology; in contrast to "horizontal race," where race is defined according to one's soul and spirit. Yockey's advocacy of "horizontal race" derives from his commitment to the philosophy of Oswald Spengler.

[18] Indeed, during the Depression era, when Gerald L. K. Smith was in his heyday, he worked with the popular "radio priest," Father Charles Coughlin, whose mass circulation newspaper, *Social Justice*, published Yockey's first political article, "The Tragedy of Youth."

erance for these survival types, but I never disturb them in their mental graveyards. It is they who attacked me.

I am taking the liberty of sending you half a dozen sets of *Imperium*. You may use them in any way you think fit—they are yours. What you say is true, that even hostile criticism of the book by the enemy is good, and I have tried to get this, by sending the book to prominent enemies. So far I have not succeeded in getting a review this way. In general, I favor sending and giving it only to those who are already with us in their **instincts**. It will give them a firm foundation, and make them more articulate. If you ever want more sets of the book, merely let me know.

I still don't know when I shall be able to return to Europe, but when I do, I shall go via Montreal if possible.

Best wishes,
Front Heil!
Varange

JANUARY 17, 1950, BRUSSELS, BELGIUM

Mon cher M. Arcand,

I received your valuable letter yesterday, and have read it carefully. You must never think that any suggestions you make to me would ever possibly be received in the wrong spirit. *Tout a fait au contraire*,[19] as I value them highly, and hope that you will always not only feel free to tell me anything you wish to, but that you will continue to do so from time to time.

About the word "fascism" I should like to say this: I, no more than you, am not particularly attached to the *word*. I prefer the word *Imperialism*. This word has the strongest possible organic roots, is a synonym for organic health, and describes alone the entire tendency of our Cultural stage, the stage of Imperium. Imperialism described now, not only the expansive tendency itself, which has been present ever since the rise of Spain, but also the feeling, the rationale, the philosophy, and the doctrine of

---

[19] "Quite the contrary."

this great, wordless, undeniable instinct.

I shall always devote my energy to trying to supplant the word fascism—during this fluid stage. I am no *Wortgläubiger*,[20] but I do believe the word fascism is simply a tactical handicap for us. Imperialism is not: the Marxists have never been able to take the magic, and pride, and the strength out of this fundamental word. Words too have a destiny, and through the decades and centuries their meanings change. Compare the meaning of the word democracy in 1800—everything bad—from its meaning in 1920—everything good. The Marxists are losing out in the terminological struggle, and it is merely a coincidence that they have used some of the words which we now use—with the opposite sign. This coincidence will be one day forgotten.

However, another problem arises: suppose that at public meetings, or in the press, or officially, we are asked: "Are you fascist?" What can one answer? *Heroic* is to say, "Yes, make the most of it." Clever is to say: "What do you mean by fascism? Tell me that, and then I shall answer." We cannot deny, without injuring ourselves, that we have the same fundamental doctrine as Mussolini and the Hero,[21] that we stem from them and are loyal to their spirit. We shall not raise the issue, but the enemy will, and he controls the organs of public information. Thus, the public will call us "fascists" and "Nazis." It is out of the question that we can pursue Mosley's stupid tactic of saying, "I am no longer a fascist; I am beyond fascism." I told him at the beginning that this tactic, pregnant as it is with negative suggestion, would cost him everything, and it has done so—he is finished in England. The other possibility is to evade the question entirely and try to focus on other issues. It is questionable whether this can be successfully done in view of the fact that the recent past is still so very much with all of us, including the enemy.

There comes a time in such circumstances when the object of the obloquy simply adopts the name and thus deprives the op-

---

[20] Literally, "believer in words," seeming to suggest someone who believes that words have a power in and of themselves.

[21] An allusion to Adolf Hitler, "the hero of the Second World War" to whom Yockey dedicated *Imperium*.

ponent of its pejorative force. Examples: the *Gueux de mar*, the *sans culottes*.[22]

As Patrick Henry said to the cries of "treason!"—"If this be treason, make the most of it!" This sort of reply restores the true issue to its place and necessitates a new term of abuse.

As a matter of fact, the term fascism has had, or will have, its own destiny, and it is largely beyond our control. If history imposes it on us, we will accept it, even though at this moment we do not wish to tie ourselves to the word.

About the idea of a world-front against Jewry, I only wish to say this. Only an *organism* can carry on political activity, and only organisms can form an alliance. "The world" is not, and can never be a political organism. Our task at present is to work within the framework of a Cultural organism, a *potential* political organism, in order to constitute it as a political unit. After that it will be time enough to talk of alliances. I am strongly in favor of a horizontal war against the Jew, but this can only be done within the framework of the Western Civilization, i.e., Europe above all, and to a less intense degree, the colonies. In this process Africa, India, China do not figure at all, and after the recent miserable performance of the Arabs against the Jew, who can say that Islam has big potentialities of this kind?

You are quite right about the Italians, they are not clear. There are two schools of thought in Italy, the one Imperialist, represented by Julius Evola, who is still alive. These are European, Prussian, Imperialist—they regard fascism as a means of conquering the world, as a spirituality, as Europe. The other school is the Gentilian[23] one; they regard fascism as a means of *saving* the world. They continually talk of the world, humanity,

---

[22] References to the lower classes during the French Revolution, which became significant factors in it.

[23] Referring to Giovanni Gentile (1875–1944), who was an Italian philosopher and educational reformer and was among the most important theoreticians and intellectual spokesmen of Italian Fascism. He applied the Marxist/Hegelian dialectic to the idea of the State, believing that in Fascism the oppositions which comprised the various elements of the State were reconciled within the overarching unity of the State's authority.

etc. They iterate "fascism is universal," completely changing the real meaning of Mussolini's famous dictum. Mussolini meant universal-European, universal-Western, but never meant to include India, China, Russia, Islam, Indians, and Negroes in one conception. This attempt stultifies Mussolini, who was first a *realist*, an artist of the possible, not a theological word-juggler. This second school in other words contains vestigial remnants of Ultramontanism,[24] whose significance is past.

There is another aberration in Deutschland, which would marry politics to ethics (specifically, the ethics of chivalry), now that politics has been divorced from race.

You mention an Ulrich Fleischauer[25] in your letter. I do not know anything of him. Would you tell me about him in your next letter? If he belongs to our race, I shall see that *Imperium* is sent to him.

Would you do me a great favor, cher Arcand? I have been trying to get into personal touch with G. L. K. Smith and have not succeeded. I have a very wonderful tract written for America which he would surely want to publish, but I do not wish to send it until we hear from him personally. Would you write to him, mentioning me and Westropa, telling him that we are bona fide, and all that? I should appreciate this contribution to our efforts greatly.

I believe I have forgotten to thank you for your Christmas greeting. If you received none from me, it is because I never send them. But be assured always that I think of you cordially and that I wish you, in 1950 and thereafter, the greatest success for the Idea and for yourself.

Front Heil!
Varange

---

[24] Ultramontanism was a current within the Catholic Church which held that the Pope's authority, both within the Church itself and in some cases also in politics, is supreme.

[25] A First World War veteran who had founded a publishing house, Welt-Dienst, focusing on Jewish issues, and which created an international network of correspondents. It became a significant factor before and during the Second World War.

JULY 28, 1950, ST. LOUIS, MISSOURI

Cher Monsieur Arcand,

I have just returned from the Convention in Los Angeles. I see now why you did not feel any urge to go. You already know, apparently, that which I had to find out—viz. that the movement in this form and under this leadership is devoid of a future. The magazine, the newsletters, the World News Service which Lohbeck[26] and I are founding—these indeed are valuable, but of themselves they are not *politics*. At most they are useful adjuncts to politics.

I met Smith—in company with his wife and with Lohbeck—and he delivered a speech at the lunch table. He had not read *Imperium* nor the London "Proclamation," because, as Lohbeck tells me, he reads *nothing*. I delivered him a short memorandum I had prepared outlining the offer which I was bringing to him to form a supra-national, supra-continental white Imperialist organization, with him as leader, setting forth the mutual advantages to his organization and to mine. He was to be leader, and was to furnish financial assistance to the Europeans' organizations for the immediate future until the people come out of hiding and a large enough effort can be made to attract the attention of all Europe in spite of the conspiracy of silence on the part of the press.

This memorandum he did not even care to discuss with me, for reasons unknown to me.

When he introduced me to speak, he washed his hands of me, saying he did not know what I was going to say, he had only just met me, etc. etc. I then gave my speech, and despite the time

---

[26] Don Lohbeck was originally a classical pianist who joined the America First Committee before finally coming to work with Gerald L. K. Smith full-time in 1944. Lohbeck was Yockey's primary contact with the Christian Nationalist Crusade. Lohbeck and Yockey shared an apartment in St. Louis during the summer of 1950, although they soon had a falling out over Lohbeck's perception that Yockey was a Communist rather than a nationalist. In 1960, upon hearing of Yockey's arrest, he contacted the FBI to volunteer information about him that he had gained during their brief acquaintance.

I delivered it—the morning session, the worst possible time—it was received by the audience very well indeed. To me alone, of some thirty speakers, the audience gave a spontaneous standing ovation. The first part of my speech was on the horrors which America has committed in Europe, how the American flag and uniform have become hateful symbols of Jewry etc. The second part was on the glorious past of the true American type and the necessity for the seizing of America's destiny by this type. The third part was the mutuality of the cause of the true America and the true Europe, the fight for Liberation from Jewry, democracy, class-war, finance-capitalism, social degeneration, liberalism, and the ethical syphilis of Hollywood. I ended with the call to *war* against the Jew and his democracy, the refusal to engage in any other war than the war against the Jew, and the demand for unlimited white Imperialism, the natural and organic way of living of the white race, and spirit of the Teutonic Knights and the Vikings, whose descendants we are, and whose spirit we must once more live in.

Immediately after the speech, Smith delivered one of his own, attacking me, and saying that Americans love democracy, that he would not unite with me in my hatred of the Jew, nor in my love for the Western Civilization, but only in the principles of Jesus Christ. Exactly what that means I do not know, but perhaps it was only a way of calling attention to the fact that I had not mentioned Christ. The entire Convention was primarily Christ and Christianity, and secondarily anti-Jewish, mostly on the basis that the Jews are anti-Christ.

Smith also refused to allow me to display the flag of the European Liberation Front, the banner of the sword, even during my speech.

There is one other thing that I must tell you, an unfortunate thing. It concerns Elmhurst. When I met him he was very cordial and friendly and gained my confidence by talking as one European to another about these American goings-on, so different from the stern and serious creative spirit of Europe, the center of the world. We discussed Smith, and Elmhurst was most strong in his statements that he was no follower of Smith, and had always told Smith just that, that Smith was a charlatan, solely interested in money, that Smith was a coward and had retreated to Los Angeles instead of being on the real political fighting fronts—New York, Chicago, etc., that Smith would not be interested in my proposition since it entailed financial assistance, and that Smith would only give anything if he could be assured of a threefold return. These things he said not once, but many times. He went over Lohbeck the same way. He told me that my speech was the only one delivered with any value—and his of course. (By the way, his speech was a discussion of Anglo-German relations for the past generation, and thus could not hold the audience, which constantly diminished.)

Then he went to both Smith and Lohbeck—this was the last day of the Convention—and told them that I was an impostor, that I was not the author of *Imperium,* that *I* had said about them all of the things which he had said about them. All of this puzzled Smith, who did not know what to think. Lohbeck of course knows that I am no impostor and am the creator of *Imperium,* but he did tend to believe that I had criticized him personally. For the time being, this has damaged the relations between Lohbeck and me, which were excellent, and which were beginning to bear fruit. Lohbeck is actually interested in power, and his organization in St. Louis is entering the elections this autumn. He also has a streak of European consciousness in him.

Elmhurst is supposed to be here (St. Louis) next month, and Lohbeck and I shall see him at that time.

As to the explanation for Elmhurst's conduct, I can only think of suspicion-mania. This is further borne out by the fact that he warned me—and others—against certain other people at the Convention as agents for the enemy. These people, I am convinced, were not agents. Such morbid suspicion could arise in a case like Elmhurst's, for he has indeed suffered long and hard persecution, and he lives in the environment of New York, where, he says, Jews are constantly trying to poison him. I thought that you should know these things, for the future.

I do not believe Elmhurst did much damage to the relations between Smith and me, since I believe Smith's attitude did not change, that he is not yet ready for the kind of political thinking that I brought to him, and that, in any event, he is not political.

In his beliefs, he is undoubtedly sincere, but in his actions, so to speak, he is not. His person, his family—in every speech he mentions his wife, mother, and father at least ten times—"the clean loins of my father, and the pure womb of my mother who carried me," etc.—and himself at least thirty times—his security, physical and financial, are of the very highest importance to him. He lacks entirely what we call in Europe the heroic world-outlook. He explained to the audience at one point that he does not live in St. Louis because there was a plot to kill him in St. Louis, and that under these conditions, his mother could not visit him in his home, nor could he enjoy peace and quiet with his wife. One of the strong points which he makes to his audiences is that he and his wife are as happy a couple as could be found in America. In the closing speech of the Convention, he talked for four minutes about his stomach, his digestion, and the fact that he does not need to take laxatives.

If Adolf Hitler and Mussolini had pursued these tactics, they would have both gone to *la Suisse*[27] and there carried on a mutual admiration society, and put out a radical magazine, raising money all the while from old ladies of both sexes. For all of these reasons, and a hundred others I have not detailed, no movement can be expected in America led by Smith. In his deepest depths, he is not really after that. I have no word to say against his information service, to the extent that it prints and exposes facts not elsewhere to be found.

Nor does any of this apply to Lohbeck, who is a different kind of man, and who has to a large extent come under the influence of *Imperium*—something that could never be true of Smith, because the intellectual basis is not there. Lohbeck has political ambition, and I have persuaded him to carry his fight in St. Louis onto the streets, leaving the secure halls, where old ladies of both sexes foregather to hear the Jews damned. Street meetings are themselves victories, but a speech in a hall of old ladies, from which the enemy is excluded, is a political nullity. He sees this; Smith never will.

By the way, in Los Angeles, Kurts of New York and I went in-

[27] Switzerland.

to Pershing Square (in the center of L.A.) and there spoke of Communism, Jews, and the Korean war. This is possibly the **first** time that this message was ever heard in that square, hitherto given over to reds and crackpots. Jews and other guks[28] who tried to intervene were silenced by the audience. Guk, by the way, is our new word for anyone who does not belong to the white race and Western Civilization. It is our word corresponding to the Jewish word Gentile or *goy*—any non-member. It is the word the American soldiers use to designate all Koreans, north and south. Gannon will introduce the word in England, and it must enter all languages.

This has been a long letter. I hope none of it has been superfluous. Let me close with an expression of my highest esteem and my

Best wishes,
Varange

AUGUST 9, 1950, ROXANA, ILLINOIS

Cher Monsieur,

Since I last wrote to you, I have seen Elmhurst, and I am writing therefore without waiting for your reply to my last, to inform you of what developed.

Elmhurst stopped in St. Louis on his way back to New York, and Lohbeck detained him in St. Louis until I could get over to there. I interrogated him in the presence of Lohbeck and two other people. After about half an hour or so, I actually began to feel sorry for him, because he could not stand up at all to the situation he had created. He made a compete ass of himself, to put it in the most charitable way possible. That very evening, before my arrival, he had circulated new slanders about me, and other statements tending to throw suspicion and discredit upon me. For instance, I did not know German (when I had actually con-

---

[28] Yockey spells the word "guk," rather than "gook," as it later became popularized.

versed in this language with him, and when I have translated Spengler's *Preussentum und Sozialismus* for the first time), that I told him of a woman who gave a large sum to the Christian Nationalist Party, which sum was defalcated by Lohbeck, etc. etc. Such stories were of course total falsehoods, and Lohbeck and the other persons present realized it at once when he stammered, stuttered, evaded, attempted to change the subject, and generally gave every possible sign of the discomfort of the liar confronted with his lie.

Since that time, I have heard from Gannon, in regard to Leese's campaign against me—of which I believe you have heard—that Leese is working with someone in America to try and find out something which he can use against me. It is of course possible that this is true, and that Elmhurst is acting as the thing of Leese in circulating these lies about me. Fortunately, I learned of it at once, so that Elmhurst was not able, despite his efforts, to effect any damage in my relations with Lohbeck and the Christian Nationalist Party. These relations are closer than ever, and the Liberation Front is now officially affiliated with the CN Party.

Gannon has told me that Leese in England is displaying—or rather, citing—a letter which he claims to have from you, attacking me, questioning my bona fides, and the like. I do not believe this report. I believe that poor senile Leese is either lying or imagining, out of the depths of his suspicion—and persecution-mania. Nevertheless, in order to clear it up, I should like to hear from you to this effect. Leese, in case you have not heard the details, is writing in private letters about England and elsewhere that I am a Jewish agent and a Bolshevik agent. Some of his supporters, in order to cover every possibility, are also saying that I am an American agent provocateur.

I might say that Leese—whom I have never met—wrote to me in London some two-and-a-half years ago, a long letter against *Imperium*, saying that he read only as far as page 80, Volume I, and that he could not read further, as it was (*sic*) "a wilderness of words." He interprets *Imperium* as a Jewish book, and says that the Liberation Front is "all in the Jew plan."

Since Leese has brought you into this controversy, may I have your opinion about all this?

Now as ever, you have
My highest regard,
Varange

NOVEMBER 13, 1950, ROXANA, ILLINOIS, P. O. BOX 336

Cher M. Arcand,

I have just learned from Gannon that you are under the impression that I did not answer your last letter. There must be either a mistake, or else a letter of yours to me has miscarried, for I have written you twice (both times in August, I believe) and had no reply. I did not write again, since I took your silence to mean that you had been duped by the idiots Elmhurst and Smith.

I now learn from Gannon, with deep joy, that you have not been duped by these two, and that you have weighed *Imperium* and the "Proclamation," on the one side, against the ungrammatical drivel of the illiterate Smith and the persecution-mania of poor Elmhurst, on the other.

The facts about Smith—and even more about Lohbeck—are that both are simply self-seekers. Lohbeck has just been engaged in a so-called campaign for office, and in the course thereof, he was on the radio some ten or fifteen times. His radio talks were 85% old-fashioned, negative, Republican-type propaganda, 10% anti-negro, and 5% anti-Jewish. It is also sad that he is a very ineffective speaker, with a precise, school-boy type of delivery. This, coupled with his talk about "freedom" and against Russia, completely undermined any good that the 5% anti-Jewish propaganda might have had. Smith became an anti-Semite in 1946, and is still today anti-German, anti-European, and anti-fascist (three words for the same thing).

Smith did not tell you, in his scurrilous letter to you, that my speech at his "convention" was the *only one*, of some twenty-five speeches given there, which was given a spontaneous standing ovation by the audience. Smith himself was not given this recognition, and this is his real grievance against me, which he translates into his stupid emotional statement to you that I am an agent of the Jews.

Enough of this personality-matter. It is unfortunate that our great Idea has such miserable pseudo-adherents as this *canaille*[29] *sans* brains, courage, and character. Smith expressly said to his audience that he did not dare live in St. Louis because the negroes had a plot to kill him there, and under those circumstances **he could not enjoy peace and quiet with his wife and mother**.

Only one other point remains to be cleared up: you wrote to Gannon about this matter, telling him about your correspondence with Smith and Elmhurst. This was supposed to be in confidence. There can however be no confidence in a political matter which would exclude Gannon's reporting to me, as I am his political chief. I was the European leader of the European Liberation Front, its co-organizer, and the sole source of its doctrine and ideology. In our previous correspondence, we had not discussed this point, perhaps, and therefore no blame whatever attaches to you in the matter, nor to Gannon. I made this point merely to explain how it happens that I know of the correspondence between you and the Smith person.

I should like to answer one point that Elmhurst made to you, namely that I had interrogated him. This is ridiculous, and the truth is the other way around. I asked him nothing save such conversational questions as his opinion of Smith, and the like. He branded Smith as a money-maker, Lohbeck as the same, told me that Lohbeck was stealing from the organization, that he (Elmhurst) was no follower of Smith, that Smith was obviously jealous of me, or the success of my speech, of *Imperium*, etc. etc. etc. He asked me a thousand questions, purely personal, of my political significance (e.g., where did I learn history?). When he told me about Jewish plots on his life, I should have known at once where to classify him, but I am a generous man and tried to retain my respect for him on the basis that he was a front-fighter in the First World War. I still have nothing against him, as I regard him as ill, from the ordeal he went through during the recent War.

[29] French: "commoner."

And now, cher M. Arcand, I hope that this debris has been cleared away. I am still not sure exactly when I return to Europe, as the event is contingent upon the sale of some real estate of mine. I should like to say that my esteem for you, which I never concealed, has been further heightened by your conduct *vis-à-vis* these slandering swine. I therefore look forward more than ever to the time when our mutual acquaintance will be perfected by a personal meeting. Please let me hear from you.

Yours in comradeship and respect,
Varange

VARANGE SPEAKS!

1950

EDITORS' NOTE

The article "Varange Speaks," which was written by Yockey under his most common pen name, was published in the fourth issue of *Frontfighter*, dated August 1950. The issue was largely concerned with attacks on Yockey by the Arnold Leese faction of British National Socialism. That and other issues are reproduced in this volume in the appendices, although Yockey's article for the fourth issue has been abstracted for inclusion here to stand alongside Yockey's other writings.

Yockey had been disappointed by Sir Oswald Mosley's rejection of his *magnum opus*, *Imperium* (albeit, despite the bitterness and rivalry between the Union Movement and the European Liberation Front, and rumors and assumptions to the contrary, Sir Oswald spoke with high regard for Yockey's intellect in private correspondence, when asked). However, when it came to Arnold Leese and his allies, and the continuation of their prewar Hitlerism after 1945, matters were particularly vitriolic, not only because of the regressive dogmatism of Leese and his colleagues, but because Yockey was not inclined to let the slights of such people go unanswered.

Leese had founded the Imperial Fascist League (IFL) in 1929. Although the British Fascisti (BF) had been established in 1923, its ideology did not go far beyond anti-socialism, while Leese advocated what he called "racial Fascism," and adopted the swastika within the Union Jack as his symbol. If the British Fascisti did not reach much beyond opposing socialists, Leese's primary focus was on Jews, although he had been well-versed in financial matters by the banking reform advocate Arthur Kitson, who joined the IFL. As for Mosley's founding the British Union of Fascists in 1932, Leese eschewed collaboration, regarding Mosley as a "kosher fascist."

A project with which Leese did maintain a close relationship before and after the war was The Britons Publishing Society, established by Captain Henry Beamish in 1919, again focusing on Jewish matters. Indeed, Beamish served as a Vice President of the IFL, and Anthony Gittens, who ran The Britons from 1949 to 1973, also joined. It was this strand of "Fascism," overwhelmingly preoccupied with Jews rather than developing a philosophy, which provided the foundation for British "neo-Nazism," the most well-known representative of which was Colin Jordan, who was mentored by Leese. This British "neo-Nazism" was largely antithetical to both Mosley's post-war "European socialism" and Yockey's "Western imperialism."

While Mosley quietly rejected *Imperium*, Gittens and Leese were unrestrained in their vehemence. Gittens wrote of the "Varangeites" and of *Imperium*:

> When the late pioneer anti-Jew fighter Henry H. Beamish founded The Britons in 1918 it was not to criticise but to help those who had similar ideas but who preferred to work on their own. When however the ideas behind a Group or Book are based on a fundamentally wrong premise and the sponsors are anonymous, it is our duty to warn all Jew-wise patriots.
>
> Such is the case when the book *Imperium* (2 vols. 12/6 each Westropa Press) written by an American lawyer of unknown origin with the alias 'Ulick Varange' who claims to interpret the 'Soul of Europe' to the Europeans. Based on the inflated philosopher Oswald Spengler, *Imperium* gives long paraphrases of Spengler's eulogies on the 'will to power', but is aimed at a new public.
>
> Spengler preaches Prussian domination of a type gratifying to those elements in Germany whose egoism and narrow class feeling was worked up to prevent race consciousness among the Aryan population. Varange's philosophy attempts to adapt Spengler to present day politics—to build up a spurious 'aristocracy' irrespective of race or creed. Even here Spengler pointed the way in his later works on the 'stupendous game' for world power.
>
> Varange's Hollywood version is a 'mammoth' creed

intended to appeal to those who feel frustrated in the genuine and very necessary efforts to cleanse their own countries of the present corrupt system. *Imperium* accentuates Spengler's arrogant, ignorant and fatuous rejection of racial truths. Just as World Jewry found a useful and possibly unexpected ally in Spengler, Varange would today be most useful to World Jewry by condemning the racialist movement as 'materialistic' and false, and by opening the way for an arrogant 'aristocracy' of mixed blood.

Spengler clung to his theories obstinately in face of all the scientific discoveries of such men as the English Galton, the Americans Grant and Stoddard, the Germans Günther, Bauer, Fischer, and Lenz, the Frenchman Gobineau; and the Law of the Augustinian monk, Gregor Mendel. Varange following in the footsteps of the discredited Spengler resurrects his crazy ideas in order to destroy nationalism and create a Super State stretching from the Urals to Europe. Already there are Varangeites who tell us that 'the soil of Europe will change the shape of a man's skull' (and presumably his brains!) and others who mistake Military Band records worked by some Jew from a Moscow Radio station for the 'march past of anti-Jewish storm troops'!

Our advice to patriots is therefore—not to accept this unknown 'Imperium' on its face value but to apply a simple test:—Any project in Europe should be judged according to the policy of: 'One-People, Many Nations.'[1]

Gittens was an expert on subversive movements and had infiltrated Communist groups at the time of the General Strike in 1926 on behalf of the British Secret Service. This was a time when the anti-socialism of the British Fascisti was quite acceptable to the British Establishment. The BF did not propose any radical policy, in contrast to the maverick socialist Mosley.

---

[1] Anthony Gittens, "An Unknown Authority," *Free Britain*, London, no. 69, July 23, 1950, p. 2.

Gittens confused Spengler and Yockey's observation that the new *Zeitgeist* for the twentieth century and beyond would change focus from nineteenth-century English economics to a German *ethos*. He assumed that Spengler and Yockey were referring to German or Prussian supremacy, whereas in *The Hour of Decision* Spengler, no less than Yockey, called for white world unity. An Englishman, Frenchman, or American could have the "Prussian" ethos if attuned to the new *Zeitgeist*, regardless of one's skull length.

In a letter to Keith Stimely dated September 7, 1980, Yockey's English colleague Anthony Gannon said of Leese:

> I am sure that Yockey never met Arnold Leese. Leese detested FPY without ever having known him.
>
> For Leese, vertical race was everything; for FPY horizontal race was the deciding issue. Perhaps, Leese was too old and too rigid in his thinking to ever be expected to grasp such a new approach to race. After all, he was born in the nineteenth century, which for FPY was, almost, a total disqualification for a true understanding of his thinking. Anyway, Leese abused FPY in his propaganda and accused him of being all sorts of mongrel, even a Yaqui Indian . . . To which FPY replied in *Frontfighter* citing Leese as 'Leese or Louse'. Guy Chesham and I once met two of Leese's collaborators to see if any kind of co-operation were possible, but it was not. It puzzles me to observe that FPY is now so widely acclaimed by vertical race merchants, and it occurs to me that they have accepted *Imperium* without having read it, and FPY without ever having known him. FPY, and I, never did indulge in fratricide with our old-fashioned 'comrades', but merely defended our position when under attack. We both regarded vertical race as having significance and value, for aesthetic reasons and others, but also *knew* that only horizontal race could explain the situation. After all, if every blue-eyed blonde was a friend, and every dark-eyed brunette an enemy—how simple life would be. Life is otherwise, and all history proves it!

The issue of *Free Britain,* the newsletter of The Britons, came out at the same time as Leese's *Gothic Ripples* in which Leese denounced Yockey in the same terms. Leese entitled his anti-Yockeyan article "Lysenkoism Comes to Town."[2] This was a reference to the Soviet Russian biologist T. D. Lysenko,[3] who declared that characteristics acquired through changes wrought by the environment on an organism would be inherited by the next generation.

Leese called *Imperium* the "doctrinal basis" of a "world propaganda drive." Identifying Varange as Yockey or "Jockel," an American lawyer "of unknown mixed races and equally unknown past," Leese stated that Yockey was being funded by Mrs. Alice von Pflügl, "who is reported to have a Jewish grandfather." The possibility of the Baroness having a Jewish grandfather would have meant for Leese, Gittens, and the others that Yockey was being financed by a Jewish conspiracy. He had previously regarded the Mosley name as having been derived from the conjunction of "Moses Levy." Furthermore, Alice von Pflügl was reported to be "a von Paulus devotee favouring an Eastern Zone mentality." Von Paulus was the German Field Marshal who had commanded the German Sixth Army at Stalingrad, and who had gone over to the USSR while a POW during the Second World War, establishing a pro-Russian committee among the German POWs in the USSR. Naturally, to Leese and Gittens, the USSR was completely under Jewish control, and Stalin's natural name, Djugashvilli, meant "son of a Jew" in Georgian—or so the myth went. The conflict between Stalin and Trotsky was seen by such doctrinaires as just a family squabble among Jews. Leese stated that "the European Liberation Front, as the drive is called in Britain, dallies with the Jew Menace as Mosley did to attract Nationalists but the main object is the Jewish one of a European Superstate."

Leese wrote that "the ridiculous doctrine, which is the foun-

---

[2] Arnold S. Leese, "Lysenkoism Comes to Town," *Gothic Ripples,* Guildford, Surrey, no. 66, July 15, 1950.

[3] Zhores A. Medvedev, *The Rise and Fall of T. D. Lysenko* (New York: Anchor Books, 1971).

dation of *Imperium* draws largely on the discredited anti-racial philosopher Spengler resembling the theories of Soviet Prof. Lysenko. Spengler always sought to belittle racial science and to discredit National Socialism earning the gratitude of World Jewry."[4] How Spengler received the gratitude of World Jewry is not explained. Leese claimed that it was symptomatic of Spengler's anti-racism that in "Prussianism and Socialism" he praised the sound political instincts of the Jew Benjamin Disraeli as British Prime Minister.[5] In Spengler's last book, *The Hour of Decision*, he alludes in passing to Disraeli as being among those conservative prime ministers who served as a defensive reaction against the renunciation of the state by liberalism.[6] It seems predictable that Leese should dismiss Spengler with a quip on a Jew, Disraeli, and found no other significance in Spengler. Leese concluded, "That this Lysenkoism should deceive any that understand race or the spelling of the word *Jew* is tragic. 'What does it matter?' say Lysenkoists 'if the Russians overrun Europe since they will absorb Culture?'—Aryan, get your Gun!"[7]

What Yockey rejected as outmoded and divisive was what he called "vertical race," precisely what Leese was promoting in dividing Europeans into sub-races: Nordic, Mediterranean, Dinaric, Alpine, and East Baltic. Only the Nordic has created civilization, wrote Leese, concluding, "Can the Nordics recover Europe? That is in the laps of the Gods. But through no other channel can Europe itself recover." To Leese, certain sub-races of the European might as well have been Kalahari Bushmen.[8]

Frontfighter's editor, P. J. Huxley-Blythe, described these attacks as "loathsome," stating that they opened with a letter to him by Leese. It is unfortunate that Huxley-Blythe was to parrot some of those "loathsome lies" when he later became the British representative of the German-based Natinform.[9] However,

---

[4] Leese, *Gothic Ripples*, op. cit.

[5] Ibid.

[6] Spengler, *The Hour of Decision*, p. 118.

[7] Leese, *Gothic Ripples*, op. cit.

[8] Leese, *Racial Inequality in Europe*, Guildford, ca. 1950.

[9] For more on Natinform, see my Preface to the "Letter to Wolfgang Sarg" in this volume.

many years later, Huxley-Blythe returned to Yockey in a fulsome tribute in *The Barnes Review* and stated that he had been wrong.

Yockey's response to Leese was characteristic of the contempt he had for "leaders" who did not match his intellect, but who sought to ridicule ideas they could not understand. Yockey quite rightly observed that Leese had "never been known to espouse any positive cause or idea, but has contented himself with shadow-boxing with his beloved Jews."

Several years later, Leese was still condemning the European Liberation Movement (*sic*) because of the influence Yockey was having on some sections of the American Right. Leese suspected that sinister forces were funding the Front, and that those involved "look like Dagoes and Wops." They will integrate Britain into "a Europe composed of similar Dagoes and Wops, and to 'play off' Russia against America." Leese hearkened back to the fourth issue of *Frontfighter*.[10] Leese's quips about Italians and Spaniards, which he made despite the fact that both were among the forefront of the European vanguard both during and after the war, were the result of precisely the kind of "vertical race" theories that Yockey rejected.

Despite being repudiated by Mosley, Leese, and Gittens, *Imperium* sold between a thousand and fifteen hundred copies, mostly in Britain[11]—which is to say, most of the copies that were published, a considerable achievement for such a group operating a few years after the World War.

VARANGE SPEAKS!

A curious tirade by a certain Leese has been drawn to my attention. His name comes back to my mind as the author of a letter, in my possession, in which he says that he could not read *Imperium*, the book which he is attempting to attack despite a total lack of comprehension of its thesis. He widens the attack

---

[10] Arnold Leese, "Colleagues," *Gothic Ripples*, no. 98, March 12, 1953, p. 3.

[11] FBI report, February 20, 1956, p. 10, file no. 105-2889—2.

and brings in Oswald Spengler, the greatest European thinker of the twentieth century. Strangely he tries to make Spengler into an agent of the Jew, although the American Jewish press in 1945 repeatedly said that if Spengler were alive they would try him as a War Criminal.—To leese the idea of Europe constituted as one Culture-State-Nation-People-Race is also a Jew idea. This was the great leading idea of Adolf Hitler, and is the Destiny of the Western Culture, clearly portended by the present inner development of Europe, an Idea so universal and irresistible that even the churchills, the carping little enemies of Adolf Hitler, have adopted the Idea and are presently presenting their perverted and distorted version of this Idea to the world in the hope of riding this great, suprapersonal, European, Hitlerian idea. Thus, in the "logic" of leese, Adolf Hitler becomes an agent of the Jew, as well as Spengler and Mussolini.—It is obvious that this man leese has never read Spengler any more than he has ever read *Imperium*, which is written entirely in the spirit of Spengler and which is dedicated to the Hero of the Second World War—Adolf Hitler!—The counterpart of leese in the race with which he is obsessed is the New York Jew Walter Winchell. Both are evil-minded slinking males who think that they have achieved something when they unearth some trivial fact of a personal nature. Thus, leese crows like a cock on a dung-hill when he discovers my passport name, a name known to everyone with whom I am well acquainted. This he chooses to call my "real" name, although a pen-name is just as "real" as any other. The determining thing about a name is whether one can be proud of it or ashamed of it. The man leese can only be ashamed of it, for he has made it synonymous with the lowest kind of prurient Jew obsession. Never has he fought the Jew *politically*, never has he struck a blow for White European Civilization—while others fought the Jew he sat on the side, interrupting constantly to say: That one's great-great-grandfather was a Jew—that one has a Jewish mistress, and other idiocies.—He says that I am a man of unknown mixed races, whereas my race is perfectly clear and definite, whereas the race of leese is a matter of grave doubt. I have been told that the man leese has mongoloid and negroid ancestry, but it is not upon this point that I base my determination of his race. I note that his entire old-age has been spent in a Jew-obsession, but without any attempt to defeat the Jew *politically* or to *really* injure him in any way. He has never been known to espouse any positive cause or idea, but has contented himself with shadow-boxing with his beloved Jews. When a man devotes himself to a negation thus, he inevitably turns into a carbon-copy of that which is supposedly resisting. All of the world to him is simply the Jew. If there were no Jews in the world, leese would lose his reason for existence. He has now been driven into the arms of Hollywood Bolshevism, and is angry because *Front* rejects Washington and Hollywood along with Moscow. In truth, race is a horizontal classification of men, and not a vertical one, and in this meaning of race, leese must be classified as a Jew, since his life is devoted to Jewry. He attacks all *real* opponents of the Jew, but never *effectively* attacks the Jew. It is of little import that he prefers the Frankfurter branch of his Jewish world to the Kaganovich branch,[12] for his world-outlook is exclusively Jewish in either case.—Whenever anyone announces and formulates an Idea which cuts across all older classifications and theories, he may expect that petty-raceless dimwits from the day-before-yesterday, survivals from the previous century, will fail to understand, and will greet with great hatred that to which they are not equal. However, none of that alters our course. The Liberation Front will continue to resist the Judaization of the West, and to fight for the Liberation of the sacred soil of Europe from Jew, Russia, and America.

Ulick Varange

---

[12] Felix Frankfurter was an advisor to Franklin Roosevelt, whereas Lazar Kaganovich (1893–1991) was one of Stalin's key supporters.

AMERICA'S TWO WAYS OF WAGING WAR

1950–51

EDITORS' NOTE

This essay appeared in German in the July 1952 issue (vol. 5, no. 7) issue of the Buenos Aires-based journal *Der Weg* (*The Way*), which was edited by Johann von Leers, a former senior staffer in the Third Reich's Ministry of Propaganda who had escaped from Germany at the end of the war and was at the time living among the German émigré community in Argentina. He later moved to Egypt, where he worked as an advisor for the Information Department in Gamal Abdel Nasser's government. *Der Weg* enthusiastically supported Yockey's work and occasionally reprinted excerpts from his *Frontfighter* journal. *Der Weg* indicates that this text is an excerpt from an essay originally published in two parts in the December 1950 and January 1951 issues of *Frontfighter*, which are no longer extant. Curiously, it bears the same title as an undelivered speech that Yockey ghostwrote for Senator Joseph McCarthy a year later, and which is included in this volume. However, a comparison of the two texts makes it clear that the present essay is not from the same text that Yockey later provided to McCarthy. It appears that Yockey simply reused the title.

We would like to thank Thomas Francis for the translation.

AMERICA'S TWO WAYS OF WAGING WAR

The following is excerpted from an essay that appeared in the *Frontfighter* (December 1950 and January 1951), British Monomark Westropa Press, London, W. C. 1.

America has two ways of waging war: one when it goes to war against Europe, and another when it is fighting against

Asia. During the Second World War, it applied one type of warfare against Europe, and another type against Japan. The fact that nothing has changed in this respect over the past five years is shown by the war America waged in Korea.

During the entire course of the war, the press and the wireless reported hourly the identity and position of American troops, as they do even now. Communist military intelligence had its mission accomplished for it by the American military command. Did anything like this occur during the conduct of the war against Europe?

During the conflict, the anti-Communist [Louis A.] Johnson was removed as Secretary of Defense, and replaced by the pro-Communist [George] Marshall,[1] who then proceeded with the destruction of the Chiang Kai-shek regime, and handed over China to the Reds. Throughout the whole duration of the Second World War, Marshall sacrificed American efforts in the Pacific War to the aims of Bolshevist Russia.

When Jewish Communist spies involved in handing over technical data to the Russians are arrested, the American press reports only the bare facts. Of 1,500 Soviet spies on a list which the Canadian Prime Minister delivered to the American President, only eight were taken into custody. This is in stark contrast to the mass hysteria provoked by the Haupt case, in which six of the eight Europeans who had been sent to America on a sabotage mission were killed.[2]

During the Second World War, all Germans in the United

---

[1] George Marshall (1880–1959) was Secretary of State, and later Secretary of Defense, under Harry Truman, and was the initiator of the Marshall Plan for reconstruction and economic recovery in Western Europe under US auspices.

[2] This is a reference to Operation Pastorius, a plan developed by the Abwehr, German military intelligence, to send operatives to the United States to carry out terrorist attacks and sabotage in an effort to demoralize Americans in the early stages of the Second World War. The agents were delivered to the US by U-Boat in June 1942, but two of them turned themselves in to the FBI shortly after their arrival, and the rest of the team was soon rounded up and sentenced to death. Herbert Haupt was one of the operatives.

States were interned in concentration camps.[3] During the Korean adventure, no Communists were interned or persecuted in any way, or even required to report to the authorities. An anti-Communist law was passed by Congress—with Truman's veto and the opposition of the administration—which required Communists to register with the government; yet no legal provisions were made for that, nor were penalties proscribed for failure to comply.[4] The result is that all Communists (ninety percent Jews) are able to move about freely, despite their provocative refusal to register with the authorities.

Not just Marshall, the creator of Red China, the co-perpetrator of Pearl Harbor, the destroyer of European cities; not just Truman, the old admirer and personal friend of Stalin, who performed on the piano for him at Potsdam, the confirmed opponent of anti-Communist legislation, the executor of Roosevelt's hate and annihilation policies; not just [Dean] Acheson,[5] who openly acknowledges the Russian spy [Alger] Hiss[6] as his friend, who during the War was chief of the pro-Russian clique, the friend of Red China—not just these, but every member of the Washington regime showed sympathy for Bolshevism during the Second World War.

Not one of them opposed the policy of setting up the mon-

---

[3] This is incorrect: the Japanese in America were interned, but those of German origin were not.

[4] The Smith Act was enacted by the US Congress in 1940, rendering advocacy of the violent overthrow of the government a criminal act. Yockey's claim is not accurate, given that eleven leaders of the Communist Party of the United States were charged under the Smith Act in 1949, and were ultimately convicted.

[5] Dean Acheson (1893–1971) was Secretary of State during President Truman's administration. He was a key player in the Marshall Plan, in determining US foreign policy during the early years of the Cold War, in setting up NATO, and in bringing America into the Korean War.

[6] Alger Hiss (1904–1996) was an official with both the US State Department and the United Nations who was convicted of espionage on behalf of the Soviet Union in 1950. He had been involved in setting up the UN.

strosity that is currently called the Communist Empire. Not one of them advocated aid to Europe in its struggle against Bolshevism. Not one of them supports the Liberation of Europe. Not one of them is capable in any way of waging war against Russia, because they are all involved in the machinations of Bolshevism, are all tainted with Bolshevism, and sympathize with Bolshevism. In this they resemble their deputies in Europe; for example, [Clement] Attlee,[7] [John] Strachey,[8] [Manny] Shinwell[9]—outstanding Bolsheviks the lot of them.

Can any European still take seriously the planned American war against Russia? It is no different than Russian leaders assuring Europe that Russia's plan is to free Europe from American influence. The two Bolshevisms, that of Washington and that of Moscow, to which is now added a third, that of Tel Aviv, are so entwined with each other, and have so much recent history in common, that all Europeans can do is lump them together in one stinking heap.

Historians and scholars, if so inclined, can spend their lives elucidating these connections and explaining the differences between these three forms of Bolshevism. But those to whom the call is sounded to prepare for battle, for Washington against Moscow, for the stooge Truman against the *muzhik*[10] Stalin, for Frankfurter against Kaganovich, for American black dancing

---

[7] Clement Attlee (1883–1967) was Labour Party Prime Minister of the United Kingdom from 1945 to 1951.

[8] John Strachey (1901–1963) was a British Labour MP and known Communist sympathizer who served as Secretary of State for War during the final year of Attlee's government.

[9] Manny Shinwell (1884–1986) was a Jewish Labour politician who served as Minister of Fuel and Power, Secretary of State for War, and as Minister for Defence during various periods of the Attlee government. As Minister of Fuel and Power, he mismanaged the nation's coal supply such that scores of British people froze to death during the winter. An enthusiastic supporter of British intervention in Korea, he raised defense spending to the point that funds had to be taken from the National Health Service, leading to the imposition of NHS charges. By the 1980s, he was an immigration proponent.

[10] Russian: "peasant."

and jazz against the factory sirens of Shostakovich, for idolization of the dollar against deification of the machine, for America's Marxist practice against the Marxist theory of Russia, for the hardware dealer Eisenhower against the cannibal Budyonny,[11] for Sam Goldwyn against Lunacharsky[12]—*those to whom that call is sounded can give only one answer, and that answer is the one given in* The Proclamation of London: *No! Europe is no more interested in this projected war than in a struggle between two Negro tribes in the Sudan.*

Ulick Varange

---

[11] Semyon Mikhailovich Budyonny (1883–1973) was a Bolshevik cavalry commander who became a hero of the Russian Civil War and was one of Stalin's top allies. In 1935 he was appointed Marshal of the Soviet Union.

[12] Samuel Goldwyn (born Szmuel Gelbfisz, 1879–1974) was an American film magnate. Anatoly Vasilyevich Lunacharsky (1875–1933) was a playwright and critic who became head of the Soviet People's Commissariat for Education.

CORRESPONDENCE WITH VIRGINIA JOHNSON

1950–52

EDITORS' NOTE

In 1953, the FBI opened a file on Yockey in regard to letters he had written to Virginia Johnson in the United States.[1] It was noted that Francis Parker Yockey was also using the name Frank. He also refers to himself as Franz. The recipient, whose name was blacked out in the FBI file, was Virginia Johnson. The letters were made available to Special Agent Donald M. Holland on October 16, 1952, by Dr. Warren Johnson, who had known the Yockey family. They relate to correspondence dating from 1950, 1951, and 1952. Warren Johnson, whose wife Virginia had left him for Yockey, had found the letters during their divorce. After Virginia had left Yockey, she continued to maintain contact with him and serve as a go-between, mainly with his sister, Vinette Coyne. She also maintained contact with Yockey's backers, Frederick Weiss and H. Keith Thompson. In the letters to Virginia, Yockey uses another alias, Warren, giving the impression that the letters are from her husband, Dr. Johnson.

CORRESPONDENCE WITH VIRGINIA JOHNSON

The first entry begins with an FBI synopsis of part of a letter, which is dated by Yockey as "July 30 I think," and postmarked Roxana, Illinois, on July 31, 1950. The first letter refers to a speech that Yockey had given at a large convention of the Christian Nationalist Party during the previous month, as described in Chapter 8. The magazine referred to is Smith's long-running *The Cross and The Flag*. The FBI synopsis reads:

Subject Yockey describes a "tremendous speech" he had

[1] FBI Baltimore office, March 2, 1953; file no. 105-8229-64.

> recently made in California. He referred to one Smith and states that Smith does not want to have anything to do with him since the talk he gave. Yockey stated that he, Smith, puts out an excellent information service magazine, etc., "but personally I do not think he will get anywhere as his line is all wrong."

The FBI quotes the rest of the letter verbatim:

> Don't worry about Korea. As I have told you numerous times there will be no great war for ten years. After the end of the Second Worldly [*sic*] War I told all my—shall I say—friends that it would be at least fifteen years. Five years have gone by, *ergo* ten. Remember it.
>
> Since I have written to you last I must tell you one thing more. You are to destroy this letter and all others I may ever write to you. If not, I shall write no more. I write to no one who keeps my letters. *Entendu*?[2]

In the next letter dated "Aug. 9 or so," postmarked Roxana, Illinois, August 12, 1950, Yockey refers to a Hollywood film and alludes to a name, presumably of a lawyer of his acquaintance, which appears to be "Recker." The film to which Yockey refers with disgust, as he believed Hollywood to be a bastion of the Culture-distorter, is likely to have been *Mr. Imperium* (1951), a romantic musical produced by Metro-Goldwyn-Mayer:

> America always did fill me with a terrible feeling that I didn't know where I was, a feeling of being on the edge of the world, of being isolated—.
>
> I saw old Recker yesterday. Took him a possible law suit against the film gang who have stolen the sacred name of Imperium for a stinking cinema effort. I can't be bothered with it, and he likes that sort of thing.

One sentence is extracted from the next letter, dated Decem-

---

[2] "Understand?"

ber 26, postmarked Battle Creek, Michigan, December 26, 1950, presumably indicating the FBI's interest in Yockey's employment with the Red Cross, which enabled him to return to Europe and continue cultivating contacts:

> The Red Cross is an anti-Fate organization and hence finds small favor in my eyes.

In the next letter, dated January 5, postmarked January 8, 1951, Battle Creek, Michigan, it is apparent that Yockey took employment with the Red Cross to secure his return to Europe:

> I am at Ft. Custer, Michigan with the Amercian Red Cross—If, in a few months, I am not on my way I would feel that my transportation idea failed, and I shall leave this thing and proceed alone.

In the next letter, dated March 6 and postmarked Battle Creek, Michigan, March 17, 1951, Yockey discusses his use of the name Frank:

> With Frank one can be frank. I have the Americans in my environment call me Frank. It blurs their impression of me and that is precisely as it should be.

Yockey's next letter is dated April 23, postmarked April 24, 1951, Battle Creek, Michigan, and deals with General Douglas MacArthur. What is surprising is Yockey's lack of any sympathy for MacArthur, given that less than a fortnight previously, the General had been relieved of his command of the United Nations forces in Korea by President Truman because MacArthur had wanted to pursue a more vigorous military offensive there that would have included confronting China. MacArthur was a hero of the American Right, with Gerald L. K. Smith himself taking up the leadership of a pro-MacArthur campaign, but Yockey had no regard for most of the American nationalist milieu. Quotes from Yockey are embedded in the FBI's paraphrase:

> The above letter refers to General MacArthur as "an ancient ass" that he could have made himself king of this island. According to the writer of the letter, five years ago MacArthur was anti-German and pro-Russian, now he is anti-Russian. "No matter how much one sympathizes with American nationalism—which is not directed against Europe (see *Imperium*) he cannot wish MacArthur well, for he is a thoroughly unworthy representative of it. During the greatest drama, up to now, that has been enacted on the world stage, this idiot cast his sympathy to the stupid Russian clod and the slinking, sneering usurer—Jew. This I do not forget."

From a letter dated "June 2 or so," postmarked June 4, 1951, Battle Creek, Michigan:

> I am familiar with the foul book *A German Talks Back.*[3] I saw it in 1945 or so. I found no back-talk in it, but only the usual filthy Jewish propaganda. If it were a real book, it would be confiscated and proscribed, as *Imperium* has the honor to be—in three countries. People have been held in jail for possessing *Imperium*. *Imperium* is more deserving of the title (subtitle let us say), *A German Talks Back*, than is that dirty little piece of Jewish-liberal-Masonic propaganda by the weak and despicable traitor Hauser.
>
> Forgive me for my enthusiasm about *Imperium*. It is growing on me. When I finished it, I was slightly disappointed, but now when I pick it up I ask myself how could it have been written through such an unsure instrument as me, for in very truth its truths are superpersonal and the

[3] Heinrich Hauser, *The German Talks Back* (New York: Henry Holt & Co., 1945). Hauser (1901–1955) was a Berlin-born writer and journalist who had been a Rightist in his youth. He was briefly supportive of National Socialism when Hitler first became Chancellor but soon turned against the movement and ultimately fled to the United States in 1939. *The German Talks Back* was his attempt to distinguish between the National Socialist conception of German identity and what he regarded as the genuine German identity.

real author is the spirit of the age, the *Zeitgeist*.

From a letter dated August 1, postmarked US Army, August 1, 1951:

> I am in a God-forsaken village named Baumholder, or rather in a camp above it. It is not too far from the French border in the Hunsruck Mountains.

From a letter dated August 18, Stuttgart, postmarked US Army, August 20, 1951:

> I do not yet know whether my new position will mature. Two different sets of secret police have to clear me for it and a certain section of one of the two I know has me listed as an undesirable. It is frightful that I have to expose myself in this stupid fashion. No one can simultaneously try to do big things and be obliged to devote all his time and energy to the little thing of earning a living.

From a letter headed "Garmisch, September 4," postmarked US Army Postal Service, September 4, 1951:

> I am *en route* to Rome today. I had a disaster and lost my job. I resigned in the expectation—more, assurance—of having another at once, twice as good financially. But the secret police told the prospective employer (Judge Advocate, Seventh Army) that they wanted to investigate me for six months, and he became frightened.

Yockey, having left the Red Cross and the US Army, proceeded to Italy as an organizer for a large Fascist convention, at a time when the neo-Fascist movement was already burgeoning in Italy. This effort was referred to previously herein in terms of abortive plans for establishing a "European League" based in Italy and incorporating the European Liberation Front.

The review of *Imperium* in South America to which Yockey alludes was carried in *Der Weg*, a periodical published in Argentina by German émigrés, prominent among whom was Dr. Johann von Leers, formerly of the Reich Ministry for Public Enlightenment under Dr. Joseph Goebbels. While British Hitlerites such as Arnold Leese were dismissive of *Imperium*, German and Italian veterans embraced it enthusiastically. Von Leers himself wrote that *Imperium* could inspire "the next big European revolution." He urged that *Imperium* be published in all the languages of the West, as it was "more important than all the books published by the 'Left' in the world—because it's ours and it shows where the march must go."[4]

In the above letter Yockey indicated that his next address would be in care of American Express Co., Rome.

From a letter dated October 3, postmarked Napoli Ferry, 1951:

> I am staying in one spot for about three weeks and thus if you answer today air mail I shall receive your letter. I am in Naples organizing the foreign part of a Fascist convention to be held 25–28 October. As you know, I do not believe in conventions, I believe in the lonely agonies of superior men, but I have ulterior motives, not the least of which is the fact that my expenses of living are being paid during this month, and thus for a short while I am relieved from the terrible pressure of economics.
>
> I have soon a good review of *Imperium* for South America. The reviewer calls it the bible of the next great European revolution.

In the above letter Yockey gave the address, c/o the American Consulate, Naples, Italy.

From a letter dated October 12, postmark unreadable, Italian stamps on envelope:

> Everyone now is beginning to say the things I said six years ago. The Korean War has proved and vindicated the

---

[4] Johann von Leers, "Ulick Varange: Imperium," *Der Weg* (Buenos Aires), vol. 5, no. 9, 1951, pp. 662–63.

> proclamation.[5] It has shown all Europeans that the Washington regime is incapable of fighting against Russian Bolshevism, being itself the very same thing, only in a different form. It has undermined the military prestige of America, and all over Europe, the people who matter are saying with the Germans "*Ohne mich.*"[6]
>
> Little Franz[7] was however the first to say it, to write it, and now again he is five years ahead of the other members of his race.

The next three letters refer to Yockey's association with the artist, Professor Egidio Boschi, a veteran of the Fascist "March on Rome" in 1922 who won acclaim for his detailed landscape paintings rendered on pin-heads. Yockey does not refer in these letters to the actual reasons why he and Boschi were in Canada, which was to assess the political situation and to visit Adrien Arcand. Despite Yockey's reference to Boschi being in bad health, he was still exhibiting his pin-head paintings around the world in 1958.[8]

Letter dated December 3, postmarked Montreal, Canada, December 4, 1951:

> I am back on the wrong continent again.
>
> The strangest thing has brought me back here. I am managing an enterprise for an artist. This chap is an Italian

---

[5] *The Proclamation of London of the European Liberation Front* (1948), reproduced in this volume.

[6] *Ohne mich* means "without me," a popular "neutralist" slogan in Germany during the Cold War. German veterans, among the most vocal of whom were Major General Otto Remer and the Socialist Reich Party, were among the many who adopted a "neutralist" and even a pro-Russian line during the Cold War, in opposition to the American occupation. Yockey became a primary influence in this direction and was avidly supported by his German mentor in the United States, Frederick Weiss.

[7] Franz, that is, "Frank" Yockey.

[8] "Pinhead Painter," *The Independent Record* (Montana), August 24, 1958, p. 12.

from South America. He came to Europe last year with his paintings to exhibit them, and he visited Gannon, having heard of *Imperium*, etc. When he learned I was in Naples he came down there to see me, qua author of *Imperium*, which he regards as a bible.

He is also a very sick man: cardiac, pleurisy, bronchitis, high blood pressure.

Write to me care of Coyne at Roxana.

I am in Canada because Boschi is waiting still for a visa to go to USA. Perhaps he won't get it.

From a letter dated January 1, postmarked January 2, Montreal, Canada:

I am in great difficulties with this artist mad man this pin painter. He is in a terrible state of moral deterioration, not to say physical and mental as well.

Letter dated January 22, postmarked January 22, 1952, Washington, DC:

I come hither to find myself some base economic employment, after my Boschi enterprise showed itself no longer feasible.[9] I was counting heavily upon old Jaeger[10]—about whom I told you, as you will remember and I learned with one telephone call that he is in Florida until the end of the month.

I shall be here all week, at least up to Saturday, staying

[9] Yockey had unsuccessfully attempted to act as an agent for Boschi in selling his paintings.

[10] Walter Jaeger was a world-eminent Professor of Law and International Relations at Georgetown University when Yockey was a student. He was a Rightist who opposed American entry into the war against Germany, and after the war he associated with Senator Joseph McCarthy. Despite his position on American neutrality, during the war he served with the Army Judge Advocate General's Office in Washington. (See: "Walter H. E. Jaeger Dies," *Washington Post*, October 15, 1982.)

at the YMCA Hotel, 18th and G Streets, a block away from the infamous State Department.

In a letter dated "February 5 or so—, Tuesday anyway," postmarked Washington, DC, February 5, 1952, Yockey refers to his having met with Senator Joseph McCarthy in regard to his speechwriting job:

> I called on Patterson who arranged an appointment for me with Senator McCarthy for Saturday P. M. He wanted me to write a speech for him, based on a whole batch, a huge corpus of material, to have it ready by Monday.
>
> There are still several things to settle with him but it looks as though I have a job. Really quite unbelievable that it should be this particular job. Everything else orally.
>
> I am usually in my room, Tel: National 8250, ext. 860.

Letter headed Thursday, no envelope:

> I am enclosing a letter to Vinette[11] the [*sic*] which please mail for me. It is written as though it comes from Warren, in case the enemy starts reading her mail in the Roxana Post Office. This is entirely within the realm of possibility, as is telephone tapping. Vinette, of course, will understand the letter perfectly. In it I suggest indirectly that she get herself a new mailing address, a post office box in a different place or an arrangement with the neighbors. I mention nothing in the letter concerning Atl. City, or pins. I also tell her, speaking as Warren that I have just had a card from her brother, Francis from Mexico City, saying he is *en route* to Buenos Aires on business. In case the enemy comes to you as he probably will—after checking her telephone calls—this should be your line with him: I visited you for a while, and then left, and then next you heard was the card from Mexico City. If asked about the card, naturally you destroyed it, since you do not collect post cards.

---

[11] Yockey's sister, Vinette Coyne.

> Tell Warren you had a call from Vinette so that he will be alerted for a visit from the enemy and will tell them the same story. Treat them distantly and firmly; make them produce their credentials, ask them exactly what they want, and do not be helpful at all. Show great surprise that they are seeking poor Franz, a model member of the community, etc.

From a letter dated May 16, postmarked Atlantic City, May 16, 1952:

> You ought to write to Vinette and tell her—make it clear that you are speaking for me, but do not mention my name—to get herself another mailing address. Do not mention A. City but tell her that things look good over here—. She has my address here and I have had a letter from her.
>
> I want you to call me, you should go to a pay station. I really think these precautions are justified because before this I have had this sort of wrong interest taken in me, and I know their standard procedures.

In the above letter,[12] Yockey mentions Perry S. Patterson, Sandy Spring, Maryland, as a contact of his.

From a letter dated May 20, postmarked Atlantic City, May 20, 1952:

> The main reason of course for the Buenos Aires-Mexico City story was the FBI but it does not harm if Dog thinks the story is straight. This is about the third of fourth time the FBI has sought poor Franz, each time without success, so each time they will look more intensely and each time I

---

[12] Patterson was a lawyer associated with Senator McCarthy, and represented the *Washington Times-Herald*, one of the few pro-McCarthy newspapers. Yockey had known Patterson while they were law students at Georgetown University, according to Kevin Coogan's biography (*Dreamer of the Day*, p. 25).

must be more cautious. Remember, do nothing which will leave a record on paper that will connect you to me. Very soon, or perhaps already, they will connect your house to Vinette because of the long-distance phone calls and perhaps also because of mail.

THOUGHTS PERSONAL & SUPERPERSONAL

CA. 1950

EDITORS' NOTE

This is a collection of random thoughts on culture and religion. Yockey refers to "Prussianism and Socialism," the title of a work by Oswald Spengler from 1919. From that essay Yockey derived his idea of "ethical socialism," which he alluded to in passing in some of the previous writings in this volume. Spengler pointed out that this is not only the true antithesis of capitalism, but also its transcendence, while Marxism, as a reflection of the nineteenth-century English materialist *Zeitgeist,* is merely a reflection of it.

Here Yockey also speaks of skepsis, as he did in "Life as an Art," as the basis of a new religious outlook. Yockey's skepsis is quite unlike the "skepticism" of nineteenth-century materialism. Indeed, it is contrary to the skepticism of the age of Darwin and Marx, of scientism and positivism that continues to cast a pall over the present.[1]

These "Thoughts" are post-war. There is an allusion to "the sieges of Stalingrad and Berlin," and several times the year 1950 is mentioned, although it cannot be assumed that this is the precise year that this was written, as Yockey, like Spengler, tended to round out years.

THOUGHTS PERSONAL & SUPERPERSONAL

No European can ever know the precise quality and intensity of the love which a colonial brings to the history and the works of the Western Culture. No matter how sensitive he is by nature,

---

[1] See Oswald Spengler, *Prussian Socialism and Other Essays*, annotated and introduced by K. R. Bolton (London: Black House Publishing, 2018).

no matter how high the cultural-historical focus to which he can attain and hold, the European—and I have in mind just such beings as Goethe, Fichte, Carlyle, and Leonardo—must of necessity take many things for granted. The houses, the streets, the society, the universal diffusion of culture—he grows up in this atmosphere, having nothing with which to contrast it. Not only concepts, but feelings also, form themselves by polarity. Hence it is that weak heads in Europe—like Lafayette, Ortega, Keyserling, the English plutocracy of the XXth century, Ferrero, Santayana, Croce[2]—not being able, through complete lack of imagination, to *compare* Europe with that outside, fail utterly to realize the rarity and exquisiteness that are Europe. They lack the sense of *value*. This sense is born, but it can be sharpened and intensified by privation. Thus it is that the colonial—and *all* colonials have a certain plane of their being which is susceptible to the centripetal attraction of the Mother-soil—when he does have the sense of value and the creative hypersensitivity that have always characterized higher Europeans, from Hohenstaufen to Hitler, has a heightened love of everything European which rises almost to the pathological. For him every paving-stone, every street, every European human type, every place that has been a focus of Destiny, even in the most recent times, has a magic force.

A new type of love and affection can even arise in the colonial who returns to the soil of his spiritual origins. He can experience warm feelings even for those individuals and types which would be repellent for him according to his personal taste, but who are clothed also with their quantum of the magic which bathes everything European. *He can love a person as a product and a part of Europe*. Such a feeling is of necessity unknown to the native European.

---

[2] José Ortega y Gasset (1883–1955), Count Hermann von Keyserling (1880–1946), George Santayana (1863–1952), Benedetto Croce (1866–1952). Probably Gilbert du Motier, Marquis de Lafayette (1757–1834). Possibly the historian Guglielmo Ferrero (1871–1942).

On the other side, there is a lack of feeling in the colonial: owing to his generalized love of the entire organism, he may be unable to feel the inner poles, the inner discord of the Culture. In the XIXth century, both Washington Irving and Emerson evinced this lack. In the Age of Absolute Politics, this lack is no defect, but an asset. Absolute Politics means politics between a Culture and extra-Cultural forces. This struggle for power is unmitigated, unconditioned, the total Culture against the totality without. To such a struggle, the colonial brings the true, synthetic, creative feeling; for him the Culture is a perfect unity, while for the natives, the memories of past discords linger: Versailles versus Potsdam, Habsburg versus Bourbon, Socialism versus Capitalism.

In one word: for the colonial who is capable of creative and appreciative feelings, *the Culture is Religion*. Culture embraces the totality: the soul of the organism, every event in its life, every product of its soul, every possibility it still contains of creation. Religion is the form of all awakening creative life; it *is* creation, it is youth. Religion is the formulation of the deepest feelings of harmony, which turn themselves into truths in the process of developing.

The feeling of Culture-as-Religion is the interim religion of Europe. It is itself a highly refined autumnal product of the Culture. It is the last but one of the religious phases of the Culture. It is a bridge, from the larger standpoint, over the debris of critical-atheist-materialism of the Age of Rationalism, connecting the Gothic origins to the Gothic future. But for those of us who live at this period, this moment is a life. This is our religion, and if any religion in all the history of High Cultures was ever exclusive, it becomes almost popular compared to this. How many souls can make of the materials of history and skepticism a profound and divine world-outlook? They are counted in Europe in hundreds.

❖ ❖ ❖

Perhaps there are a few souls in Europe who feel within them the religious imperative of the future. Unlikely, but possible, just as Nietzsche and Carlyle were utterly improbable in the desert of mechanistic criticism that was the XIXth century. If so, they are the summit of the religious pyramid of Europe. Beneath them is the stratum of our precious and strong interim religion, making out of skepticism a Faith, and out of History a sacred philosophy. Beneath this is the great mass of the population which is still in the "religion" of the XIXth century, that grotesque materialization of the spiritual, profanation of the divine, mechanizing of the organic, and insolent disrespect to the Awful and the Unknowable. This God-killing mockery took two forms, in Europe, Christian-social politics, and in America, compulsory social entertainment in the Sunday meeting-houses. These forms it still has, and this is what today calls itself religion in the Western Civilization. Below this stratum in the religious pyramid—not in any absolute spiritual sense, but only in a chronological sense—is the Jesuit level, the plane which regards religion as a matter of knowledge, formula, law, and in case of doubt, of authority. This is simply the Counter-Reformation, and includes members of both sides of that era. Below this is the Reformation level. Still today in Germany there are many, and elsewhere there are some who have remained permanently in the Lutheran stage. To that they attained in their personal forming, and there they stay. Below them—are there any left who feel the old, pure, monastic religiousness of the pre-Renaissance period of true religion? Yes, there must be, although they are not to be found in the offices of the Church, wearing the purple, or engaging themselves to the hilt in those banking operations which constitute religious administration today. They would be in some monastery, in an isolated rural district, the plains of the Romagna, or the Spanish Sierras. This type simply could not survive in a city. But these, together with those others of problematical existence, the religionists of the XXIst and XXIInd centuries, are the only true religionists in Europe; for these two groups—and for them alone—religion is directed to the transcendent, it knows and loves the Unknowable, it personalizes the impersonal, it cares for the indifferent.

❖ ❖ ❖

For the other aspect of our interim religion is that the object of its tremendous feelings is unworthy of it. God and the Gods are still asleep, still in the deep slumber into which the Counter-Reformation lulled them. For when Western man introduced militarism and politics into religion, he expelled God and the Gods. Religion is the window of the Culture looking out into the cosmos, and when the Culture becomes obsessed with the surface of the Earth, that window is closed. But it is only the cosmos—the entirety of all things, organic, inorganic, man, Culture, and meaning—that is the proper object of religion. Culture is not worthy. But there is nothing else; the divine aspect of the cosmos—God and the Gods—cannot be violently reawakened. It is slowly awakening, but not for us, for those who come two or three generations after us. Every religion has its mysteries, its idiom, and even its painful point. This is ours, that our religion takes the form of a yearning which sees its satisfaction beyond its grasp, that the last perfection of religious feeling is forever denied us, moving across our dark golden-brown autumnal bridge of Culture-religion, bathed in the dying light of the second twilight of our superpersonal Western life.

❖ ❖ ❖

Just as every religion has its point of unbearable sensitivity, so does it have its peculiar joys. The joy of our religion is precisely in its *radical* aristocracy. If only few are capable of complete *skepsis*, fewer still can make a faith of their skepticism.

❖ ❖ ❖

But it is precisely this that is the organic necessity for those who *will* to be the creators, and, like the historicists that we are, we know and love this necessity.

❖ ❖ ❖

The present is the point of tension between the past and the future. This fertile insight is the source of another of the heightened joys that are reserved for us believing skeptics: while all other religious feelings whatever present anywhere in the West are directed to the past—or toward the future—we alone are the present, the noon. One can labor for the future, dream it, build for it, deliver it—but not live in it. Thus ours is *the* religion of the times. All others belong to the blind and the inferior.

❖ ❖ ❖

Our fourth joy: we *know* the coming religious forms, but after they have come and taken up their sway, those in their service will no longer know them, but will be in them and surrounded by them. What to them will be the totality is only to us one more item of knowledge. We know their world, and they will not know it.

❖ ❖ ❖

We are thus Classical and Romantic in one. We are the synthesis of everything past, the prefiguration of everything future, we are the highest attainable point of the Western free spirituality. Classical: ours is the religion of the Age; Romantic: the active side of our religion is a labor and a yearning for the future, an affirmation, a conservation, a love and a yearning for our Past.

❖ ❖ ❖

Our religious interregnum, alone of all the religious phases of our Culture, will have no descendants. Jesuitry, Enlightenment, Atheism—a certain form of physiological inferiority—all will continue to have some form of existence at least two centuries from now. But the felling of Culture-as-Religion will have disappeared then, and it will leave no memory, for the possibility of seeing things our way will have disappeared. The other religions all represented possibilities more widely diffused in human nature than the possibility of skepticism. Think of Friedrich Hohenstaufen, alone of the ice-cold skeptical height which was his dwelling-place.[3] Think of Socinus, who had not the courage of his skepticism and lapsed into vulgar belief.[4] Ours is thus a great collective loneliness. We have no ancestors on this plane, for no previous High Culture ever had our archaeological tendency which alone is the source of our intense historicism. We shall have no descendants—as far as we can see. Once more—our uniqueness.

Never before has a superpersonal feeling so completely subjugated the world to such a profound and total knowledge. We are thus the highest form to which Culture-man has ever attained, since Culture-man is the creature who *knows*. We know that knowledge is not knowledge, that it is belief, and in our knowledge we believe, we will to believe, we are impelled to believe. We know that words destroy thoughts, and thus we leave the formulae and the words to the believers without faith, retaining for ourselves, the devout skeptics, the thoughts without words.

Skeptical historicism is at once the greatest affirmation and the greatest negation. It is thus capable of the most extravagant creation and of the most complete destruction. It combines delicacy and barbarism, Crusades and Rococo. It is the synthesis of

[3] Friedrich II (1194–1250) was a Holy Roman Emperor who came into conflict with the Church for holding that Imperial power was superior to that of the Pope. This led to a series of wars, and the two factions became known as the Guelphs, who supported the Pope, and the Ghibellines, who supported the Emperor. This conflict was often referred to by Julius Evola as an archetypal distinction between those who view either sacred or temporal power as being preeminent.

[4] Faustus Socinus (1539–1604) was an Italian Protestant theologian. Born a Catholic, he became a nontrinitarian (one who denies the reality of God in the form of the three persons of God, Son, and Holy Ghost), and eventually left the Church, ultimately becoming the primary theologian of the short-lived Minor Reform Church of Poland and giving rise to the doctrine of Socinianism.

all the ideas and mores of the Culture.

❖ ❖ ❖

An example: the tasks of our time are frankly irreligious tasks. No religionist of any older variety is equal to them; the true religionists of the future are not yet here, nor will they interest themselves. We skeptics alone can bring to them the necessary religious zeal, for all older religions are stifled in logic and mechanism. Our feeling alone is once more pure; ours is the clean slate, the primitive chaos side by side with over-refined urbane intellectuality. But this purity is itself true religion.

❖ ❖ ❖

If the Inscrutable permits the West to fulfill itself, we shall undertake such projects, erect such structures, create such a State, and hew such deeds, that our remote descendants, hearing the legends of our race, and gazing at its remains in walls and monuments, will tell their children that once a race of Supermen dwelt on the Earth.

❖ ❖ ❖

The most pressing of all the projects we must undertake, for it involves the physical security of our holy soil and therewith its entire future and destiny, is the causeway linking the continent with the island, and as an additional security, linking Ulster with Scotland. The second is a subsidiary undertaking. The Great Causeway must be undertaken at the earliest possible moment, and it must continually be widened for a century. This must be done on principle, even though no apparent need for it exists.

❖ ❖ ❖

Two other grand projects have less immediacy. As to which will, or can, be undertaken first, incident will decide. But both have the Destiny-quality. First, the Europeanization of North Africa. To effectuate this, the conversion of the Mediterranean into two lakes: causeways at Gibraltar, and from Italy to Tunisia, dams at Dardanelles and Bosphorus, closing of Suez. Irrigation of the African continent as far inland as possible with the power resources of the Gibraltar, Tunisian, and Egyptian dams. Settlement of the new area with Europeans from the overcrowded petty-states of Europe. Total expulsion of all indigenous populations.

Second, the Europeanization of the hither Slavic lands. This includes the Balkans, Bohemia, Poland, the Baltic, White Russia, Little Russia, Muscovy, the Ukraine, and the Caucasus.

To a certain extent, the two projects are substitutes for another. If either one could be completely accomplished, it would assure Imperium of security in one direction. Viewed however from the viewpoint of the next three centuries, both projects are necessary, if Imperium is to remain forever as the great monument of the West. From the standpoint of one century, one will suffice. Either one will take fifty years to actualize.

Great things can be expected of England—Prussian things—with the Liberation of Europe and the erection of the Causeway. The Great Causeway will destroy the island, the insular mentality, the remnants of exaggerated nationalism, the possibility of the repetition of the American stab in the back of 1944, Capitalism, what remains of it, Calvinism, Puritanism, the Spirit of Money, the inner America within Europe. The stock inhabiting the island still contains a good deal of Northern Barbarian in it. It was not only the English National Idea which undertook the continent-wide racial extermination of Australia and Tasmania, it was also the Northern Barbarian, who has gone in history under a hundred different names: Sea People, Aryans, Kassites, Norsemen, Danes, Kelts, Varangians, Prussians. Only this Northern Barbarian can accomplish the tremendous cruelties which alone can form the foundation of Imperium. At the moment, the Barbarian in England is in the service of the exotic regime of Washington. After the erection of the Great Causeway, the Barbarian from the island will feel a mission impelling him toward Slavia, a mission of conquest and clearing. The entire project of course is one which only the Northern Barbarian could entertain, and these elements of all Europe will participate. There is, however, no ground for despair that the island population will continue during the two centuries to come, as during the two centuries past, to misuse the security that the Prussian created for it. The Great Causeway will liberate the island just as it will liberate and secure the mainland.

❖ ❖ ❖

Northern Barbarian is redundant: there are not, cannot be, Southern Barbarians. Southern means contented, social, refined, above all, delicate in conception and usage and manner. Only from the Northern mists, and not from the Southern sun, can come the rough man, the man of loneliness, discontent, inner tension, the grand destroyer-creator. Barbarian does not mean primitive; barbarian is the transition from primitive to High Culture. All primitive organization is based on suggestion, nuance, and delicacy; the barbarian is blunt, crude, destructive.

❖ ❖ ❖

The three forms of knowledge as the three forms of the Causality-Principle.

Superstition—remote causality;
Religion—divine causality;
Science—profane causality.

Superstition is basically human. The other two are Culture-human, found only in men under the impress of a High Culture, thus they are the creations of the High Culture itself. Superstition always exists, the others only during the life-course of the High Culture. Religion is the beginning and the end knowledge-form of a High Culture. Science is the counterpoint to Religion; for seven centuries it is the bass, and then for a brief period, it ascends into the treble, carries the Culture-melody, and then dies out forever, followed closely by its parent-religion. Superstition exists before the Culture, underneath it, and after it. All knowledge succumbs in the end to superstition.

Here is the key to skepsis. The skeptic has no knowledge; he needs none. Explanations do not interest him, nor suffice him.

Self-expression alone, and that in deeds, is his need.

❖ ❖ ❖

The skeptic is the bravest man. He needs no rationalized equipment like the religionists and the scientificoes. He suffices in his feelings of race, honor, inner imperative, and mission. Explanations are meaningless in this realm. Explanation is breaking-down into simpler things, but honor and the mission are themselves elements, cannot be broken down.

❖ ❖ ❖

The skeptic can see the outer world as void, enigmatic, meaningless. He is not overmastered by his fear. He does not run to gods of his own creation, nor to natural laws, to give his life an intellectualized meaning, to hide from Fate.

❖ ❖ ❖

The skeptic has no need of these intellectualized devices for escaping from metaphysical fear, for one simple reason: the strength of his ascendant instincts themselves overcome his world-fear. The skeptic is the man with absolute confidence in himself—metaphysical self-confidence. This is the highest formula for honor and race, and for the heroic world-outlook. His substitute for knowledge—which is always mediate—is feeling, which is immediate. He *feels* his aim in life, and he feels his life-ethos. Beyond this, he feels the sublime accident-quality of everything outside the data of his feeling.

❖ ❖ ❖

This type of skepticism has nothing whatever in common with what the clerical people call skepticism. They mean not believing in their particular distillate of fear-antitoxin. Absolute skepticism, however, is the disbelief in all explanations, simply because of the precedent inability to believe in the power of the intellect to achieve satisfactory results in the realm of the last and deepest things.

❖ ❖ ❖

Intellect is a practical thing; it is a weapon, a tool. It is for the purpose of accomplishing terrestrial things, making steel, building bridges and ships, navigating the senses and skies, producing food. But it can only work in submission to something higher, just as a tool can only be plied by a hand. This something higher is the instinct, which demands that the problem be solved. The solution of the ultimate problems, however, can only be bungled by intellect. Instinct of higher men refuses to accept any such botched product as an explanation of Life and World. This instinct refuses all explanations, because they are all so pathetic, and even the possibility of an explanation, because the world is so sublime.

❖ ❖ ❖

Intellect is to the beast-of-prey man what claws and teeth are to the tiger. Intellect is the most flexible and powerful of all tools and weapons. This is its distinction, and in this let Intellect be humbly satisfied.

❖ ❖ ❖

It is also a shield; it can protect one from traps. It is also a tonic; it can remind a tired and suffering soul of that which it well knows, and can thus renew it.

❖ ❖ ❖

The Instincts of the Northern Barbarian, the highest order of intellect sharpened to the keenest edge by historicism and a resolute skepsis: these are the human treasures which we higher men of the period 1950–2050 bring to the Destiny of Europe, and which we put into its service in all religion.

❖ ❖ ❖

An army at any one moment has five components, in order of descending importance:

Morale

The officer corps
The supreme leadership
Fighting material
Equipment.

The officer corps is more important than the supreme leadership, for it can survive mistakes there, whereas the supreme leadership can do nothing without the officer corps equal to the execution of the task. Fighting material means the human material. It refers thus directly to racial qualities; horizontal race, needless to say. Morale, from the larger standpoint, is a function of the Destiny of the Culture. Hence the morale of the German armies which gave their performance in two World Wars. Hence the morale of the French Army, 1940. No mission, no morale. Morale is thus mystic. *Vide* Valmy,[5] where the French won by morale alone, or Narva, where Charles XII won by morale alone.[6]

Navies must be infused with the continental army spirit. Army ranks must be introduced. Sea and land functions must be interchangeable on higher levels. Air, sea, and land branches—all must be known and felt as **the Army**.

From one standpoint, the world-situation is an endurance contest between the tension in America and the perseverance of

---

[5] The Battle of Valmy was fought on September 20, 1792 between Prussian troops and the French army. The Prussians were attempting to get to Paris in order to put down the French Revolution and were unexpectedly and soundly defeated by the previously untested new French army. This was the first major victory of the fledgling French Republican government.

[6] The Battle of Narva was fought on November 20, 1700, when Charles XII of Sweden was attempting to lift a siege by the Russian army of the city of Narva, Estonia, which was then part of the Swedish Empire. Although the Russian force was four times larger, the Swedes dealt them a crushing defeat.

the spirit of Prussia. The situation in America cannot last; neither can Prussia continue to fight and go down. Only America has twice frustrated Prussia and the Destiny of Europe. In 1917, with the peace of Brest-Litovsk, we were the victors. Without America there is no question whatever, no possibility other than, that England would have made peace. This peace would have had to be a victory for us. Everything subsequent had been different; the Second World War could not have taken the form it did. Or even if it had, without America, Prussia-Europe would still have won, and we would now be living in the first crude, provisional form of Imperium. Everyone would know his place, his task, his mission. Europe would be a bee-hive of creative activity. There would be no Russia in political existence. Only America frustrated this.

If the American ascendancy continues for fifty years, there will no longer be any possibility of Imperium. The reason is that America is civilizing the entire colored world, introducing Western technics everywhere. But this technical superiority is our only hope. Granted, they can never have our originality. But this originality is not absolute, and when the outer world *approaches* a technical par with us, numbers will come into play. The colored world outnumbers us five to one.[7]

---

[7] Yockey's prediction has in recent years loomed large *vis-à-vis* the emergence of China, which has mainly been built up by America: (1) primarily as a means of containing Russia, and (2) secondarily through the motive of simple, crass greed for Chinese labor and Chinese markets. This has dramatically changed the world situation from that in which Yockey wrote: Russia (and the Slavic lands), far from being the "outer enemy" whose soil would provide the *Lebensraum* for the European Imperium, is—or must become—the bulwark of Europe against the "outer enemies": China and America. (See K. R. Bolton, "Geopolitical Realignments: USA-Israel-China versus Russia-Europe-Arabia," *Foreign Policy Journal*, September 19, 2011.

Additionally, so far from the North of Europe providing the "Barbarians" who would invigorate a decaying civilization, like the "Vandals" and others in decadent Rome, the northern folk have so

❖ ❖ ❖

The case of America shows better than anything the meaninglessness of happening outside the High Cultures. The monstrosity called America can intervene in Europe, can frustrate it, can perhaps destroy it. This Europe has been the most sublime of all the High Cultures, the most passionate and intense, the most masculine, barbarian, and its future was to have been the grandest single spectacle ever played out on the world-stage: the foundation of Imperium and the embarkation on the conquest of the world as an absolute mission. This was, is, our Destiny. Up to now, twice in a generation, this mighty denouement has been effectively frustrated by the boundless stupidity and empty malice of the American monster. The element in the situation which tortures the soul is the fact that this mechanical thing cannot be tracked down to its lair and destroyed. It can lose in the field, but the field will always be thousands of miles abroad. Europe can defeat it, but the defeat will at most only give Europe security. We cannot have the satisfaction of standing over this misbegotten product of blind forces, sword in hand, watching its final convulsions, watching its heteroclite human material scatter like nomads over the empty landscape.

Cruel paradox: America, with no mission, enjoys absolute political security. Europe, with the only mission in the world, lies

---

completely succumbed to the hegemony of the Culture-distorter and the Culture-retarder that, again, it is the Russians who stand as the only remaining possibility of forming a cleansing Barbarian mass to regenerate Europe and provide a pivotal role in forming what must now be seen as a Eurosiberian Imperium.

Yockey himself, shortly before his death, recognized the dramatically changing world situation. See Yockey's final essay, "The World in Flames," herein.

Yockey later referred not to the dispossession of the Slavs and the colonization of "Slavia," but rather to a "new Europe-Russia Symbiosis." See K. R. Bolton, *Yockey & Russia* (Kapiti, New Zealand: Renaissance Press, 2009), p. 14.

crushed between the two formless monsters without purpose or mission.

Nietzsche has changed his mind—no frivolity, he has merely changed his position. No longer in 1880, when Winckelmann[8] was still culturally alive, but in 1950, after the world has seen the sieges of Stalingrad and Berlin. The spirit of Nietzsche now gives us *our highest formula of affirmation*: the world-as-drama. I call this the dramatic *Weltanschauung*. The formula of Eternal Recurrence no longer moves us: we suspect that it came from the Darwinian half of Nietzsche.

Two modes of seeing the world have always separated themselves out: the world as beauty, or the world as goodness. They correspond to the heroic and the saintly. This Age is a heroic one, an age of politics, of irreligion and amorality. Its regnant *Weltanschauung* on the highest level therefore can hardly be one of the-world-as-goodness.

And it is precisely the-world-as-drama that bears itself in upon us as the appropriate one because we have in our bloodstream the *Fifth Act feeling*. This dramatic *Weltanschauung* is one of affirmation of Life and Fate; who as the tragedy heightens, however unbearably, would cowardly order the play to cease?

Also *dramatic*: we feel instinctively that a man's end is the only thing that matters. This was *not* so in the XIXth century. In a drama, it is only the end that matters. We do not know whether every man is the poet of his own biography, but we do know—in our way of knowing—that the honorable end is the one thing that cannot be taken from a man.

---

[8] German art historian Johann Joachim Winckelmann (1717–1768).

❖ ❖ ❖

The masculinity of this age is another reason for its instinctive creation of the dramatic *Weltanschauung*. Masculine is dramatic, it is play within rules, deliberate non-seriousness, or otherwise put, seriousness on a higher level. It is disregard of seriousness on the cosmic plane—this is where woman is serious and practical—and a preference for the non-seriousness of the plane of artificial situations, which one knows are artificial.

❖ ❖ ❖

Man is an eternal child. The higher the man, the more this is true. The child at play, however, knows that it plays, and this is hardly kept secret from the highest man, who suffers from that most human of all diseases—the disease of unremitting consciousness.

❖ ❖ ❖

But this is the age wherein the higher man attains to a superpersonal plane on which he has never stood before, and never will again, for the religion and the existence of the higher man of Europe 1950–2050 is *radically* aristocratic.

❖ ❖ ❖

This, because the age is a heroic one, because it is an age wherein things will be done once and for all, because the higher man embodies in him the highest formulation of masculinity and of his Age, he chooses henceforth the dramatic *Weltanschauung* for his. He recognizes the World-mystery and participates in it deliberately, consciously, and with reverence for himself.

The human race as a whole is a woman; old people of both sexes figure as women, and for most purposes, children also. Man is thus a variation. Man is a revolt. Higher man is the greatest defiance of the revolt, and thus at this century-moment of history, it is not only the highest point of the most intense Culture, but the highest point of the Idea of Man itself that is here attained.

❖ ❖ ❖

The Americans are *psychologically* socialists; so are the aborigines of New Guinea and the Solomon Islands. This means merely that within each individual the social impulses predominate over the individual impulses. In this environment, individualism is stamped out, and higher types become almost impossible, because a higher type can only be individualized, psychologically egoistic. This is true also of saints, all of whom were psychologically egoists, even though they were spiritually altruistic. In America, instinctive altruism predominates, but spiritual egoism.

❖ ❖ ❖

Prussian Socialism[9] is the opposite of American socialism. Prussian Socialism, arising as it does in a land and Culture of psychological individualism, absolutely requires an aristocracy to actualize it. An aristocracy is an expression of individualism. Thus Prussian Socialism encourages automatically the arising of higher individuals, since without them, there can be no Prussian Socialism, but only chaos. Prussian Socialism is *spiritual* socialism, not, like the American variety, psychological. In Prussia, Socialism is a value, a conscious ethic, an ideal, an organization-form, a means of accomplishment. In America it is unconscious, an inhibition, a negation, an inability to be individual, thus a denial of the human in man and an assertion of the herding animal in man.

❖ ❖ ❖

Money: the well-known American orientation to money, according to which *everything* is assessed in terms of dollars and cents, including religion, art, politics, social life, and individual life, does not arise from greed and covetousness. These things

---

[9] Oswald Spengler, "Prussianism and Socialism" (1919). The concept is original to Spengler, and Yockey also refers to it as "spiritual socialism" and "ethical socialism." It can be summed up in the word duty.

are human, not national. This method of comparing all things with one standard is simply an expression of the *uniformity* of America: this uniformity is adjusted to a very low level, specifically to the animal level of man, the plane on which health, happiness, and comfort are the greatest problems. But all of these problems—and there are no others in America—can be easily resolved in terms of the great money common denominator. To an American—whose acquaintance with, say, the aesthetic side of the Western Culture is as slight in comparison with a European as would be that of a present-day-European in comparison with a European of the Rococo—it is no strain of the mind to assess Frans Hals[10] and Ruysdael[11] in terms of money. To him these things come under the heading of "beautiful surroundings," in other words, comfort.

Three different orientations to money: American, English, German.

To the American, money is *life*.

To the Englishman (the true Englishman, a type now almost extinct, the historical Englishman), money was culture.

To a true Prussian-German, money is preservation.

The whole German economy, even though it still uses money—I am speaking, of course, of the Third Reich—is a systematic attempt to defeat money.[12] The effort of German social creations is to make the amount of money an individual receives directly proportionate to his needs. The only role played by money in the process is that of facilitating it. Money dispenses with the administration that would be necessary to operate a

---

[10] Frans Hals (1582–1666) was a portrait painter of the Dutch Golden Age.

[11] Salomon van Ruysdael (1603–1670) was a landscape painter of the Dutch Golden Age.

[12] For the practical measures by which the Third Reich "defeated money" while also providing for the needs of its folk, see K. R. Bolton, "Breaking the Bondage of Interest: A Right Answer to Usury," *Counter-Currents*, August 10, 2011.

non-money economy.[13]

In England, need never played any part in the money-outlook. The aim of everyone was to have as much as possible. As long as the upper stratum retained its sense of a world-mission, this concept of money-as-culture (culture means here: higher life) did no damage; it effected no degeneration. Granted, it ruined the lowest classes, but they did not matter to the world-mission.

---

[13] Yockey is alluding to a fundamental truth, albeit one that is today seldom realized: that money should serve merely as a convenient token of exchanging goods and services, not as a commodity upon which the profits and power of the plutocrats are founded.

Miscellaneous Notes

Ca. 1950–53

Editors' Note

The specific date of composition of these notes is unknown, but as with Yockey's other notes for essays and random thoughts, the style and format of these suggest the early 1950s. As can be seen in this and other writings, Yockey had a habit of noting down pithy comments from various sources.

Unsurprisingly, Spengler appears here, too. Yockey again refers to Spengler's 1919 essay "Prussianism and Socialism" as "P. and S." Yockey drew numerous elements from this essay, not only on "ethical socialism" as the socialism of the West, but also the concept of the "Michel" stratum of Europeans, which Yockey often uses in his writings, and which Spengler defined as a class of bourgeois liberal conformists who were obstacles to the coming of the new spirit of the age.

Another interesting reference is to Spengler's Introduction to Richard Korherr's thesis in *Decline of the Birthrate*.[1] Spengler regards population decline as a primary symptom of culture decay, especially noted in *The Decline of the West*. Dr. Richard Korherr, a population specialist with the Reich Bureau of Statistics, had contacted Spengler in 1926, addressing him as "Highly honored Master"! He had read *The Decline of the West* in 1920, and had "not been able to escape from its spell." In 1925, he made Spengler's *magnum opus* the basis of his doctoral thesis, *Geburtenrückgang* (*Decline of the Birth Rate*), and sought Spengler's permission to dedicate it to him as "the greatest thinker of our time."[2] Spengler replied that, having read the thesis, he accepted the dedication with his "best thanks," adding, "I will tell

---

[1] For Spengler's Introduction to the Korherr thesis, see Spengler, *Prussian Socialism and Other Essays*.

[2] Letter from Korherr to Spengler dated October 21, 1926, in *Letters of Oswald Spengler: 1913–1936* (New York: Alfred A. Knopf, 1966), p. 203.

you honestly that up to now I have read nothing which has completed and deepened a suggestion in my book into such knowledge and understanding."[3]

In 1927, Korherr had visited Spengler and wrote stating that he had given him the means by which to oppose depopulation: returning to the ethos that marriage means children, and that woman is "regarded in the first instance as a mother." Like Spengler, Korherr sought analogies in other civilizations and found that Confucius gave China the ethos that "the man who dies without descendants receives no social recognition among the living." Western Civilization therefore needed a "Western Confucius." Korherr regarded Spengler as that individual, and anyone lesser as only causing harm.[4]

Korherr's work had a major influence on Fascist Italy's population policy, where it was translated in 1928, with a Preface by Mussolini. Korherr's influence prompted the formation of the National Organization for the Protection of Motherhood and Infancy in Italy. Korherr became Inspector of Statistics in the Third Reich, and survived "denazification" after the Second World War to pursue his academic career. He died in 1989.

MISCELLANEOUS NOTES

Leonardo Demetrius (Ms. published 1891, Milan) used to say that there was no difference between the words and voice of the unlearned and ignorant and the sounds or noises from a belly full of superfluous wind. And he said, not without justice, that it seemed to him to make no difference from which part they emitted their voice, from the mouth or from below, since both were of the same value and substance.

There are men who deserve to be called nothing else than passages for food, augmenters of filth, and fillers of privies, be-

---

[3] Letter from Spengler to Korherr, October 28, 1926, ibid.

[4] Letter from Korherr to Spengler dated May 30, 1927, ibid., pp. 219–20.

cause nothing else in the world is effected through them, and they are without any virtue, since nothing is left of them but filled privies.

❖ ❖ ❖

Keyserling[5]—*America Set Free,* Page 135.

Accidents and individual variations mean little. No defeat has ever changed the destiny of a nation inwardly strong if it was not annihilated. Nor has any victory which was not founded on moral and intellectual superiority ever lasted.

❖ ❖ ❖

The more the means of communication improve, the more chance there is that localisms will survive and the more they will mean. For great facility and frequency of intercourse counteract mutual influence, nor is like-mindedness any longer the necessary premise for friendly intercourse.

❖ ❖ ❖

Indeed, culture stands and falls with differences perceived and recognized. Only where the law of polarization as opposed to equalization obtains can there be culture.

❖ ❖ ❖

Goethe: Reverence, which no man brings into the world with him, is yet that upon which everything depends, if man is to become a man in every sense.

❖ ❖ ❖

Varange—Youth: independently functioning parts; maturity;

---

[5] *America Set Free* (New York: Harper, 1929). Count Hermann von Keyserling (1880–1946) was a Baltic German and philosopher who travelled widely and sought a synthesis between Western and Eastern doctrines. An opponent of German militarism and nationalism, he criticized the National Socialists on the grounds that they lacked spirituality.

the integrated whole.

Logos—the principle of masculinity, of fatherhood, of distance, of tension.

Eros—principle of femininity, or love, of motherhood, of nearness, of rest.

Keyserling—op. cit. If a man meeting another man begins by thinking, "I am as good as he is," and accordingly treats him with familiarity, he will never learn from him, even though the other one be a god. On the other hand, if reverence is the primal attitude even the greatest can learn, and always does learn even from the humblest.

Varange—Women are first women and only then human beings; men are first human beings and then men.

Courtesy toward women: in Europe the respect of the strong for the weak; in America the respect of the inferior for the superior.

Even if a tired and effete mankind wishes to renounce wars, like Classical mankind of the latest centuries, like the Indians and Chinese today, it can only become—from having been the wager of wars—the object about which and with which wars are made by others. Spengler—P. and S.[6]

No parliamentary babbling or party-politics are equal to our tasks, but only personalities, who know how to force themselves and their decisions through. Spengler, from Introduction to Korherr's Essay on the *Decline of Births*.

---

[6] "Prussianism and Socialism" (1919).

Woe to the general who comes onto the battlefield with a system. Napoleon[7]

Will, character, industry, and boldness have made me what I am.

The ambition to rule souls is the strongest of all passions.

Self-interest is only the key to commonplace transactions.

---

[7] Paraphrased from *Napoleon in His Own Words: From the French of Jules Bertaut* (Chicago: A. C. McClurg, 1916), p. 116.

THOUGHTS UPON WAKING

CA. 1950

EDITORS' NOTE

In these quite rough notes, Yockey seems to be attempting to develop a new dialectic beyond that of Hegel, a type of Western Tao for the new epoch. The basis of this paradigm is that of polarities, rather than the Hegelian thesis and antithesis, with each polarity being both positive and negative, and interacting. The dialectic is not between positive and negative polarities as thesis and antithesis, but between polarities and diffusion. One gives form, while the other leads to formlessness.

One might see how Yockey's theory works out in history, as in for example when considering hierarchy, with its caste social structure (polarity) in conflict with equality; and in an ideological sense, aristocracy, which gives form, in conflict with Marxism, which causes diffusion, and one might add dissolution. One might discern something similar in Jung's *anima* and *animus*; in the conscious and the unconscious, polarities giving form through the individuated self. In such a context, both capitalism and Marxism can be seen as examples of diffusion, and the ideological counterparts of schizophrenia, leading to diffusion.

D. H. Lawrence set out an analogous dialectic of polarities in his concept of the dual nature of life. Lawrence's polarities are symbolized by the lion (the mind and the active male principle) which is in eternal strife with the unicorn (the senses and the passive female principle). But for one to completely kill the other would result in its own extinction, and a vacuum would be created around the victory. This is so with ideologies, religions, and moralities that stand for the victory of one polarity and the repression of the other. The crown belongs to neither. It stands above both as the symbol of balance. Into this, Yockey projects diffusion, which is a type of cultural pathology.

The following notes were likely written in the early 1950s, as the concepts, although not evident in *Imperium* (1948), are presented in Yockey's *The Enemy of Europe*, published in 1953. In that book, Yockey lists two columns of polarities, comparing, for example, "Imperialism" (the Yockeyan Idea) with "Capitalism":

Imperialism	*Capitalism*
Faith	Rationalism
Primacy of spirit	Materialism
Idealism	Sensualism
Will-to-Power	Will-to-Riches

Etc. . . .[1]

After the lists of polarities, Yockey states that "the reigning forces of Culture-retardation make use of the ideas and instincts of Imperialism whenever and wherever they find it necessary and possible," such as the preaching of "democracy"[2] while establishing an authoritarian occupation regime over Europe, and replacing the traditional hierarchy with an inverted version in the name of equality. This is because even the Culture-retarder and the Culture-distorter must act within the context of the Age, or what we can more precisely call the *Zeitgeist*; just as the *Zeitgeist* of the nineteenth century had been materialism, and hence the "polarity" of capitalism, Marxism, was as materialistic as its opposite.

The same situation pertains today, as it did in the post-Second World War era of Yockey's time, with the "new world order" of the post-Cold War era proclaiming the principles of "democracy" and "human rights" while suppressing with whatever brutality is required any regime, culture, faith, or movement that does not subject itself to the international regime. That is because, despite the fact that Yockey's Imperium did not triumph over the extra-European forces in his projected timeline (ca. 1950 onwards), he is nonetheless right that this is the "Age of Absolute Politics," and conflicting polarities must all be ex-

---

[1] Francis Parker Yockey, *The Enemy of Europe* (York, S.C.: Liberty Bell Publications, 1981), p. 51.

[2] Ibid., p. 53.

pressed within that *Zeitgeist*, including those that call themselves "democratic."

THOUGHTS UPON WAKING

Wherever there is polarity, there is always a wider reality which includes [illegible], which is served by both poles. The poles define, express, and make real this inclusive reality, but nonetheless they are the parts. In many cases, since the poles are so strong in their expressing and defining power, so intensely felt, the inclusive concept is lacking in our speech. Thus, love and hatred are polarized, and the inclusive reality is *feeling*, pathos. Catholic theologians try to rationalize love as a positive, and hatred as a mere negative, "the absence of love." But polarized entities or ideas are *never* related as positive and negative; each pole is equally positive, equally negative, equally creative, equally destructive, equally **necessary** in every sense of the word, organic and inorganic. Each pole exists as such only by virtue of the other.

Polar-thinking is historical thinking. Nicolas Cusanus[3] thus an anachronism, a spirit essentially belonging to the entire history of the Western Culture, and not merely to his age, like Thomas Aquinas. Hegel's thought is always polar, even though he (in this the child of his age, delighted with its new plaything called electricity, and its arbitrarily named "positive" and "negative" poles) mistakenly used a terminology which assumes a "positive" force for the Thesis and a "negative" for the Antithesis.

Every statement, every movement contains *ab initio*[4] its own contradiction. Every affirmation is also a denial. Every denial

[3] Nicholas of Cusa (1401–1464) was a German theologian and astronomer. He favored reforms in the Church and also believed that political power had to operate with the consent of the governed.

[4] Latin: "From the beginning."

contains an implicit affirmation.

❖ ❖ ❖

The principle of diffusion which obtains so clearly in the physical world, so that even the comparatively inert metals like gold and silver will in time, placed side by side, mix with one another, rules also in the world of life. *It is the opposite pole to polarity.*

❖ ❖ ❖

Polarity shapes, defines, creates, makes tense, generates. Diffusion renders formless, obliterates, enervates, anaesthetizes, kills. Example: the polarity of the sexes. The higher the state of Culture, the more pronounced the accompanying polarity of the sexes. Among primitives this polarity hardly exists, in comparison with its epitome of development in XVIIIth-century Europe. But even in [the] highest intensity of sexual polarity, there are always the intermediate types, which leave the poles and wish to return to the middle. Diffusion, the opposite of polarity, polarity's other pole.

❖ ❖ ❖

We can classify thinkers also as polarized and diffuse. In our age, Spengler is polarized, Keyserling, Toynbee et al., diffuse. Nietzsche is polarized, Haeckel diffuse. Goethe, here as in most things, combines all tendencies in an equal rhythm. Kant and Leibniz are polarized, as are Berkeley, Hobbes, and Spencer. Voltaire, Rousseau, Mill, Hume, and Pascal are diffuse. English thought **in general** is diffuse—naturally I refer primarily to England's age of glory, the XIXth century—and English action (again the XIXth century) is polarized. Hence cant, the universal hypocrisy of England, the land of the culture of **hypocrisy**. Parliament, victory of the principle of diffusion over the polarity of King and subject, leader and led. Appropriately this principle of negation of monarchy came to victory under King Oliver, more absolute than the Charles he beheaded in the name of republicanism.[5] Parliament, the principle of diffusion, however, succumbs at once again to the polarity of leader and led, in this case, however, the leaders are semi-anonymous, semi-visible, but they **lead** nevertheless, since polarity and only polarity *creates*.[6]

❖ ❖ ❖

Needless to say, every polarity creates within it its own diffusion.

❖ ❖ ❖

The interworkings of the poles upon one another are perfectly simple and infinitely complicated. Thus in the polarity of the sexes, in any one individual, a strong inner opposite pole to his actual sex **heightens** his actual sexual polarity. Ultra-masculine figures like Cesare Borgia, Wallenstein, Olivares, Richelieu, Napoleon, Bismarck, Hitler, have **necessarily** within them a strong feminine pole, and it is this which sharpens their feeling for the Idea of masculinity. The limiting factor enters when the inner feminine pole is so strongly marked that it *neutralizes* the masculinity of the man. Among men this happens often, since the masculine pole is the pole of the dynamic, thus of *variations*. Among women, this occurs seldom if ever—namely such an inner masculine excess that it neutralizes the femininity of the woman.

❖ ❖ ❖

Just as the man with the strong inner feminine pole is more masculine, so is the woman with [text missing][7]

---

[5] King Charles I of England was executed at the order of Oliver Cromwell during the English Civil War, after which the short-lived republican Commonwealth of England was established. Yockey is using the term "King" sarcastically, since Cromwell's official title was Lord Protector.

[6] Yockey has handwritten here, "Leonardo, Michelangelo, Tiziano are polarized, Raphael is diffuse. Velazquez is polarized, Murillo diffuse."

[7] Either Yockey left this sentence unfinished, or else the text is

The fact that no man is *purely* masculine, no woman *purely* feminine, is the principle of diffusion accompanying the principle of polarity.

❖ ❖ ❖

One will understand all this better when he never for a moment ceases to remember that in the physical world there is no such thing as "The Principle of Polarity." This is our thinking, which has two poles: passive receptivity, and active forcing of full-blown theories onto the physical world (i.e., our **picture** of the physical world). In the actual world of life there never was such a thing as "Evolution," but in the brain of every true Englishman in the XIXth century, it was self-evident that "Evolution," gradual, orderly, parliamentary development, governed the entire world of life.

❖ ❖ ❖

When passive receptivity dominates our thought, we attain to that "shuddering awe" of which Goethe spoke.[8] When force governs our thinking, we develop a **system**, like the philosophers, and the philosophasters (Marx, Darwin, Freud & Co.). It was owing to the great strength of his passive-receptive pole that Goethe never attained to any **system**. At the last moment in every orgy of thinking, he realized suddenly that it was only his **picture** that he was forming.

❖ ❖ ❖

Polarity is the one principle which describes equally well—i.e., to our satisfaction—the physical world and the world of life. Why is this? Because the world of life and the physical world are themselves **polarized**. Life equals spirit; physical world equals matter.

---

missing from the copy that survives.

[8] "Beneath your sacred shades, ye ancient groves, with shuddering awe I walk." Johann Wolfgang von Goethe, *Iphigenia in Tauris*, Act 1, Scene 1.

This is the supreme formula for us late men, historically and skeptically oriented, of the relationship of spirit and matter. No longer do we see a conflict, as did earlier centuries. We see the interaction of two poles, mutually destroying, mutually creating. Remarks appear in the pages of the philosophers, like Spengler's "Whoever separates soul and body has neither." In Gothic times nothing was more self-evident than the absolute disjunction of body and soul, and the absolute primacy of soul. To us, in my formula, the soul and body are identical, the soul is the inside, the body is the outside. Old age is the triumph of the outside over the inside, the victory of matter over soul, this being again an example of diffusion. Death is the diffusion of matter and spirit, and if we can use the expression, absolute Death would be the utter extinction of **both** matter and spirit.

Life (i.e., spirit) is a denial of the world—polarity—but at the same time it is tied to the world—all poles are tied to one another. World becomes life and life slowly becomes world—old age and death.

Life and World are two poles, and thus both serve a wider reality. This inclusive reality is Being. Here we can get no further, with words, since all thought from now on is **verbally** contradictory, e.g., if Being is also polarized its opposite pole is non-Being, which thus—the weakness of words—has to **exist**. From this point on, thought must proceed without words, and we are only one or two thoughts removed from the state of "shuddering awe."

The emergence from the state of shuddering awe (maximum of passive receptivity) proceeds at once into activity for its own sake—polarity again.

❖ ❖ ❖

Matter and spirit arose together (like all poles) and they will go down together. Mythology of all cultures fills out its picture of beginnings (the best-known myth of origins is Genesis, the best-known myth of the end is *Götterdämmerung*) and endings. Before, and after, is **nothing**. With the idea of **nothing**, thought comes to an end, since there is nothing with which we can polarize it.

❖ ❖ ❖

Always remember, neither matter or spirit exists, save as *concepts*. These are two words, two ideas, two thoughts—i.e., they are both emanations of **spirit**. Everything that is not spirit, spirit labels, collectively, "matter." Possible polarities within the realm of "matter" do not exist for us (i.e., polarities equally fundamental as that of matter-spirit).

Two Reflections

1950, 1953

Editors' Note

The first of these reflections was written in June 1950. It shows that Yockey had already adopted a "neutralist" position for Europe *vis-à-vis* America and Russia during the "Cold War." He certainly did not think, as was common—and still is—among "anti-Semites," that there was a covert collusion between Jewish capitalists in New York and Jewish commissars in Moscow to rule the world.

While he continued to regard Russians as barbarian invaders from the Asian steppes, he saw the American occupation of Europe as the greater danger because of its spiritually and culturally corrosive impact. He states here a later major theme: "To urge a crusade against Moscow, Bolshevism simply plays into the hands of the Washington regime."

This 1950 memorandum gives credence to an FBI report that cites Yockey, at the 1949 inaugural meeting of the European Liberation Front, urging the formation of a partisan organization in West Germany that would act against the "Western Occupation Powers," in collaboration with the Soviet military authorities.[1] The cultural contamination from the American occupation was a greater danger to Europe than Soviet military occupation, and Yockey was to later consider the possibilities of a European-Russian symbiosis.

While Yockey suggests that historical laws indicated that within five years, Europe would either resist or "throw away" the opportunity, the latter occurred, and "Marshall Aid" for the rebuilding of Germany had replaced the Morgenthau Plan for the annihilation of Germany, as the United States presented itself as Europe's protector against the Soviet menace. The analo-

---

[1] FBI Memorandum, 100-25647, Passport and Visa Matters, November 24, 1953, p. 1.

gous situation today is America's role as "protector of the West" against the new "enemy," "Islamic terrorism." We might therefore now understand why Europe acquiesced in the aftermath of the Second World War to the domination of New York, Hollywood, and Washington, just as the present generation acquiesces to American hegemony.

It is of note that Yockey was writing in 1950, when the Morgenthau Plan for the extermination of Germans was still in effect.[2] There was reason to believe that unless Germany resisted, a large proportion of the German folk would literally starve to death in a calculated genocide hatched in Washington, had this policy not been reversed with the Marshall Plan to reconstruct Europe, including Germany.

An additional factor in blocking Yockey's vision of a regenerated and united Europe was that Europe did unite, but under the terms and ideology of the "outer enemy," along Masonic and plutocratic lines;[3] what might be called "Anti-Europe," as it per-

---

[2] See James Bacque, *Crimes & Mercies: The Fate of German Civilians under Allied Occupation, 1944–1950* (London: Little Brown & Co., 1997).

[3] See Dr. Marian Mihaila, "European Union and Freemasonry," *Masonic Forum*, web.archive.org/web/20080323071233/http://www.masonicforum.ro/en/nr27/european.html; and Dr. Corneliu Zeana, "The European Union—A Masonic Accomplishment," *Masonic Forum*, web.archive.org/web/20091022120219/http://www.masonicforum.ro/en/nr20/zeana.html.

Count Richard Coudenhove-Kalergi, acknowledged by the European Union as its ideological father, was backed by the Rothschilds and Warburgs. In his book, *An Ideal Conquers the World* (London: Hutchinson, 1953), Coudenhove-Kalergi stated regarding this:

> Early in 1924 Baron Louis Rothschild telephoned to say that a friend of his, Max Warburg, had read my book and wanted to meet me. To my great astonishment Warburg immediately offered a donation of 60,000 gold marks to see the movement through its first three years. Max Warburg was a staunch supporter of Pan-Europe all his life and we remained close friends until his death in 1946. His readiness to support it (the movement) at the outset contributed decisively to its subsequent success. (p. 99)

sists today. The Destiny that Yockey saw for Europe five years hence was thus aborted, in favor of a *counterfeit* "Europe."

The 1953 note on intellectualism demarcates the outlooks between Western Destiny Thinkers and modern academia. The latter has limited horizons caught in the *Zeitgeist* of nineteenth-century materialism. "Scholarship" is weighed as a set of figures and calculations, as a merchant would count his money. There is no "feeling" for history, which would be regarded as lacking empiricism, and therefore little understanding of the extra-material forces from which history unfolds.

THOUGHTS, DISTILLED FROM A MEMORANDUM WRITTEN IN JUNE 1950

The world-situation of the moment takes the form of war-preparations between the two remaining powers. Such a war would be a great war, and would be begun with corresponding caution. No "incident" in Berlin, Trieste, or elsewhere could precipitate such a war.

It is obvious that neither power is prepared. Preparation means something quite different to both powers. To Russia it means a much higher state of **technical** organization, for America's sole advantage *vis-à-vis* Russia is the technical one. To America it means possession of vast masses of infantry.[4] Both powers will need years of preparation. I do not mean absolute preparation, for that never exists, but only the feeling of preparedness.

The stake of the war will be possession of the soil of Europe, the center of the world.

Russia can win only with higher technical development; America only with infantry-masses far greater than it alone can raise.

---

[4] The United States eventually solved this problem of superior Soviet manpower by resorting to the construction of a massive nuclear arsenal to counteract the threat of Soviet aggression in Europe, forcing Moscow to follow suit. This led to the largest, most expensive, and riskiest arms race to have occurred in the history of the world thus far.

To urge a crusade against Moscow, Bolshevism simply plays into the hands of the Washington regime.

Imperialism now supplants the older word, fascism. Fascism was still infused with petty-stateism to a greater or lesser degree.

The enemy is organized **internationally** on all levels. For us to fail so to organize is to insure that our several struggles, however gallant and heroic, will be severally doomed. It is simply the reign of terror in Europe that keeps Europeans out of active politics and in their homes.

By the ordinary cycles governing such things, it can be known that in about five years, approximately 1955, the initiative will pass to us, for us to exploit, or to throw away.

OCTOBER 1953

All of the intellectuals and critics who have read Spengler almost without exception have misunderstood him. They missed that highly important sentence: "What I have written here is *true*, that is, true for me and for the leading minds of the time to come."[5] These scholarly idiots all put the question to themselves: Is this philosophy **true**? Naturally, in an age of criticism, nothing is considered objectively true, as all the scholars, again almost without exception, rejected Spengler, although all borrowed his method and his terminology and conclusions in great part to reach philosophical conclusions in perfect harmony with the Pollyanna spirit of 1900.[6]

Anyone in the XXth century who thinks that a philosophy is objectively true or objectively false is an anachronism, and an idiot. A belief is true if it makes me more efficient, more dangerous, more coordinated. In this sense Spengler is *true*—his phi-

---

[5] The exact quotation reads: "I can then call the essence of what I have discovered 'true'—that is, true for me, and as I believe, true for the leading minds of the coming time; not true in itself as dissociated from the conditions imposed by blood and by history, for that is impossible" (*The Decline of the West*, vol. I, p. xiii).

[6] Derived from the name of the main character in a series of children's books from the early twentieth century, Pollyanna refers to someone with an extremely optimistic attitude.

losophy corresponds to our deepest metaphysical instinct, makes us thus harmonious in feeling and in deed and in word.

The scholar-idiots demonstrated also in their senseless fault-finding with Spengler their total incompetence in the aesthetic realm: a philosophy is a *picture*—here again, Spengler said it for them, but this they did not read, and if a picture is a *whole,* if it *lives,* if it *works creatively* on the observer, it is aesthetically *true*. It does not matter whether in the foreground the shadows fall right and left in the background.

We live in an age when mental refinement, like everything else rare and beautiful, has apparently died out. The statesmen are miserable self-seekers, almost without exception, the so-called thinkers are merely erudite mouthpieces of the party-politician, the scientists are fakirs who change their theories every few years, there are no religionists, no artists, no universal minds here.

THE DEATH OF ENGLAND

1951

EDITORS' NOTE

This is the second part of an essay, "The Death of England," the first part of which had been published in *Frontfighter*, no. 12. Here, Yockey calls for the end of petty English nationalism and exhorts the English to see themselves as Europeans and England as an integral part of Europe. This second part was published in *Frontfighter*, no. 13, June 1951.

The intent of the essay is, firstly, to refute the old rivalries, especially aggravated by the World War, between European states, including England. All of these states in the post-war era were being run by those serving alien interests, whether in Germany, France, Italy, or England. It was outer forces that had created the war against Europe, not Englishmen or Frenchmen. Nowadays, Italy and Germany are just as much in thrall to these outer forces as were and are England and France. The European elite must be a unified body in resisting the outer forces for the common Idea of Europe, and not merely committed to the aggrandizement of one state.

Secondly, Yockey insists it is not Russia that poses the greater threat to Europe, but America, a theme he continued to develop for the rest of his life. An anti-Soviet policy was merely playing into the hands of America and maintaining its alien domination. America is the common enemy against which the entirety of Europe must unite to expel it. This is a position that was adopted by the most advanced thinkers in Italy and Germany, where the ELF considered its major allies to be. Indeed, this same issue of *Frontfighter* (reproduced in an appendix) celebrates the electoral victories of the Italian Social Movement and the Socialist Reich Party, the latter soon to be banned exactly because of its quick successes. Yockey's book, *The Enemy of Europe*, which he regarded as the third volume of *Imperium*, developed these ideas in detail, in particular for the leadership of the Socialist Reich Party.

However, the German translation, *Der Feind Europas,* was quickly suppressed by the German authorities. It had to wait several decades before being published, and then only in an English-language edition in the United States, first serialized by the magazine *TRUD,* and then finally as a book produced by Liberty Bell Publications. It has remained in print to this day. In the following second part of Yockey's essay, these ideas are presented in a broad and straightforward outline.

POLICY TOWARD THE ISLAND

(Continued from "The Death of England" in issue no. 12.)

It is necessary to formulate a clear and definite policy in the minds of members of the European elite, both on the mainland and in the island.

Once it is realized that the so-called "government" of England is no more "English" than the bidault regime[1] is "French" or the sforza regime[2] is "Italian," or the adenauer regime[3] is

---

[1] Georges Bidault (1899–1983), a veteran of the French Resistance, served briefly as the President of the Provisional Government of France for four months in 1946, and as Prime Minister for two months in 1946 and for eight months in 1949–50. At the time Yockey was writing, he was Defense Minister and advocated for the Marshall Plan and France's participation in a strategic alliance with the United States. In the 1950s, he supported France's retention of its colonies in Vietnam and Algeria. In 1962, he was accused of conspiracy with the Secret Army Organization, a subversive movement which sought to prevent Algerian independence at all cost, and was discredited, although he always denied being a member of the group. He was also briefly a member of the Front National during its founding in October 1972.

[2] Carlo Sforza (1872–1952) was an Italian anti-fascist politician who served as Italy's Foreign Minister from 1947 until 1951, and was a supporter of the Marshall Plan and of Italy's strategic alliance with the United States.

[3] Konrad Adenauer (1876–1967) was the first Chancellor of West Germany, from 1949 until 1963. Yockey most likely disliked him for his opposition to National Socialism and Prussianism, as well as the

"German," it follows clearly that the enemy of Europe is the alien power which maintains all these puppet regimes in order to keep Europe in subjection; to thwart its destiny; and to strangle the great XXth century Idea of the creation of Europe and the Resurgence of Authority.

It is *America* which controls ninety percent of Europe: the other ten percent is controlled by Russia. No part of Europe is controlled by any other force. It is *America* which by its war-time assistance to Russia created the present Russian empire; it is *America* which delivered some thirty million Germans to the Bolshevik fury of Russia, Czechia, and Poland; it is *America* which destroyed the German-Italo-French State structure which promised the flowering of the XXth century European Idea; it is *America* which destroyed the English Empire and reduced the forty-nine million inhabitants of the island to beggarly dependence on Washington.

In all those occurrences *England* played not the slightest role. It is true that America found English tools: churchills, edens,[4] and attlees[5] to enforce its policy—traitors to Europe.

But America also found sforzas and gasperis,[6] adenauers and heusses,[7] bidaults and de gaulles for its work. But traitors to Europe are not Europeans, and traitors to England and Europe, like Churchill and Attlee, are neither Englishmen nor Europeans.

---

fact that he sought closer ties between West Germany and the Western Allies, and accepted the division of Germany imposed by them.

[4] Anthony Eden (1897–1977) was Foreign Minister of the United Kingdom on three occasions, the last being from 1951 to 1955.

[5] Clement Attlee (1883–1967) was Labour Party Prime Minister of the United Kingdom from 1945 to 1951. He strongly supported the Marshall Plan.

[6] Alcide De Gasperi (1881–1954) was Prime Minister of Italy from 1945 until 1953. He probably earned Yockey's ire for being an anti-Fascist, as well as for being supported by America, which regarded him as a bulwark against Communism, and indeed he took loans on Italy's behalf from the US government to bolster his popularity against them.

[7] Theodor Heuss (1884–1963) was the first President of West Germany, from 1949 until 1959.

The population of the island is no longer English, but simply undifferentiated European. English nationalism is actually weaker today than German or Italian nationalism. The elite of the island is as ready as the rest of the European elite for the Idea of *Europe*. The Fascist possibilities of this population are considerable and are only beginning to be exploited by the Liberation Front in England.

The policy which emanates from London, like that from Rome, or Bonn, or Paris, is simply a reflection of American policy. Let us not attack phantoms, let us attack the *real* enemy of Europe: *America*. The spiritual union of Europe begins in our own minds. The entire European elite everywhere, on island and mainland, must unlearn the old habits of nationalistic and petty-state thinking and must begin to think of itself as undifferentiated European.

Only thus will Europe be born.

Ulick Varange

America's Two Ways of Waging War

1951

Editors' Note

Around late 1951, Yockey was approached by a member of Senator Joseph McCarthy's staff and was asked to write a speech for the Senator. Yockey himself stated of this:

> I called on Patterson, who arranged an appointment for me with Senator McCarthy for Saturday P.M. He wanted me to write a speech for him, based on a whole batch, a huge corpus of material, to have it ready by Monday. There are still several things to settle with him but it looks as though I have a job. Really quite unbelievable that it should be this particular job.[1]

An examination of the text of the speech makes it readily apparent that Yockey was indeed the author. This is evident by such phrases as describing Western Civilization as a "superpersonal force," references to the "inner enemy" and the "divine plan," and the use of lower case when writing the names of "acheson" and "marshall"—a Yockeyism used in several of his other writings. Indeed, the paragraph halfway through the speech, where the "divine plan" is discussed, is essentially a simplified rendering of Yockey's philosophy.

One of Yockey's primary English supporters, John Anthony Gannon, confirmed that Yockey definitely met McCarthy.[2] Gannon said that Yockey had a "considerable relationship" with McCarthy, "and found him to be well-informed on the Culture-

---

[1] Letter by Yockey dated February 5, 1952, cited by Keith Stimely in a letter to John Anthony Gannon, "More Questions on Francis Parker Yockey," no. 10, ca. December 1981.

[2] Letter from Gannon to Stimely, March 31, 1982.

distorters issue." Yockey also had "some considerable respect" for Richard Nixon's abilities in regard to his role in exposing State Department eminence, Alger Hiss, as a Soviet agent (albeit one who seemed to have most of his mentors among Washington's upper echelons). Yockey felt that the "Culture-distorters" would never forgive Nixon for ending the meteoric career of Hiss, "which they never did."[3]

The association between Yockey and McCarthy drew the attention of the FBI. However, they regarded this speech as the work of McCarthy, and they did not know the precise character of their association. But the style is certainly Yockey's. McCarthy did not end up delivering the speech due to another engagement.

While the speech was never used, and perhaps never even seen by McCarthy himself, it is notable that Yockey's theme was later taken up as a major theme by the conservative movement when describing the Vietnam War as a "no-win war" being fought for the United Nations. And indeed, in relation to the Korean War, General Douglas MacArthur was removed from his command of the American forces in Korea because of his deter-

---

[3] Gannon to Stimely, February 15, 1982. Despite the pervasive presence of Henry Kissinger, Nixon probably formed his attitude regarding Jews at an early stage of his political career, when they were conspicuous among Soviet agents and in the Communist Party. However, by the time he was President and working for US-Soviet détente, Jews had become vociferously anti-Soviet, especially in agitating for increased Jewish emigration from the USSR to the US and Israel. Nixon commented to Kissinger that if Jews sabotaged his efforts, he would publicly expose them: "Let me say, Henry, it's gonna be the worst thing that happened to Jews in American history. I won't mind one goddamn but to have a little anti-Semitism if it's on that issue. They put the Jewish interest above America's interest, and it's about goddamn time that the Jew in America realizes he's an American first and a Jew second." Nixon to Kissinger, Oval Office tapes, April 19, 1973. Of Nixon aide Leonard Garment: "Goddamn his Jewish soul!" On appointments: "No Jews. We are adamant when I say no Jews." Nixon to presidential counselor Anne Armstrong, June 14, 1973. See Elspeth Reeve, "Some Newly Uncovered Nixon Comments on the Subjects of Jews and Black People," *The Atlantic*, August 21, 2013.

mination to press on to victory over Communism, including in China. This likewise became a major point of contention for certain other military figures such as Major Arch E. Roberts, whose 1966 book, *Victory Denied,* became a primary text on the subject. And yet another intriguing fact is that McCarthy himself developed these themes that same year in his 1951 book attacking General Marshall, *America's Retreat from Victory: The Story of George Catlett Marshall.* But there should be no doubt that this present speech is Yockey's work, not McCarthy's.

The FBI knew that Yockey had been employed to ghost-write for McCarthy by Perry Patterson, legal counsel to the conservative-oriented *Washington Times Herald* and a friend of Yockey's from his law school days,[4] and Kevin Coogan cites correspondence that Yockey had himself sent to the FBI regarding his employment.[5] Why the FBI was so ill-informed about the authorship of this speech, only a year later, is therefore perplexing.

However, Coogan also cites evidence that Yockey had been in contact with Senator McCarthy as early as 1948–49, soon after Yockey went to England, when McCarthy was involved in the plight of German prisoners-of-war,[6] who were being tortured to extract confessions in relation to the "Malmedy Massacre."

Yockey "approved" of senators Robert Taft, an old-time American isolationist, and McCarthy, "with the usual reservations." He regarded McCarthy as a "shoot-to-kill" politician. Although after the war Yockey had given up hope of an "American nationalist revolution," many on the radical Right saw McCarthy as a figure around which an American nationalist revival might occur. McCarthy, even before his famous Senate investigations into Communist and Soviet subversion and espionage, had made a name among nationalists for his forceful criticism of the American-run war crimes trials in Germany in 1949.

What is especially of note about the speech is Yockey's placement of America within the context of Western Civilization, having McCarthy state—at least hypothetically—his

---

[4] Letter from Stimely to Gannon, February 28, 1982.

[5] Coogan, *Dreamer of the Day,* pp. 238–39.

[6] Ibid., p. 240. Coogan cites John Anthony Gannon as his source.

commitment to the "future of the Western Civilization, of which America is an integral part," and to sharing that Civilization's "great world mission."

It seems that the speech was intended to be used by McCarthy at a meeting in Yorkville, New York, which was also to be addressed by German-American conservative luminaries such as Dr. Austin App, and to appeal primarily to German-Americans.[7] Hence the focus by Yockey in the speech on contrasting the attitude of the American regime towards fighting Germans with fighting Asiatic Communists. After intense pressure from the media, however, McCarthy withdrew in favor of another engagement.

Yockey was *not* primarily an "American patriot." His first loyalty was to the Destiny of Western Civilization and to the Mother-soil of Europe, to the point of later advocating collaboration with the Soviet Union against the American occupation of Europe. It seems reasonable to conclude that, within the broader context of Yockey's thought, he would seek out possibilities within the mass movement behind Senator McCarthy and General MacArthur that might set up a reaction against the inner and outer enemies of America which could eventually be identified as something other than merely Communism.

However, McCarthy was soon destroyed by the "inner enemy"—not by "Communists" or "Soviet agents," but by those representing the wealthiest and most powerful interests led by the likes of international banker Herbert Lehman in the Senate, *The Washington Post*, the Anti-Defamation League, Goldman Sachs banker Sidney Weinberg's Business Advisory Council, and others.[8]

AMERICA'S TWO WAYS OF WAGING WAR

My fellow Americans:

Our meeting here tonight is symbolic—symbolic for a deep

---

[7] Ibid., p. 243.

[8] K. R. Bolton, "Joe McCarthy's Real Enemies," *The Occidental Quarterly*, vol. 10, no. 4, Winter 2010–2011, pp. 75–102.

and wide unrest now going through the American people. This growing unrest arises from an awareness throughout all of our people that somehow, somewhere, **something is wrong.** It does not fall to everyone to devote his life to the service of his people, but it is the duty of him who has made this decision to represent—truly to represent, in the most spiritual sense of that word—his nation. It is for him to actualize the innermost feelings of the national soul; it is for him to make clear and articulate that which everyone dimly feels. It is his duty, because he is himself only the voice of his nation and his people.

Therefore, I am not going to burden you with purely personal ideas—I am only going to answer the question in your minds and hearts: **what is wrong in our land?** Nor will I use the alien terminology of the Marxists, whether from Moscow or Washington. Our enemies like to use involved and complicated explanations [for] why their policy abroad is necessary, why America must continually retreat before advancing Communism, why American blood must be spilt in a war in which American victory on the battlefield is forbidden by the American government. But I will use only your language, which is my language; when I mean war, I shall say war, when I mean peace, I shall call it that, and when I mean treason, I shall say treason.

Have you ever noticed that the Truman-Acheson regime says war when it means peace, and says peace when it means war? In Korea, tonight, American blood is being spilt in defeat and Americans are dying in cold, in isolation, in despair. What does the Washington regime say to this? It says: "By our clever diplomacy we are preventing the Third World War." Fellow Americans, they lie! Korea **is** the Third World War, and our rulers are leading America to a defeat in that war!

It is a shocking thing to say, and to contemplate, is it not? To think that men, entrusted before God and the world with the conduct of America's destiny would coldly and deliberately prefer the interests of America's enemy to the interests of this American nation. Because of the enormity of this crime, most of us hesitate even to think of such an explanation of events, and we only realize it with the greatest reluctance, when every other explanation is excluded.

As an American who has watched the steady descent of his country from its high point of 1945, when the human affairs of nine-tenths of this Earth were under the control of America, as an American who has felt himself humiliated as he has watched his country's humiliation at the hands of the Communist Barbarians of Moscow, as a veteran of America's armed forces who is forced every day to read in the press a new list of hopeless American casualties, I have no joy in recounting to you the vicious story of treason in our country. It gives me no pleasure to tell you things which ought never have happened within our land. But, regardless of everything else, my first duty is to tell you the truth—and in particular that very truth which the Washington regime is so intent upon concealing.

I would like to think, as would you also, that the explanation of America's continuous and endless succession of defeats and humiliations, America's progressive loss of power in the world, is simple incompetence on the part of the Executive branch of the government. Perhaps these people simply do not know how to seek and acquire allies, perhaps they do not understand how to strike salutary fear into the hearts of the Kremlin barbarians as they proceed on their self-appointed task of the conquest of the world. Perhaps the Truman-Acheson regime would like to win in the present war with China, but they do not know [how] to manage a war.

This explanation could possibly be accepted if we did not still have before us, present in the memory of every person in this meeting, the entire Second World War. In that War, the entire Communist faction in the Washington regime was wholeheartedly in favor of victory.

In this War, as we all know, the Communist faction desires an American defeat. Let us compare the two wars, and we shall see develop before us America's Two Ways of Waging War.

First of all, what was the objective of the Second World War? It was given to the world as **unconditional surrender**! They wanted total victory, and they said so. But what is the objective in the Chinese War now going on? In Acheson's words, it is "a just truce." Not even peace! Much less victory. No question of unconditional surrender. Marshall as Secretary of Defense visited the battlefront and there announced to the press that the American mission in Korea is "to prevent the enemy from coming below the 38th parallel." Did he make a similar announcement when America was fighting Germany and Italy? No, when he wanted victory, he said so, and he subscribed to the "Unconditional Surrender formula."

Next, during the present Chinese war, the whole regime in Washington says we must prevent the conflict from spreading, we must localize the conflict. What did they want in the Second World War? They wanted a continual extension of the front, continual involvement of other powers. They exerted every conceivable pressure to bring other powers in on their side. When they had two fronts, they wanted a third, when they had that, they wanted a fourth. They wanted to **win** that war.

Next, did they refuse any offers of troops in the Second World War? On the contrary, they used every pressure on neutrals to extract troops from them to use against Germany and Italy. But in the present war against Red China, they have refused Chiang Kai-shek's[9] standing offer of five hundred thousand combat-ready troops. Not only do they refuse his offer, but they have ordered the American Navy to blockade Chiang Kai-shek so that he cannot strike the Chinese Communists. Yes, tonight, as we meet here, the American Navy is protecting Red China.

On the same point, South Korea under Synghman Rhee, our ally in the war against Red China, does not even have conscription of its man-power to defend the soil of Korea, nor has the Truman-Acheson regime put any pressure on South Korea to raise more troops by conscription. Not like the Second World War, is it? Then, they sought to get troops even from neutrals. Now, they refuse troops, even from allies. The difference is, that

---

[9] Chiang Kai-shek (1887–1975) was the nationalist President of the Republic of China from 1928 until his death. He fought alongside the Allies against the Japanese in the Second World War, and also against the Communists. When the Communists took control of China in 1949, Kai-shek retreated to Taiwan, where he continued to rule as the President of the Republic of China until his death.

they wanted to *win* that war. You see, Russia and the Communist faction also wanted victory in that war.

Next, when the Second World War was finally brought about by the ultimatum to Japan which precipitated the Pearl Harbor attack, every cabinet minister was loud and positive about his support for the war. But when the war in Korea started, Secretary of State Acheson could not even be prevailed upon by the press to make a statement for several days. American troops were ordered to resist the Red onslaught only through channels of military command, and Acheson was not in on it. Then, as now, he was thinking only of ways to stop the war, to stop the resistance against Communism. The reaction of George Marshall, the Defense Secretary, to the war in Korea was similarly lukewarm. No fire breathed from him, no talk of **unconditional surrender**, no talk of victory. He knew how to work for victory in the Second World War, but in the war which began in Korea in June 1950, George Marshall and his entire faction did not talk about victory.

Perhaps the reason that Marshall and Acheson are lukewarm about fighting Red China is that they themselves called this political monster into being. In June 1946, the Marshall-Acheson group even sought in Congressional sanction to send an American military mission to train and equip the Chinese Red Army, whose only enemy then was the Chinese government of Chiang Kai-shek, the ally of the United States. Think of it, American officials daring to advocate the arming, training, and equipping of Communist armies against America's allies, and thus against America. If Marshall had been so stupid as to do such a thing unawares of the treasonable nature of his activity, he never would have had sufficient intelligence to graduate from military school. If Acheson had been that stupid, he could never have entered the Bar Association.

Let us compare further the conduct of the Second World War, in which Russia and the Communist faction in Washington wanted victory, with the Third World War, in which Russia and the Communist faction in Washington want defeat of American arms.

In the present war against China, tourist traffic is still permitted to the Far East, including Japan, the staging area of our Far Eastern forces. Was tourist traffic permitted on the oceans during the Second World War? Of course not, for every cubic foot of space was required for war transportation. You see, they wanted to win that war.

In every war mistakes occur, and they occurred in the Second World War. More than once, American land forces and American air forces fired upon one another. More than once, American field headquarters were bombed by American planes. But these incidents were not magnified out of all proportion and spread across the land in great headlines. But, remember the scandal that was created out of the incident in Korea in the winter of 1950 when certain American units did not receive their proper winter clothing? It is the operation of the Communist faction in press and government which resolves this riddle. In the Second World War, they wanted no military scandals to undermine public confidence in the command, to damage public morale. In the current war, the exact opposite is true. They *want* scandal which will break down public confidence and morale, which will lay the groundwork for defeat.

Next, remember how the press, in the Second World War, continually told us of the imminent defeat of Germany, Italy, and Japan? We were told every day—it won't be long now, our victory is assured, we only need keep up the fight a little longer. Now what is the line, now that we are fighting Communism and Red armies? Now we learn that the war would be endless if it were extended, that we can never gain victory over the enemy, that Russia is getting stronger day by day, that Russian plane production exceeds ours, that their planes and tanks are better, their man-power is greater, that the best we can hope for is to pay them tribute to let us live in peace.

Do you see how the pattern emerges, in unmistakable clarity, in utter simplicity? No wonder the inner enemy wants us to be confused by a thousand viewpoints, distracted by scandals, and twisted into knots by his perverted explanations of his treasonable diplomacy. All you need to do is sort out the facts, and the big issue is there: in its stark greatness, it dominates the entire American political landscape. Involved in this issue is the entire future of our land, our nation, our people. Either we meet this challenge, or our nation and everything that has ever been known in world history by the name America will go down into permanent darkness.

Fellow Americans, look once more at the Second World War, the war against Germany. In selecting the leadership for that war, political and military, did our rulers select men with pro-German backgrounds, with a long record of affiliation with Germany, men who had dealt publicity and privately with Germany's leadership? On the contrary, any such persons were purged at once from positions of leadership, and only pronounced anti-Germans were entrusted with conduct of the war against Germany. Regard now the present war against Red China, especially the moment of its beginning: in their theory, who are the participants in the war? The United Nations on the one side, the Republic of North Korea on the other. But who is entrusted with the conduct of the war, in theory? The Security Council of the United Nations—and in June 1950, at the beginning of the Korean War, this organ was presided over by a Russian delegate, the personal representative of Stalin. Here then we had American armies fighting under the command of an alien organization called the United Nations, and under the theoretical command of its Security Council presided over by the enemy. When we fought Germany, were we ever a member of an alliance which embraced Germany, and presided over by a German representative?

Look for a moment at these men who are leading, or who have led, the American war effort against Red China. There is Truman, whose pet name for Stalin is good old Joe, the man who played the piano for Stalin at Potsdam, even as he was giving him half a world. Look at Acheson, the leader of the pro-Russian clique during the entire Second World War, the member of a law firm which has represented Communist interests for twenty long years, the co-architect, with Marshall, of the Red Chinese State with which we are now at war, the bitter opponent of General MacArthur, whose first offense was that he refused to kowtow to Russia in the Far East. Look at Marshall, the man, who as Chief of Staff of a great world-power in a time of crisis did not remember where he was on the morning of the Pearl Harbor attack, the man who continually during the Second World War sacrificed the needs of MacArthur's command in the Pacific to Russian needs in Europe, the man who undertook the mission to destroy the state of Chiang Kai-shek, the firm ally of America, the man who gave decisive aid to the Chinese Reds in the Civil War and thus at one stroke lost one-quarter of the world to Russia, the man who has had private conversations with Stalin, and has not thought it necessary to tell the American people what was discussed in those secret conversations. In the Second World War, they did not choose men of backgrounds friendly to Germany and Germany's leadership to carry on the war, but for the Third World War against Russian-directed Communism, the crusaders to lead it are men who have been distinguished by pro-Russian activity.

A hollow and stinking crusade! A crusade in a vacuum! A crusade which does not want to win!

Look again at the United Nations: the Secretary-General of this—should I say—organization, is a man named, most appropriately, Lie, spelled L-I-E.[10] This man was nominated for his position by Russia and he has continued during his tenure of office to merit the confidence of the Russians. His mission there is to see that Russian interests are not damaged, and he visits the Kremlin from time to time to report and consult.

Yet this is the organization under whose artificial flag American blood is being daily spilt, spilt heroically as far as the individuals are concerned, spilt in defeat as far as American national interests are concerned. When the American Navy bombards the enemy coast of Korea, the United Nations flag is run up, and American land forces fly this alien flag over their headquarters. Compare it with the Second World War. Were American soldiers told they were fighting for some abstraction, some League of Nations or other? No, because every leader knows that his nation will only give its best and sacrifice the most in the name

---

[10] Trygve Lie (1896–1968) was a Norwegian politician from the Labor Party. He was the first Secretary General of the United Nations, from 1946 until 1952.

of its own nation, a living, breathing reality, and in the sign of the symbols of that nation, clothed with its history, drenched by its blood, bound up with its honor. In the Second World War, they wanted victory, so they used the American flag, which has always been attended with victory. In the present war against Communism, they want a defeat of American arms, so they use an abstract flag representing nothing more than an office building in New York, the second League of Nations, doomed, as we all know, to go the way of the first League of Nations.

During the Second World War, against Germany, no part of the press, and no one in the government, spoke of a truce, or of a peace. It was treated as quite self-evident that whoever sought peace was approaching treason. Now, however, when we are fighting against world-Communism, our rulers talk of a "just truce," whatever that is.

When the Red enemy finally consented to enter into truce talks—for his own purposes—he stipulated that the American delegates approach the conference through a gauntlet of Red bayonets, and carrying the white flag. This vile and dishonorable sight was then photographed and spread over all Asia as the sign of America's surrender to Asiatic Reds. The illiterates of Mongolia, Burma, and India, to whom a newspaper means nothing, nevertheless understand the language of pictures, and know the meaning of the white flag. Why was this abject and vile performance kept from the American people? Compare it with the Second World War: did anyone ever suggest going to the Germans with white flags? If he had, the Democratic administration would have prosecuted him for treason.

Another point: do you remember those first months of the war in Korea, when the only enemy in the field was the North Korean Red Army? During that period, the entire American press, and members of the administration prompted them, continually spoke of the possible intervention of China in the war. It was treated as natural and normal that China would intervene against us, and no measures were contemplated, suggested, or discussed to prevent that intervention. Was there anything like this in the Second World War? Was it not treated as self-evident that if anyone entered the war it would be on our side? After all,

Red China was created by the Truman-Acheson administration, and Marshall was the mid-wife who delivered this monster into life. No, the threatened intervention of China—not threatened by China, but by the Washington regime and by the Communist faction in the American press—was used as a further reason for inculcating defeatism, and for mollifying America's conduct of the war.

Where in all this clear pattern of events do we now find any ambiguity? How could mere stupidity, however gross, account for this systematic and continuing anti-American conduct? Look at the picture: American troops are in the field, they are fighting for their lives against huge odds, dependent for their bare survival upon their technical superiority in weapons and transport, dependent for their victory upon that same superiority. These American troops are armed—thank God for the technical superiority of the Western Civilization!—with atomic weapons against which the Red Chinese enemy cannot retaliate. This superior weapon, which brought about [the] surrender of the Japanese Empire within a week of its employment, is held back by our rulers. Did they hold back any weapon in the Second World War?

What reason do they give for this refusal to exploit every possible means to give victory to American arms, power to America, and life to American soldiers who tomorrow may be dead in this treasonable war in which victory is **forbidden**? They say: "We don't want to anger the enemy, or the neutrals, like the pro-Communist Nehru.[11] We don't, above all, want to spread the war, because Russia might intervene, and then, naturally, we would lose." Did they refrain form the mass-bombing of German and Japanese cities because it might make anybody angry? They would have pushed anyone aside who didn't like it. They were determined on victory and unconditional surrender, and they were prepared to use any amount and any form of armed

[11] Jawaharlal Nehru (1889–1964) was the first Prime Minister of India following its independence from Britain. Although officially non-aligned, India had a closer relationship with the Soviet Union throughout the Cold War.

force against anybody whatsoever to achieve their purpose. From the beginning Nehru has been the spokesman for Red Chinese interests, so in that quarter we have no sympathy and no neutrality to lose. As to the argument about Russia: it is a crass and vile lie that Russia could defeat the United States in a military contest, and those in high places who say it know that it is a lie. If they believed it, they would be cowards, but they are worse than cowards, they are liars, using their lies to support their treason.

I am not yet finished with this matter of the atomic bomb. Fellow Americans, God made this world as it is, and in its ever-recurring forms we dimly perceive his divine plan. World-history, in which America is now caught up, involved for its very life in the tempest of events, is the history of **nations**. The units of history are **nations**. Those individuals who lead those nations owe their primary duty to that nation whose destiny God has placed temporarily in their hands. It is not allowed to a ruler to sacrifice his people on the battlefield to abstract aims like United Nations of some kind or other, like humanitarian principles of one kind or another—it is the duty of every government of every form to serve the national interest, and no government has the right to expend one single soldier for any other purpose.

It is thus the **duty** of the American military high command—and Truman, with Acheson hovering over him, is the supreme commander-in-chief—to bring victory to American arms in order to save American lives. In that duty, every reasonable means of achieving victory must be pursued, including the use of atomic weapons to the utmost.

Six years ago, to justify the atomic bombardment of Japan, did not Truman officially state that it was done to terminate the war quickly and thus save American lives? His reason was sound then—why is it not sound today?

It is not sound today, to the minds of the Truman-Acheson regime, because the aim of the present war against Red China is *not* victory, it is *not* unconditional surrender, it is *not* to save American lives. Six years ago this regime knew how to fight—can we believe that today it no longer knows how to fight? Would Truman, Acheson, and the entire Communist faction dare to appear on this platform and answer the questions of this audience here tonight?

Fellow Americans, I say to you now, and beyond this audience I say it to the entire American people and nation, and I say it with every ounce of seriousness and purpose I possess: the war in which America is now engaged is being waged not for American victory, but for Communist victory, and these in America who are ultimately responsible for the conduct of this war are guilty of black, damnable treason.

Think of the Second World War on the question of prisoners-of-war: if any American legal officer had announced that Germany had killed five thousand American prisoners-of-war, would he not have had a favorable and continuous press, would not the high command have given him every assistance in his task of investigation and proof?

We know they would. Yet how was it when Col. James Hanley, the Judge Advocate of the Army in Korea, announced that he had proof of Communist slaughter of five thousand American war-prisoners?[12] He was immediately summoned to Tokyo for discipline. The Command in Tokyo stated that he should have made his announcement under their conditions, that he was injuring their plans by exposing Communist atrocities at that particular time. It was given a poor press, and Truman's reaction to it was "*If it is true,* it is the worst thing that had happened in the century." Note that "If it is true—." It prepares the public to disbelieve it, to greet this American officer's statement with suspicion, to wait and see. Editorials in the American press, slipped in by members of the Communist faction, counseled the public not to get excited, to wait and see—in other words: wait and *forget*. And up to now, what has been done about this massacre of American soldiers, surrendered and disarmed? Abso-

[12] James Martin Hanley, Jr. (1904–1999) was Judge Advocate of the US Eighth Army during the Korean War. He publicized a report in November 1951 which stated that the executions had taken place during the Eighth Army's strategic withdrawal from northeast Korea, and that soldiers of other nationalities had been massacred as well. He testified regarding the atrocities before a Congressional Committee headed by McCarthy in 1953.

lutely nothing. The Communist enemy has in no way been deterred from future massacres.

And yet, my friends, I know what Washington, Hamilton, or Andrew Jackson would have done.

During the Second World War, the Washington regime was not faced with a great problem of an inner enemy. Nevertheless, it interned and uprooted all the Japanese on the West Coast and numerous German-born men and women all over the land. The vast majority of all internees were American citizens, but nobody worried much about their "civil liberties."

During the present war with Red China, however, everything is different. The inner enemy is numerous, highly organized, thoroughly indoctrinated, with a literature of class war, proletarian dictatorship, and world conquest going back a century. At the very narrowest, the inner enemy includes the Communist Party and affiliated organizations; more realistically it includes also the Communist sympathizers and backers of Communist-front organizations, many of whom are in high positions in the Executive, Legislative, and Judicial branches of the Federal and State governments. Although we are in a state of actual war with Communism, with Red China backed by Red Russia, no measures have been taken against the dangerous and powerful inner enemy, who is actually in a position, as every day's news tells us, to destroy the American war effort and kill American soldiers on the battlefield from behind.

One feeble measure was attempted: an "anti-Communist bill" was passed by Congress, over the powerful opposition of the Executive branch of the government, requiring all Communists to register. Truman vetoed this anti-Communist bill, and it was passed over his veto. When it went into effect, however, all Communists publicly and openly defied its provisions, and refused to register. Nothing was done to them, because the whole bill was drafted in such a way that it could not be enforced because of [the] vagueness of its provisions, and because there was no penal sanction to the measure. Was this an accident?

Why was it impossible to draft a real anti-Communist law?

Did they proceed this way during the Second World War against Germans and Japanese?

Think again of the Second World War: were American troops, in the presence of the enemy, and without a truce being in effect, ever ordered to cease their fire? And yet this happened not three months since, in Korea. Company units, in the face of the enemy, received an order of which press correspondents there on the spot were informed, to refrain from firing on the enemy, except in self-defense. The order, once given, attributed to the "highest sources of command," was suddenly revoked and its very issuance was denied, as a result of the strong reaction of the American nation to this unbelievable scandal.

Is there anyone so blind that this glaring Red light does not illuminate the American political scene for him?

Look at the list of Communist spies: Eisler, Hiss, Coplon, Gubitchev, the Rosenbergs.[13] Not one of them has received a punishment commensurate with his crime and sufficient to deter others from engaging in espionage. Eisler was allowed to escape. Hiss was tried on a charge minor in comparison to his real offense of espionage and given a short term from which he will soon be free. Coplon was released on a foolish technicality. Gubitchev was set free to go to Russia. The Rosenbergs were condemned to death on a charge of treason, but it was clear at the time and it is clear now that these spies are being protected: they will never receive the death penalty, and their case will be reversed on appeal.[14] Note what I say, and then observe your newspapers.

Was there ever an instance, in the Second World War, in which an American general, who had held the highest military commands within the power of his nation to confer on him, covered with the glories of his numerous victories, was removed from his command **because he wanted to win the war**? Of course there was not—the Washington regime wanted to win

---

[13] Gerhardt Eisler (1897–1968), Alger Hiss (1904–1996), Judith Coplon (1921–2011), Valentin A. Gubitchev (dates unknown), Julius Rosenberg (1918–1953), and Ethel Rosenberg (1915–1953) were all spies for the USSR against the United States.

[14] The Rosenbergs were executed on June 19, 1953, but Judith Coplon's convictions were overturned on appeal.

that war, so it encouraged and honored victorious generals. But in the Third World War, in which we are now engaged, which we are daily losing, and in which every day we are faced with a new scandal, a new lie, a new treason—everything is different. General MacArthur was disgracefully removed from command, and his offense was *that he wanted to win the war.*

In very truth, America has two ways of waging war. One for victory, and one for defeat.

Fellow Americans, we have stood in the presence of some awful truths tonight, we have contemplated some terrible things, we have witnessed the foulest of all crimes, the crime of treason. We have looked into the form of events and the events have yielded up their mystery to us. Now that we know precisely what is wrong in our great land, what is our response?

It is one of the things for which we must be grateful that the Communist faction does not yet have sufficient power to prevent free elections, nor to stifle the public voice, nor prevent public organization in self-defense against the Communist advance within America. Twenty years ago, if anyone had foretold that in the time to come an American military commander would be dismissed for trying to bring victory to American arms, he would have been called a lunatic. Yet we have seen just that. If this pattern of events continues, twenty years from today the Communists will be embarking on their final mopping-up operations in their total destruction of everything that the idea [of] America has stood for in the history of nations. Perhaps they would have the assistance of barbarian troops from Russia, perhaps that would not be necessary. If Americans are nothing but peace-seeking slaves who will pay tribute for peace, who will pay ransom to an enemy who kidnaps American airmen, the destruction of America from within will be easy.

But that is not to be, and one proof of it is this very gathering here tonight.

Tonight I have been only your voice, saying what you feel and think. If these were only my personal thoughts, they would not be interesting, but these thoughts correspond to the feelings of the great mass of our people stretching from ocean to ocean, from the deserts of the Southwest to Maine's rocky coast. If that which has been said here were only my personal ideas, you would not have come, nor would I be here. When I went into public life, I did not enter it for my own advantage, and in public life I have always had the choice of saying the popular thing and getting praise from America's powerful enemies, or of saying the truthful thing and being smeared and calumniated by those enemies, enemies of America, of you, and therefore, of me.[15] They have invented a word, McCarthyism. A clever trick, they thought. The idea was to make everybody think that I am something unique, some sort of wild individualist, somebody all alone. Their trick has not worked. I give it the lie right now. There is no such thing as McCarthyism—what they mean is **Americanism.**

When I give voice to an idea which is not in accord with the entire spirit of America and its history, an idea which is not in furtherance of America's destiny, of America's power, prestige, and honor in the world—then, but not until then, will there be such a thing as McCarthyism. Up until that time—no matter what America's internal enemies chatter about, your enemies and mine—I shall speak only in the American spirit.

Part of the campaign of treason is defeatism: Russia is too strong for us, let us be careful, don't use our superior weapons, someone might not like it if we win, let's ransom our soldiers and be quiet about it, a new Communistic day has dawned in Asia, Communism means hope for the Asiatic masses. You have heard it all, and it has nauseated you.

I am not such a fool, nor such a contemptible coward to bring you any brand of defeatism. If I thought America were doomed to defeat and Communist extinction, I would still continue to fight to my last breath. But I don't believe in any such thing: I believe in the spiritual resources of this nation, I believe that far from being exhausted, they have scarcely been tapped. America has only written its first pages in history, and not its last. I believe in the future of the Western Civilization, of which America is an integral, organic part. I know, deep down inside me, that

---

[15] The text, from this point to the end of the following paragraph, is crossed out in the surviving copy.

the future belongs to us who are part of this Civilization and who share its great world mission.

I summon you, not to a Korea-type war in which to seek, and find, defeat, but to a war for victory. This, our immediate war, is not far beyond our shores, it is here, in our own land, against the inner enemy. How can we conscientiously ask an American soldier to fight a foreign enemy under the command of the Truman-Acheson regime which has been guilty of such monstrous conduct, whose members have been pro-Russian all of their lives, a regime which cannot possibly be trusted to lead a war against Communism, honeycombed with Communist sympathizers and agents as it is?

It is not a part of the divine plan that a great superpersonal force working for order and creativeness in the world, like the Western Civilization, is to be overcome by an onslaught of barbarians against an America weakened by corruption and betrayed by a horde of achesons.

The inner enemy, like the Red Chinese Armies in Korea, has not earned any of his victories. They have been presented to him by the marshalls and achesons. But America is coming back. We shall pull ourselves and our nation out of this swamp of treason, corruption, and disgust.

We shall liberate our land from the domination of traitors, and then, by the help of the Almighty God, we shall restore the word America to its old meaning in the world before all nations.

By the deluge of our votes, by the irresistible storm of our organized protest, we shall sweep America clear of its inner enemies and onward to its God-given Destiny.

Finis

AMERICA'S TWO POLITICAL FACTIONS

1952

EDITORS' NOTE

Yockey wrote this essay in 1952 under his *nom-de-plume*, Ulick Varange. It appeared in two parts in *Frontfighter*, the newsletter of the European Liberation Front, specifically issues no. 22 (March) and no. 23 (April), 1952. Only the second part has been preserved, while the extracts and comments from the first part are taken from an FBI analysis. The second part survives in a copy that was retyped by Keith Stimely from a photocopy of the issue.

Yockey here advocated a "neutralist" line in regard to the "Cold War," and states that neither the "Communist" (i.e., "Jewish") nor the "military" factions running the United States were friends of Europe.

The American intelligence services would have had particular interest in Yockey at this time, and in regard to these ideas, because there was widespread concern among the Allies of a resurgent German nationalism under the leadership of the war hero, Major General Otto Ernst Remer, and the Socialist Reich Party. Remer was also advocating a "neutralist" position for Germany.

An FBI report on Yockey dated November 24, 1953 alludes to Yockey's association with Remer and the Socialist Reich Party, and to Yockey being "anti-United States." The report also cites one of Yockey's key American contacts, Frederick C. F. Weiss, as possibly accepting funds from Soviet sources and as having rejected an anti-Soviet stance. The FBI report further cites Yockey as having advocated, even as early as 1949, an underground resistance movement in Germany which would collaborate with the Soviet Union to oppose the Allied occupation authorities.

In December 1952, only about half a year after writing

"America's Two Political Factions," Yockey attended the so-called "Treason Trial" in Prague, Czechoslovakia, which he regarded as the epochal turning point in Russia's total break with Jewish world hegemony. The Jewish and military factions were soon conjoined, and many from the "Jewish faction" who had pursued a Communist course became some of America's most avid champions of opposition to the USSR during the Cold War.

On the other hand, "neutralist" Third World regimes, such as that of Nehru's India, whom Yockey had previously criticized as being pro-Communist, would be praised a few years later for their statesmanship in opposing Judeo-American hegemony. Today, the American military acts as the policing arm of what Yockey had once called the "Jewish," Communistic faction. There is no longer any differentiation.

AMERICA'S TWO POLITICAL FACTIONS

PART ONE

(FBI summary of Part One, from Chicago, Report dated July 20, 1953 [CG 100-25647], made by Agent Lloyd O. Bogstad.)

The author states that Europe and South Americans are baffled by the United States' rapid change in foreign policy.

Contained on page one:

> The American inner-political scene is dominated by two factions, neither of which at this moment exercises dictatorship. The first, presently the more important of the two, is the Jewish or Communist faction (the two words are interchangeable in America). It is well organized, coherent, conscious of its power, conscious in its policy. It knows its objective, and even when temporarily set back, it continually returns to it. The second is the Army or military faction.

Varange believes that the Jewish politics is everywhere and that it spells the destruction of Western civilization. He believes the Jews were instrumental in giving Communist spy Hiss a light sentence, as were the Communist leaders who were sentenced in this country.

Found on page two:

> An "anti-Communist" law required all Communists to register, but no penal provision was attached to it. It was defied by all Communists with impunity. All this testifies to the efficiency of the Communist organization in America.

Contained on page two:

> The Cabinet minister Forrestal,[1] who resisted the official policy *vis-à-vis* Israel, was killed, and his murder portrayed as a suicide. It is now known everywhere that shortly before his death, Forrestal was warned by Baruch[2] to abandon his resistance to the Israel policy.

On page three:

> In order to enroll the masses of intellectuals—those who believe that because they can talk therefore they can also think—the Jew uses the ideology of Marxism.

---

[1] James Forrestal (1892–1949) was the first US Secretary of Defense who resigned in March 1949 after he became mentally unstable. He was hospitalized and was soon found dead, ruled a suicide as the result of depression. Some have alleged that he was in fact murdered, one theory holding that this was because of a statement he had made in relation to the recently-established state of Israel, that "no group in this country should be permitted to influence our policy to the point it could endanger our national security."

[2] Bernard Baruch (1870–1965) was a Jewish international banker and philanthropist who was a perennial advisor to presidents, including both Franklin Roosevelt and Harry Truman. He was often called the "elder statesman" of the United States. He was Chairman of the War Industries Board during the First World War, and was prominent in the formation of the United Nations.

The author believes that the Army is lacking in political plans. The top military leaders do what they are told, but they do not know or realize what the objective is of what they are doing.

On page four:

> There are traitors within it, like Eisenhower and the infamous Marshall.[3] It was Marshall who, in 1941, when he was chief of staff, brought about the Pearl Harbor disaster. Though knowing when and where the attack was coming, he absented himself from his post and deliberately refrained from alerting the garrison in Hawaii. For this direct treason, he received a promotion.
>
> American foreign policy has become weaker and weaker because of the actions of our military in Europe and Korea.

The author believes that America cannot help Europe. Europe must help itself and develop its own resources.

Noted on page six:

> Europe will not fight under the banner of its enemy.

PART TWO

It was the military faction which insisted on the economic help to the Serbian butcher Tito, whose revolt against Moscow occurred through no connivance of the Washington regime, and who was at first denounced in the American press. It was the military faction which insisted on the imposition of a war-alliance on Greece and Turkey. It was the military faction which intervened in Korea—it will be remembered that Acheson refused all comment during the early days of the war in Korea, for his Communist faction was still fighting hard against American

---

[3] After the Second World War, a Congressional investigation accused Marshall of having been negligent in delaying the transmission of intelligence regarding the impending Pearl Harbor attack to American forces stationed in Hawaii.

intervention. It is the military faction which is still fighting for the imposition of an alliance on Spain, and the Communist faction continues to sabotage all efforts to make this alliance real.

With the knowledge of the existence, the identity, and the interests of these two factions, the otherwise insoluble riddle of American policy becomes clear. Thus, in the Russian blockade of Berlin, summer 1948, the military faction wanted to send armed convoys through. This of course would have brought about a political defeat for Russia, since the Russians were in no position to challenge such a military demonstration. Therefore, the Communist faction in Washington threw all its weight against such a move. The final result was the "air-lift," a compromise between the two factions, which saved Russia's face and destroyed American military prestige in Europe. Europeans no longer believe, even the democrats and America-lovers, that America has either the will or the guts to oppose Russia. It is the military faction, again, which is reoccupying prostrate Europe and going through the forms of rebuilding European military forces, including a German Army. And it is the Communist faction which opposes, now openly, in debate and propaganda, now secretly, in sabotage and undermining, all these measures. Here is manifest the terrible weakness of this politically-unconscious military faction: at the very head of its wish-thinking so-called European army, it allows the enemy Eisenhower to make sure that under his regime at least, there will be no real European army. Eisenhower belongs by his _____ and his _____[4] personal history to the Jewish-Communist faction, and he could no more be relied on to fight Russia than could Nehru or Togliatti.[5]

The Communist faction ties the hands of the American forces in the Chinese War, refuses to use superior atomic weapons against the Communist enemy, and talks even now, in the American press, of the wisdom and expediency of extending

---

[4] These blanks are in the original manuscript.

[5] Palmiro Togliatti (1893–1964) was the long-time leader of the Italian Communist Party and a member of parliament from 1948 until his death.

diplomatic recognition to China in the middle of a war. Similarly, during the "air-lift," friendly diplomatic conversations continually went on between Communists from Moscow and State Department Communists from Washington, to keep everything within bounds and make sure that all incidents would be minimized in order to assure Russia's diplomatic victory.

The only question of interest to us is: what is the significance of these two factions to Europe? The objective of the Communist-Jewish faction is the destruction of the Western Civilization, including America. The military faction has no *political* objective whatever; its purely military objective is preparation of a successful war against Russia, securing in the process all possible strong-points and bases, and utilizing to bring about its victory the man-power of Europe. In its official doctrinal publications, this faction has referred to the former nations of Europe as "pawns" in the war-front against Russia. The military faction at the moment is stronger than it has been at any time since the War, as shown by its forcing through the Spanish rapprochement and by its progressive reoccupation of Europe. Its conception of Europe is a heavily industrialized area of a numerous population, politically and spiritually will-less, whose only rational formation is that of a group of mutually hostile protectorates, united only in common allegiance to America. Europe's main function in this estimate is that of furnishing military support—principally in man-power—to the plans of the American generalate in its self-imposed task of conquering the world. *Pari passu*[6] with the American reoccupation of Europe proceeds an intensification of the persecution of European nationalist elements: in France and Belgium the secret police are ordered by the American colonial administration to discover "plots" and make arrests; in Rome thirty-five are arrested by the churchill regime; in Germany a new wave of repression is begun by the local churchill, Adenauer. All this is testimony to the spiritual leadership of the Liberation Front, the first European nationalist organization, whose policy is gradually being adopted all over Europe by the elements of tomorrow, and is therefore being at-

[6] Latin: concurrently; at the same rate; side by side.

tacked all the more bitterly by the elements of yesterday.

Both factions mean the subjection of Europe, both mean the thwarting of its organic destiny, both are animated by jealousy of Europe and the wish to prevent the coming Imperium of Europe. Future developments in the intensifying struggle between these two factions are unpredictable. In no case can Europeans play the role of spectators in a foreign struggle rather than actors in the poetry of their own destiny. Let no misguided European beguile himself into an utterly misplaced sympathy with the American generalate as an American *nationalist* group, for this it most certainly is not. It is no more nationalist than is the Ford assembly line at Dearborn. Nationalist means: placing the interests of one's nation before the interests of a class, and before the interests of other nations; it is a *political* word, and in the political realm, it cannot be repeated too often, the American generalate is unconscious. It would as soon fight Europe as China—in fact a comparison of American tactics in 1941–45 and in 1950–51 indicates it would *rather* fight Europe; it would as soon bombard London as Berlin, Buenos Aires as Moscow. These generals are not men of the stamp of Moltke, Schlieffen, and Clausewitz,[7] but rather of the stamp of Henry Ford. Their contribution to warfare is the assembly line; their military faith is not in morale, love of Fatherland, and iron discipline, but the belief that with enough industrial production, Destiny itself can be set aside and History be made to come out the end of a tube.

The true American nationalism is not constituted as a party, nor a faction, and not even yet as a movement. It is still a mere *feeling* distributed among a certain spiritual level of the American population. This American nationalism is a spirit that recognizes America's colonial status *vis-à-vis* Europe, that has no wish to destroy the mother-soil and father-culture of Europe, that could be counted upon always to assist Europe against Asia and the world Colored Revolution.[8] This America still existed politi-

[7] Helmuth von Moltke the Elder (1800–1891) or Younger (1848–1916), Alfred von Schlieffen (1833–1913), and (1780–1831) were all Prussian Generals or Field Marshals.

[8] A reference to an essay in Oswald Spengler's 1933 book, *The*

cally in 1900 and in that year sent an expeditionary force to China, there to act in concert with European forces, in the smashing of the Boxer Rebellion, the whole under the command of a German field marshal. But at this critical moment of our Destiny, this America has no *political* existence. Europe cannot look to it for hope, leaderless, unorganized, unconscious as it is.

Friendless and alone, Europe is thrown upon its own resources for its own salvation. But these resources are mightier than all the accumulations of matter, and biological units to operate the matter, of which the enemy disposes. In addition to its unassailable superiority in will, instincts, and intelligence, Europe possesses within it that which the enemy cannot even understand: the invincible Destiny of the Western Civilization. The arrogant products of America's human assembly line who call themselves at present the Allied High Command have no past, they contain no unifying Inner Imperative, no Idea, they represent no Nation and no State, they have no future.

At this moment both of America's factions are the enemy of Europe. Europe will not fight under the banner of its enemy.

Hour of Decision, entitled "The Colored World Revolution." In it, Spengler predicted the rise of the non-white world as the Western Civilization continued its demographic and spiritual decline, and believed it could only be countered by the rise of Caesarism in the West.

CORRESPONDENCE WITH DEAN ACHESON

1952

EDITORS' NOTE

For four months during 1951–1952, the German veteran Major General Otto Ernst Remer was jailed for his criticism of the post-war regime. In July 1944, Remer, as commander of the Berlin garrison, had aborted the plan by a clique of army officers to overthrow Hitler. For this he was given the command of Hitler's personal bodyguard.

After the war, Remer was one of the luminaries of the Socialist Reich Party (SRP), which was causing much consternation among the occupation authorities due to its popularity among the "denazified" Germans. The party was also noted for its anti-Americanism and advocacy of a neutralist line *vis-à-vis* the Soviet Union at a time when the "Cold War" had destroyed American illusions that the USSR would continue in the post-war world as a subordinate partner in a United Nations-led new world order.[1] In October 1952, the SRP was banned.

H. Keith Thompson held a law degree from Yale. He had been active in Rightist politics in the United States prior to the Second World War, and after the war, he was closely associated with the German émigré group in Argentina which established the journal *Der Weg*, of which he was the accredited American agent. The émigrés included air ace Colonel Hans-Ulrich Rudel and Goebbels' deputy, Dr. Johann von Leers. Thompson was a central figure in what has been variously termed *Die Spinne* or ODESSA—the clandestine network that operated to assist German officers in escaping from Europe, and thus imprisonment

---

[1] K. R. Bolton, *Foreign Policy Journal*, "Origins of the Cold War and how Stalin Foiled a New World Order," *Foreign Policy Journal*, May 31, 2010.

and Allied prosecution, at the end of the Second World War.[2] His colorful life included participation in Admiral Byrd's expedition to the South Pole, service in Rhodesia as a mercenary, and giving legal representation to Muhammad Amin al-Hussein, the Grand Mufti of Jerusalem, Cuba's Batista, Lee Harvey Oswald's mother, and so on.

The correspondence between Thompson and the US State Department, addressed to Secretary of State Dean Acheson, was undertaken on behalf of alleged German "war criminals" and political prisoners. The final letter, dated October 15, 1952, is both a cogent expression of Yockeyism and a legal argument against "war crimes" trials. Although written under Thompson's name as Executive Secretary of The Committee for International Justice and The Committee for the Freedom of Major General Remer, the influence of Yockey in that final letter is evident. However, the evidence for this is not only stylistic. In an interview with Keith Stimely, Thompson related the circumstances of the letters to Acheson:

> Well, at the time I was a registered foreign agent, representing Generalmajor Otto-Ernst Remer and his party, the Sozialistische Reichspartei (SRP), a very strong post-war German political party. And as a registered agent I was at the time drafting a letter to Acheson on behalf of the prisoners incarcerated at Spandau, and I was in Yockey's presence at the time as I recall, and he made some emendations and suggestions as to wording, and things that might be added, all of which I incorporated into the final draft. Yockey knew that I was required by law to mention anyone who assisted me in the furtherance of my activities as a registered foreign agent. So I did so in my foreign

---

[2] David McCalden, *Revisionist Newsletter* no. 21, June 1983. This is an article strongly critical of Yockey and Thompson by a former disgruntled director of the Institute for Historical Review (IHR) who seemed to be trying to undermine the IHR. Nonetheless, the information is generally accurate, according to Thompson, who only noted one correction regarding a minor error.

> agent's registration reports: reported that I had been assisted by one "Frank Healey," which was the name that Yockey was using in New York at the time.[3]

This was at a time when Yockey's whereabouts were of much interest to the FBI, the CIA, military intelligence, and Interpol as he toured the world on numerous passports, Thompson stating, unsurprisingly, that Yockey was "very secretive in his movements."[4]

The letter of October 15, 1952 remains of relevance insofar as "war crimes" trials have now become a significant factor in maintaining the "new world order" with the same hypocritical morality that was inaugurated with the defeat of Germany in 1945. Under the shadows of the Nuremberg gallows, heads of state who have in some manner fallen afoul of American global hegemony are targeted with the sheer weight of America's technical might, tried before kangaroo courts under the same conditions and jurisdiction established at Nuremberg, and punished for "crimes" that are being committed wholesale and continually by their accusers. Hence the hanging of Saddam Hussein, the badgering to death of former Serbian President Milošević, the ongoing proceedings against Serbian political and military leaders, and the overthrow and murder of Libya's Gaddafi as a "war criminal."

It should be noted that in 1952, the US State Department claimed that it would not intervene in the internal affairs of other states and that no such jurisdiction is sanctioned by the United Nations. That was, of course, nonsense, as the "United Nations" had established a legally and morally groundless jurisdiction over the political and military leaders of a defeated state, whom they sentenced to hanging on the basis of proceedings that had no precedent in legal history, unless one refers to the Inquisition.

Today, the "United Nations" and NATO no longer make any

---

[3] Keith Stimely, Interview with H. Keith Thompson on Francis Parker Yockey, March 13, 1986, *Counter-Currents*, August 4, 2014.

[4] Ibid.

pretense about interfering in the internal affairs of supposedly sovereign states: it has become a regular feature of international affairs. Conversely, no action is taken against presidents George W. Bush and Barack Obama, Prime Minister Tony Blair, or American and British military personnel complicit in the torturing of Afghans and Iraqis, and the regular "war crimes" committed by Israelis against Palestinians and others, even though these heads of state bear ultimate responsibly under the terms established by the Nuremberg precedent. Therefore, if the Nuremberg precedent was implemented impartially, the aforesaid would be liable to being tried as "war criminals" and "hanged by the neck until dead."

Likewise, the hypocrisy derived from Nuremberg means that while elderly folk such as John Demjanjuk[5] and Frank Walus are physically and financially ruined trying to prove their innocence in the face of forged documents and perjured testimony, Jewish NKVD veterans responsible for bestial atrocities against Germans, Latvians, Ukrainians, and so on are given safe haven in Israel.[6]

While cynics might dismiss the Thompson-Yockey letters to the US State Department as the outraged rhetoric of the politically impotent, such a presumption would be inaccurate. When Grand Admiral Doenitz, Hitler's designated heir to the leadership of the Reich, was released from Spandau in 1957, Thompson launched an international campaign to rehabilitate Doenitz's reputation. The campaign was successful insofar as the Bonn

---

[5] Yoram Sheftel, *The Demjanjuk Affair* (London: Victor Gollancz, 1994).

[6] "Israel Refuses to Cooperate in Lithuanian Genocide Case," *RFE/RL Newsline*, February 21, 2000. This refers to the Israeli Prosecutor-General's Office refusing to assist Lithuania in the case against Nachman Dushansky, a former KGB officer accused of participation in the deportation of families to Siberia. Lithuanian authorities met the same refusal in regard to Semion Berkis-Burkov, who had been a local NKVD chief. Shlomo Morel, commandant of a concentration camp for Germans in post-war Poland, who was responsible for particularly vicious atrocities, was indicted for crimes against Poland in 1998 but remained safely in Israel.

government was pressured into paying Doentiz his full pension rights.

The letters deriving from the campaign were published by Thompson in 1976 under the title *Doenitz at Nuremberg: A Re-Appraisal,* and indicate the important contacts Thompson had been able to cultivate. They comprise about four hundred letters from esteemed military officers, jurists, educators, and diplomats throughout the world, all attesting to their opposition to the Nuremberg Trials, and many to their support for Doenitz. For example, William O. Douglas, Supreme Court Justice and Professor of Law at Yale, stated an opinion of the trials that is similar to the opinions expressed by Thompson and Yockey in their letters to Acheson, the venerable Justice stating that:

> I thought at the time and still think that the Nuremberg trials were unprincipled. Law was created *ex post facto* to suit the passion and the clamor of the time. The concept of *ex post facto* is not congenial to the Anglo-American viewpoint on law . . . there has never been a code of International Law governing aggressive wars . . .[7]

Yockey had himself worked for a "war crimes" tribunal in 1946 at Wiesbaden, where he spent eleven months preparing reports on the cases. Following a complaint that his reports were objective rather than following the party line, he retorted to his superior officer that he was a "lawyer, not a journalist," and said the tribunal would have to "write its own propaganda."[8]

Correspondence with Dean Acheson

June 20, 1952, Department of State, Washington

My Dear Mr. Thompson:

---

[7] H. Keith Thompson and Henry Strutz, *Doenitz at Nuremberg* (New York: Amber Publishing Co., 1976), p. 194.

[8] Willis A. Carto, Introduction to Ulick Varange, *Imperium*, pp. xi and xii.

The receipt is acknowledged of your letter of June 16, 1952, addressed to the Secretary of State and referred to this office for reply, in which you request the presentation of a petition for the release of Herr Remer.

The arrest and confinement of Herr Remer is a matter lying wholly within the jurisdiction of the Federal Republic of Germany. The United States Government therefore intends to take no action to intervene in this case.

Furthermore, nothing in the Charter of the United Nations authorizes that organization to intervene in matters which are essentially within the domestic jurisdiction of any state.

Sincerely yours,
Henry B. Cox
Officer-in-Charge
Division of German Information
Office of German Public Affairs

JULY 30, 1952

Honorable Dean Acheson,
Secretary of State
State Department
Washington, D.C.

Honorable Sir;

I address this appeal to you personally, Mr. Acheson, as an expression of the apprehensions of an American citizen concerning certain events in the world and the part which the United States State Department is playing, or in some instances fails to play, therein. I well realize the pressure of your work, and that you cannot read every letter which is addressed to you. In this instance, however, I feel these issues are of sufficient importance to the future of the United States to warrant at least your fair consideration. It is in this spirit that I appeal to your sense of fairness and justice in asking you to hear me out. We are both graduates of, and interested in the affairs of, Yale University; my class is the Class of 1946. I state this not to appeal to any feeling which you might have towards a fellow alumnus, but to convey my feeling that Yale grounds her graduates reasonably well in history and international affairs, and that an honest exchange of ideas between fellow graduates is never out of order.

Requesting your indulgence, Mr. Secretary, I would like to place before you, in one communication, my ideas on four (4) problems of worldwide concern. They are as follows: (1) the problem of the German "war criminals"; (2) the case of Major General Otto Ernst Remer; (3) the plight of the German Rightist, anti-Communist political parties; and (4) the present Austrian laws restoring property and civil rights to some 34,000 former "war criminals."

There are at this moment 1,045 German soldiers held as "war criminals." They are being held as follows:

Landsberg Prison	- 344	Denmark	- 11
Werl Prison	- 140	Luxembourg	- 6
Wittlich Prison	- 120	Italy	- 3
Belgium	- 5	Norway	- 22
Holland	- 80	Switzerland	- 15
France	- 299		

There are, in addition, the seven highest-ranking officials held at Spandau, and the countless German "prisoners of war" still held by the Soviet Union.

The Review Board, for which provision has now been made, to consider the "war criminal" cases is, in my opinion, an incomplete and unworkable structure. Its defects are as follows: (1) the establishment of the Board has been made contingent upon ratification of the Bonn Conventions and the European Army Treaty by all the parliaments concerned; (2) the Board will not question the validity of the convictions; (3) the favorable voice of all six members of the Board are required to make the decision of the Board binding upon the nation having custody of the prisoner; (4) the Board is to confine itself to prisoners held in West Germany and (5) the Board will not concern itself with the seven major "war criminals" held in the four-power prison at Spandau, West Berlin. This group includes Grand Admiral Doenitz, legally the last Head of State under the Third Reich.

I respectively submit to you, Mr. Secretary, the following considerations: that the position of the future German military officer is made exceptionally difficult by the war crimes convictions; that a German cannot justifiably be asked to fight for or with an Alliance of which other members are holding Germans as prisoners for war-time acts (World War II) which the Germans believe the Allies also to have committed; that the presence of Soviet "judges" at the Nuernberg Proceedings tend to render such proceedings invalid in view of subsequent disclosures concerning the Soviets (particular reference is made to the matter of the Katyn Forest Massacre);[9] that when men act as agents of a Government representing the collective will of a nation, there is a definite incongruity involved in later convicting such men as individual "war criminals."

Mr. Secretary, I urge you to consider the fact that many young people in America, as well as Germany itself, do not have confidence in the humbug formulae which have served as the basic orientations of official thought and propaganda lines in the matter of the "war criminals." The cold fact is that the "war criminals" remain connected in the popular mind of Germany as men connected with a great National effort which had the overwhelming support of the people. United States policy will be more popular abroad when it begins to take cognizance of these facts instead of basing itself on what would certainly appear to be the empty academic dreams, often the veritable philosophic nightmares, of biased minor professors.

It is therefore urged, Mr. Secretary, that the United States government immediately take the initiative in urging the unconditional release of all war criminals, including the Spandau group, if for no better reason than as evidence of good faith towards the German people.

I have viewed with growing concern the matter of the apparent persecution of minority political parties, of the anti-

---

[9] The Katyn Forest Massacre refers to the murder of over twenty thousand Polish military officers and members of the intelligentsia carried out in the spring of 1940 by the Soviet NKVD, or secret police.

communist Right, by the Government of the Federal Republic of Germany. The particular, but not the exclusive, target has been the Socialist Reich Party of which Major General Remer is an official. The history of the actions of the Bonn Government, and local administrators, against the SRP is too lengthy to set forth in this letter. I take the liberty of enclosing a partial history of such actions. This has been followed in recent weeks by an injunction prohibiting the SRP from conducting public meetings, distributing its publications, or otherwise bringing its case to the people. As a climax, the Bonn Government is seeking a legal ban against this party, contrary to the [illegible] interests of the United States in that it (1) is indicative of an attempt within Germany to restrain free speech and freedom of political expression and (2) tends to destroy unity amongst the conservative political parties which will be our strongest sources of strength in any anti-Communist endeavor. I submit that the United States has responsibilities in Germany in view of the presence of our troops there and in view of the extent of United States influence, direct and indirect, in German affairs.

On June 16th, 1952, I sent to you, Mr. Secretary, a request for the presentation of a petition in the case of General Remer to the United Nations Organization by means of the United States Delegation thereto. In reply to my sincere request, I received a letter over the signature of Mr. Henry B. Cox (File CAI 762A.00/6-1652) stating very curtly that since the case of General Remer is "wholly within the jurisdiction of the Federal Republic of Germany" the United States Government intends to take no action to intervene in this case.

I note, however, that on July 18th, 1952, the Austrian Parliament passed three laws restoring property and civil rights to 34,000 former "Nazis." On July 19th, a Jacob Blaustein of Baltimore,[10] President of the "American Jewish Committee"[11] sent

[10] Jacob Blaustein (1892–1970) was the founder of the American Oil corporation in 1910, as well as the President of the American Jewish Committee. An advisor to the American delegation to the formation of the United Nations, he also advised presidents Harry Truman, Dwight Eisenhower, John F. Kennedy, and Lyndon B. Johnson, as well as Da-

you a telegram stating as follows (as reported in the *New York Herald Tribune* of July 19th, 1952): "The United States still has responsibility in Austria and should do its utmost to redress the acts taken and to prevent further shameful steps. The Austrian Parliamentary acts and plans not only are unjust and undemocratic, but also provide excellent material for further Communistic propaganda.—We urge you to take all possible counter measures."

Whereupon, on July 28th, 1952, the United States State Department made public its disapproval of the Austrian laws in question. Mr. Lincoln White, a State Department spokesman, said that the State Department has communicated "its fairly strong" views on the subject to the Acting High Commissioner for Austria.

Apparently the United States State Department is willing to intervene in the affairs of another country when urged to do so by the "American Jewish Committee," but will not intervene in the interests of justice in the case of General Remer, the persecuted Rightist political parties of Germany, and the 1,045 "war criminals." The United States has far more at stake in intervening in the aforementioned cases than in serving the cause of international Jewry by adversely intervening in a small administrative matter restoring rights to persons plainly entitled to hold such rights. I realize that it might be argued that some "legality" exists whereby interference in Austrian affairs is permissible. However, this is a matter of principle, and some degree of consistency is certainly desirable.

It is therefore urged, Mr. Secretary, that the United States Government immediately intervene with the West German Government against the persecution of General Remer and minority Rightist political parties. It is further urged that the United States Government not seek to veto the Austrian laws

---

vid Ben-Gurion of Israel. He also negotiated the payment of Germany's reparations to Holocaust survivors with Konrad Adenauer.

[11] The American Jewish Committee was established in 1904 and still exists today. The group was active in the Civil Rights Movement of the 1950s, and their research was cited in the decision to desegregate public schools.

restoring property and civil rights to certain lesser former Nazis.

I enclose a copy of my letter to you of June 24th, 1952 which has never been acknowledged by your office. I assume that this was due to the position of Mr. Cox stated in his letter of June 20th. However, Mr. Secretary, if, after fair consideration, you find that you are willing to assist me in my fight for justice in the Remer case, I will be more than willing to prepare suitable briefs for presentation.

It is sincerely hoped, Mr. Secretary, that you will give serious consideration to the views presented in this letter and that you will be able, in the best interests of the United States, to incorporate these views in some measure into a really practical, effective foreign policy.

With all best regards, I am—

Respectfully yours,

H. Keith Thompson

SEPTEMBER 2, 1952, DEPARTMENT OF STATE, WASHINGTON, D.C.

In reply refer to
GER:GPA 762.00/7-3052

Mr. H. Keith Thompson
380 Main Street, Apartment 13,
Chatham, New Jersey.

My dear Mr. Thompson:

The receipt is acknowledged of your letter of 30th July 1952.

That letter, as well as your earlier ones, has been fully considered by those officers in the Department who are concerned with the subjects you discussed. I do not desire to dismiss your letters and arguments with a conventional or curt reply. Nevertheless it is patent, I believe, that the views which you hold are so much at variance with the concepts behind the policy which has been pursued in Germany that little would be accomplished by an attempt to respond to your comments in detail. Perhaps the point of view of the Department can be sufficiently illustrated by a few remarks.

In your approach to the problem of war criminals, you appear to be prepared to put aside questions of fact and law, of right and wrong. You advocate, apparently for purposes of political opportunism, the release of all these people, including the group of leading Nazis held in Spandau. The Department, on the other hand, holds the view that if there is to be any release of these convicted criminals or any modification of their sentence it should be accomplished on the basis of established principles of clemency and parole and in accordance with the merits of the individual case. As you are doubtless aware, an exhaustive, months-long review of the cases of all war criminals held under American jurisdiction, did take place last year. There will be ample opportunity for continuing review by the Board to be set up under the recently signed agreements with the German Federal Republic. This is the only sound approach to the question and is fully consistent with traditional Anglo-Saxon standards of justice. Moreover, the Department is convinced that very important elements of the new Germany understand and welcome this policy as one calculated to help protect the new democracy from those who were enemies of humanity and democracy.

The other problems to which you chiefly addressed yourself is the status of the Socialist Reichs Party and the imprisonment by German authorities of one of its leaders, Otto Ernst Remer. Here again it is obvious that there is little or no common ground for a discussion of the issue. You apparently feel that Herr Remer leads a worthy cause and is being persecuted for it. You also consider that support for him and his party would greatly advance the cause of anti-Communism and United States policy in Europe. You are well aware, however, that the State Department holds entirely different views. From Remer's speeches, from the known views held by him and the other leaders of the SRP, and from other information available to the Department, there seems to be every indication that this man and his movement are neo-Nazi in character. You make the common mistake of considering that because a man is not a Communist he is a good democrat. Far from being in league with anti-Communist parties, Remer and his partners are bitterly hostile to the moderate democratic forces in Germany. Under these circumstances, the Department can scarcely be expected to intervene with the German Government on Remer's behalf, even if it had the technical right to do so. It is no part of American policy to assist Nazism to arise once more in Germany.

Finally, you refer to recent expressions of disapproval by the United States Government of certain Austrian legislation concerning amnesty and property rights for former Nazis. I do not consider it necessary to reply to the virtually open charge in your letter than this action was taken to please a certain religious segment of the American people. The fact is that the Department considers these Austrian laws to be intended to benefit former Nazis before the restitution and general claims problems of victims of National Socialism have been satisfactorily resolved by the Austrian Government. This is a problem of simple justice, not of race or religion.

Sincerely yours,
For the Secretary of State:

Perry Laukhuff
Acting Deputy Director
Bureau of German Affairs

OCTOBER 14, 1952, DEPARTMENT OF STATE, WASHINGTON, D.C.

In reply refer to
L/GER 662.0026/10-652
Committee for International Justice,
380 Main Street, Apartment 13,
Chatham, New Jersey.

Sirs:

The receipt is acknowledged of your letter of October 6, 1952 and enclosures concerning the Krupp[12] case.

The law which authorized the United States High Commissioner for Germany to modify the sentence on Krupp expressly provides that he "may not increase the severity thereof." It is believed that that case is not now subject to further action which would impose a new penalty on Krupp.

Very truly yours,
For the Acting Secretary of State

John M. Raymond
Assistant Legal Adviser

October 15, 1952, Committee for International Justice

380 Main Street
Chatham, N.J.
H. Keith Thompson
Executive Secretary

Honorable Dean Acheson,
The Secretary of State
Washington, D.C.

Dear Mr. Acheson:

The receipt of your letter of September 2, 1952 is herewith gratefully acknowledged.

We should state at the outset of our reply that our Committee does not have simply a personal objective. Our interest in General Remer, while it includes the personal, is primarily in the

---

[12] Alfried Krupp (1907–1967) was the head of the historic Krupp dynasty of industrialists during the Second World War, when the materiel their factories provided was of crucial importance to the German war effort. He was convicted of crimes against humanity because his factories had made use of slave labor and sentenced to twelve years' imprisonment, although he was pardoned by the American High Commissioner after serving only three years.

great superpersonal Idea and movement of which he is a symbol, and it is in this light that we should like the work of our Committee to be appraised.

In your letter of September 2nd, you demonstrated that you are in error on many points as to our general philosophy of politics, and to our specific views on United States policy in Germany since 1945. This is written to clear up these errors.

First, we should like to deal with the specific points, namely the "war-criminal" problem, the status of the Socialist Reich Party (which includes within it the problem of internal political freedom in Germany), and the question of Jewish influence on the United States attitude toward the Austrian amnesty legislation.

In the democratic Germany you mention, the authoritarian Adenauer regime has found it necessary to make it a criminal offense for anyone publicly to write the word "war-criminal" in quotation marks. This was necessary because, generally speaking, all Germans regard the use of the word "criminal" in connection with their political and military heroes of the War as a cowardly and vile slander by a dishonorable victor, and because the Adenauer regime, supported only by American bayonets, is necessarily obliged to enforce, by all possible means, the internal policy relayed to it through you. Until the forces you represent are able to pass similar legislation here, we shall continue at all times to write this phrase in the manner which is forbidden in democratic Germany.

"War-criminal" is an illicit phrase for the simple reason that there exists no legal definition of this term in any authoritative treatise. It is legally impossible for an American or Russian soldier, or a soldier of any of the American vassal-states in Europe or Asia, to commit a "war-crime." Any crime which could be committed by an American soldier is set forth in the Code of Military Justice, and it is cognizable by an American military court. Any conduct not precisely described in this Code as criminal cannot be charged to a soldier as a crime. The soldier knows these crimes in advance, and he knows the nature of the tribunal to which he will be responsible. The substantive and adjective law by which he will be tried is codified and he has the right to qualified counsel of his own nation and of his own choosing.

Before he can be charged with an offense, his conduct must be such as is described as an offense in the Code, the court must have jurisdiction of the subject matter, and jurisdiction of his person.

In the case of the "war-crime" terror in Germany (the corresponding program in Japan was a mere token effort, an elaborate lip-service to the principles of the terror in Germany, and no "war crimes" organization was even instituted in any other country conquered by America, such as Italy or Siam) there was no legal system in existence which defined any such "crimes." The accused were not tried under German Law, nor under American law, nor according to the terms of the Geneva Convention regulating trial of war-prisoners. On this point, see the opinion by the reviewing authority on the Dachau case, December, 1945. They were supposedly tried under International Law but, as every school-boy knows, International Law has no penal provisions whatever, and never has had, and never could have, by its very nature, since it has always rested, in its entirety, on comity and never on force and authority. Nations, and not individuals, groups, classes, or elites, are its sole and unique subject matter. Its fundamental principle was, and is—as the Russian delegation daily reminds you in the "United Nations"—the sovereignty of nations. Never before 1945 did anyone allege, and up to now, no scholar of recognized authority has yet alleged, that one nation has the legal right to review the internal policy of another nation and the legal right to massacre the leadership of another nation.

Since there was no pre-existing legal system, there cannot possibly be a properly constituted tribunal, nor an offense, nor jurisdiction of the subject matter or of the person, nor a trial. Therefore, what did ensue was simply a series of mock-trials, not the first in history, but the most prolonged, the most scientifically cruel, the most cold-bloodedly vicious, the most vilely dishonorable.

It would be easy to recite from the mass of injustices in the gruesome killings from the beginning with arrest by Colonel Straight's[13] police through the trial by his appointees where

[13] Lieutenant Colonel Clio Edwin Straight (1904–1991) was put in

Colonel Straight's prosecutors opposed the defense counsel appointed by Colonel Straight to the review by Colonel Straight's appointees and the final signing of the execution order by Colonel Straight himself, thus bringing to a triumphant conclusion, a democratic conclusion, a foul process that had been under his strict military command from the beginning, a hideous caricature of the American constitutional principle of separation of powers. The universal principle of impartiality in the court was naturally absent in "judges" under military orders to convict, and in conditions in which the accused and the members of the court were legally in a state of war with one another. The accused were tortured to obtain their pre-trial confessions, which they were not later heard to deny. A man was hanged for a crime when there was no evidence before the court that the crime had been committed, no *corpus delicti*[14] has been shown. Judge Leroy A. van Roden of Pennsylvania found, in his official investigation, that it had been routine pre-trial practice for American officers, in the torture-cells at the Schwäbisch-Hall prison, to kick all interrogees in their private parts.

But these injustices, which still stink in the nostrils of mankind, and which still cry out to Heaven, are not what History will remember from the satanic debauch. History forgets detail. No, the real historical fact which the "war-crime" terror has produced is this: America was victorious—America hanged the defeated leaders and heroes, disarmed and surrendered in its custody. This has destroyed, once and for all, for History is irreversible, the ancient Western usages of honor in warfare, those usages which were merely codified in the Geneva Convention of 1929. American soldiers may in future expect to be used as America used other soldiers, and the same is true of American political leaders. Remember, the German leaders and heroes were not slain in haste and anger by irresponsible elements—they were deliberately humiliated, insulted, calumniated, and tortured before the world for more than a year, while honorable

---

charge of the prosecution of war criminals in Germany during the first few years of the occupation.

[14] Physical evidence of a crime.

men everywhere in the West, powerless to stop the satanic proceeding, averted their heads. The final stupid touch of ineffective malice, that of distributing the ashes of Herman Goering and the other slain heroes over the landscape by airplane was supposed to prevent a cult of the memory of these heroes. Despite this silliness, the name of Herman Goering will loom larger before the eyes of posterity than the name of Dean Acheson, and monuments will be raised to him, but not to his persecutors.

At this very day, in the law schools and in the courts of every State in the United States, it is taught as a fundamental principle that domestic law takes precedence over international law when the two conflict. Nonetheless, on the political level, the level of your Department, the contrary principle is enthroned, and if tomorrow the leadership of China decided to try American soldiers for "war-crimes," you have deprived yourself of any fundamental grounds on which to intervene and to remonstrate. Both the Russian and Chinese governments accuse your regime of cruel and frightful methods of warfare in Korea. On what grounds would you protest a trial of American soldiers by a Chinese court of charges of "war-crime"? At the Mauthausen Trial, a member of the court (Colonel Rosenberg) asked one of the accused why he was on duty at Mauthausen,[15] and to the answer that those were his orders, the judge replied, "You could have deserted." You are bringing American soldiers closer to this position. Was that the intention, or did the general language of the system you promulgated serve merely to cover a particular scheme, namely, the genocide of the German elite? It must be one or the other.

To conclude this point, the "war-time" terror is contrary to policy, to political and military honor, to Christian morality, to social ethics, to International Law generally and the Geneva Convention of 1929 in particular, and to the basic law of the United States: policy obviously prescribes that one conciliate and refrain from insulting a people which one seeks as an ally; both political and military honor prescribe magnanimity to a conquered foe, such as Grant showed to Lee, such as Bismarck

[15] A concentration camp that was located in Upper Austria.

showed to Napoleon III, such as Adolf Hitler showed to Schuschnigg, Daladier, Reynaud, Blum,[16] Jakob Stalin, and a host of others; Christian morality forbids all revenge, whether or not masked by elaborate lynching and mock-trial ritual; all social ethicians, from Aristotle to John Stuart Mill, exclude revenge in all forms, legalistic or otherwise; International Law has no penal provisions and could not be the basis of any prosecution in any court whatsoever, and furthermore, the Geneva Convention specifies the procedure for the trial by a captor of prisoners-of-war, which procedure was illegally evaded by the "war-crime" terror; the United States Constitution specifically outlaws *ex post facto* legislation and by every implication outlaws *ex post facto* judicial quasi-legislative proceedings.

We come now to the second question, that of internal political freedom in Germany and of the status of the SRP in particular. First of all, the outlawing of the SRP and the persecution of General Remer, General von Bothmer, Wolfgang Hedler, Dr. Fritz Dorls, Dr. Gerhard Krueger, Rainer Klagges, Frau Heinrich Himmler, Graf von Westarp, and Dr. Fritz Roessler are definite, public proof of the fact that the Adenauer regime you have set up on American bayonets is not democratic in any sense of the word. Before the entire world, it outlaws its opposition, except that purely formal opposition which substantially agrees with it. Whether or not the cause of General Remer is a worthy one, the *fact* is that your regime in Germany persecutes its opposition, outlaws it, and deprives it of freedom of activity. This fact cannot be gainsaid or explained: either internal political freedom exists, or else it does not. When certain parties, regardless of what they are, are outlawed, internal political freedom does not exist. The act of your agent Adenauer, within the scope of his authority, binds you politically, and you are thus an opponent in *fact* of the freedom you advocate with your words.

You make the statement that Remer and the other leaders of the SRP are "neo-Nazi" in character. In the next sentence, you

---

[16] Kurt Schuschnigg (1897–1977) was Austrian Chancellor before the *Anschluss*. Édouard Daladier (1884–1970), Paul Reynaud (1876–1866), and Léon Blum (1878–1950) were French Prime Ministers.

say that Remer and the SRP leaders are not in league with *what you call* the "anti-Communist parties." While Remer was supporting the war of Europe against Bolshevist Russia, those who today persecute him were hoping, and working, for the victory of Russia. In that war, you too supported Bolshevism against Europe, the heart, home-soil, head, brain, and soul of the Western Civilization. In this constellation of facts, no one can be heard to say that General Remer and the SRP are not anti-Communistic. The spirit of the German National Socialist Revolution was the strongest anti-Communist, anti-Bolshevik force to arise in Europe after the Bolshevik Revolution of November, 1917. What you call the forces of democracy allied themselves with Bolshevist Russia, and stabbed the European armies in the back, and destroyed the power of Europe. And yet those European armies were fighting then for the entire Western Civilization, just as much as they would be tomorrow if they were to be reconstituted in their own spirit and under their own leadership. Under the hegemony of these "democratic forces," Soviet Russia has increased steadily in world power. While the Resurgence of Authority was spreading itself over Europe, however, Soviet Russia was steadily declining in world power.

The German National Socialist Movement was only one form, and a provisional form at that, of the great, irresistible movement which expresses the Spirit of our Age, the Resurgence of Authority. This movement is the affirmation of all the cultural drives and human instincts which liberalism, democracy, and Communism deny. General Remer's movement is a current expression of the irresistible Resurgence of Authority in the Western Civilization. This movement is against all inner degeneration in the West, against the hegemony of finance-capitalism, of class-war and trade-union dictatorship, against the ideology of liberty, equality, and the "pursuit of happiness" as embodying the human mission on Earth, against the domination of private individuals, of pressure groups, and especially alien elements within the West. Liberal democracy is related to Communism as the evening twilight is related to night. The basic values of liberal democracy are identical with those of Communism, and your policy in the current Chinese War demonstrated to the world, and above all to Europe, that it is more than values that your system has in common with the Moscow regime. The significance of the American Fleet blockading Formosa, and directly helping the Russian-Chinese coalition, directly injuring the American military effort, while American troops are engaged on the mainland with Chinese troops in critical battle, is not lost on Europe which, in its millennium of history, has seen many wars conducted for victory, and has even seen wars conducted for defeat.

The Resurgence of Authority has both its inner and its outer aspect. The inner has been touched upon in the preceding paragraph. Its outer aspect is the creation of the European-Imperium-State-Nation, and therewith the reassertion of Europe's historically ordained role, that of the colonizing and organizing force of the entire world. This role is historically necessary and no other force in the world can be substituted for Europe in this mighty Destiny. Either Europe brings peace and order to the world, or else the world will remain in darkness and chaos. Compare the sunlit and serene world-conditions of 1900, when almost the entire planet was under the direct or indirect control of Europe, with the confusion and increasing primitivity of the present. And yet, there are forces in the world which prefer the conditions of 1952. Among these forces there could not possibility, by definition, be anyone who serves the great mission of the Resurgence of Authority, as General Remer and his associates do. These leaders, like all other members of the European elite, reject the domination of Moscow, of Washington, and every other extra-European force.

It is an attractive error to think that everyone not in favor of your domination of Europe is *ipso facto* pro-Russian. Europe remembers with incisive clarity that when it was engaged to the hilt against Barbarian Russia, your regime stabbed it in the back, and Europe—this means, of course, the elite of Europe—is quite incapable of waging a war in which it would supply ill-armed cannon-fodder to one enemy to be used against another enemy. True, a helpless mass of spiritless, ill-armed conscripts can be scraped together by democratic compulsion, but this army, without the feeling of a mission, without morale, without its organic elite, will melt away under combat conditions. There are those who want a German-European army of this caliber, and who want the result to which such an army would inevitably attain: the delivery to the Siberian tundras of the military manpower of Europe.

Communism is the collective name for the attempt to destroy the Western Civilization from within. This movement, led by class-war and race-war within the West, is two centuries old, and thus long antedates the Russian Bolshevik Revolution, and is no mere subsidiary phenomenon to that Revolution. The Russian barbarian threat to Europe exists independently of the Communist movement within Europe, and if another Adolf Hitler were to arise and liquidate the Communist movement within Europe, that outer threat of mobilized Russian barbarism would still exist. All his life, General Remer and his associates have opposed both threats, that of Communism within and barbarism without. The Adenauer type, his regime, and the parties which support it definitely worked, during the Second World War, with the inner Communist movement in Europe and with, and for the victory of, the outer barbarian forces over Europe. By their detestation of the Resurgence of Authority, which is the organic answer to the problems of our present stage of evolution, Adenauer and his ilk are still supporting European Communism and thus furthering the cause of the extra-European threat to Europe. *It is fantastically unrealistic to believe that a group of armies officered with liberal democrats and led by adenauers can give the military performance of even a single army corps indoctrinated with "neo-Nazism" and commanded by General Remer.*

We come now to the third question, the Jewish influence on your Department's intervention in Austria's internal affairs regarding the Nazi amnesty question.

As you know, and every schoolboy knows, the Jew has, as barriers between him and his host-peoples, not only Culture, but has as well his own State, Nation, People, Race, Religion, and Society. Thus the Jewish organism is a Culture-State-Nation-People-Race-Religion-Society. Deriving as it does from a different Culture from the Western Culture, its fundamental world-feeling is different from ours, and thus every basic value and concept is different from ours on the corresponding point. Thus its idea of a nation is entirely dissociated from the idea of a specific territory, and *according to the Jewish nation-feeling,* the Jew from Russia, from America, or from England all belong to the same State and Nation—this in complete disregard of what the Russian, American, or English idea might be on this subject.

To our question concerning this influence, your letter states with democratic arrogance that you "do not consider it necessary to reply." Does this mean that you regard such influence as beyond the bounds of possibility? Do you think the boasts of the Jewish press and Jewish leaders on the extent of their influence in your regime are merely braggadocio? Presumably you will concede that the Jewish entity exists, since every Jewish spiritual leader considers himself in the first place with this organic entity and the reasons for its strength and advancement among the host-peoples, their word for the alien Western nations among them from the most part the Jewish entity is dispersed.

You will also concede that its members are human, and that they are thus quite naturally striving to advance their own interests, that they have been openly hostile to Germany—which includes the *Ostmark*[17]—since 1933, that the policy of the State of Israel (of which all Jews everywhere, including those in your Department, are *de jure* members if they find it politic to so signify) is openly hostile to Germany, that the said State is supported almost entirely by Jews in America and that the said State therefore necessarily follows the policy of its sponsors. These things are unquestionable facts, none of which, presumably, you would wish to deny.

Presumably you do not affirm, in the face of a mountain of Jewish political literature to the contrary, in both the declarative and the imperative moods, that a Jew holding political office or power in a non-Jewish State ceases to have his spiritual connections with the Jewish entity. Anyone gifted with an elementary comprehension of human psychology knows the universality and the power of cultural-political-racial-national-religious-

---

[17] The name used in the Third Reich for Austria following its unification with Germany in the *Anschluss* of 1938.

social drives, and thus knows that a Jew holding public office in America does *not* cease to be a Jew, that he is *not* indifferent to the fate of the Jewish entity, and he does, from *human psychological necessity,* endeavor to steer American policy into channels favorable to his own ideas and feelings.

We understand how little freedom your circumstances leave you to discuss the Jewish question, but would like to say that this burning question will not be resolved by any pretense, however elaborate, that the question does not exist.

Our letter draws to a close. The tone of your letter in accusing this Committee of political opportunism would indicate that you are unaware of our fundamental philosophy. For ourselves, our associates, for the elite of the Western Civilization, and for millions of others whom democratic persecution has deprived of voice and even of civic status, we should like briefly to state our world-view.

First, we believe in God and accept the world as a divine idea; we thus reject totally the materialism which first triumphed in the XVIIIth century and which now ends by spawning the world-outlook of your regime and that in Moscow. Together with materialism we reject the idea that human and superpersonal evolution can be regulated by a piece of constitution-paper, as well as the vain notion that there can exist such a thing as a legal system which overrides the destiny of men, nations, superpersonal ideas, and cultural development, the notion expressed in the meaningless phrase about "government of laws, and not of men." We reject the superannuated idols of liberty, equality, and the idea that "the pursuit of happiness" is the meaning of human life on this planet. We reject liberal-capitalism and *laissez-faire,* whether that of the supra-national banker or of the labor-dictator, and the parliamentarism and class-war which serve its purpose. We reject world-weary pacifism and the defeatism which fails to oppose and thereby encourages the word-wide revolt of the primitive and the barbarian peoples against the hegemony of the Western Civilization everywhere in the world.

These rejected values—openly professed by your regime, the Moscow regime, and by the Jewish Nation-State—are simply historically dead. Whether or not they are "true" or "false" is a question without meaning for actual History. In the period from about 1750 to about 1900 these values were still effective—they could still inspirit men, generate an inner imperative, serve as battle-cries, but today they are mere skeletal material of once-living historical facts. Deriving as they do from the century of Anglo-Saxon supremacy, the century of liberalism, parliamentarism, economic individualism, the domination of trade and chauvinism, they bear the common hallmark of materialism. But that era has irrevocably passed, its values are dead and utterly incapable of ever again setting Western men in irresistible revolutionary motion, and your posthumous support of these cold and rigid formulae puts you in the position of Metternich, who also devoted himself to the sterile and hopeless task of building a wall against the Future, and who pursued, as do you, the policy of intervening everywhere to prevent the stirring of the Future and to silence by persecution the voices of the Future.

But it is impossible successfully to oppose the historically necessary. Your bayonets are mere mechanical appurtenances, but the forces of History are far beyond mere mechanics. The XVIIIth century Revolution of Materialism is succeeded today, with irresistible historical necessity, by the XXth century Revolution of Faith and Resurgent Authority. Against the charnal values of your and Stalin's "Democracy," we pit those of our mission: Faith, Authority, Discipline, Duty, Ethical Socialism, Honor, Responsibility, Order, and Hierarchy. To your policy of assisting the barbarian revolt against the West, we set our policy of crushing that revolt and affirming once more the world-mission of the West. To your policy of atomizing and destroying Europe, of perpetuating XIXth century petty-stateism, we oppose our policy of the total unity of Europe, the creation of the Imperium-Culture-State-Nation-People of the West, and the liberation of all Europe and the entire Western Civilization from every form of Bolshevism, whether yours of Stalin's. To your policy of hamstringing Germany, we oppose our policy of rebuilding, in its own spirit, Germany, the heart of Europe, the strongest defense-potential of the West.

On the point of your European policy, our view is stated by

Varange in *Imperium* (volume I, p. iii):

> I condemn here at the outset the miserable plans of retarded souls to "unite" Europe as an economic area for purposes of exploitation by and defense of the Imperialism of extra-European forces. The integration of Europe is not a subject for *plans*, but for expression. It needs but to be recognized, and the perpetuation of nineteenth century economic thinking is entirely incapable here. Not trade and banking, not importing and exporting, but Heroism alone can liberate that integrated soul of Europe which lies under the financial trickery of retarders, the petty-stateism of party-politicians, and the occupying armies of extra-European forces.[18]

The imperative integration of Europe takes the form of unity of People, Race, Nation, State, Society, Will—and naturally also—economy. The spiritual unity of Europe is there, its liberation will automatically allow the full blooming of the other phases of the organic unity, which all flow from the spiritual.

Your values dominated the XIXth century, the age of Economics, but our values will dominate this century, the Age of Absolute Politics. Your Metternichian attempt to oppose the advance of History will end as did his. The last age was that of Democracy, the coming age is that of the Resurgence of Authority.

In the spirit of the above, and the hope that it has been of help, the Committee and I are

Very truly yours,

The Committee for International Justice
The Committee for the Freedom of Major General Remer

H. Keith Thompson,
Executive Secretary

---

[18] In the Noontide edition, p. xlvii.

WHAT IS BEHIND THE HANGING OF THE ELEVEN JEWS IN PRAGUE?

1952

EDITORS' NOTE

The trial of the leaders of the Communist Party in Czechoslovakia in 1952 was of seminal importance to Yockey's perspective during the Cold War. Yockey had written in *Imperium* of the distinction between the Russia of the mystically-inclined Slavic masses and the Bolshevik Russia of Jewish technocrats. In his view, the 1952 "Prague Treason Trial" was primarily a symbolic public break by the Slavs with "Jewish-Bolshevism."

The essay was published in the United States under the title "Prague Treason Trial" as a "press release" dated December 20, 1952, as well as in the December issue of the *NRP Bulletin*. This was the newsletter of the National Renaissance Party (NRP), led by James Madole, which was often used as a mouthpiece by Frederick Weiss, Yockey's German-born mentor in the US, who provided funds to both Yockey and the NRP. Yockey had even briefly joined the NRP while in the United States, under the pseudonym Frank Healy, but his membership was unknown to Madole until after Yockey's departure from the country.

This essay was also reportedly published widely in the Rightist press throughout the world, including in *Der Weg*. Most significantly, many nationalists in Germany were adopting a "neutralist" line towards the Soviet Union, and this was of real concern to the American authorities. Many German veterans did not see why they should fight for the US against the USSR a few years after having come out of a bloody conflict against the Russians and their then American allies. In particular, Major General Otto Remer and the burgeoning Socialist Reich Party were promoting a "neutralist" and often outright pro-Soviet line.

"Prague Treason Trial" was one of the "four essays" republished in 1971 by Douglas T. Kaye, along with "The Tragedy of

Youth," "The Destiny of America," and "The World in Flames."[1]

WHAT IS BEHIND THE HANGING OF THE ELEVEN JEWS IN PRAGUE?

On Friday, November 27, there burst upon the world an event which, though small in itself, will have gigantic repercussions in the happenings to come. It will have these repercussions because it will force a political reorientation in the minds of the European elite.

That event was the conclusion of the treason trial of the Jews in Prague, and their condemnation to death. During the years 1945 and 1946 the coalition Jewry-Washington-Moscow functioned quite perfectly and frictionlessly. When the Israel "State" was established as the result of armed Jewish aggression, the entire world, dominated by Moscow and Washington, sang hymns of praise and congratulation. Washington recognized the new "State" *de facto* within a few hours of its proclaimed existence. Moscow outbid Washington in pro-Jewishness by giving *de jure* recognition. Both Washington and Moscow vied with one another in seeking to please the Israel operetta-state and aided it by all means moral and material. Russian diplomats boasted that at last, in Haifa, they had a warm-water port.

And now, after a few short years, Israel is recalling its "ambassadors" from Russian vassal-states, and intensifying its anti-Russian policy from its American citadel. Volatile Jews in Israel and America cry out that Stalin is following in the footsteps of Hitler. The entire American press boils with fury at anti-Semitism in Russia. Anti-Semitism, warns the *New York Times,* is the one thing America will not tolerate in the world.

WHY THIS *BOULEVERSEMENT*?

It began early in 1947 with the Russian refusal to surrender a part of its sovereignty to the so-called "united nations" for purposes of "control" of the atomic weapon industry. Jewish

---

[1] Francis Parker Yockey, *Yockey: Four Essays* (Essex Fells, N.J.: Nordland Press, 1971).

statesmen, being materialistic in their metaphysics, believe strongly in the "absolute" military power of atomic weapons, and considered it thus indispensable for the success of their policy that they control these weapons unconditionally. This control they already possessed in America through the Atomic Energy Commission, specially created and constituted so that it is beyond the reach of Congress, and responsible only to the President, who is, by the practical rules of American inner-politics, an appointee of the Culture-State-Nation-People-Race of the Jew. They sought the same degree of control of atomic weapons in Russia, and used the device of the "united nations" to submit an ultimatum to the Russian leadership on this question.

This was in the latter part of 1946, when the tide of atom-worship was at its height, and the minds of nearly all of the poor crop of statesmen who today conduct the political affairs of the world were fantastically dominated by a mere explosive bomb. A similar mania reigned for a short time after the invention of dynamite, after the invention of the machine-gun. The Russian regime also believed in atoms with the same religious faith, and thus regarded the abdication of its "atomic" sovereignty as equivalent to the abdication of its entire sovereignty. Thus the Jewish-American ultimatum in late 1946 was rejected, and in early 1947 the preparation for the Third World War began.

This Russian refusal stymied the plans of the Jewish leadership, which aimed at a surrender of both Russian and American sovereignty to the "united nations," an instrumentality dominated by the Jewish Culture-State-Nation-People-Race. Even supine, politically-unconscious America could hardly be expected to give up its sovereignty when the only other world-power unconditionally refused, and the entire policy had to be scrapped.

The next policy of the Jewish leadership was to persuade the Stalin regime by the encirclement and pressure of the "cold war" that it was hopeless to resist. The same tactic was used against the regime of Adolf Hitler from 1933 until 1936, when war was decided upon at the earliest feasible moment.

Because of the Russian rejection of the atomic weapon ultimatum, Russia now found its policy opposed everywhere, in Austria, in Germany, in Korea, in Finland. Those same American publicists who had become so deft at explaining Russia's need for "security" as Russia seized one landscape after another, suddenly turned against Russia the accusation of "aggressor." The faithful Russian servants in the West, like Truman, Acheson, Churchill, Attlee, Gaulle and the rest, became suddenly—almost—anti-Russian. Naturally they did not use the same sort of language against Russia, the peace-loving democratic people of yesterday, that they had used against Germany, and—naturally again—they did not yet use the language of "Unconditional Surrender" when it came to a military test, in Korea. Although they had eagerly sought Russian aid against Germany, they did not now seek German aid against Russia. That would be going too far, and it is one of the political weaknesses of the Jew that he is the victim of *idées fixes*. The leading obsession of the Jew is his unreasoning hatred of Germany, which, at this present stage of Europe's cultural evolution, means: unreasoning hatred of Europe.

For several years there have been grumblings and undertones in the American press against "anti-Semitism" in Russia. These dark mutterings began after the Russian rejection in late 1946 of the Jewish-American ultimatum on the atomic weapon question. It was then that the Stalin regime began its inner-policy of dropping its numerous Jews from the highest positions, then working on down to the lower positions. Elastically, the Stalin regime tried all approaches to the Jewish leadership: it offered aid to Israel; it withdrew the offer and shut off emigration to Israel; it tried every policy, but still the Jewish-American encirclement policy continued. Wooing the Arabs did not change the mood of the Jewish-American leadership, nor did spurning the Arabs. The press campaign against Russia continued in America and all its European vassal-states. "Russia is anti-Semitic"—thus thundered the American press, and, as political initiates know, this is the worst epithet in the American arsenal of political invective. As Eisenhower said, when accused by Truman of being an anti-Semite: *"How low can you get?"*

❖ ❖ ❖

The treason trials in Bohemia are neither the beginning nor

the end of a historical process, they are merely an *unmistakable* turning point. Henceforth, all must *perforce* reorient their policy in view of the undeniable reshaping of the world-situation. The ostrich-policy is suicide. The talk of "defense against Bolshevism" belongs now to yesterday, as does the nonsense of talking of "the defense of Europe" at a period when every inch of European soil is dominated by the deadly enemies of Europe, those who seek its political-cultural-historical extinction at all costs.

That same barbaric despotism called the Russian empire and presided over by the fat peasant Stalin—Djugashvili, who rules by his cunning a Khanate greater than all those gathered together by the mighty Genghis, is today the only obstacle to the domination of the entire Earth by the instrumentality called "united nations." This vast Russian empire was created by the Jewish-American hatred of Europe-Germany. During the Second World War, in order to prevent Stalin and his pan-Slav nationalist-religious entourage from concluding peace with Europe-Germany, the Jewish-American leadership gave Russia military equipment in unheard-of masses, and political promises, gifts, and advantages with unheard-of largesse. With the 14,795 airplanes, 375,883 trucks, and 7,056 tanks given it by America, Russia occupied all Eastern Europe for itself, and advanced into Magdeburg, Weimar, and Vienna. The American Secretary of State Marshall acted consciously and openly as a Russian agent in undermining the Chiang regime in China and delivering quietly to Russian vassaldom a quarter of the world's population. It was only later that this conduct of Marshall's seemed reprehensible; at the time, he was regarded as a distinguished diplomat, like Churchill and Roosevelt at Tehran, and was decorated for his service to Russia.

Gradually the picture changed, there was more talk of "anti-Semitism" in Russia, and American public opinion, in prompt and unconditional obedience to the American press, switched over from being anti-German and pro-Russian to being anti-German and anti-Russian.

The epoch marked by the trials in Prague is not absolute; Russian papers still explain that the Jews condemned to death for sacrificing the interests of Bohemia to the interests of Jewry were "enemies of the Jewish people." The American Jewish Committee takes the same line, so that people elsewhere in the world, in places like America and its English appanage, will not develop the idea that it would even be possible for a Jew holding public office in a host-country to behave like a Jew, and not like a loyal member of the host-country. The American Jewish Committee, however, gives no explanation whatever, not even in mere words, of what possible reason Russia would have for charging loyal Russian subjects with sacrificing Russian interests to Israeli interests. They give us no clue. Apparently they would have the world believe that the canny peasant regime of Stalin is embarking on entirely unmotivated adventures in the same realm of world-politics which destroyed the political power of National Socialist Europe; the power of the Jewish Culture-State-Nation-People-Race.

The question of "guilt" or "innocence" in these, or any other political trials, like the stinking horror of Nürnberg, is historically meaningless. The Jewish victims in Prague, like the Rosenbergs[2] in America, merely did not understand how late it was in the development of the "cold war." The fashion of yesterday, of being pro-Russian in word and act, has changed. The Rosenbergs were not *au courant*.[3] The Jewish officials in Prague also were living in yesterday and felt far more secure than they were. In 1952 they behaved as though they were in 1945.

Anyone who knows the simple meaning of the world "politics" knows that these trials were not spontaneous outbreaks of "race prejudice" on the part of politically wide-awake Stalin and his power-hungry entourage. These men want *power*, and they will not attack on a front where, in the event of victory, no power could possibly be gained. For thirty-five years, Stalin has been pro-Jewish in his inner- and outer-policy, and if he now changes, it is for well-considered reasons of state-necessity.

The same Jewish press which says Stalin is "anti-Semitic"

---

[2] Julius and Ethel Rosenberg, the American Jewish couple who were executed by the US government in 1953 for passing American military secrets to the Soviets.

[3] French: up to date; well-informed.

says that his Jewish victims are "enemies of the Jews." If they really believed this of his victims, the trials show that Stalin is pro-Jewish, not that he is anti-Jewish.

However, nothing is easier than to catch the Jewish leaders in contradictions during these times when they are frantically realizing that perhaps their atomic ultimatum, their "united nations" front against Russia, their "cold war" encirclement of Russia, and their Korean war were gigantic blunders.

Up to now their objective within Russia has been to replace the Stalin regime, which the Jews consider as a traitor to the fundamental principle of Bolshevism, by a new Trotsky. Just as they constantly hoped for an internal revolution in Germany, so they have hoped for a revolution against Stalin, a revolution to return to Trotskyism and the fundamental principle of *international* Bolshevism, a revolution to wipe out religious, pan-Slav Russian nationalist-imperialism, a revolution which would embrace the "united nations" and bring about a Jewish millennium, the reunion of Baruch and Kaganovich, of Lippman and Ehrenburg, of Buttenwieser and Eisner, of Ana Pauker and Anna Rosenberg.[4] But now, this hope has vanished. There is no way of bringing about the millennium by peaceful means, through coercion of Russia by "cold war" and "united nations."

It is possible now to record the developments which have been rendered *inevitable* by the clear break signified by the Prague trials.

❖ ❖ ❖

First, and most important of all to those of us who believe in the Liberation of Europe and the Imperium of Europe: this is the beginning of the end of the American hegemony of Europe. The shoddy structure of Morgenthau Plan and Marshall Plan,[5] of

---

[4] Bernard Baruch (1860–1965), Lazar Kaganovich (1893–1991), Walter Lippmann (1889–1974), Ilya Ehrenburg (1891–1967), Benjamin Buttenwieser (1900–1991), probably Kurt Eisner (1867–1919), Ana Pauker (1893–1960), Anna Rosenberg (1901–1983) were Jews prominent in liberal or Communist politics in the United States, Europe, and USSR.

[5] The Morgenthau Plan, put forward by US Secretary of the Treas-

Schumann Plan and Strassburg Plan,[6] of the American flag flying over European capitals, of NATO, of the systematic subjugation and spoliation of Germany, of the satanic project of constructing a German Army to fight Russia on behalf of the occupying Jewish-American enemy, an Army without a General Staff, officered by democrats and armed with the weapons of 1870, the whole prolonged democratic holiday of churchills, gaulles, spaaks, gasperis, adenauers, and schumanns. For Europe, the Prague trials will act as a historical cathartic to flush out the historical waste-matter of churchills and their liberal-democratic-communist dirt.

The American hegemony is doomed because all Europe realizes with a start—what *Imperium, The Proclamation of London,* and the *Frontfighter* have preached for years—that the power on whose behalf Europe is asked to fight "Bolshevism" is none other than the Jewish State-Nation-People-Race, that entity which itself is the historical creator and leader of political Bolshevism.

It is obvious that events which were strong enough to force Stalin to reorient his entire world-policy and to become openly

---

ury Henry Morgenthau, Jr. (1891–1967), proposed to eliminate Germany's industrial and military capabilities in the aftermath of the Second World War. It was not adopted but did influence occupation policy. The Marshall Plan, which was adopted, was a massive infusion of American cash into Western Europe designed to allow the region to rebuild and head off the rise of Communism.

[6] Robert Schuman (1886–1963), who was France's Foreign Minister at the time, issued the Schuman Declaration on May 9, 1950, calling for France and West Germany's steel and coal production to be placed under one common authority. The proposal was greeted with great enthusiasm and was soon joined by several other nations, culminating in the Treaty of Paris the following year, which established the European Coal and Steel Community, which is regarded as the first step toward the establishment of the European Economic Community, the precursor to the European Union.

The Strasbourg Plan (Strassburg being the German spelling, given that the city is located in Alsace) probably refers to the Council of Europe, which was established in 1949 and operates to uphold human rights and democracy in Europe, and which is headquartered in Strasbourg, France.

anti-Jewish will have the same effect on the elite of Europe. For the American hegemony to endure, it is necessary that the European elite be quite passive—it is of course quite impossible that the European elite would ever actively cooperate with primitive human material like McCloy,[7] Truman, Acheson, or Eisenhower—and the Prague trials have gone off with an explosive roar to waken this elite to active resistance against the death plans being hatched for the European organism in Washington by the Jewish-American leadership.

America cannot undo the Prague trials any more than Russia can. From these trials there is now no going back. They are a war-declaration by Russia on the Jewish-American leadership, no matter whether or not the Russian press still wraps its explanations in woolly words disclaiming "anti-Semitism." What matters, in politics above all, is not what one *says*, but what one *does*. The fact is: the Russian leadership is killing Jews for treason to Russia, for service to the Jewish entity. Nothing can gainsay or reverse this fact. The European elite will *perforce* note this fact and be governed accordingly. Russia has publicly before the world named its power-enemy, and has thus removed all controversy on the question of who is the real power-beneficiary of the American hegemony of Europe.

In the dark days of 1945, many Europeans embraced the American occupation as the lesser of two evils. During the past seven years the comparative destructiveness of Russian barbarism and American-Jewish Bolshevism has appeared in its true proportions, the proportions set forth in *Imperium*, Volume II: a Russian occupation would be far less dangerous to Europe because of the abysmal cultural gulf between Russia and the West. This gulf would render impossible the erection of a vassal-state system, because there are no religious pan-Slavs in Europe, and the Russian barbarian leadership trusts no one else. The notion—fostered by wild American propaganda—that Russia could kill off the two hundred fifty million people of Europe

---

[7] John J. McCloy (1895–1989) was an American lawyer and banker who served as Assistant Secretary of War during World War II and US High Commissioner in occupied Germany.

need not be taken seriously. It is a vile insult to European spiritual resources and masculinity, as well as being a historical nightmare and originated no doubt in the brain of some American writer of science-fantasy stories.

For political purposes, and increasingly for total cultural purposes, America is dominated absolutely by the Culture-State-Nation-People-Race of the Jew. America in Europe appeals to all the forces of Culture-Retardation and reaction, the forces of laziness and degeneracy, of inferiority and bad instincts. From the spiritual sewers of Europe, America can siphon up an endless number of churchills to do its dirty work of dividing, despoiling, and destroying Europe in a suicidal war.

Henceforth, the European elite can emerge more and more into affairs, and will force the Jewish-American leadership to render back, step by step, the custody of European Destiny to Europe, its best forces, its natural, organic leadership. If the Jewish-American leaders refuse, the new leaders of Europe will threaten them with the Russian bogey. By thus playing off Russia against the Jewish-American leadership, Europe can bring about its Liberation, possibly even before the Third World War.

A second inevitable development from the turning-point of the Prague trials is the intensification of the American diplomatic offensive against Russia, the "cold war." The press campaign will intensify in America and in Europe; Russia will become morally blacker and blacker; the American armament will be accelerated; all potential Soviet agents will be liquidated by the "united nations." Russia will naturally retaliate: today *Pravda* says, "Zionism is a tool of American imperialism." Tomorrow it will say, "American imperialism is the tool of Zionism."

A third inevitable development: the collapse of the American-Jewish position in the Near East and throughout Islam. Since Russia will be unable to retreat from its anti-Jewish policy and the Jewish State-Nation-People-Race from its anti-Russian policy, since for each one there is no other power-opponent in the world, Russia will *perforce* ally itself with Islam, and Islam will *perforce* ally itself with Russia. Dark clouds of tragedy are gathering over the operetta-State of Israel, with its one million population surrounded by a sea of three hundred million Mohametans in whose face it has just spat, emboldened by the brawn of its big American lackey. The lackey is still big, still stupid, still willing—but he is five thousand miles away, and the concern will grow graver in Israel, and in secret places there, evacuation plans are being re-examined . . .

A fourth inevitable development is the weakening of the American position in Japan, and within a few years it is quite possible we will see the final expulsion of the American occupation troops from Japan. Even today these troops are ordered to wear mufti on the Japanese streets, and it is unavoidable that the coming intensification of Russian policy against the Jewish American regime of Washington will automatically heighten the nationalist activity of the politically-conscious Japanese elite.

Many other developments *must* follow, developments which no head in the Kremlin is now contemplating. Some are regular, and foreseeable, others are Imponderables and cannot even be imagined: one thing is sure—whoever declares war on the Jew will soon be engaged in a fight of world-wide dimensions and increasing viciousness, for the power of the Jewish State-Nation-People-Race is widespread, and the leadership of this State-Nation-People-Race conducts its policy with its emotions rather than intellectually, subject as it is to obsessions and *idées fixes*.

To us in Europe, the trials are welcome; they clear the air. The opponents have now defined themselves. America recedes now to its proper position, that of the armorer and the technician, the world's assembly line, the supplier of biological units called G.I.s to whoever is situated to pull the appropriate strings—in the First World War, it was England, in the Second it was Jewry. As far as Europe is concerned, the Jewish leaders may as well pull down the Stars and Stripes and run up the Star of David.

It was fatuous enough to ask Europe to fight for America, it was silly enough to ask it to "defend itself against Bolshevism"—under the leadership of Frankfurter, Lehman,[8] and

---

[8] Felix Frankfurter (1882–1965) was a Jewish lawyer and jurist who had served as an advisor to Franklin Roosevelt, where he was in-

Morgenthau!—but now it is too absurd to ask Europe to fight to wipe out "anti-Semitism" in Russia. Is there *one* European—just *one*—who would respond to this war-aim? But today, openly, without any possible disguise, this is the *raison d'être* of the coalition against Russia, for Russia has named its chief enemy, its sole enemy, and the sly peasant leadership of pan-Slavs in the Kremlin is not given to frivolity in its foreign policy.

The trials have made easier the task of the European Liberation Front. This Front was the first organ to warn Europe of the extinction in slavery promised for it by an alliance, supposedly with America, but actually with the Culture-State-Nation-People-Race of the Jew.

We repeat our message to Europe: no European must ever fight except for sovereign Europe; no European must ever fight one enemy of Europe on behalf of another enemy.

Europe has one aim: to actualize its Destiny. This means, to reconquer its sovereignty, to reassert its mission, to establish its Imperium, to give to the world an era of order and European peace. In the actualization of this mighty, irresistible Destiny, all extraneous events are mere material to be utilized. Inwardly, therefore, the words of the London Proclamation are as true today as they were in 1948, as they will be in 1960: "No, Europe is no more interested in this projected war than in a struggle between two negro tribes in the Sudan."

---

strumental in bringing about the New Deal, and was appointed to be a Justice of the US Supreme Court by him in 1939. Frankfurter had also helped to set up the ACLU and later called for the desegregation of America's public schools.

Herbert Lehman (1878–1963) was a Jewish politician who was elected Governor of New York when Franklin Roosevelt was elected President and served from 1933 until 1942. He was then a Senator for New York from 1949 until 1957. He was a supporter of Roosevelt and the New Deal.

LETTER TO WOLFGANG SARG

1953

EDITORS' NOTE

This letter indicates Yockey's bitter disappointment because his ideas were not only rejected but slandered by the shallowness of much of the "Right." Although his rejection by Mosley is of a different kind, that of Gerald L. K. Smith in the United States and of the veteran British "racial fascist" Arnold Leese, as well as The Britons Publishing Society, all of whom could not get much further than anti-Semitism, stunted avenues for expansion and cooperation by Yockey and his colleagues. On the other hand, those who did accept the message of *Imperium* were among the best minds of Europe. The depth of the affronts felt by Yockey from Smith, Leese, and Wolfgang Sarg also perhaps indicates the sensitivity of an artistic temperament, of someone who might have been a concert pianist had it not been for an auto accident. Yockey's humility in attempting to find a leader other than himself for the resurgence of the West—in Smith and Mosley—precludes narcissism or other sociopathic traits.

Among those most vehemently opposed to Yockey was "Natinform" (Nationalist Information), which had been intended as the opposite number to the Soviet Union's "Cominform." Founded by Wolfgang Sarg, one of H. Keith Thompson's contacts; A. F. X. Baron, a veteran of Arnold Leese's pre-war Imperial Fascist League; and former ELF colleague Peter J. Huxley-Blythe,[1] Natinform issued a "confidential" bulletin on Yockey in

[1] Peter J. Huxley-Blythe (1925–2013) in later years wrote of Yockey with esteem and came to regard him as correct in regard to the United States. He is particularly remembered in Rightist circles for his book *The East Came West*, describing the forcible return by the British of thousands of anti-Soviet Cossacks and Russians, including their families, after the Second World War to the USSR for immediate execution, under the Yalta Agreement. He later became a noted psychotherapist, and returned to politics as a contributing editor for Willis

1953, which was augmented in 1954. Signed by Sarg, a Wehrmacht veteran, the smear was written by Baron, according to Thompson.

In October of that year, Sarg was raided by the police and investigations were initiated against him as head of Natinform in West Germany.[2] Sarg was sentenced to eight months' imprisonment in 1956 for "conspiracy, libel, and fraud." According to Jewish sources, "Sarg, who is only 30, admitted during the two week trial that, together with other leading neo-Nazis in Northwest Germany, he had signed a manifesto pledging 'unconditional loyalty to National Socialism.'"[3] The Natinform document was supposedly an intelligence backgrounder, despite being littered with errors and vitriol. Some of the information later found its way into the FBI's files.

The primary allegation was that Yockey was a Soviet agent. Sarg/Baron claimed that the ELF promoted collaboration with the USSR and East Germany. Yockey supposedly joined the US Army Psychological Warfare branch and the War Crimes Commission at Nuremberg. "According to his account, upon arrival in Europe he became converted to the cause of 'Authoritarian European Nationalism,'" according to Natinform.[4] None of this information was correct. Sarg/Baron continued, "Cultivating contacts within Mosley's Union Movement, the breakaway ELF primarily included Guy Chesham, Baroness Alice von Pflügel [*sic*], and Anthony Gannon." They were of an "Eastern orientation, advocating neutralism and extreme anti-American activity." The ELF linked up with Alfred Franke-Gricksch, a German war veteran and the legal advisor to Mosley's Union Movement,

---

Carto's journal, *The Barnes Review*. See his obituary in *The Telegraph*, October 15, 2013.

[2] "German Authorities Start Investigation of Anti-Semitic Editor," *Jewish Telegraphic Agency*, October 6, 1953.

[3] "Anti-Semites in Germany Fined for Insulting Chancellor Adenauer," *Jewish Telegraphic Agency*, May 18, 1956.

[4] Wolfgang Sarg and A. F. X. Baron, "Francis Parker Yockey and the European Liberation Front," Natinform, January 28, 1953; Papers of Sir Oswald Mosley, OMD/7/1/6, Special Collections, Cadbury Research Library, University of Birmingham.

through whom contact was established with the Bruderschaft (Brotherhood) veterans' association. Sarg/Baron claimed that Karl Kaufmann and Helmut Beck-Broichsitter of the Bruderschaft had also been contacted by Yockey with the prospect of carrying out anti-American and pro-Soviet underground actions in Germany, but that they had rejected the plan.

Imperium was supposedly written with the assistance of Guy Chesham, Yockey's Oxford-educated colleague, in the overseas liaison office of the Union Movement, where both had worked. It is claimed that Yockey "likes to be considered a disciple not only of Spengler but of Moeller van den Bruck,"[5] and "completely rejected the ideas" of Nazi ideologue Alfred Rosenberg. "The style of *Imperium* is a crude imitation of Spengler's, similar to a Hollywood film production," Sarg/Baron wrote. It is claimed that *The Proclamation of London* was jointly authored by Yockey, Gannon, and Chesham.

Yockey supposedly had a meeting with an "agent" of Natinform in England, where, speaking in German, he attacked the Union Movement as being pro-American and praised Soviet policy, and in particular German POWs such as General Walther von Seydlitz-Kurzbach and Field Marshal Friedrich Paulus, both of whom had surrendered at Stalingrad and then offered their services to the Soviet side in the Second World War. Yockey supposedly asked whether this Natinform contact could organize partisans in West Germany to collaborate with the USSR. Baroness von Pflügl allegedly spoke about the soul of Germany and its eastward orientation. If Yockey's proposals were accepted, those present would be "initiated into a vast world-wide secret organization." Guy Chesham allegedly had two meetings with a Natinform agent, outlining a plan to infiltrate nationalist groups, to promote an anti-US policy, and to obtain funding

[5] Arthur Moeller van den Bruck (1876–1925) was a Weimar-era "National Bolshevik" and "Conservative Revolutionary" intellectual who, like certain other German nationalist intellectuals of the time, supported a pro-Russian policy to counter the Allies' policies after the First World War. While Yockey's stand *vis-à-vis* Russia and Western Europe after the Second World War is analogous, there is no reason to believe that Yockey was a follower of van den Bruck.

from the Soviet embassy. There would be a focus on contacting "ex-soldier organizations," such as Bruderschaft. Yockey himself was described as "small, dark, of unknown mixed races, pale and intense."

There is a tad of plausibility mixed with much nonsense in the Natinform report.

Yockey replied from Beirut, Lebanon, stating that the slanders had not caused any breach between himself and his "personal and political friend Keith Thompson," to whom Sarg had sent the memo. Yockey affirmed his authorship of the article on the "Prague Treason Trial" that had been published in the *National Renaissance Bulletin*. He countered the claim that he had been "converted" to "Authoritarian European Nationalism" in Europe after the war by pointing out that he had held these principles, which he was calling "Imperialism," since 1936.[6]

What incensed Yockey most, however, was the suggestion that the ELF pursued a pro-Russian policy and that he was a Soviet agent. From the point of view of the Russophobes of Natinform and much of the rest of the "Right" of that time, we can readily appreciate why Yockey and his followers might have been regarded as pro-Russian and worse. Yockey's friends in Germany, including the burgeoning Socialist Reich Party and its leader, Major General Otto Remer, and other war veterans, were indeed pursuing a line that was "neutralist," if not pro-Soviet. This caused alarm among the intelligence services of the United States and Germany. It is this dispute in regard to the Russian question that might explain the exception Yockey took to the Sarg/Baron claim that he had met Helmut Beck-Broichsitter and Karl Kaufmann. These two Bruderschaft officials were the least likely to be approached with any anti-American plan, and Yockey would have been fully appraised of factions within the Bruderschaft.

The Bruderschaft (Brotherhood) was formed in 1949 in the British occupation zone by former SS officers, NSDAP officials,

---

[6] Letter from Yockey to Wolfgang Sarg, January 24, 1953. Yockey is referring to "The Philosophy of Constitutional Law." "Life as an Art" further develops his philosophy.

and POWs. They advocated a united Europe independent of both the US and the USSR.[7] Hence the policy was in line with that of the ELF and the Socialist Reich Party. However, it is also the policy that caused a rift within and ultimately the end of the Bruderschaft in 1951, two years prior to the Sarg/Baron memo on Yockey. From the start, the organization was under the surveillance of the US Army Counterintelligence Corps (CIC).[8]

Yockey's contact, Franke-Gricksch, advocated an anti-American orientation for Germany. However, Beck-Broichsitter desired for Germany to align with the US as an anti-Communist ally, spoke to Allied authorities and the press, and told US High Commission members that the USSR aimed at "Bolshevizing" Germany through "phony peace initiatives" and "the offer of German unity." He stated that Germany's historic mission was to defend the West against Russia. While Beck-Broichsitter tried to align with the US, that was not the policy of the Bruderschaft, which rejected NATO. A CIC agent noted that the Brotherhood was "not pro-Allied," and opposed "protection" from both East and West. The "covert program" of the Bruderschaft was described by the CIA as a "united Europe" that would "withdraw from close political and military cooperation with the US, and although opposing international Bolshevism and Soviet interference in European affairs, could take a neutral position between the US and USSR or even enter as an equal partner into an alliance with the USSR." The fascist form of government would presumably be enacted in other European states where the Bruderschaft had contact with neo-fascist organizations.[9] Therefore, the line taken by the dominant faction in the Bruderschaft was in accord with Yockey's.

It is little wonder that Yockey was incensed at any exposure by Sarg/Baron of his communications with the Bruderschaft, which involved espionage and Cold War intrigue. Further, it is

---

[7] Richard Breitman and Norman J. W. Goda, *Hitler's Shadow: Nazi War Criminals, U.S. Intelligence, and the Cold War* (Military Bookshop, 2011), p. 53. The book is based on the US National Archives.

[8] Ibid., p. 54.

[9] Ibid., p. 57.

not likely Yockey would have communicated with Franke-Gricksch's rival, Beck-Broichsitter, given the latter's pro-American orientation. On the other hand, he was in contact with Franke-Gricksch, whose orientation was pro-Soviet. Moreover, the line of most of the Bruderschaft, like that of the Socialist Reich Party, was the same as Yockey's: to play the USSR and US off each other in order to secure concessions for Germany and Europe, with a preference for the Russians. If Yockey did talk at a meeting of the ELF about a secret order with worldwide contacts, pursuing an anti-American strategy, he was probably alluding to the Bruderschaft. For Sarg/Baron to blurt out such matters to all and sundry would have been a serious matter for Yockey and others.

Sometime in 1954, Sarg added to his Yockey memo. Sarg equated any opposition by the Right to American occupation and Culture-distortion with being pro-Soviet, and in particular as indicating Yockey's influence. Sarg and other such "nationalists" had completely thrown in their lot with the US in the cause of Russophobia and "anti-Communism." Any opposition to "America-Jewry" and the "cleansing of the soul of Europe from the ethical syphilis of Hollywood"[10] was condemned as "pro-Red." He lamented that Yockey's ideas were gaining attention among the American "Right."

Letter to Wolfgang Sarg

24 January 1953, Beirut

To Wolfgang Sarg:

By an unusual chance your letter of 28 January[11] to Keith Thompson in regard to me—the letter headed "*Confidential!*" so melodramatic—reached me here. A photostatic copy of it is in

[10] Point 5 of the ELF program.

[11] The reason for the discrepancy in dates between January 24 and 28 is unknown; it was most likely an oversight by Yockey, or else an error by Keith Stimely, who retyped it from "a dim photocopy of the original."

front of me.

It is too bad from your standpoint that your letter failed utterly of its intended effect on my political and personal friend Keith Thompson. You were apparently unaware that he is a student of *Imperium*, like dos Santos,[12] Weiss,[13] Arcand, Pirow,[14] Evola,[15] *et al*. You were also unaware of the nature of the work that Thompson and I have done together. Since I presume that he does not entrust you with this information I shall not enlighten you. Suffice to say that Thompson and I have the same *Weltanschauung*, so that your stupid and vicious attack failed, despite its cowardly "Confidential" label.

What I now say to you is not confidential. Anything in it about you or about anyone else you may publish as widely as you wish.

The article on the Prague trial of Slansky *et al*. was indeed by me, and it foretold the Russian break with Jewry which is becoming deeper and more complete every day. This development, arising as it did from the absolute identity of American and Jewish policy, is favorable to our fight for the liberation of Europe from its outer enemies, America-Jewry and Russia. The contents of the article did not reach your limited comprehension

---

[12] Possibly this is Captain Fernando dos Santos Costa (1899–1982), Minister of Defense in Salazar's Portugal. Santos Costa was an uncompromising Rightist.

[13] Frederick Weiss, a German veteran of the First World War, was a close colleague of Yockey's, ensuring him a hideout on his farm in New York. Weiss was a thoroughgoing Spenglerian, like Yockey, to the extent that their worldviews appear to have been nearly identical. Weiss, Yockey, and Thompson collaborated on many writings which were published by Weiss' Le Blanc Publishing.

[14] Oswald Pirow had been a South African cabinet minister and later formed his own political party, New Order. After the war, he collaborated with Sir Oswald Mosley.

[15] The famed Traditionalist philosopher Julius Evola had published a critical evaluation of *Imperium* in 1951 entitled "Spiritual and Structural Presuppositions of the European Union," translated into English in *North American New Right*, volume 1, ed. Greg Johnson (San Francisco: Counter-Currents, 2012).

because you, like a true Freudian, wish not to understand but only to besmirch anything superior to you.

You gave Keith Thompson a mass of lies beginning with an incorrect name for me. I know what person supplied you with this name. The same person supplied you with the birthplace for me which does not exist, and a formal educational background which is incorrect, and even went so far as to invent a career for me in the United States Army which I did not have. You state that I was "converted" to what you call "Authoritarian European Nationalism" in Europe. The fact is that my doctrine, whose principles are entirely superpersonal, is called "Imperialism," and that I arrived at its fundamentals in the year 1936,[16] before I had ever visited Europe.

You misinterpret in a stupid fashion my relations with Mosley. I was interested in his possibilities because of his pre-war orientation as Hitler's voice on the island.[17] When I discovered that he was pro-Churchill and pro-American, and anti-Russian *à outrance*,[18] even to the extent of mobilizing Europe to fight for American-Jewish victory over Russia, I left him.[19] Mosley is an effective American agent, just as Adenauer is, just as you are. It is entirely unimportant whether or not you and Mosley are paid as well as Adenauer.

I have never read, or quoted, Moeller van den Bruck. You lie about the publication of *Imperium*. You lie about the London *Proclamation*. Only an idiot like you could believe that such a work could be the work of *four* authors.

These harmless, unmotivated lies, concern me little. More se-

---

[16] See herein Yockey's first known political essay, "Life as an Art."

[17] No Mosley adherent would accept that designation.

[18] French: "to the furthest extreme."

[19] Mosley continued to view the USSR as the greater enemy to Europe than the US, whereas Yockey regarded the Culture-retardation and -distortion purveyed by American occupation as a deeper malady than military invasion. Hindsight allows us today to consider who was correct: Indeed, the European Right is strongest in the ex-Soviet states, where the people lived under Spartan conditions largely uncontaminated by the "spiritual syphilis of Hollywood," as Yockey put it.

rious is the lie which would link me with Chesham, who was expelled from the Liberation Front in 1949 for intrigue with stupid and vicious elements.[20] Serious also is the lie that I have met Beck-Broichsitter and Kauffmann, and the attempt to link me with Mrs. von Pflügl of London, who is a psychopath, and who has never had any connection, nominal or otherwise, with the Liberation Front.[21] Most serious of all is the suggestion, which you conveyed only by innuendo, being too cowardly to state it outright, that I am a Russian agent and that the Front pursues a pro-Russian policy. To the extent that you have spread this lie, you will be required to retract it.

Your entire letter to my friend Thompson was a tissue of lies. A part of it is mere misinformation, and I recognize the identities of the people who supplied you with each separate lie.

One last point remains to be made on the negative side: you inject a personal note into your vicious letter to Thompson when you try to insult my race. You wrote to my friend, who knows me personally, that I am "small, dark, of unknown mixed races, pale . . ." My height is that of Adolf Hitler, my complexion is white, my race is exclusively European. For this stupid attempt at a personal slander, you will give me satisfaction if I am ever in

---

[20] Guy Chesham had been Mosley's university student organizer. He left the Union Movement with Yockey to form the European Liberation Front. According to Yockey's primary colleague in Britain, Anthony John Gannon, Yockey originally had a falling out with Chesham because he regarded Chesham as lacking commitment by putting family before the cause. Chesham continued, however, to promote *Imperium* among the British nationalist Right.

[21] Why Yockey is denying any involvement with Alice von Pflügl, who provided funds for the first edition of *Imperium*, is unknown. She remains an enigma; little is known about her, even by her son Johnny von Pflügl, who recalls Yockey with affection when he stayed at their plush household. The daughter of a wealthy cotton merchant who married an Austrian of noble background, what is known is that during the Second World War she was detained under Defence Regulation 18B at Holloway Prison, where Lady Diana Mosley was also jailed, although the two did not meet. Her imprisonment caused much hardship for her sons.

your vicinity. If you refuse out of cowardice, I shall flog you before witnesses.

On the positive side I have this to say to you, and to the forces which you represent:

You and your kind—I refer to the European *Michel* stratum, and in particular to its leaders, the churchills—are Europe's most dangerous enemies.[22] You and your kind would make Europe into a Sarg.[23] You are a whited sepulcher, uncreative, uncomprehending, and full of malice and crooked jealousy of those with life in them, those who would lead the West forward on its great mission. You and your kind alone make possible the looting and despoiling of Europe by the American-Jewish forces. You and your kind alone made possible the victory of the Jewish-American-Russian coalition over Europe. With your talk of petty-nationalism, you are helping to perpetuate the conditions in Europe which make possible the continued Jewish-American domination.

I now state—not confidentially—that you are an agent of America-Jewry charged, on a lower plane, with the same mission as Gasperi, Gaulle, Adenauer, Zeeland, Mayer, Churchill *et al.*,[24] namely, the maintenance of the Jewish-American hegemony over Europe. Your method is the same as theirs: the attempt to identify American-Jewish interests with Europe's interests. Your propaganda is the same: you label all European Imperialists as Russian agents.

My policy, and the policy of the European Liberation Front, aims at the unconditional liberation of Europe's soul and Europe's soil from America-Jewry and from Russia. America-Jewry controls ninety percent of Europe's soil; Russia controls ten percent of Europe's soil. Elementary political tactics reveal from whom Europe can gain power over its own Destiny once more.

---

[22] The *Michel* element, a term which Yockey borrowed from Spengler's "Prussianism and Socialism" essay, designates the "inner traitor": the Westerner who betrays his Civilization.

[23] *Sarg* means "coffin" in German.

[24] Paul van Zeeland (1893–1973) was a Belgian Minister of Foreign Affairs from 1949–1954. René Mayer (1895–1972), a French Jew, was briefly Prime Minister of France in 1953.

Publish this if you dare, you vile coward. I give you my permission. My policy is not "*Confidential!*"

Note well, my attack on you is not because you are dark and pale, nor because of your vertical race. These things do not interest me, and I know nothing of your vertical race. I merely know from your name that your ancestors practiced a particularly loathsome and disgusting trade, and from your letter that you continue in their tradition. I attack you because of your political orientation: I repeat, you are an agent of America-Jewry; you are a miserable spy, a professional liar, a traitor to Europe, a Culturally-retarded idiot, an agent of Culture-distortion, a wretched *Michel*, a foul conniver, a crooked, effeminate gossip.

Copies of this letter are going to those members of my race who should be warned of your hateful mission and your vile character.

Meanwhile, swine Wolfgang Coffin, retract all your lies about me and about the Front. I shall be kept informed as to your poisonous letter-writing activities. You have been warned.

Yockey

Brotherhood

1953

Editors' Note

"Brotherhood" appeared in 1953 as a four-part series under the name of Frederick Chas. F. Weiss, over four issues of the *National Renaissance Bulletin* (June, July, October, and December). It is apparent that Yockey had considerable input into this essay, if not the majority of input. Yockey was back in the United States in late 1952, departing to work at the propaganda department of the Egyptian government in early 1953. In 1952 Yockey met Weiss[1] and was assisting Weiss' colleague H. Keith Thompson with writing to the US State Department regarding the jailing of Major General Otto Remer and the banning of the Socialist Reich Party in Germany, under the name of the Committee for International Justice, as discussed in the correspondence with Dean Acheson included in this volume.[2] It seems plausible that Yockey would have assisted Weiss with the writing of "Brotherhood" in late 1952, a time during which the FBI noted that they had received information that Yockey was writing Weiss' material, although joint authorship seems more likely.

Again, the theme is Spenglerian, in particular the theme of a Bolshevik-led "class war" and a race war of the colored world (through both internal and external revolts) against the white nations, which is a major theme of Spengler's last book, *The Hour of Decision*.[3] However, in "Brotherhood," the focus is on the subversive character of modern Christianity, with its worldly ideology that has become a tool of the "Jewish Consensus" and its Left-liberal allies, an antithesis of the "Gothic Christianity" that Yockey described in *Imperium* and elsewhere as providing the

---

[1] Kerry Bolton, *Yockey: A Fascist Odyssey* (London: Arktos, 2018), p. 236.

[2] Ibid., pp. 296, 300–306.

[3] Spengler, *The Hour of Decision*, the chapters "The White World-Revolution" and "The Colored World-Revolution."

foundations of Western High Culture and the defense mechanism against Jewish culture-pathology and usury. Now, the religion of the churches had become that of "Brotherhood," and the vitality of the West was (and is) being sapped to oblivion.

In terms of style and content, Part 4 of "Brotherhood," is markedly Yockeyan. Yockey's thinking is most evident in the discussion of constitutions as expressing a race-soul. Compare the passages on constitutions and state-formation here with Yockey's college essay, "The Philosophy of Constitutional Law," where he writes, for example:

> The kind of law is dependent directly and completely on the kind of lawgiver, and therewith on the society in which he has matured—whether primitive or cultured, whether feudal or cosmopolitan, aristocratically or democratically ordered, industrial or agricultural, whether Russian, Western, Chinese, Indian, Egyptian, or Classical. A nation is as much a legal unit as it is a political or economic unit. In the law of a people its world-outlook finds pure and clear expression (there are outstanding exceptions, but in these cases the alien-ness of the law dominated the legal picture, and eventually the law was either spiritually transformed [Roman law by the Arabian Culture], or became the object of a violent political abrogation [Roman law by Germany in 1935]).

According to "Brotherhood," in writing the US Constitution, the Founding Fathers "had to act consciously or unconsciously under the spell of the culture of their ancestors. For their soul would not let them do otherwise. They responded to the spell of the same culture which had produced the peoples of Europe, but not of a culture which had been produced by these peoples." Further, it is held that the American nation was born not only through a common spiritual feeling, and certainly not through a political or even a zoological bond, but "through an *idea* of our spiritual Elite which had to act under the spell of a Western culture."

Again, from Yockey's college paper on constitutionalism:

> It is in the national soul, preserved in tradition and expressed anew at every epoch, that we must look for the source of the living constitution—that constitution that exists (in any Western nation) for nine hundred years before the brief interlude of rationalistic written constitutions and will continue, after their inevitable demise, to the end of Western history.

Since the early 1950s, the "Brotherhood-Babblers" have become predominate in all the churches of the West. It is called the "social gospel," and the banal cries for "social justice" show no semblance whatever to the traditional social doctrine of the Catholic Church that had been expressed through papal encyclicals until *Quadragesimo Anno* (1931), and had formed the Gothic edifice of the Western High Culture until the Reformation, which started to undermine the old sanctions against usury.

From the "Right" of the churches there is a "prosperity gospel" that is particularly avid in its support for the "Jewish Consensus"; from the "Left," "Brotherhood" has become the predominant gospel, with the focus being on feminism, homosexuality, "racism," and open borders, and one does not even have to profess faith in Jesus as the supernatural Son of God, nor in "God the Father" (patriarchy), not only to be a "Christian" but even to become a minister of the new social gospel. While Protestantism showed the first signs of rot in its very foundation, the Catholic Church finally succumbed to it with Vatican II during the 1960s.[4] What remains is the spirit of Bolshevism. The following is a fairly typical example, taken from the Uniting Church, a major church body in Australia and New Zealand:

> The Give Hope campaign for asylum seekers is an initiative of the Social Justice Forum and its partners. It was founded in response to growing community concern about how asylum seekers and refugees were being treated in Australia. The plight of refugees and asylum

---

[4] See Joseph Roddy, "How the Jews Changed Catholic Thinking," *Look*, vol. 30, no. 2, January 25, 1966.

seekers was identified by Forum affiliates as a key concern for their members.[5]

BROTHERHOOD

Part 1

A religion is that which the soul of the faithful is. A church is worth just as much as the priest-material of which it is composed is worth. All priests are human beings. The fate of churches therefore becomes dependent upon the human material of their continuously changing personnel. The vulgar instincts and vulgar thoughts of many of our clergy seem to become predominant now in these times of our social degeneration and revolutionary demolition. A priest-rabble drags the dignity of the church through the mud of petty politics, allies itself with an international, landless, boundless, and alien Consensus in our midst, and by sentimental talk about Brotherhood, eggs on our misguided mob and so destroys the social order—that order with which the church is irrevocably and fatally bound up.

And here we ask: Does the outcry for brotherhood and World-Reconciliation of many of our clergy not actually mean our abdication from history at the cost of dignity, honor, and liberty? Is not life war? Can we dismiss its meaning and yet retain it? When our priests shout from the pulpits: Love your neighbor and help the poor, down-trodden peoples of Asia and Africa . . . these yellow-brown-black men on the shores of the Yangtze and Senegal rivers see through us! They scent our unfitness and lack of will to defend ourselves! They do not cling to a life whose length is its sole value! Once they feared us; now they despise us! Once they were filled with terror at our power; now they look down upon us as a thing of yesterday! But, that is not all. In Asia and Africa, the extraordinary public profiles will increase still more enormously now that European

[5] Uniting Church, "Social Justice," ume.nswact.uca.org.au/links/social-justice/

and American medicine has been introduced to check disease, which was so strong a selective factor. In contrast to this, the apparent increase of the white population all over the world, little as it is in comparison with the volume of the colored increase, rests upon a temporary illusion: the number of children grows ever smaller, and only the number of adults increases, not because there are more of them, but because they live longer.

Yet, the mob element in the priesthood continues unabated its raid upon whatever there is left of our "Race" qualities. And the Consensus sees to it that our masses live so under the bombardment of their intellectual artillery that hardly anyone can acquire a clear view of the present monstrous drama. What the Press, Radio, and Television wills, is true. For our masses, Truth is that which they continually read, hear, and see by media of communication which the Consensus controls.

Yet nobody tells them that all Communist systems in the West are in fact derived from Christian theological thought. The Consensus' terrible censorship of silence sees to that. It sees to it that nobody dares to tell our masses that Christian theology, as taught in our schools and distorted from the pulpit, is the grandmother of Western Bolshevism: that all abstract brooding over economic concepts that are remote from any economic experience (like the Four-Point[6] raising of the standard of living of the Hottentots[7] to that of our own) will lead in one way or another to reasoned conclusion against State and Property. Were we to understand this, we then could easily comprehend why the Bolshevism of our priesthood, fostered by the bolshevistic teachings of our cosmopolitan Intelligentsia, is ten times more dangerous than Asiatic Bolshevism: that it is

---

[6] President Truman announced his "Four Point" program as the fourth foreign policy objective he outlined in his inaugural speech of 1949. Its purpose was to provide technical assistance to the nations of the Third World as part of an effort to win them over to the American side in the Cold War.

[7] A term coined by the Dutch colonists in South Africa to describe the Khoikhoi, non-Bantu nomads who were indigenous to the region. In later centuries it had a derogatory connotation.

more dangerous because it hides behind the mask of religion.

And so, nobody tells us, that to put into effect the Brotherhood ideal which our One-World apostles shower upon us from the pulpits, requires dictatorship, a reign of terror, armed force, the inequality of a system of slaves and masters, men in command and men in obedience—in short: *Moscow.*—

When Jesus was taken before Pilate, then two worlds were facing each other in immediate and implacable hostility: a world of *facts* and a world of *truth.* At this appallingly distinct scene, overwhelming in its symbolism, human tragedy took the highest conceivable form. In the famous question of Pilate: "*What is truth?*"—lies the entire meaning of history, the exclusive validity of *truth,* the prestige of State and war and blood.

"*What is actuality?*"—for Pilate actuality was all; for Jesus nothing. How—otherwise—could pure religiousness stand up against history or sit in judgment on active life?

"*My Kingdom is not of this world.*" This final word admits of no gloss. A statesman can be deeply religious, a pious man can die for his country—but they must, both, know on which side they are standing. When the statesman ridicules the inward thought-process of the ethical philosopher in a world of fact . . . or the pious man discards all ambition in the historical world as sinful and as lacking any lasting value . . . then for the onlooker it is meaningless to argue which one of the two is right or wrong.

But if our present administration wishes to "improve" the religious feeling of our masses in the direction of political, practical, purposes—then these *ten-, twelve-,* or *fourteen-point acrobats* stand before History as absolute fools.

And equally, when our *Brotherhood* Preachers try to bridge the course of History and the existence of a divine world-order—they are fools also. They'd better leave this experiment to those champion prestidigitators whose nation-feeling over the last four millennia comprised neither more nor less than what was and is covered by the Ideas of the Church of their *landless, boundless Consensus.*

Part 2

The idea underlying this alien "brother-nation" in our midst is the result of an immense mission. Whereas the history of the Jewish Consensus has been for its members the progressive actualization in and through mankind of a world plan laid down by God and accomplished between a creation and a cataclysm, history in our eyes is a single grand willing of conscious logic in the accomplishment of which nations are led step by step and represented by their Presidents, Leaders, Kings, and Kaisers. Whereas our nation concept, though necessarily bound up with a particular religiousness, is not so with a particular confession, the nation-feeling of the Consensus comprises neither more nor less than is covered by the idea of its church. Thus, the Jewish Community embraces the whole of the world-"cavern," the here and the beyond, and within this community their "state" only forms a smaller unit of the visible side, a unit, therefore, of which the operations were governed by the major whole. Consequently, in the Jewish world the separation of politics and religion is theoretically impossible and nonsensical, whereas in our Western Culture the battle of Church and State is inherent in the very conceptions: logical, necessary, unending!

Jesus' final words: "My Kingdom is not of this world" and "Give unto Caesar the things that are Caesar's" are absolutely nonsensical to the elect, just as they appear nonsensical to the governing horde in the Kremlin . . . and to our own babbling Brotherhood apostles, for that matter. Whereas our nations are inwardly linked with a landscape, the Consensus knows neither fatherland nor a mother tongue. Our country as a region whose boundaries an individual cannot see, but which he will nevertheless defend and die for, is something that in its symbolic depth and force the elect in "exile" can never comprehend. To us, on the other hand, the inwardness and hidden force of the Consensus, its tacit, self-secure cohesion based upon a purely metaphysical impulse, but by no means on a deliberate, visible organization, is something entirely enigmatic. If our nation contains a great proportion of folk-elements of varied provenance to whom state-majesty, a life symbol of the first order, means absolutely nothing, it is not so with the members of the Consensus. They, too, are of varied provenance, yet the energy of the Consensus long ago has completely overridden the older tribal arrangement. They therefore no longer constitute an obstacle to the closest world-wide cohesion, for they are all co-believers, they all belong to one body which knows the "right" way to salvation. Whereas the plurality of the elect venerate their "State" as a matured form of high symbolism, the plurality of our people look upon our State as a vehicle to serve their private, selfish ends. But the deepest element of separation and bitterness is the difference in phase. Where we experience the short, crowded epoch in which our history and destiny now take decisive turns, for the Jew, all this lies thirty generations back. He lives these experiences, not really as something of his own, but as a partisan, a supporter, or as an interested spectator. A Jewish cavalry general fought in the Thirty Years' War[8]—but what did the ideas of Luther of Loyola[9] mean to him? Certainly not more than our ideas mean today to our Jewish generals, admirals, and to our "consulting statesmen."

But there is also a statistical aspect to the matter. For every human being alive today there are ten million ancestors who lived around 1000 AD. Consequently, each and every one of us of Celtic-Germanic stamp is without exception a blood relative of every Nordic European of the age of the Crusades. But in the cases of the Consensus with its thousand years of ghetto life, the relationship becomes a thousand times more intensely close, and this especially so in the case of its Western European members. And if we look carefully into this phenomenon of mysterious resemblance, we begin to comprehend why we can

---

[8] The Thirty Years' War, between 1618 and 1648, was fought primarily in Central Europe between Catholic and Protestant states of the Holy Roman Empire, expanding to become a war between the Habsburgs and France.

[9] A play on Martin Luther and St. Ignatius of Loyola, the founder of the Jesuit Order. Weiss and Yockey seem to be suggesting that both Protestantism and Catholicism are meaningless to Jews.

hardly exaggerate the formative power which created the immense race energy of this alien people, so that in utter unconsciousness it has been able to fulfill to this very day its will of the race.

Even when the force of "cohesion" between the elect and the institutions of his host people exercises an outward attraction upon him, to the point of induced patriotism, the "party" he supports is always that of which the aims are most nearly comparable with the essence of his boundless, landless nation. Hence, "by nature," he is today a "Communist" of the Trotsky brand; a One-World-Apostle, that is. And it is certainly a fatal misunderstanding if *we* regard these "Democrats" or "Republicans" as kindred spirits—that is as "constitutionalists" in our Western sense. For, if there is inward alienness, a man destroys even where his desire is to be constructive. And, if he does no longer possess the material power to enable him to act in the cadre of his own Culture (as we see it today in Stalin's "Russia"); if he no longer can ignore or manipulate the destiny of the Russian people (as he did in Trotsky's time); he stands helpless in the midst of events and his cohesion falls apart. Hence, it is quite natural that today he subtly professes to be an "Anti-Communist" . . . by which he, naturally, means only to be opposed to "Stalinism" (which he regards today—and righteously so—as his most deadly enemy)!

The Machiavellian genius of these few alien go-betweens and cosmopolitan mediators, have now set the stage to bring about a climax in the fulfillment of their mission: the final achievement of their World-rule with the help of a pyrrhic victory *à la* Korea by *either* East *or* West; fought out in the land of those they dread the most: *the German nation!* That is, however, if not before, their *Berias* and *Judins* should have succeeded in the liquidation of the *Molotovs* and *Stalins*: For, that would be the day when our babbling Brotherhood Apostles would smoothly and silently (the Potsdam, Yalta, and Teheran way) sign away our historical rights; when we—without a shot—would abdicate, not in favor of everlasting peace, but in favor of a supernational UN, which then would automatically become the maximum conceivable field for the exploitation by the only remaining world power: the landless, boundless, cosmopolitan *Consensus!*

We now comprehend why it is impossible that the two metaphysics can ever come closer to one another. Yet, our Brotherhood-Babblers shout from their pulpits that only our religious confession would separate us from these aliens in our midst! Incapable of feeling the metaphysical hatred, which is the beat-difference of two currents of being and which settles deep in the blood—these deplorable babbling priests, those doctrinaires and Utopians, these lawmakers and shoemakers—for sheer want of "race"—no longer are able to register as such the unbearable dissonance between the two Cultures; they are no longer able to feel these fundamental differences because they themselves—in contrast to the majority of the members of the Jewish Consensus—have ceased to be metaphysical at all.

And so from their pulpit, they poison the mind of our "Fourth Estate,"[10] the *mass*, which now rejects our Tradition, our Culture, and its matured forms—lock, stock, and barrel!

Shall we now pass from history into the historyless? Will it be the end, the radical nullity?

Part 3

Slowly now, to our horror, there rises before our inner eye a *Trinity*: Father, Son, and Ghost. All unholy, to be sure, but unholiest of the three is the Ghost.[11]

---

[10] Before the French Revolution, European civilization was understood to be divided into three estates: the clergy, the nobility, and the commoners; in modern times, some have added the press to this as a "fourth estate."

[11] Two alternate versions of this issue of the *National Renaissance Bulletin* exist, typed and distributed in mimeographed form. They both contain the following paragraph inserted after the one above. One version contains only part of the paragraph, beginning with the words, "The Son represents the forces of Stalinism . . ." The other version contains the whole paragraph.

The Father represents World Jewry, that international race of

For, whereas the Jew fathers World-Bolshevism for the "holy" task of fulfilling his mission; whereas the ungrateful son in the Kremlin—again for the "holy" purpose of shaping his own destiny—threatens now to murder the Father, lest the Father murder the Son, the Ghost causes his obsessed victim to commit suicide.

Both Father and Son are masters in the art of the possible. Their eye for possibilities assures them of victory. They both are masters of fact. And so they sensed the possibility of making an end of our White World and promptly—with the help of the Ghost—began to let us tear down what centuries had built

---

people whose intellectuals and financiers created World Communism as an effective instrument with which to gain control of the economic, political, and cultural life of the Gentile nations. Communism also provided a lure for the barbarian hordes of Asia and Africa, allowing the Jew to rally the entire colored world for an onslaught against Western Civilization. Not since the days of Genghis Khan has the Aryan World been in such mortal peril. The Son represents the forces of Stalinism which have sought to usurp the power of the Jew behind the Iron Curtain. The forces represented by Stalin and Malenkov have sought to replace the Jewish ideal of an international World State consisting of a racially mongrelized Gentile population dominated by Jewish intellectuals with a dynamic form of Russian Imperialism. For this reason the Jews would like to destroy the Russian Imperialism of the Malenkovs and Stalins and replace Malenkov with a new Leon Trotsky (Bronstein). This would insure the fact that the Communist Philosophy would remain a completely Jewish monopoly. The Ghost, for whose existence both Father and Son are to blame, is the spirit of Nihilism which stalks the hapless Twentieth Century World. Nihilism is defined as an extreme socialist movement in Russia to destroy existing institutions and found a new order of things, with Communistic rights of land and property. Nihilism is the blood-stained Ghost, conceived in the minds of the Jewish theorists like Marx and Engels, which stalks our era and seeks the destruction of Western Civilization.

A handwritten note in one of the copies that survives indicates that this addition was an editor's note.

up, both here and in Europe. The result is that we have now become mere objects of a supranational "progressive" government.

The warning that this progress actually meant constitutional anarchy, and the negation of every kind of authority, was met with contemptuous laughter by our "liberals," by our Brotherhood-Babblers and World-Reconcilers, all of whom were obsessed by the most frightful thing our White World has ever experienced—*nihilism*, that is.

Thus, the Father and Son joined forces with a Ghost in our midst that had obsessed our "enlightened" doctrinaires and Utopians since the middle of the eighteenth century, but which now—with the help of Father and Son—turned its attention successfully from the theological systems of Christianity and traditional world philosophy of our Western scholars—to the fact of actuality: the Western State with all its sacred institutions. And how easily we let Father and Son win over our Nihilists: our literary and political Bohemia, our wastrel "nobility," our spiritually shipwrecked academicians, our adventurers and speculators, our criminals and loiterers, our halfwits and sunken priests . . . mixed with pathetic enthusiasts for the abstract ideal of universal Brotherhood.

With the media of a "subsidized" press, International News Service, and above all, with the Father's own Radio and Television systems, the unholy Trinity now forms at will the consciousness of our "Fourth Estate," the Mass, under a deafening drumfire of theses, catchwords, standpoints, scenes, and perverted feelings. Above all they tell our spiritually poor, downtrodden mass that a new era—"democracy of the Century"—had dawned. They flatter and organize the mass of our wage-earners in the cities and industrial centers and drive them by means of a cynical propaganda into the class war against the majority of our people. Whenever the agents of this unholy Trinity are able to assemble corporeally a mass; whenever the millions of our families are gathered around their television sets, they subject them to an influencing process, unknown even at the time of Caesar and Cicero. For their bodily near and sensuous means, and their rhetoric that works upon every ear and eye, have no parallel. Their shameless flattery, fantastic lies, brilliant phrases, and resounding cadenzas, their "games" and presents, their Jazz music, rhumbas, and Negro dances . . . and even when necessary—their rehearsed sob-effects, outmatch everything that the democracies of other centuries had to offer!

This process of "conversion," this *veryiddeln*[12] of the spirit of our masses, goes on and on; it does not stop before the Titans of our Beaux Arts,[13] not even before Science (who did not hear of Einstein, whoever heard of Planck?).[14]

Whether our Western States in their present form would be able to hold their own over the next decisive years . . . no one dares to question. All that matters, they tell us, is that we hang on fervently to the words (but not to the meaning) of our Constitution and so to secure for the Father his special "God Given" right to freedom from every kind of restriction of our soil-bound life and his absolute freedom to exercise at will his worldwide monopoly of mediation.

All that matters, they tell us, is that we should bleed ourselves white and permit the Father's own supranational government to shower our blessings and resources in the form of "universal rights" over our drum-beating and rhumba-dancing brown-black-and-yellow brethren; over those who had not ever thought of claiming them.

Is there any wonder that we live so cowed under this bombardment of the intellectual artillery of our unholy Trinity that hardly anyone of us can attain to the inward detachment that is required for a clear view of the present monstrous drama? The will-to-power of this Trinity, operating under a pure "democratic" disguise, has finished off its masterpiece so well that our masses' sense of freedom is actually flattered by the most thor-

---

[12] *Ver-yiddeln* is a German anti-Semitic term, and seems to be a diminutive form—essentially, "to yid-ize"—of *verjuden* ("to judaize"). It is undoubtedly a reference to the famous 1936 Yiddish musical, *Yiddle with Her Fiddle*.

[13] French: fine arts.

[14] Max Planck (1858–1947) was a German physicist who made the discoveries that laid the foundations for quantum physics.

oughgoing enslavement that has ever existed. So successfully is this deceit manipulated that our multitude now placidly goes its way in the belief that it has won for itself the famous four freedoms;[15] that phrase which we express so proudly in "Liberal Constitutions" is now nothing but anarchy become a habit. For, no nation can govern itself . . . any more than an army can lead itself. What we call democracy, parliamentarianism, government "by the people" . . . is in fact nothing else than the mere non-existence of a conscious responsible authority, a government that is, a true *State*.

Nobody dares to lift a finger when—upon command of Father and Son—our Ghost-obsessed Brotherhood-Babblers, detached from the pulse of our blood and being, tell our masses that they can no longer find any "reasonable" connotation for the Nation idea; that the time is now ripe for Universal Brotherhood and . . . that gone forever are the days when a white man held a bit of soil to be worth dying for.

Unobserved by the majority of us, we now have ceded the choice of the hour to Father and Son; to Asia, whose frontier now lies along the Elbe River. For the first time since the siege of Vienna by the Turks, our white world again has been put on the defensive. Where yesterday we would have commanded, we now have to flatter if we are even to negotiate and nobody among us is even aware of this sad fact.

Deprived of our most powerful ally since 1776—distance, deprived of every potential powerful European ally after our pyrrhic victory over Central Europe, Fate now knocks at our door and demands that we take over the leadership of our white world in the last struggle for all or nothing.

In this Hour of Decision, this gravest task of ours no longer can be pushed into the future as an unavowed commitment

---

[15] On January 6, 1941, President Roosevelt outlined what he termed the "four freedoms" which he felt all peoples everywhere in the world should have: freedom of speech, freedom of worship, freedom from want, and freedom from fear. The speech has been seen as part of the case that Roosevelt was building for US intervention in the Second World War.

upon the shoulders of our heirs' heirs. Too heavy now has become the centrifugal pressure emanating from an Asiatic focus of power; too obvious has become the will of the unholy Father in our midst to deny us the man who in the last moment could muster every possible resource of spiritual power that is still left in our white world; too great has become the power of this unholy Father in our midst, who at will unleashes the mass of his readers and listeners—that *mass*, which at any time, upon the command of its true master, will storm through the streets and hurl itself upon the "Fascists," "Nazis," "Bigots," and "Hate-Mongers," the moment the few who are left of our elite dare to offer resistance.

And so we see the eventual physical death of tens of millions and the certain political death of all of us to be near at hand . . . that is, if the store of excellent blood that still exists in a great part of the American people can no longer be roused and spiritualized to meet the stupendous challenge of Father, Son—and our Ghost-obsessed Brotherhood-Babblers and One-World Apostles.

At this decisive moment, the ghettoes of New York City now have become the *point*, where the whole life of our entire Western World is collecting while the rest dries up. What does it signify? It signifies that London, Berlin, and Paris, together with our own big cities, including our "Capital," have become provinces! It signifies the approach of the end. From now on, the great intellectual decisions take place, not in the whole Western World where yesterday no hamlet was too small to be unimportant, but in the world-city of New York where the Father of World-Bolshevism has absorbed into itself the whole content of our Western History, while the old, wide landscape of the Culture—here as well as in Western Europe—has become merely provincial and is fighting a losing battle against the chosen Big Brains in the World Capital of New York.

If we fearlessly try to comprehend the great crisis of the present, we have to concede that from this moment on, all our great conflicts of world-outlook, of politics, of art, of science, of feeling, are now—not only here in America, but throughout our Western World—under the opposition of the Father; that the hallmark of our Western politics today is journalism and broadcasting rhetoric, both serving that abstract which represents the real *power* behind everything—*money!* And, worse still, here in America this money-spirit penetrated unnoticed the historical forms of the people's existence—without destroying or even disturbing these forms, so that our great parties, though still in being, have ceased now to be more than the reputed centers of decision. The decisions in fact lie elsewhere. A small number of superior heads—those champions in battles fought with the coldest and most abstract means—in the Father's consensus, whose names are hardly known, keep skillfully alive the illusion of popular self-determination.

May the following chapter help in comprehension.

Part 4[16]

We will attempt now to show why all this *had* to come; why it *had* to happen . . . because we let it happen; how we tried to adhere to this or that, but *not* to the necessary . . . and why now we are confronted with the nothing: with our final abdication from the political platform! For, what the individual will not do, Fate (and what a Fate) will do for him! . . .

"Historical" man is the man of Culture, that is in full march towards self-fulfillment. Before this, after this, outside of this, man is historyless, and the destinies of the people to which he belongs matter as little as the Earth's destiny matters when the plane of attention is the astronomical and not the geological.

Culture is the being of nations in State-form. A nation, a living and struggling unit flowing in the stream of history, possesses above all a State as an Idea. Even very lowly animal genera, not to speak of ants, bees, migrating birds, beavers, etc., have "constitutions" of some sort.

Peoples as States are the real forces of all human happenings; they are destiny. Every State that emerges in History exists as it is but once and for a moment; the next moment it has,

[16] For this chapter, the title was written as "Brotherhood?" in imitation Hebrew lettering.

imperceptibly, undergone a mutation, whatever the rigidity of its legal constitution. The systematically planned State of the theorist will ever contrast with the State of actuality. *For no real constitution, when taken by itself and committed to paper as a system, is complete.* The description of a State or its constitutional archives cannot give us even the silhouette of that which underlies the living actuality of a State as its essential form. For the unwritten, that is the indescribable, yet so unusual, so readily felt, so self-evident, by far outweighs everything else. If we seriously subject an existence-unit of history to the constraint of a written constitution, and then critically fix our eyes upon its form, we soon find out that it is no longer "in condition" to wrestle successfully in and with history. This holds equally true for the smallest as for the largest unit in the stream of history, for a family as well as for a nation.

However different their ideas of a State were from the concept of their forefathers, the idea which underlaid the historical manifestation of our Founding Fathers, they had to act consciously or unconsciously under the spell of the culture of their ancestors. For their soul would not let them do otherwise. They responded to the spell of the same culture which had produced the peoples of Europe, but not of a culture which had been produced by these peoples.

And so our Nation was born, not merely by a strong common spiritual feeling of our people, and certainly not through an already existing linguistic, or political, or zoological bond, but mainly through an *idea* of our spiritual Elite which had to act under the spell of a Western culture.

But what has become of this Constitution? In this Hour of Decision, the destiny question for us all now is whether our State exists in the effectiveness of the spirit of our Constitution, not in the moral of an impractical dreamer and Brotherhood-Babbler, but in the steadiness, sureness, and superiority of political leadership, or whether the strength of our constitutional leadership has been shattered and our Nation has already become the victim of an alien policy . . . forever. The question is, whether our leaders' responsibility is still above all to a minority, to our spiritual Elite, that possesses the instinct of statesmanship and represents our Nation in the true spirit of our Constitution—or whether our "leaders" feel themselves responsible to another minority in our midst: To those spiritual members of an international, boundless, and landless Jewish Consensus, to those Jewish subjects of an alien nation, whose nation-consciousness, derived from a particular and defined world-feeling, is entirely different from ours as we have seen before.

Over the last six millennia and up to this day, the savants of the Consensus shaped their Nation's fate by feeling for, and ascertaining, the general conviction of their associates, which could not err because the mind of God and the mind of the community are the same . . . while we, nations and individuals alike, sought to shape our future, each for himself, and fought one another—nay, annihilated one another!

So long as the world powers were without exception European powers, so long as these powers fought one another, sometimes over miserable scraps of land; so long as our own coal, industry, bank, and bourse element fought our settler and planter element in the South, the members of the Consensus could not possibly understand the passion with which we Westerners livingly experienced the decisive turns of our history and destiny. For them all this lay thirty generations back.

But things changed fundamentally when, with the beginning of our century, the *visible* decay of one Western state after another set in; when with the disappearance of *Staatshoheit*,[17] the repressive force of one state after another in Europe vanished, when we so crowned our suicidal effort and obliged the Consensus by tearing down what centuries had built up. That was the time when the savants of the elect knew that their hour had come. At least twenty-five years before our deplorable statesmen could see it, the Consensus began to comprehend that with our entry upon the age of world wars, the transition from the eighteenth-century world of states to the *imperium mundi*[18] had set in. Even today our "leaders" have not realized this hard fact. For

[17] German: "state sovereignty."

[18] Latin: world empire.

how otherwise could be explained their state-destroying wish for "universal Brotherhood" by abdicating in favor of a supernational government?

After the Consensus in launching against all of us a yellow-brown-black offensive under a Red leadership; after stirring up a class war from below and a race war from without; after his "glorious recapture" of Jerusalem, can we now only assume that this alien nation is willing to renounce her aspiration for world domination or give up the desire to fulfill her mission? Are we really to believe that, because a few members of the upper stratum of the elect have lost every kind of inward cohesion, the Consensus will regionally fall into parts or willingly give up his worldwide cohesion; once our famous UN will declare Universal Peace, once our own world pacifists and Brotherhood-Babblers, our theorists and professors, our utopians and humanists, our lawmakers and shoemakers, will have signed away our historic rights and our freedom?

Once on this globe we all have become brethren, will the Consensus give up the accomplishment of the task that in its belief historic necessity has set for him? Would not Universal-Brotherhood presuppose the absurd assumption that Yahweh, in order to become Jesus' benign and Heavenly Father of all humanity, undergoes a sudden and extraordinary transformation? That wrathful, irascible, unforgiving God of our Jewish brethren; that Yahweh from whom the elect expects that "he crushes the unrighteous . . . that he lay waste the country of the unbelievers . . . that he destroys—with a rod of iron—their being . . . that he breaks their pride like a potters' vessel . . . that he makes nations flee before him at his threatening . . . that he will gather his 'holy people' and rule over them in righteousness . . . that neither settler nor stranger shall dwell among them (in Palestine!) . . . that, so long as they serve him, he will hold the Gentiles in yoke" (Psalm of Solomon, Ps. 17).

Does anybody believe in such an absurd transmutation? Will the majority of the elect follow the small minority, the stubborn and zealous few, and return to the "Israeli homeland" and leave us in peace? When, on the other hand, history teaches us how in the "Exile" this alien nation increased enormously beyond the old small clan limits, when she destroyed the political power of one after the other of her host peoples by manipulating at will their economic potentialities, when the dispersed majority turned so successfully to "conversions" as the only form of conquest open to a landless nation? Do we not have right here the best proof of the immense aggressive power of this "conversion"? When we can daily witness how the Consensus succeeds in the more and more radical political elimination of our own spiritual Elite, of those few who alone would still be able to find their way from thinking in terms of party lines to thinking in terms of statesmanship? The more radical this elimination, the more completely is our electoral mass delivered by their party leaders into the hands of the Consensus.

And so with that, the Consensus has now succeeded in changing the name of our Republic to the finest sounding of all, freedom and democracy, but in reality it has turned it over to the worst thing of all, to the mob, ruled by the Consensus. Yet, not satisfied with their "remodeling" job over here, our wire-pullers now even force us to impose their "paradise" of a State upon our brother nations and to reject every refusal of acceptance with the warning: *"Und willst du nicht mein Bruder sein, so schlag' ich dir den Schädel ein!"*[19]

But what are the upper strata of our society and our "leaders" doing to stem this progressive Bolshevization of our masses? Where is the opposition of graded social structure against our town-masses, of tradition against mob-rule, of the higher existence of the few against the lower of mass-labor, when at best we can see only our Me-Too-Politicians seeking in vain a conciliatory middle course against the radical tendencies of our misguided masses? As if this radical age would permit compromises! As if this will to the middle way was nothing else but the senile wish

---

[19] "If you won't be my brother, I will smash your skull in!" This is a famous quotation which was originally coined by the German revolutionaries in the 1848 revolution as a play on the French Jacobin slogan, "brotherhood or death." Bernhard von Bülow (1848–1929), who was Chancellor of Germany from 1900 until 1909, also used the expression during a speech in the Reichstag on December 10, 1903.

for peace at any price, even the price of our liberty! Can we discern as yet any other focus of resistance against this diabolically organized mob-rule? Is this revolution not striding unchecked towards its ultimate decision with the historical recklessness of a terrible destiny to which we and all the other white peoples must inevitably succumb . . . if not checked by a handful of thoroughbreds, by some individuals who make history? Or are we waiting with our counter-measures for a real "emergency" — for the day, that is, when the Consensus will have succeeded in its effort to join physically the force of class war from within with those of race war from without? Neither of these two Revolutions will disdain the aid of the other because it despises its supporters, for a common hatred against the white man extinguishes their mutual contempt.

Can we for one moment doubt that this planned joining of these forces would have been accomplished long ago had it not been for a temporary miscarriage of the Master Plan! When with the appearance of the Red Fascist (!) Stalin and the "abdication" of Trotsky, the Consensus' State within the Red State had to go more and more underground; when Marxian Bolshevism retreated before the furor of an Asiatic "Horde," led by a new Genghis Khan.

Frederick Chas. F. Weiss

CULTURE

1953

EDITORS' NOTE

With the December 1953 essay "Culture," Yockey develops a theme that repudiates rationalism, positivism, and other such nineteenth-century materialistic philosophies, presenting the post-rationalist era of History as the unfolding of a great drama that is beyond rational or scientific interpretation, because Life, and hence History, shaped by the "higher man" is itself part of a *mysterium*. Here Yockey incorporates his previous themes of the "higher man," or what has been termed "heroic vitalism," as a foundation of History, and his doctrine of polarity as a post-Hegelian dialectic. The foundations of Life and History are shaped by irrational forces, and the actors, the great men of History, follow a script according to historical laws, rather than writing their own. They must act within the theme of the drama according to how their epoch's *Zeitgeist* has scripted it, as if by a Divine or Unseen Hand.

Here we might also recall the concept of the "Myth" as the motive-force of History, as explicated by Georges Sorel, although Yockey has recourse not to Sorel, but to the German scholar Hans Vaihinger and the great Spanish dramatist Pedro Calderón.

We might also be reminded of Shakespeare's oft-quoted opening line, "All the world's a stage," but it is worth quoting the entirety of the Bard's lines, which poetically antedate the morphology of History of Spengler and Yockey:

> All the world's a stage,
> And all the men and women merely players:
> They have their exits and their entrances;
> And one man in his time plays many parts,
> His acts being seven ages. At first the infant,
> Mewling and puking in the nurse's arms.

And then the whining school-boy, with his satchel
And shining morning face, creeping like snail
Unwillingly to school. And then the lover,
Sighing like furnace, with a woeful ballad
Made to his mistress' eyebrow. Then a soldier,
Full of strange oaths and bearded like the pard,
Jealous in honour, sudden and quick in quarrel,
Seeking the bubble reputation
Even in the cannon's mouth. And then the justice,
In fair round belly with good capon lined,
With eyes severe and beard of formal cut,
Full of wise saws and modern instances;
And so he plays his part. The sixth age shifts
Into the lean and slipper'd pantaloon,
With spectacles on nose and pouch on side,
His youthful hose, well saved, a world too wide
For his shrunk shank; and his big manly voice,
Turning again toward childish treble, pipes
And whistles in his sound. Last scene of all,
That ends this strange eventful history,
Is second childishness and mere oblivion,
Sans teeth, sans eyes, sans taste, sans everything.[1]

CULTURE
DEC. 1953

Culture as play—the thought is not precisely new, but it is immensely important, and has not been seen in its **fundamental** significance. The "let's pretend" of the child is the proto-human asserting itself: similarly with savages—they too "pretend" that this action is sacred, will bring favorable consequences, while that other action is evil, will bring disaster. But children growing up in a culture-atmosphere are already vastly above savages, for they **know** they are playing, while the savages—except for the witch-doctors, the medicine men, the proto-priests—actually believe in the collection of totems and tabus which make up

[1] William Shakespeare, *As You Like It*, Act II, Scene VII.

their primitive culture.

❖ ❖ ❖

The drama is the pretense that the artificially arranged events on the boards are **real**. All of us accept this pretense, most obviously during the performance, and—literature and conversation show—even to a great extent thereafter.

❖ ❖ ❖

Music presupposes the attitude: "Let's pretend that the world of sound is orderly, pleasing, and beautiful—like this:." The inner-world of symbols is then projected into sounds.

❖ ❖ ❖

Religion is the pretense: "We can understand the totality of things, so completely that we can even assign with perfect security that which we cannot understand to an orderly place, under the heading: "Mystery." Every religion can make everything come out without remainder, because the will-to-play (here, the will-to-believe) is stronger than any mere intellectual weapons—logic, contradiction, etc.—that can be brought against it. Philosophy is religion—except that the compartment for "mystery" is smaller, and progressively less respected. Science is mere fact-ordering until the will-to-play abates to the point where it becomes world-outlook, and then it is the pretense that the sum total of things is nothing but the things themselves.

❖ ❖ ❖

Ethics is the pretense: "We can be as perfect as our play-ideas of perfection if we just observe the right rules." This describes both types of ethic, that aiming at goodness, and that aiming at beauty.

❖ ❖ ❖

Painting is the expression of the play-feeling: "Let's pretend that landscapes, people, and things, really look like *this*."

❖ ❖ ❖

Vaihinger's *Philosophy of As If* was an early form of the idea of Culture as *play*.[2]

❖ ❖ ❖

The dying out of culture is the dying out of the will-to-play, and its attenuation in ever-cruder games. The nineteenth-century society said to itself: "Let's pretend that we are clock-work figures, and create our codes, our buildings, our dances, our inner lives accordingly." The twentieth century says: "Let's pretend we are gangsters"—but what is the gangster—a crude individualist, a savage desocialized, without the tabus of the savage. That is to say, for *mere* man to pretend to be a savage is no pretense, the game is thin. Almost the only play-element left in the gangsters' code is the insistence on courage to be observed in the ideal gangster.

❖ ❖ ❖

The twentieth century finds the Baroque and Gothic orientation in architecture silly. It stresses instead the "Principle" that "function must govern form." This is the ideal also of the aborigines of Australia and the Congo. This is the aggressive and deliberate declaration of war on culture. In this architecture is not isolated. In the realm of morale a quack-doctor like Freud, or a prurient statistician like Kinsey, can find a hearing **as an ethi-**

---

[2] Hans Vaihinger (1852–1933), a scholar of Kant, considered in his primary work *Philosophy of As If* the vital role of "fictions"—what he called "fictionalism"—in both individual and collective life. Hence the world was not governed by "truth" but by the impact of an idea. For example, we might say that the "value" of Darwin's evolutionary theory is not that it has been "proven" but that it served the *Zeitgeist* of nineteenth-century materialism and English economic theory.

Yockey's reference to Vaihinger was written in by hand in what seems to have been an after-thought. One might conjecture that he read Vaihinger's work after having typed the manuscript, and that it was closely in accord with the idea of life-as-drama that Yockey was propounding.

cian in the twentieth century. Instead of Kant's magnificent Categorical Imperative, which tells us how we *should* act, quite regardless of how anyone else does act—again, the will-to-play—we want to know how most people *do* act, with the latent idea already there: if this is the way people act, then I too can act this way.

❖ ❖ ❖

In warfare, the nineteenth century—to say nothing of the eighteenth—still treated war as a game with strictly permitted and forbidden measures, of which the fundamental principle was: civilians are excluded from warfare, both actively and passively: they may not fight, nor may they, as such, be made the object of warfare. This was still culture-warfare. Its last appearance was in the German conduct of the Second World War, and in that same War, it was brought to an end by American primitivity. American fliers, *en masse* and individually, made war solely against civilians **as such**, and individual fliers were instructed to murder even isolated civilians. In pursuance of these orders, American fliers murdered civilians fleeing from railroad trains, running in the streets, in parks, working in the fields. From this, there is no way back to culture-warfare of the highly developed type. And yet—all large-scale warfare is culture *per se*, since culture is the totality of human thinking and activity above the plane of economics and reproduction, for in all large-scale warfare **power** is the stake, and the will-to-power on this scale is thus culture. What we are witnessing, in this cultural interregnum, this Concert of Bolshevism, the domination of the world by the American-Russian coalition, is the transition from culture-warfare to warfare once-more-primitive. In the future, even European warfare will be steadily increasingly primitive.

❖ ❖ ❖

Rousseau is the break with the will-to-play which is synonymous with Culture. With his idealization of the savage, the peasant, the shepherd, the milk-maid, he expresses, on the cultural plane, Culture's fatigue with itself, Society's fatigue with the demanding and exhausting game, the ever-intellectualization of the game, and, on the individual plane, the outburst of the jealous and inferior individual with **moral** indignation and **moral** hatred directed against that to which he is not equal. In a previous century Rousseau would not have burst out, nor would he have been heard. There are always Rousseaus—there is one in every class-room.

❖ ❖ ❖

It must never be forgotten that the chief revolutionary in eighteenth-century France was Louis XVI.[3] It was he who at every decisive turn frustrated the men and measures who would have put it down. This cipher-personality, with his pathetic rationalistic belief in "the goodness of the people" was a fate for France and the West, by his very rationalistic creed. Historians who treat this Revolution neglect the didactic value of his role.

❖ ❖ ❖

Rousseau says, "Let us play no longer—let us merely be what we *are*, namely what we are at bottom, simple creatures with merely basic needs." It was an expression of the strength of Culture, and also of the principle of polarity, that this revolt against the will-to-play was immediately adopted by the Culture-bearing stratum and was made into a lovely game, a play: Marie Antoinette as shepherdess, the triumph of the English garden-style over the French.

❖ ❖ ❖

Play makes life *magic*. It polarizes life, makes it tense, conscious, aware, demanding. One relaxed moment—and ruin supervenes. The Prince of Homburg[4] falls asleep—what more nat-

---

[3] The last monarch prior to the French Revolution.

[4] A reference to the eighteenth-century play by Heinrich von Kleist. In it, Frederick II, the Prince of Homburg (based on an actual historical figure), sleep-walks, during which the Grand Elector of Brandenburg plays a trick on him by making him steal one of the gloves belonging to the Elector's niece, using it to fabricate a story

ural? Yes, but according to the rules of the culture-game (the military regulations) he **may** not sleep at this moment of his life, and for this all-too-human moment he finds himself condemned to death. His pardon by the King was a concession by Kleist to the revolutionary spirit: already people found it too **cruel** to bring such sacrifices to Culture.

❖ ❖ ❖

We today can no longer feel the **immensely** strong play-urges of Gothic men, the culture-bearers of their time. These knights errant were ready at any moment for any **significant** trifle, to risk their lives. Granted, no actual Parsifal[5] ever lived. Yet, the Parsifal ideal was present in generations of knights, rulers, and warriors, and worked there **formatively**, just as in our day literary-gangster ideals work formatively. Some respond more than others to ideals, to the *Zeitgeist*—all respond to some degree.

❖ ❖ ❖

All of these thoughts have been wrong—for Culture-man does not play—he is **played with**. Culture-man is the creature of the Culture-organism, one of its cells, its units of structure and fulfillment. He does not play, for the simple reason that he **does not know or feel that it is a game—to him it is dead earnest**. Only the refined intellectuals, the Calderóns,[6] the Shakespeares,

---

that he is in love with her. Later, during a strategy meeting, he is confronted with this, which causes him to become distracted and inadvertently disobey an order from the Elector during a battle, even though doing this causes the Prince to win it. The Elector condemns the Prince to death for disobeying orders, but just before the sentence is to be carried out, the other officers persuade the Elector to pardon the Prince.

[5] Parsifal, or Perceval, is one of the Knights of the Round Table in Arthurian mythology, who goes on a quest to find the Holy Grail so that it may be used to restore the wounded Fisher King to health.

[6] Pedro Calderón de la Barca (1600–1681) was one of the greatest of the Spanish playwrights. His leading play, *Life is a Dream*, considers the conflict between free will and predestination, while other plays were themed on honor, including blood-honor. The example by

the Goethes—these know that it is a game. Among men of action, the two Frederick II's[7] had their moments of insight in which they knew that Culture is a game, but Napoleon was the first who was so clear about it, for already he extended into the time when the game had passed its highest development.

❖ ❖ ❖

Children play, but know that they play. Culture-man plays, and does not know it. Civilized man consciously revolts against play, but there is still a great deal of historical necessity, i.e., **unconscious** play, still latent in him, and **this he will play out**, whether he wants to or not, whether he knows it or not.

❖ ❖ ❖

Play not only makes magic—it is magic. The theater always works magically: every successful theatrical piece contains the polarization between that which the players instinctively would like to do, and that which, for any reason, they feel they should, or should not do.

❖ ❖ ❖

Magic is the one pole of a polarized entity. The entity is polarized: possible-impossible. Magic is identical with impossible. What is magic to you is routine to me. Hence the magic of culture: all culture working within an individual is an expression of the polarity between his natural wish or tendency and his feeling of a higher imperative. We are all lazy, for proto-man is lazy, and all culture requires *effort*. Already this generates a tension, a polarity. Successful effort makes a man capable of that which others, unequal to the effort, find impossible. Hence he possesses *magic*.

Yockey is apt for his concept of Culture and History as unfolding, predestined drama.

[7] Presumably, Frederick II (1194–1250), the Holy Roman Emperor who expanded the Empire to its territorial peak; and Frederick II (1712–1786) of Prussia, otherwise known as Frederick the Great, who won many victories during his long reign.

❖ ❖ ❖

All great men, all higher men, affect us *magically*. Polarization attracts us, but so does diffusion. We are drawn to the polarized man by our own higher desires, our own wish to do something with our lives above the plane of the proto-human; but so also does the kindly, gentle, diffuse man attract—he is soporific, and is as pleasant as the green, sunlit meadow. But the higher man is like the snow-covered mountain peak.

Napoleon owed his victories on the battlefield to the fact that he departed from the game of warfare as hitherto played. So did Frederick, a generation before him, but Napoleon's break with the game was more fundamental. Napoleon represents Rousseau applied to warfare—away with the rules, if victory is the aim, let us pursue it regardless of any **form** in which it is supposed to be attained. On St. Helena, with his remark, "Nowadays, war is all rose-water . . ." he showed that he could envisage an even more total departure from the rules than he had been able to effect on European battlefields.[8] No man can compel the *Zeitgeist*. It does not **let** itself be accelerated.

The German armies that went into Russia in 1941 had gained easy victories over the Belgians, English, and French, because all were within the same Culture and played the game according to the same rules. German superiority in the game was so manifest that the others promptly surrendered, with their forces largely intact. In the case of the English, the Hero, playing too subtle a political game, allowed a withdrawal, allowed the feeling of a sort of negative victory, because he was looking a long step

[8] "At the time of Cannae, the Romans redoubled their efforts, but that was because every individual stood in fear of death, of rape, of pillage. That is making war, but in modern campaigns, everything is sprinkled with rosewater." R. M. Johnston (compiler), *The Corsican: A Diary of Napoleon's Life in His Own Words* (Boston: Houghton Mifflin, 1930), p. 496.

ahead, a **political** step. On the battlefield itself he was thinking about the peace-conference. Even fifty years before, this would have been quite in order. In 1940 it was too subtle for the *Zeitgeist*. There was no England in 1940—there was only America, and America did not know or play this game.

❖ ❖ ❖

In Russia it was otherwise. The Russian armies, even when defeated according to the Western rules of the game, did not surrender. They had to be destroyed piecemeal. Their primitive ignorance of the rules of the Western game of warfare conferred on them thus a **superiority**, just as Napoleon's breaking of the rules had conferred on him a superiority *vis-à-vis* his more cultured opponents. Napoleon's advantage lasted until—"Do not fight," says Sun Tzu, "too often with one enemy, lest you teach him all your art of war"[9]—his opponents caught up with him. Archduke Charles was the first, then Scharnhorst, Blücher, Clausewitz, and yes, him too, Wellington. Russia's advantage will last only so long. Perhaps already, 1953, it is gone. Are we now primitive enough in warfare to lay aside our rules and fight like Russians? Or are we too weak, too pacifistic? Can we fight to **kill**, and not merely to defeat the opponent? Have we understood the significance of Roosevelt's bloodthirsty lust, which he displayed openly, for "killing Germans"?

❖ ❖ ❖

In the eighteenth century, it was tactically inferior to fight to kill. It was a waste of precious time. In the twentieth, it is tactically necessary to fight to **kill**, not merely to defeat. As far as numbers of the dead go, the difference is not as vast as one would think. One may fight to **kill**, but this does not mean that one is **able** to kill the entire enemy force—this is impossible, when large numbers are present. The difference in one of tactic, of the approach to the battle, of one's intention as it governs his battle-conduct—and not one of casualties.

---

[9] This was actually said by Napoleon. It is found in Ralph Waldo Emerson's *Representative Men: Seven Lectures*.

❖ ❖ ❖

Inner tension in a man, polarity, magic, attract, but, in the usual case, repel in the end. Distance is decisive here—the mountain peak in the distance is imposing and attractive, but after it is scaled, the winds and snows and ice tell . . .

In this age, we can only apprehend the world **historically**. Since history is like a play, it therefore works *aesthetically*, and thus our world-outlook can only be an **aesthetic** one, rather than a **moral** one. This is the answer—although of course they will not understand it—to the small minds who wail, "If the Western Culture will die in any event, why should we try to accomplish anything whatever in it, or with it?" In the vast drama called history we play the role assigned us, even though we know it to be only a role, a part of an agreed game. It is also permitted us to leave the stage if we are not assigned the role that **we** feel **rightfully**, **aesthetically**, belongs to **us**.

Once more: the highest formula of affirmation: **the world-as-drama**.

DER FEIND EUROPAS:
TRANSLATOR'S PREFACE

1953

EDITORS' NOTE

This "Translator's Preface" was intended to be published in the German edition of *The Enemy of Europe* (*Der Feind Europas*), but was never used. Although Yockey wrote the Preface, it was supposed to be ascribed to his close American collaborator and patron, Frederick C. F. Weiss, a German émigré who operated Le Blanc Publications and issued many essays through it, especially on Russia, and often with the assistance of Yockey and H. Keith Thompson. Weiss was also a financial patron of James Madole's National Renaissance Party, utilizing the *National Renaissance Bulletin* to assist with the circulation of his publications and articles.

Yockey had written *The Enemy of Europe* particularly for the edification of the German nationalist leadership in 1948, with minor revisions in 1952. It had been intended as the third volume of *Imperium*. The book had a particular influence on Major General Otto Remer and the Socialist Reich Party, which adopted a "neutralist" and even pro-Soviet attitude during the Cold War, much to the alarm of the American occupation authorities, who in addition to banning the party and jailing Remer, suppressed *Der Feind Europas*.

The intention was to ascribe the German translation of *The Enemy of Europe* to Weiss. This did not happen. Weiss was in a precarious position insofar as he was not a naturalized citizen, and the FBI maintained an interest in his activities and associates, especially in regard to their activities in Germany. However, at one point, based on information from an "informant" ("T3"—"of known reliability," according to the FBI report), the FBI discussed the possibility of *The Enemy of Europe* being the work of Weiss, and that, "Weiss has allowed one Ulick Varange to be listed as author of this book as Weiss does not desire to become known as the writer. The informant said that Weiss has stated that since the American authorities cannot reach Varange, 'I'll let him sign as author, otherwise the FBI would be on my heels.'"[1]

Ironically, while the English manuscript of *The Enemy of Europe* did not survive, a photocopy of the German edition did. Therefore, when it could finally be published in English, the German edition had to be translated back into English. The satirical Yockeyan journal *TRUD* serialized *The Enemy of Europe* during the 1970s, but this lively journal became defunct before the project was completed. Thomas Francis then undertook the task, and an English edition was published by George Dietz's Liberty Bell Publications in 1981. Interestingly, Francis did utilize a Preface written by Yockey, which included the following paragraphs, slightly altered in several places, with further paragraphs added, before and after, making it about twice as long.

TRANSLATOR'S PREFACE

The translation of this work has been a proud duty, to the final execution of which I feel impelled to add some words of my own. The book is complete in itself, and its thesis about the nature of America is true without qualification.

Having lived for several decades in America I have seen with my own eyes the distorted development of that country since the Revolution of 1933.[2] For the most part, the resistance to the progressive distortion of America is merely passive—the resistance which any material whatever opposes to that which is acting upon it. The dimensions of this resistance are scanty. Where the resistance is active, it finds little support, since idealism and heroism do not grow in an atmosphere wherein economics is the ruling spirit.

---

[1] Edward A. Brandt, "Frederick Charles Ferdinand Weiss," FBI-New York (Report 100-111893), February 3, 1954, p. 3.

[2] The "Revolution of 1933" was the assumption to the presidency of Franklin D. Roosevelt, which was considered by Yockey, and indeed many on the Right at the time, as the completion of the domination of the "Culture-distorters" over the United States.

For world-political purposes, Europe can attach no hopes to this resistance in America. The "white America" which still existed in its strength in the 1920s has today ceased to exist, for practical proposes. Whether or not this submerged spirit can ever rise again in some remote future, too far ahead to be within the range of practical planning, is unforeseeable. In any case Europe cannot allow itself the luxury of dreaming that a revolution in America by the pro-European elements will lead to Europe's liberation.

Europeans are familiar with the American propaganda for export, but less familiar with the internal propaganda within America. The volume of this propaganda utterly dwarfs, in its scale as well as in its effect, anything that Europeans can readily imagine. The leading internal thesis of the Washington regime—which has not changed since 1933—is that Americans must be "tolerant" of the alien elements (which how number roughly fifty percent of the population), since after all, these aliens are "brothers." "Brotherhood" is glorified on all public occasions, by all public officials, is taught in the schools, is preached in the churches, which have been completely coordinated into the master-plan of the culturally-alien regime in Washington. Newspapers, books, magazines, radio, television, films—all vomit forth the same "Brotherhood." The "brotherhood" propaganda is a ghastly caricature of the Christian idea of the Fatherhood of God and the Brotherhood of Man, but there is no religious purpose to the propaganda. Its sole intent is to destroy whatever exclusiveness, national feelings, or racial instincts may still remain in the American population after twenty years of national leprosy. The result of the "tolerance" and "brotherhood" campaign is that the alien enjoys a superior position in America—he can demand to be "tolerated"—the American cannot. The tragic fact is that the attenuation of the national instincts has proceeded so far that practical vision does not let us see how a nationalist revolution would be even possible in America.

So long as America was populated by stocks from culture-European soil, it was a European colony, even though sometimes vocally rebellious. But the America that has been deformed by the Revolution is lost to Europe. Let no European dream of help or cooperation from that quarter.

Frederick C. F. Weiss

EDITORS' NOTE

The following text is a handwritten note to F. C. Weiss that Yockey appended at the bottom of the typescript of the Editor's Preface. "Pappali" was presumably a code name or nickname for Weiss. Many thanks to David Yorkshire for the transcription and Thomas Francis for the translation.

Lieber Pappali.
Sie sind scheinbar der Übersetzer.
Ich habe angefangen, den Drucker zu bezahlen. Er
sagte ungefähr 1300 DM, d.h. $325. Die Hälfte is ungefähr
$165.
Auch der Übersetzer braucht noch $45.
Sie sind also jetzt schuldig $165+$45 — $210.
Wenn Sie das Sparkonto verkaufen, dann erwarte ich
noch $210 von Ihnen fürs Übersetzen u. Drucken. Die
Postgebühre werden auch etwas kosten, wie viel weiss ich
nicht.
1. Schreiben Sie mir wie viele Exemplare Sie wollen.
2. Schicken Sie mir auch Adressen von deutsch-lesende Leute —
nur die Auslese die das Buch bekommen sollen.
Nur 200 Exemplare werden gedruckt werden.
Der Drucker fängt jetzt an.
3. Bitte nicht vergessen: $210. Geben Sie das bei
Virginia — sie wird es mir schicken. mit herzl. Grüssen
V.

Lieber Pappali:

Sie sind scheinbar der Übersetzer.

Ich habe angefangen, den Drucker zu bezahlen. Er sagte

ungefähr 1300DM, d.h. $325. Die Hälfte ist ungefähr $165.

Auch der Übersetzer braucht noch $45.

Sie sind also jetzt schuldig $165 + $45 – $210.

Wenn Sie das Sparkonto verkaufen, dann erwarte ich noch $210 von Ihnen fürs Übersetzen u. Drucken. Die Postgebühre werden auch etwas kosten, wie viel weiss ich nicht.

1. Schreiben Sie mir wie viele Exempläre Sie wollen.

2. Schicken Sie mir auch Addressen von deutsch-lesende Leute – *nur die Auslese* die das Buch bekommen sollen.

Nur 200 Exempläre werden gedruckt werden.

Der Drucker fängt jetzt an.

3. Bitte nicht vergessen: $210. Geben Sie das Geld an Virginie sie wird es mir schicken.

mit kamerad. Grüssen
V.

Dear Pappali:

It seems you're the translator.

I've just begun to pay the printer. He says about DM 1300, i.e., $325. Half would be about $165.

The translator also needs another $45.

So now you are in debt $165 + $45 = $210. When you liquidate the bank account, I shall be expecting another $210 from you for the translating and printing. The postage will also cost something – how much I don't know.

1. Write me how many copies you want.

2. Also, send me the addresses of German-reading people – *only the elite* – who are to get the book.

Only 200 copies are going to be printed.

The printer is starting now.

3. Please, don't forget: $210. Give the money to Virginia[3] – she'll send it to me.

With comradely greetings,
V.

---

[3] Probably Virginia Johnson.

Oswald Spengler, the American Jewish Committee, & Russia

1954

Editors' Note

Written shortly after the death of Stalin, this estimate of Russia and the United States is reminiscent of *The Enemy of Europe*, and could be seen as a sequel to "What is Behind the Hanging of the Eleven Jews in Prague?" The book's primary thesis was that "the enemy of Europe" was "the Washington regime" as the harbinger of "American-Jewish Bolshevism."

This "American-Jewish Bolshevism" was the means by which the cultural, physical, and spiritual life of Europe would be destroyed. In contrast, "Russian Bolshevism is simply barbarism"; its destructive mission towards the decaying West is that of traditional Russian, pan-Slavic religiosity, although at times using the verbiage of Marxism.

The message of Yockey for Germany was for it to not fight in any war for the United States. Occupation by Russia would be preferable to occupation by the US. Either Russian's occupation would be so brutal as to arouse and unite all of Europe, and thereby achieve Imperium in the face of the "barbarian invasion," or, more likely, that Russia would seek an accord with Europe and, as in other "barbarian" occupations in history, the occupiers would enter into a symbiotic relationship with the occupied.

Yockey points to the barbarian invasions of Egypt by the Hyksos, Babylon by the Kassites, China by the Chou, and Rome by the Germans and Gauls. "In none of these historical instances did the invasion of the barbarians destroy the body of the Culture; in each case the result was finally the absorption of the barbarian elements into the Culture-body or their expulsion."[1] "Russian Bolshevism is therefore less dangerous to Europe than American-Jewish Bolshevism, for no aspect of its menace corresponds to a weakness in Europe's spiritual armour."[2] Another advantage to Russian occupation would be the purging of Europe of its "inner traitors."

What Yockey, like Spengler, meant by "barbarian" is not derogatory: "The barbarian is to be distinguished not only from Culture-men, but from savages, primitives, fellaheen,[3] and decadents as well. Barbarian is a word full of promise, for the barbarian is inwardly in motion. The Germanic tribes that occupied Imperial Rome were barbarians, and from this Germanic stock came, many centuries later, men who wrought the Western Culture."[4] This is why Spengler suggested that after the West had fulfilled its life-course, the next civilization on the world-stage would be Russia.

This essay was originally published as a pamphlet by Le Blanc Publishers under its standard moniker, "X. Y. Z." Comparing the ideas and style of this 1954 essay with the 1948/1952 *Enemy of Europe*, the "Russia" chapter in *Imperium*, and the essay "What is Behind the Hanging of the Eleven Jews in Prague?," written in December 1952 and, like this essay, issued as a "press release" by Weiss,[5] we can be relatively confident of this essay being written by Yockey under the pseudonym. This is further confirmed by the fact that, during this same time period, the FBI reported that an informant stated, "Since December 3, 1952, it appeared to him that Weiss' writings have been composed by a man by the name of Francis Parker Yockey. He said he believes that Weiss may be putting out writings under his own name

---

[1] Yockey, *The Enemy of Europe*, pp. 80–81, "The Concert of Bolshevism."

[2] Ibid., p. 79.

[3] Used by Spengler, and here by Yockey, fellaheen means those peoples that have become historically passé, having already gone through the periods of cyclic rise and fall.

[4] Yockey, *The Enemy of Europe*, p. 75.

[5] Issued as a "press release," according to D. T. K., publisher of the Yockeyan journal *TRUD* and of *Yockey: Four Essays*, who knew Frederick Weiss well during the 1970s.

which have been written by Yockey and that it is these writings that seem to favor the pro-Russian viewpoint to some extent although they do not come out in favor of Communism as such."[6]

Le Blanc Publishers
Box 155
208 East 86th Street
New York 28, N.Y.

Press Release
To be released April 1st

OSWALD SPENGLER, THE AMERICAN JEWISH COMMITTEE, & RUSSIA

In volume II, page 196, of his monumental philosophical work, *The Decline of the West*, Oswald Spengler wrote as follows in 1918:

> The real Russian is a disciple of Dostoevsky, although he may not have read Dostoevsky or anyone else, nay, perhaps because he cannot read, he is himself Dostoevsky in substance; and if the Bolsheviks (Trotskyites),[7] who see in Christ a mere social revolutionist like themselves were not intellectually so narrowed **it would be in Dostoevsky that they would recognize their prime enemy.**[8] What gave this revolution its momentum was not the intelligentsia's hatred. **It was the people itself**; which, urged only by the

[6] "Frederick Charles Ferdinand Weiss," FBI-New York (100-111893), December 7, 1953, p. 4.

[7] "Trotskyites" has been added by X. Y. Z. to distinguish between the two types of Bolshevism: the international Bolshevism of Trotsky and his oligarchic patrons of Wall Street, and the National Bolshevism that Spengler could even in 1922 see taking the upper hand in Russia. See Spengler, "The Two Faces of Russia and Germany's Eastern Problems," Essen speech, 1922, available at besbosh-nik.wordpress.com/2013/02/09/the-two-faces-of-russia-essay-by-oswald-spengler/.

[8] Emphasis added by X. Y. Z.

> need of throwing off a disease, destroyed the old Westernism[9] in one effort of upheaval, and **will send the new (meaning Trotskyism) after it in another** . . .[10] Tolstoi's "Christianity" was a misunderstanding. He spoke of Christ and meant Marx. But **to Dostoevsky's Christianity the next thousand years will belong.**[11]

And may we add here: **"Dostoevsky spoke of Christ and meant a Russian world-mission."**[12] The above paragraph was written by Spengler only one year after Jacob Schiff sent his ambassador Bronstein (Trotsky) to Moscow with sufficient funds to launch the Red Revolution.[13]

---

[9] "The Old Westernism," which Spengler called "Petrinism" after Peter the Great, who sought to Westernize Russia, shackled the Russian soul with a foreign outlook. The Marxism of Trotsky and other largely Jewish revolutionists sought to replace the Westernism of the Czars with Marxism, which had arisen as a Culture-disease within the Late West.

[10] Emphasis added by X. Y. Z. Again, "meaning Trotskyism" has been added to distinguish the two factions: Trotskyism and National Bolshevism.

[11] Emphasis added by X. Y. Z.

[12] Russia as the "Katechon," the bulwark against the coming of the Antichrist, was mentioned by Saint John the Apostle and was remolded by the Russian National Bolsheviks as a messianic world-mission to reform mankind and destroy Mammon. This messianic Russian Bolshevism was more a transcendence of capitalism than Marxism, which Spengler defined as a reflection, not a transcendence, of capitalism.

[13] Jacob Schiff, a senior partner in Kuhn, Loeb & Co. on Wall Street, was widely rumored to have funded the Bolsheviks. Rumors of twenty million US dollars given by Schiff and carried by Trotsky aboard ship to Russia can be discounted. What is certain, however, is that Schiff funded George Kennan, the anti-Czarist American journalist and author, to distribute Marxist propaganda among thousands of Russian POWs who had been captured during the 1905 Russo-Japanese War, and that Schiff was a patron of the US-based Friends of Russian Freedom, which sponsored revolutionists of sundry types. Trotsky was facilitated in his journey from New York back to Russia by the head of British military intelligence in the US during the First World War, William Wiseman, who after the war became a partner in Kuhn, Loeb &

In volume II, page 295, of his *Decline of the West,* Spengler wrote about the spiritual character of the Russian people as follows:

> **That all are responsible for all!** . . . is the metaphysical fundament of all Dostoevsky's creations. That is why Ivan Karamazov must name himself murderer, although another had done the murder. Mystical Russian love is the love of the plain, the love of brothers under equal pressure all along the earth, ever along and along, the love of the pure tortured beasts that wander on it, the love of plants—never of birds, clouds and stars—[14]

And Spengler concludes this particular paragraph with the words: "What sort of Christianity will come forth one day from this world-feeling?"

But, already it should dawn upon us why the Soviet Union now has become a going concern. It would have been far better if we had not discounted the socialized order over there as "visionary" or "utopian" or "ready to explode." The Soviet system will not collapse. It will not collapse simply because it is part and

---

Co. The enigmatic international banker Abram Zhivotovsky, Trotsky's maternal uncle, maintained close contact with his nephew and other Mensheviks and Bolsheviks. A century of rumor, exaggeration, misinformation, and inaccuracies has finally been overcome by a definitive scholarly work on the subject: *Wall Street and the Russian Revolution, 1905–1925* (Walterville, Ore.: Trine Day, 2017) by Dr. Richard Spence, Professor of History at Idaho State University. Significantly, Spence dates the end of the era of collusion between international finance and the USSR to 1925, which was the beginning of Trotsky's fall and the rise of Stalin.

[14] From footnote 1 on page 295 of the George Allen and Unwin edition. Spengler is here explaining the difference between the space perceptions of the Western, Faustian soul towards infinite space, and that of the Russian, who looks to the infinity of the horizon. It is this sense of brotherly solidarity expressed in Christian Orthodoxy, as brother Christians, that the National Bolsheviks transformed into a Russian socialism that had been forming since the conflict between Karl Marx and Russian socialists in the International during the nineteenth century.

parcel of the mysterious Russian soul. It is the Russian mass itself which carries the Revolution![15]

But, we also begin to understand, why that "vicious, sworn enemy of the Trotsky-Revolution and democratic revolutionary," Dostoevsky would have best understood the mentality of the Russian masses of today. He would have understood the feelings of the Russian people much better than other Russian mental giants like Tolstoi, Saltykov-Shchedrin, Gogol, and Pushkin who—unlike Dostoevsky—were pruned on to the Soviet ideological totem pole.

But let us pause here for a second and consider what another "mental giant," one in the Schiff-Baruch camp,[16] had to say about the meaning of the great Russian upheaval in 1917. Our readers are urged to peruse carefully what may be regarded as the classic statement of Jewish illusion (and that of our own "statesmen")—Ex-Ambassador Joseph Davies' conclusion to his book *Mission to Moscow*:[17]

---

[15] As we know, the Soviet system did collapse half a century later. However, Yockey predicted that Bolshevism would be thoroughly transformed and held that Marxism was being used only as a tactical but ineffectual "export article" that would probably be discarded. But there remained an inner friction between imported Marxism and National Bolshevism that was not entirely resolved or synthesized; hence an internal weakness of the Soviet bloc that the "inner traitors" and "outer enemies" could utilize.

Culture-pathology with the power of corruption of the "inner traitor" and "outer enemy," and decades of Culture-distortion aimed at the Soviet bloc, contributed to the implosion. On how this was implemented, see K. R. Bolton, "Václav Havel: The 'Inner Enemy,'" *Counter-Currents*, December 27, 2011.

This has not destroyed Russia, however. Apart from the brief Yeltsin interregnum, the return to the authoritarian style was prompt, and Russia remains as much an enemy of the "Washington regime" as had the USSR, but unencumbered by vestiges of Marxism, and more likely with a clearer vision of its messianic world-mission.

[16] Like Schiff, Bernard Baruch played an important role in trying to harness Russia.

[17] Joseph E. Davies (1876–1958) was Franklin Roosevelt's Ambassador to the Soviet Union from 1936–38, during the time of the Stalinist

> The Russia of Lenin and Trotsky—the Russia of the Bolshevik Revolution—no longer exists. Through gradual, stern, and often cruel evolution that government has developed into what is now a system of state socialism operating on capitalistic principles and steadily and irresistibly swinging to the right. . . . The present government professes to be a democracy. It is, I believe, sincerely devoted to peace both for practical and ideological reasons. The present government further proclaims and asserts constitutional protection for civil and religious liberty. Constitutional protections do not always work perfectly in certain regions because of political and personal purposes, as we know from our own experience here. In my opinion the Russian people, the Soviet government, and the Soviet leaders are moved, basically, by altruistic concepts. It is their purpose to promote the brotherhood of man and to improve the lot of the common people. They wish to create a society in which men may live as equals, governed by ethical ideals. . . . The British Empire, the Americas, and Russia, along with China, are the great complementary powers of the earth. Their interests, their governmental ideas and purposes do not conflict.—

The events of the last few years have brought bitter disillusionment to the Jews and to our native Reds and Pinkos, who in vain have tried to combine their own "Left wing" political principles with Stalin's professed non-ideological official belief, when he let the Soviet regime appear to return to traditional normality as a national state. Before long, the acts of Stalin's policy no longer permitted even the most ardent of the Jewish admirers of Stalin's altruism to look upon the Soviets as a nation-state in the coalition with the United States and their satraps in the West. Much to their horror, the Baruch-Truman-Churchill

---

purges. Davies was extremely pro-Communist and pro-Soviet Union, and his book, *Mission to Moscow* (New York: Simon & Schuster, 1941), which was made into a film by Warner Brothers in 1943, whitewashed the purges in a pro-Stalinist light.

clique began to see how the Soviet Union used its military power after the collapse of Hitler's Empire, to put Communist parties in power outside of Russia whenever it was able to do so, and to produce tension after tension on the international scene without actually involving Russia in open warfare.[18]

Then came Stalin's death. Immediately, the Jewish commentators of Press and Radio caused us to raise our hopes for a radical change in Soviet policy. Because there were just enough peaceful gestures from the Soviet side to keep alive the sense of new promise in the Malenkov Era,[19] our dumb and dull Dulleses[20] and their coterie of career diplomats speedily returned to their wishful thinking of 1941–1945. They believed that the Soviet Union, however tough and truculent, would be, after all, just another national state and so, to this day, these ostrich philosophers of ours have refused to believe that the Russian Communist movement is actually an international conspiracy which conditions the whole world outlook of its disciples and so

---

[18] A primary cause of the "Cold War" was Stalin's refusal to acquiesce to the United Nations General Assembly becoming a World Parliament, which would have meant *de facto* global control by the United States, with its ability to buy votes.

Additionally, the Soviet Union repudiated the "Baruch Plan" for the "internationalization" of atomic energy under the UN. Again, the USSR perceived this as a means by which nuclear energy would be controlled by the US. Note how this "plan" was symbolically named after Bernard Baruch. See K. R. Bolton, "Origins of the Cold War: How Stalin Foiled a New World Order," *Foreign Policy Journal,* May 31, 2010.

Yockey was well aware of these maneuvers. In his "What is Behind the Hanging of the Eleven Jews in Prague?," Yockey writes of Russia's refusal early in 1947 to "surrender part of its sovereignty to the so-called 'united nations' for purposes of 'control' of the atomic weapon industry." This refusal "stymied Jewish plans" to surrender American and Russian sovereignty to a UN world government, wrote Yockey.

[19] Georgy Malenkov (1902–1988) was the Premier of the Soviet Union who succeeded Stalin upon his death in 1953. He held the position until 1955, when he was unseated by Nikita Khrushchev, who proceeded to destalinize the country.

[20] John Foster Dulles (1888–1959) was US Secretary of State from 1953 until 1959. He was a staunch anti-Communist.

determines their entire approach to **international** relations!

It is almost amusing to watch how Stalin's revival of patriotic feelings and his cultivation of a rabid Russian chauvinism has brought shame and confusion to the Trotskyites in our midst; to those Rosenbergs, Golds, Coplons, and Greenglasses[21] who now try in vain to combine admiration for the Soviet regime with an honest devotion to their much cherished Marxian principles. For this reason, emphasis on the regression of the "Bolshevik" Revolution to Russian nationalism has for years been part of the stock-in-trade of both the Baruch-Murrow[22] wing of World Jewry and the Rosenberg-wing, who believe that a Marxist internationalism, divorced from all patriotic prejudices, is the first duty of a truly progressive mind!

When Trotskyism in Russia first forced itself upon the attention of our diplomats, there was hardly a Jew in the entire world who did not praise to high heaven the new "International Communist Party" as the instrument for the creation of a new era—or One World. The Trotskyites, under the leadership of Leon Trotsky (Bronstein), had created an ironclad Jewish dictatorship over the economic, political, and cultural life of the Russian people. Trotsky's regime was the living incarnation of the Godless, materialistic principles set down by the Jewish theorist, Karl Marx.

However, very soon, this phase which emphasized the unity of Communists all over the world went out of use, much to the sorrow of the Jews. Too late they began to comprehend that Communism in Russia had become something quite different from what they—the authentic Marxist-Leninists—had in mind. Slowly, they began to comprehend, that what they now saw in

---

[21] Soviet spies who delivered information on nuclear weapons, all of whom were Jewish, even while Stalin was purging the Soviet bloc of Jews *en masse*.

[22] Edward Murrow, a CBS news anchor, became a liberal icon for his pillorying of Senator Joseph McCarthy. In 2005 he was honored with a film, *Good Night, and Good Luck*, directed by George Clooney; an example of what Yockey called the "ethical syphilis of Hollywood" (Yockey, *The Proclamation of London*, Part III: "The Mission of the Liberation Front").

Russia was a special Russian brand of Communism, a combination of Russian nationalism and Communism,[23] the latter only worn as a mask for convenience sake.

Let us now quote some excerpts from an article entitled, "The Return to Wishful Thinking," by G. F. Hudson, in the January issue of *Commentary*,[24] published by the American Jewish Committee.

> It has always been assumed in Western thinking about the Soviet Union that international revolutionary Communism and Russian nationalism are incompatible alternatives, so that when Soviet publicity glorifies the Russian past and sanctifies in retrospect the expansion of the Czarist empire, it follows that world revolution must have been definitively renounced. Such an assumption has indeed the authority of both Marx and Lenin, but it is nearly thirty years out of date, for the special achievement of Stalin ever since his first rise to power has been his success in combining these two superficially opposed political forces.
>
> Today it is official doctrine that the unique national genius of Russia, already for many centuries culturally supe-

---

[23] That is, "National Bolshevism." Trotsky showed this in his book *The Revolution Betrayed* (1936), particular points of outrage being Stalin's revival of the family and respect for parents, reversing Bolshevik laws on abortion, honoring women as mothers rather than as factory fodder, and so on. (See K. R. Bolton, *Stalin: The Enduring Legacy* [London: Black House Publishing, 2012], pp. 3–27). Trotsky did not live to see the extent of Stalin's commitment to reversing Marxism. Already outraged at what he saw as a revival of religion in Russia even in 1936, by the time of Stalin's death in 1953 the churches were being reopened and the Orthodox patriarchy was again reconciled with the State. See K. R. Bolton, "Saint Joseph: Was Stalin a Defender of the Church?," *Inconvenient History*, vol. 9, no. 1, 2017.

[24] G. F. Hudson, an Oxford historian, wrote extensively on Communism and the USSR for *Commentary*. This essay, "The Return of Wishful Thinking: Has International Communism Really Changed?," January 1, 1954. Boldface and italicized text is X. Y. Z.'s emphasis throughout.

rior to Western Europe and, of course, the real originator of all those scientific and technological discoveries which the West has falsely claimed, brought forth the new world of Communism as the climax of its creative activity; the essentially universal and world-embracing character of the Communist faith in its struggle against imperialism, **far from cancelling or obscuring the preeminent function of the Russian people, entitles it to world leadership and gives it a historical mission** which cannot be subject to any geographical limits. It has been all the easier to inculcate among Russians the idea of a special world-saving destiny because the way was so well prepared by the prophets of Pan-Slavism, *such as Dostoevsky,* who saw Christian Orthodox Russia as the savior, even by force, of a decadent civilization.

It was not Lenin or Stalin, **but Dostoevsky**, who, in anticipation of a Russian war against Western Europe, wrote that "so much that is new and progressive will begin in human relations that it would be useless to mourn and to hesitate on the eve of the last great struggle which will bring about the great regeneration of all Europe." The "Populist" revolutionaries of 19th-century Russia rejected **the medieval Christian inspiration of the Slavophiles**, but took over from them the idea of a **Russian world-mission**, no longer to revive and extend Slav Orthodox Christianity but to initiate a new age of socialism for all mankind.

The Bolsheviks claimed—and still claim—to derive their doctrine solely from Marx, but they were also in fact **deeply influenced by the tradition of the non-Marxist Russian revolutionaries**, particularly Chernishevsky and Nechayev; indeed, it is **impossible to understand Bolshevism from Marxist origins alone.**[25] After the Bolshevik

---

[25] As Dr. Mikhail Agursky, in his book *The Third Rome: National Bolshevism in the USSR* (Boulder, Col.: Westview Press, 1986), showed the ideological conflict between Marx and Russian socialists was a race-conflict between "German" (Jewish) and Russian factions, both reflect-

> Revolution had triumphed in Russia, but had failed to detonate the expected worldwide upheaval, the new regime became more and more closely identified with **Russian nationality** and it was found politically profitable to appeal to traditional nationalist fears, prejudices, and aspirations.

We are most grateful to the American Jewish Committee for the publication of the above article by G. F. Hudson for therein the author reveals conclusively (though mainly by implication) the bottomless abyss between our own Marxian Bolshevism and—as the *New York Times* calls the Russian movement (March 13, p. 14)—"imperialistic Communism." The author also leaves no doubt that this abyss can never be bridged—just as little as the metaphysics of the Jews and our own could ever come together; and neither can those of Tolstoi and Dostoevsky; for that matter.

For Tolstoi is the **former** Russia, Dostoevsky is the **present** Russia. Hating the West, Tolstoi hated himself and so became the father of the first phase of the Russian Revolution. Tolstoi was an event within, and of, Marxian Bolshevism. He stood midway between Petrinism[26] and Marx, and neither of these managed to get within sight of Russian earth.

---

ing opposing types of "messianic" "world-mission." Marx himself was a Germanophile and a Russophobe, who was alarmed at the possibility of an invasion of Germany by the "Russian barbarians," while the Russian socialists were often pan-Slavic (Slavophiles). This rivalry continued after the rise of Bolshevism, and was reflected in the suspicion that Russia maintained towards the German Communists.

Dr. Agursky was an adviser to the Soviet military industry, becoming a dissident who migrated to Israel and pursued a career in academia. His father, Solomon, had been the leader of the Jewish section of the Bolshevik Party, and the Party's official historian. Agursky's book is essential reading for understanding developments in the USSR.

For a review of Agursky see K. R. Bolton, "Was Bolshevism a Product of Traditional Russian Messianism?," *Geopolitica*, November 6, 2017.

[26] Petrinism is Spengler's description of the Westernizing political and cultural forms introduced into Russia by Peter the Great.

But Dostoevsky **is** Russian earth, just as the real Russian of today "is himself Dostoevsky in substance." After Trotsky's exit, Dostoevsky took over—and nobody else!

But, to come back into our own, Western camp:

When a newspaper with the prestige of the *New York Times* dares to state (March 13, p. 14): "If the mountain (McCarthy) has labored to bring forth only a mouse"[27]—and gets away with it—it goes to show to what extent we have become mere **objects** in the great game of World-Politics; and worse: it even shows that we have lost every sense of reality. For here, the real issue is NOT to catch a few card-carrying members of the old Marx-Bronstein clique. Long ago, 99% of these Reds have become "Anti-Stalinists" or "anti-Malenkovs"; hence they now meekly profess to be "anti-Communists"—and everybody believes them!

However, the all-important issue in this fight of our McCarthys is to bring home to our masses the enormity of the impact this alien clique in our midst has been allowed to exercise upon our Western institutions—here as well as in Europe. The all-important issue is to expose our Red-Herring traitors who alone made this impact possible; who alone are responsible for the fact that our most deadly enemy is now firmly entrenched *within* the walls of our White Fortress. This is a threat far greater than the one from behind the Iron Curtain!—

And now we ask: "Will the next thousand years really belong to Dostoevsky's Russia—as Spengler predicted? Or will they be-

---

[27] Alluding to the defection *en masse* of Trotskyites, Mensheviks, and other Marxists to the anti-Soviet side, becoming the most vehement of Russophobes during the Cold War, filling the ranks of the CIA's Congress for Cultural Freedom, and later replacing it with the National Endowment for Democracy to continue the war against Russia even after the collapse of the USSR. No less than Trotsky's widow, Natalia Sedova Trotsky, assured these Washington-sponsored Bolsheviks that they remained loyal to the legacy of her husband in siding with the US against the USSR, the latter being seen as the primary obstacle to "world socialism." (Natalia Sedova Trotsky, "In Defense of Trotskyism," *Labor Action*, June 17, 1951.) Other anti-Soviet Cold Warriors included Trotsky's primary spokesman in the US, Max Shachtman. See K. R. Bolton, *Stalin*, pp. 93–124.

long to our own, Marxian brand of Communism?"[28] Does it matter whether we now step down in favor of either of the two? Is it not a fact that, since we in America have equated political power with money and—at the same time—did away with the repressing force and the majesty of every White State . . . *only two* real world powers are left which now face each other in a final struggle for all for nothing? And are we now anything more than mere pawns in the hands of those who are at the helm of these two competing world powers? With the fall of Hitler's Empire, Western Imperialism came to an end also.[29] Now, what's left are two camps dominated by two Communistic ideologies, and the great question is: which of the two will now disappear?

Over the last thirty years, our deep wishful thinkers in and around the White House have discussed without end our Destiny and that of our brother nations; they have babbled about their special, well concocted, political recipes; about their four, ten, twelve, and sixteen point-theories—and run around in circles—while the tide of events swept us away.

It was enough for Baruch on the Hudson and for Malenkov in the Kremlin to ***be*** Destiny.

X. Y. Z.

---

[28] "Our own, Marxian brand of Communism" refers to what Yockey regarded as "American-Jewish Bolshevism" in conflict with Russian Bolshevism, the first symbolically represented by Baruch, with his plan for a UN world state; the second the rejectionist regime of Malenkov, and subsequent Soviet leaders until Gorbachev.

[29] The Bolshevistic policy of the "Washington regime" is particularly evident in the "Fourteen Points" of President Woodrow Wilson and the "Atlantic Charter" of Franklin Roosevelt, both presented in the aftermath of World Wars, for the reorganization of the post-war world as a World State. Primary in both is the aim of dismantling the European empires.

THE DESTINY OF AMERICA

1955

EDITORS' NOTE

This essay was first published in January 1955. It has been described as "a relatively little-known work which was issued in mimeographed format."[1] The essay made its first appearance under the name of the leader of the National Renaissance Party, James H. Madole, in the *NRP Bulletin*. According to William Goring, who infiltrated the NRP on behalf of an anti-Nazi organization, Yockey had joined the party under the name Frank Healy during a brief stay in the United States, and then informed Madole, who had not known Yockey's true identity, that he was leaving for East Germany. He then travelled through the USSR.[2]

THE DESTINY OF AMERICA

The early American arrived at a land of which he knew nothing. He did not know its geography, its fertility, its climate, its dangers. In the North, he encountered forests, rocky soil, and winters of a rigor he had not known before. In the South, he met with swamps, malaria, and dense forests. Everywhere he encountered the hostile savage with his scalping knife and his warfare against women and children. In little groups, these early Americans cleared the forests, and built homes and forts. The men plowed the fields with rifles slung over their shoulders, and in the house, the wife went about her duties with a loaded weapon near at hand. There were ships to and from Europe, and the colonials could have left their hardships and gone back—but they would not admit defeat.

---

[1] Yockey, *Yockey: Four Essays,* "Publisher's Foreword."

[2] William Goring, "The National Renaissance Party," *National Information Center Newsletter*, Massachusetts, December 1969–January 1970, pp. 3–4.

Out of these colonials was bred the Minute Man. Minute Man! These American farmers were ready at a minute's notice to abandon the plow and seize the gun. They knew that the hour of their political independence was at hand, and instinctively they prepared for it. When the moment arrived, with a British order to arrest two of their leaders, the Minute Men assembled before daybreak at Lexington to face the British force sent to seize them. Though heavily outnumbered they stood their ground in the face of Major Pitcairn's order to disperse. "If they mean to have a war," said Captain John Parker, leader of the Minute Men, "let it begin here!"

Begin it did, and for eight long years it continued. Concord, Bunker Hill, Boston, Ticonderoga, Quebec, New York, Long Island, Harlem Heights, White Plains, Fort Lee, Fort Washington, Valley Forge, Trenton, Princeton, Brandywine, Saratoga, Stony Point, Savannah, Camden, The Cowpens, Yorktown—these names recall at once the terrific odds against which the colonials fought, the low points to which their fortunes reached, and the silent and steadfast devotion of the troops. At Valley Forge, the men were but half-clad, and rations, when there was food issued at all, were slim. Sickness was rife, and mortality was high. Yet no one thought of surrender. General Washington said of them: "Naked and starving as they are we cannot enough admire the incomparable patience and fidelity of our soldiery."[3]

No nation has produced individual soldiers to excel Nathaniel Greene, General Knox, General Sullivan, John Stark, Nicholas Herkimer, Anthony Wayne, Daniel Morgan, John Paul Jones, nor greater patriots than John Dickinson, Richard Henry Lee, John Adams, Benjamin Franklin, John Rutledge. These are but a few. The spirit which animated these heroes is part of the white race, and it will last while this race lasts. It waits for its reawakening upon the coming of great events to American soil once more. When the fields of this continent are visited once again by the stern creativeness of war—war for the independence and the liberation of the pristine American colonial spirit—

[3] From a letter by George Washington to Governor George Clinton dated February 16, 1778.

the world shall see that Americans are not the weak-willed, self-interested, pleasure-mad morons that Hollywood has tried so desperately to make them.

It was the individual imperialism of the frontiersman-type that actually opened up and conquered the North American continent. Explorers like George Rogers Clark and John Fremont preceded the frontiersman into the wilderness, and he followed into the hostile land with its lurking warlike savages. With slung rifle he took wife and children and all his earthly belongings into the land ahead, unknown, unsettled, unplowed. Daily he surmounted a thousand dangers, he lived in the face of Death. This intrepid type who was at once explorer, warrior, minister, doctor, judge, and settler, advanced until he reached the Pacific, and then he looked toward Alaska and the westward islands.

The tragic defeat of the Federalists by the less worthy among the post-Revolution generation made it possible for sectionalism to arise in America, and out of sectionalism issued the disastrous "War Between the States." That war proved only that the heroic type of American occurred everywhere in this broad land. The only lesson we can learn from the sacrifice is that big-mouthed agitators of the vicious stamp of Theodore Parker and Horace Greeley[4] are capable of consigning nations to the flames in order to actualize their fantastic equalitarian theories.

During the conquest of the continent, small carping voices were continually raised against the heroic performance. Congressmen laughed at the idea of governing a region so far away as the distant Pacific coast. The Poets Lowell and Whittier and the agitators Garrison and Phillips did their best to bring about a sectional war during all of the 1840s and '50s. Calhoun's attempt to annex Texas was defeated by the Congress. Small minds were against the Mexican War and the acquisition of the Southwest. They opposed the acquisition of Hawaii, of the Philippines, of

---

[4] Theodore Parker (1810–1860) was a Unitarian minister and adherent of the Transcendentalist school of philosophy who was a popular abolitionist in the period just before the Civil War. Horace Greeley (1811–1872) was the founder of the *New-York Tribune* who worked to influence public opinion against slavery.

the Cuban protectorate. After the War Between the States, this type of mind, represented by men like Sumner and Stevens,[5] wanted to treat the Southerners as an alien and inferior people and to gloat over them while placing the conqueror's foot on their necks.

This type of mentality still survives in America. Today it still fights against greatness and heroism. Today it teaches the doctrine of liberalism with its pacifism, its love for the inferior and misbegotten, its internationalism which makes a virtue of treason, its hatred of all who possess strong national feelings, its toothless desire for racial equality, and its tolerance of everything and everyone, particularly the alien and the unfit. Today this type of mind—namely, all those to whom liberal doctrines appeal—are working for the anti-American forces, whether consciously or not. The sub-Americans are in the service of America's inner enemy.

We have seen the spirit of the white race: the spirit of divine discontent and self-help, the spirit of self-reliance, of fearlessness in the face of great danger, the feeling of racial superiority, the urge to great distances and the will to conquer all that lies between, the spirit of the Alamo. To the true American, his is a living, organic, white nation, and not a set of principles, of "four freedoms," or a "world-policeman." Of this feeling was every great American: Washington, Hamilton, Henry Clay, Robert E. Lee, Sam Houston. The American soldier shows in every war that even today this true American type survives.

But today the true Americans, the former great leaders, have been displaced by Morgenthaus, Ezekiels, Pasvolskys, Cohens, Frankfurters, Goldsmiths, Lubins, Berles, Schenks, Edelsteins, Baruchs, Goldwyns, Mayers, Strausses, Lilienthals, Hillmans, Rosenmans, Lehmanns, Rosenbergs, Eisenhowers.

---

[5] Charles Sumner (1811–1875) was a Senator from Massachusetts who was staunchly abolitionist and sought harsh treatment of the South in the Reconstruction after the Civil War. He also attempted to have the word "white" struck from all American naturalization laws. Thaddeus Stevens (1792–1868) held similar views and worked with Sumner.

We know the true American, and we know the liberal—the sub-type within the white race. Let us now look at the third group which came here only yesterday and which today is linked with the liberals, the internationalists, the class-warriors, the subverters of America's white, European traditions. This group makes use of American slogans and American ideas, but that cannot conceal its alien provenance. Let us measure the significance of the newcomers and examine their history.

The History of the Jew

The culture which produced the Jewish nation arose in Asia Minor around 100 BC. This culture produced many nations, all of them, so far as we are concerned, similar to the Jews. These "nations" were not nations at all in our sense of the word, for they had no homeland. Citizenship in this alien type of nation was gained by being a believer in the religion of the group. Jews, Marcionites, Gnostics, Mohammedans—all these were nations, and to all of them membership in the nation was gained by being a believer. Intermarriage with non-believers was forbidden, and this inbreeding for two thousand years has made it possible today to pick out the Jew by his countenance. Thus, for the Jew, race and religion became identical, and if the Jew loses his religion, he loses little for he still remains a Jew by race. The unity of the race is not destroyed even though the great masses of the Jews become atheists.

After the dispersion of the Jews throughout Europe and Russia, they were entirely cut off from any contact with nations similar to themselves. They shut themselves up in the ghettoes of the cities and lived completely unto themselves. There they had their own religion, their own law, their own language, their own customs, their own diet, their own economy. Since they were nowhere at home, everywhere was equally home to them.

The early European nations felt the Jew to be as totally alien as he felt his surroundings to be. The Anglo-Saxons, the Goths, the Lombards, the Franks, all despised the usurious infidel. A popular rhyme of Gothic times portrays the three estates as the creation of God, and the usurious Jew as the creation of the Devil. Crusaders on their way to the Holy Land carried out wholesale massacres of Jews. Every European king at one time or another robbed the Jews and drove them from his domain. For 400 years the Jew was shut out from England. When he was allowed back, centuries more passed before he acquired or wanted civil rights of Englishmen. This persecution of the Jew that went on for 1,000 years took different forms—robbery through forced fines, extortion, exile, massacre—and it has had one determining, unchangeable result: it has reinforced in the Jew his original hatred for Christian civilization to the point where it is the sole content and meaning of his existence. This hatred is the breath of life to the Jew. He wants to tear down everything which surrounds him, every Western form of life, every Western idea. For a thousand years he cringed before the European master, who was so unassailable in his superiority. The figure of Shylock, drinking his gall and biding his time, taking his usury and saving the coins which represented to him the means of his liberation—this is the symbolic figure of the Jew for a thousand years. This consuming hatred on the part of the Jew is one of the most important facts in the world today. The Jew is a world power. How did this come about?

THE RISE OF THE JEW TO POWER

It was the Industrial Revolution in Europe and America which enabled the Jew, from having been Shylock for a thousand years, the despised and cringing usurer, to become the type of the modern Jew, the cinema dictator, the tyrant of the inmost thoughts of one hundred million Americans. The Jew had been thinking in terms of economics and money for a thousand years before Europe and America began to develop a money civilization. Consequently when money stepped out as the supreme force, the Jew shot upward like a meteor. There was still a barrier however to his complete conquest of power. The heathen, the outsider, was still barred from civil rights. Of old he had not sought them, but now they were necessary if he was to conquer the master of yesterday. Nation after nation succumbed to the principles which the butchers of the French Revolution preached, and which the Jew took up and excitedly shouted over the world. A money civilization wants no aristocracy to stand in its way, so Money and Jew preached equality. Nor must there be any barriers to the employment of money, so the Jew preached liberty. He sought to lose his mark as outsider, for in his new role he wanted to be accepted as a member of whatever nation he might be among, so that he might conquer the power for his revenge. So he preached fraternity for others and the brotherhood of man.

But his "equality" meant only a new inequality—the dictatorship of the Master of Money over the economic slave tied to his bench with a wage-chain. His "liberty" meant that the Jew was free to squeeze out the life-blood of nations through usury and financial dictatorship. The "brotherhood of man"—that meant that the Jew was to be accepted as an equal—but that he was to maintain his ancient unity and desire for revenge. Now the point has been reached where he steps out and asks for special privileges—and gets them! Yesterday he denied aristocracy—today he affirms it—and he is the new aristocrat!! Did not Albert Einstein, before whom Americans are supposed to bow and scrape, write in *Collier's Magazine* an article entitled "Why the Jew is Superior"?[6] And did not the white American, afraid to think for himself any longer, read it and believe?

The Jew did not conceive nor organize modern industrialism. No more did he organize liberalism. But when these two things had become realities, he cleverly insinuated himself into the new social and economic fabric which arose, and he has now identified himself with the rapacious capitalism of the sweatshop, and with the dishonest and revolting "democracy" of the type where Tweedledum opposed Tweedledee, and the Jew cares not which wins for he nominates them both.

There was a great danger to the Jew in this removal of all barriers between him and the host nations. This danger was assimilation of the great mass of Jews. If this were to occur, the Rothschilds, Baruchs, Frankfurters, Rosenmans, Guggenheims, Schiffs, Lehmanns, Cohens—all these would be leaders without followers. They would lose their trustworthy followers who

---

[6] The claims for the existence of this article seem to be a fabrication, perhaps unknown to Yockey.

could penetrate everywhere and spread the influence of the Jew. One fruitful source of taxation would be gone. So the word "assimilated" became a term of contempt used by arch-Jews to describe other Jews who were losing their Jewish feelings and instincts. The Jew, with his two thousand years behind him, was faced with a perilous situation. No mere money manipulation could cope with this emergency. In this situation, the Jewish leaders invented Zionism.

ZIONISM & THE PINNACLE OF JEWISH POWER

It was a political master-stroke on the part of the Jew to bring out the movement known as Zionism. Its ostensible aim was to seek a "national home" for the Jew, a plot of ground to which all Jews would theoretically return and there settle. Since the idea seemed to be to make the Jews into a nation like America, one with geographical boundaries, it seemed a praiseworthy movement to Americans. It seemed to promise the end of the Jews as the shifting sand dunes among nations, and to herald their establishment as a civilized nation. Hence unlimited Zionist activity and propaganda could be carried on among the Jews by their leaders, and no suspicion was aroused in the minds of the host nations.

But the real aim of Zionism was merely to save the Jew, wherever he was, from assimilation by the Western peoples, the European and American people. It enabled their leaders to unite the Jews firmly, to prevent assimilation by giving the Jews a political aim to follow. The spurious quality of the movement is shown by the fact that almost no Jews were moved to Palestine. A few only were moved, for commercial and political reasons and to conceal the Zionist fraud, but the millions remained in America and Europe. The real aim of Zionism—to reaffirm and perpetuate the solidarity of the Jew—has been successful. Zionism has become the official policy of the Jewish entity, and its ascendancy means, as far as the simple, ordinary Jew is concerned, that he is an utter slave in the hands of his leaders. It is probably superfluous to mention that no leading Zionist has gone from his position of power in white America back to Palestine. Nor need it be pointed out once more how few out of the millions of Jews driven from Europe have gone to Palestine. Almost to a man, they have come to America, their land of promise, the last base for their power, the last place for their revenge.

The invasion of Palestine, strategically important though it is, nevertheless stands in the shade of the vast invasion of America. During the short half century since Jewry adopted Zionism, some ten millions of Jews have been dumped on the shores of North America to displace Americans biologically and economically, to live parasitically on the American organism, to distort the social and spiritual life of the nation. The volume of the invasion has been such that even the slumbering, politically-unconscious white American has begun to blink his eyes and look around him in amazement, as he becomes gradually cognizant that his native land has passed into the possession of scheming, power-hungry, money-grubbing, total aliens.

The alien has his own press, in which he reveals those things which the democratic-liberal press dutifully conceals at the behest of the Jew. Pick up at random an issue of the *Contemporary Jewish Record*—that for June 1941. On page 282 we are told how Jewish educators are combatting successfully "the un-American movement of 100% Americanism."[7] On page 260 a member of the American Jewish Committee joyfully reports that because of the hostility between American and Jew the successive waves of Jewish immigrants "will develop into a cohesive American Jewish community."[8] The article "The Jewish Emigrant—1941," describing the arrival of the Jew in America, says: "Our sole conclusion is that when the emigrant has finally arrived at his destination, he can consider himself at the entrance to Heaven" (*sic*).[9]

---

[7] 100% Americanism was an actual nativist political movement that rose during the First World War which adopted its inspiration from Theodore Roosevelt, who had called for Americans to abandon their previous ethnic and national identities and embrace the American identity, castigating what he called "hyphenated Americanism." The quotation is taken from an article by Stewart G. Cole entitled "Intercultural Education: Cultural Diversity and Education."

[8] The quotation is taken from an article by Morris D. Waldman entitled "America and the Jewish Community."

[9] The article is by Max Gottschalk, found on page 268.

Seven million of these immigrants have arrived at their "entrance to Heaven" since 1933. There is admitted hostility between them and their host-people. The Jew opposes one hundred percent Americanism. Yet he calls his arrival here his "entrance to Heaven." How is this?

THE RISING INFLUENCE OF THE JEW IN AMERICA

The North American continent was discovered, explored, cleared, plowed, and settled by the individual imperialism of members of the European-American white race. The political independence of America was won, and the industrial-technical system of the continent was planned and built by the white race. The American merchant marine was built and sent into the seven seas by white men. Every creative idea in whatever realm—political, economic, technical, religious, legal, educational, social—that has been brought forth on this continent has originated with, and been developed by, members of the white European-American race. America belongs spiritually, and will always belong, to the Western Civilization of which it is a colonial transplantation, and no part of the true America belongs to the primitivity of the barbarians and fellaheen outside of this civilization, whether in Asia Minor, the Far East, or Africa.

And yet, even though the Jew was not present at Valley Forge, even though he was not at New Orleans in 1814, nor at the Alamo, nor at Bull Run or Chancellorsville, nor at Guantanamo Bay or Manila, even though he took no part in the conquest of the continent—in spite of this complete dissociation of the Jew from the American past, it is a stark and gruesome fact that *America today is ruled by the Jew.* Where Americans hold office, they hold it at the pleasure of the Jew, and use it in deference to his policy. Baruch argues with Rosenman[10] on the steps of the White House—once the residence of Washington, Madison, Adams—and the policy of America is thus determined. La

[10] Samuel Rosenman (1896–1973) was a Jewish politician and advisor to Franklin Roosevelt who was instrumental in pushing for the war crimes trials at the end of the Second World War.

Guardia calls Lehmann by a Yiddish term of abuse in public.[11] As lawyer, the Jew brings in excessive litigation; as judge, he imports chicanery into the administration, and has the power to pronounce rules of law for Americans. A rabbi states: "The ideals of Judaism and the ideals of Americanism are one and the same." And the *Jewish Chronicle* (April 4, 1919) says: "The ideals of Bolshevism are consonant with the finest ideals of Judaism."[12] The notorious rabbi Wise[13] announces, "I have been an American for sixty-seven years, but I have been a Jew for six thousand years." The *Jewish Chronicle* tells us: "The Jews in America are 100% Jewish and 100% American." These schizophrenic percentages resolve themselves into the thesis of the rabbis that Judaism, Trotskyist Bolshevism, and Americanism are one and the same. The synagogues have a parade of liberals—sub-Americans with defective instincts—come before them to parrot back at them their own view-point.

The Jew numbers approximately ten percent of the North American population, but in the Second World War, a war fought solely for Jewish interests, a war of his fomenting, a war to increase his power, the conscripts in the American Army were only two percent Jewish, according to official records. Neither in his assumed role of American, nor in his actual status as member of the Jewish Culture-State-Nation-Race-People, was he willing to risk his blood, even in his own war. In the fighting forces he limited his participation to the administrative branches: Judge Advocate, Medical, Quartermaster, Finance. In the American Army Jewish conscripts have an unconditional right to a furlough for Passover, for Yom Kippur, for Rosh Hashanah. The

---

[11] While speaking at Seth Low Junior High School on October 27, 1941, Mayor Fiorello La Guardia of New York City was quoted as saying, "You have heard of *goniffs* stealing from *goniffs*. Well, you are hearing now of double-crossers double-crossing double-crossers. Lehmann punched himself on the chin and knocked himself out."

[12] From an article by Leopold Greenberg.

[13] Stephen Samuel Wise (1874–1949) was a rabbi in the Reform sect in New York City. A friend of Einstein's, he was a staunch advocate of Zionism and opposition to the Third Reich. As for the quotation, he said this on many occasions.

induction of Jews into the Army is delayed over Jewish holidays—"to avoid undue hardship." The Central Conference of American Rabbis in the 47th annual convention in New York addressed a resolution to the American Congress asking that Jews be exempted from conscription "in accordance with the highest interpretation of Judaism"![14]

In the publicly supported educational institutions for higher learning, the Jew is driving out the native American student. In the free universities, such as Wayne University and City College of New York, the Jew's possession is complete. The Stock Exchange presents a similar picture. The New York Exchange is dormant on Jewish holidays. The Officers' Reserve Corps is ever more penetrated by the Jew. The police forces of the large cities are under his control, and the Federal secret police enforce his bidding. He commands the National Guard in the populous states.

How has this come about? How has the native American been driven from the positions of representation, of power and respect in his own land? How has he been chased out of the professions, out of government, of the universities, out of the sources of public information? How did the interloper from Asia, the ghetto-creature from Kishnev, attain to his eminence whereupon he holds in his hands the decision of war or peace, and decides who are America's friends and who are America's enemies?

Two things are responsible for this situation in which America finds itself serving as a mere tool in the hands of an alien. First is Liberalism—the enemy of national greatness, the virus that eats up national feelings. Liberalism is the doctrine that everyone is equal, everyone acceptable, the doctrine that the

---

[14] "The Central Conference of American Rabbis reaffirms its conviction that conscientious objection to military service is in accordance with the highest interpretation of Judaism, and therefore petitions the Government of the United States to grant to Jewish religious objectors to war the same exemption from military service as has long been granted to members of the Society of Friends and similar religious organizations." From the CCAR War Draft Resolution of the 47th Convention in Cape May, New Jersey on June 25, 1936.

botched, the misbegotten are equal to the strong and the superior, that there are no foreigners and no distinctions. Liberalism gnaws away at the structure for which patriots and great leaders gave their lives and fortunes. To Liberalism, America is a "melting-pot," a dump heap for the world's human refuse. When the white race in Europe drives out the Jew, he goes to America where weak heads and inferiors who are jealous of that to which they are not equal have laid down for him the red carpet of Liberalism, and on this carpet, the Jew has advanced to supreme power in the short half a century since he first discovered that America is a fine host for an enterprising parasite. Liberalism is the inversion of that one hundred percent Americanism which the Jew hates.

But mere Liberalism alone does not account for it. The second factor has been the aggressive unity of the Jew, his cohesiveness born of hate, which has welded him together and organized his forces for his mission of destruction. By virtue of the cohesiveness of the Jewish entity, at once Culture, State, Nation, People, Race, Religion, and Society, the Jew conquered the cinema industry, the news-gathering associations which control all "news" and journalistic opinion, the periodical and book press, and the radio networks. When it became obvious the "Republican" party was about to lose the 1932 election, he cleverly insinuated himself into the "Democratic" party, and placed his candidate in the Presidency. This was the Revolution of 1933, but since it had occurred in the form of a simple change of parties, the politically-unconscious American remained unaware.

In 1933 descended upon Washington the swarm led by Baruch, Lehmann, Morgenthau, Frankfurter, Niles, and Rosenman. In their train were thousands of Pasvolskys, Messersmiths, Lubins, Berles, Fortases, Lilienthals, Cohens, Ezekiels, Silversteins *et al.*, and bringing up the procession came enough lesser Jews, deracine liberals, technocrats, and aliens to double the population of the capital city within a few years.

Between the cracks in the pavement the Jew recruited a thousand sub-Americans as "radio commentators," newspaper "columnists," and professional propagandists to disseminate the world-outlook the Jew considered appropriate for the American.

A multiplicity of government bureaus came into existence, necessarily staffed with Jews. The Jew sought to bring under his control every factor of public expression and influence, thus to make sure that never again would there be a free national election, for he did not intend to relinquish his power, so long dreamt of, and now at last real, through the free play of any constitutional game of parties and majorities. He purged the central government of whoever could not be led by the nose, or bought. Who opposed was shouted down, smeared with vile labels, and so silenced.

Thus America was given a Semitic countenance.

HANG ON & PRAY:
ARNOLD TOYNBEE, CO-EXISTENCE APOSTLE

1956

EDITORS' NOTE

"Hang On and Pray" can be dated to 1956. It was published by Le Blanc Publications, run by Frederick C. F. Weiss. Weiss' contacts reached around the world, especially among German émigrés in South America and the Middle East, and he provided funding for war veterans and political activists such as Colonel Hans-Ulrich Rudel in Germany, the famous wartime air ace who had fled to Argentina, where he assisted others who had served in the Third Reich in escaping Europe, and later returned to West Germany, where he was active in various nationalist political parties. Weiss' first publication was *Quo Vadis, America?*, issued in 1946, followed by *Germania Delenda Est?*, issued in 1947.[1] Weiss was therefore among the first in America to publicly question American policy towards Germany and Europe.

A 1953 FBI report cites an informant having stated that Weiss had been in contact with Yockey, "who wrote articles for Weiss" with what was regarded as a "pro-Russian slant."[2] Possible connections between Weiss and representatives from the Soviet bloc were of course of much interest to the FBI, and Weiss and Yockey sought to play the US and USSR off of each other to secure a more favorable situation for Germany and Europe. Of particular concern was the "neutralist" line being advocated by German nationalist veterans and political activists such as Major General Otto Remer. This informant told the FBI specifically that Yockey had written Weiss' material since December 3, 1952, and believed that it had been Yockey who had put Weiss in contact

---

[1] "Frederick Charles Ferdinand Weiss," FBI-New York, July 24, 1953, Report 100-111893, p. 7.

[2] "Frederick Charles Ferdinand Weiss," FBI-New York, December 7, 1953, Report 100-111893, p. 1.

with Soviet agents.[3]

Of the pamphlets put out by Le Blanc Publications under the authorship of "X. Y. Z.," "Hang On and Pray" is the most likely to have been written by Yockey, perhaps at the suggestion of Weiss. A Le Blanc circular refers to the "1956 edition (second printing)" of "Hang On and Pray." Along with the circular came a news article on the pamphlet's subject, celebrated English historian Arnold Toynbee. According to a report in *The New York Daily News*, Toynbee had delivered a speech to the University of Minnesota entitled "The New Opportunities for Historians." The report states that, according to Toynbee, the duty of historians is to write books that

> . . . drip the One World idea, endlessly and remorselessly, into their readers' minds. Only those events which tend to prove that One World is inevitable are to be put into the histories. Happenings which indicate that human beings are widely various, partly vicious, disunited and suspicious, and probably always will be, are simply to be passed over by Dr. Toynbee's school of historians.

The journalists at *The New York Daily News* were "shocked" that the purpose of historians, according to this most eminent of liberal internationalist academics—"one of the most famous and respected historians operating today"—was to "lie," purvey "half-truths," and "suppress pertinent facts."[4] The article and Toynbee's university lecture fortuitously confirmed the contentions of Yockey in the pamphlet: that Toynbee is not a historian or a philosopher, but a propagandist and journalist espousing a World State. Toynbee, who is often written and spoken about in connection to Spengler, was the very antithesis of Spengler. Spengler wrote of the fulfillment of Western Civilization's destiny; Toynbee looked forward to its end in a melting-pot quagmire that would establish a World State.

---

[3] Ibid., p. 4.

[4] "Should Historians Lie?," *New York (Sunday) Daily News*, April 15, 1956.

"Hang On and Pray" has the features of Yockey's style and idiosyncrasies, including the use of lower case when describing a type of "inner traitor" of Western Civilization, the type here being "the toynbees." According to Yockey's primary English collaborator, Anthony Gannon, Yockey held Toynbee in derision. Yockey's would-be biographer, Keith Stimely, asked Gannon about Yockey's library, and whether this included Toynbee's *A Study of History*.[5] Gannon replied that, "Of Arnold Toynbee he [Yockey] was derisive, saying that to write his 'philosophy' after Spengler was inexcusable!"[6] Writing such a repudiation of Toynbee, perhaps at Weiss' instigation, would therefore be a subject of relish for Yockey. The contention in "Hang On and Pray" regarding America's differing attitude towards "containing" Communism and the total war of annihilation that was fought against Germany is the theme of "America's Two Ways of Waging War."

When H. Keith Thompson was asked about Yockey's attitude towards Toynbee, Thompson stated that Yockey agreed with Weiss' view "that Toynbee was an asshole." Thompson, who printed and edited the manuscript of "Hang On and Pray," stated that:

> I am sure that some of the contribution to that stemmed from the pen of Yockey, because Weiss was really quite incapable of handling the English language, and had difficulty gathering his thoughts. I did much of that for him. But I'm not a scholar of the Toynbee school or stamp, and that came from somewhere. But I would have guessed that Yockey in some way contributed to it, and I'm sure that he would have influenced Weiss to the extent that his own views would have been expressed there.[7]

If, as Thompson states, Weiss was "quite incapable of han-

---

[5] Letter from Stimely to Gannon, January 11, 1981, Question 3.

[6] Letter from Gannon to Stimely, March 1, 1981, p. 2.

[7] Keith Stimely, interview with H. Keith Thompson, March 13, 1986.

dling the English language, and had difficulty gathering his thoughts," and Thompson did not have sufficient background in philosophy, other than definite proof to the contrary, it must be concluded that this work is Yockey's.

HANG ON & PRAY

FOREWORD

As this document is written, the curtain is rising on what may well be the last act of a great Tragedy. The Dogs of War, their atomic fangs bared, are being loosened upon an ill-prepared world. The Wars of the Races are upon us. But our "leadership" in Washington, London, Bonn, Tel Aviv, and Paris does not permit us to think, much less speak, in terms of "Race."

The Chinese feel no such taboo. To them, "Communism" is an effective dogma to be used to rid China of the long-hated "White Man." In their eyes, it is little more. Their fight is almost exclusively a struggle against the Whites. They make no secret of this fact. For them, as for their fellow-Asiatics, the Russians, the approaching death-struggle is aimed at the final destruction of the Western (White) World—military, economically, socially, and culturally.

Fools in authority tell us that this will be a "short war." They say that the Chinese will "back down," and they dream that the Russian-Mongolian Masses will soon "revolt." These dreams and august pronouncements lay bare the appalling ignorance and disgusting sentimentality which characterizes this, our most tragic hour.

Is there any hope for the Future? Perhaps. As it is certain that the Wars of the Races will be long and exhausting, it is equally as certain that the corruption of the West will ultimately cause it to crumble under the titanic exertions it will be forced to undergo.

There is one hope for the West. It is a slim hope, but there is no other. A Nationalist revival in America, in union with a revival of the European Elite, can be the only regenerative outcome of a series of catastrophes, an enraged White Race, decimated by perhaps two-thirds of its numbers after prolonged wars, might rise in blind fury against its tormentors.

To "win" the war without catastrophe is not only an impossibility in these days, but it would also be worse than useless since no dynamic change in Western thinking or political forms would result. To "lose" the war, and thereby be subject to prompt extermination, would spell the End.

The only hope for the preservation of Western Civilization lies, therefore, neither in "victory" nor in "defeat," but in a stalemate—a long and costly stalemate during the course of which both contestants would progressively disintegrate from within.

Without such a stalemate the Western World is doomed to perpetual slaughter in stupid wars and to inevitable miscegenation with colored races. Civilization will crumble, music will even more revert to that of the jungle, literature will be cast aside, history will be unread, and our cities will decompose as the dark inhabitants stalk the decaying streets.

Who are the Prophets of the West in this crucial hour? What shall be the battle cry? Shall we follow our toynbees and embrace their "philosophy of the hour"? Shall we believe Toynbee as he babbles his "philosophical" instruction to the West: **hang on and pray**? Let us instead cut through the steel armor of the mighty Rockefeller-financed propaganda machine which is promoting and deifying this little gnat of an Englishman. Let us see our "Hang On and Pray" Toynbee as he really is!

The Publishers

ARNOLD TOYNBEE, CO-EXISTENCE APOSTLE

The fashionable philosopher of the moment is Toynbee. His effusions are printed everywhere, the fashionable intellectuals quote him, and he quotes them. The great propaganda organs encourage their captive audiences to read him, or at least to revere him.

THE SUPER SCHOLAR

Toynbee passes now, in the modish world, as a super-scholar, as the arbiter of Freedom and Necessity. Fashion has taken him at his own evaluation. In his essay, "Does History Repeat Itself?,"[8] this modest man explains why history does "on occasion" repeat itself:

> ... the value of such repetitions is, after all, not difficult to discern. Creation could hardly make any headway at all if each new form of creature were not represented by numerous eggs distributed among numerous baskets. How else could a creator, human or divine, provide himself with sufficient materials for bold and fruitful experiment and with effective means of retrieving inevitable failures?

Thus, quietly, in his self-effacing manner, this retiring scholar tells us that the means available to God are only such as he, Father Toynbee, can visualize.

Toynbee can hardly pretend to be a historian; he has never written a history. He claims to be a historical philosopher, and this is the face he presents to the intellectuals and the scholars. His fashionable rank as "super-scholar" rests upon this aspect of his work.

PILFERED FROM OSWALD SPENGLER

His entire "system" is derived from Spengler: it is at one and the same time a pastiche, a massive plagiarism, a caricature, and a distortion of Spengler. To demonstrate Toynbee's larcenous relationship to Spengler, we need only to quote Toynbee himself:

> What was it that ... had set in such vigorous motion ... those few societies that had embarked upon the enterprise called civilization? ... This question was simmering in my mind when, in the summer of 1920, Professor Namier ... placed in my hands Spengler's *Untergang des Abendlandes*. As I read those pages teeming with firefly flashes of historical insight, I wondered at first whether my whole inquiry

[8] From Arnold J. Toynbee, *Civilization on Trial* (London: Oxford University Press, 1946), pp. 29–41.

> had been disposed of by Spengler before even the questions, not to speak of the answers, had fully taken shape in my own mind. . . . But when I looked about in Spengler's book for an answer to my question about the geneses of civilizations, I saw that there was still work for me to do, for on this point Spengler was, it seemed to me, most unilluminatingly dogmatic and deterministic.

It is quite obvious that the *origin* of a civilization is of no practical importance. The entire purpose of Spengler's work was to arrive at *the form of our future,* in other words to orientate ourselves historically, so that we realize unshakably what we can do and what we cannot do, what is to be, and what is not to be. Not even Toynbee has suggested that a man or group of men, by taking thought, or by studying Toynbee, could set a new "civilization" upon its legs. Why then attempt the impossible task of finding origins? But Toynbee lacked the reverence of mysteries that all deep philosophers have felt. He lacked the depth of Remy de Gourmont, who said, "Origins are forever hidden from us."[9] As Pieter Geyl saw at once, "*Toynbee's system is useless.*"[10]

As individuals, we are not fundamentally interested in our own pre-natal life, and as organic parts of a High Culture, we are fundamentally interested in whither we are going, but not in whence we came, except insofar as that may shed light upon our future. But Toynbee's aim was not this. His aim was to discover *why* our Culture arose in the first place, an utterly abstract, useless, practically meaningless question. Spengler, not Toynbee, said, "Every line that is not written to serve active life I regard as superfluous."

It was Spengler who discovered that a High Culture is an or-

---

[9] Remy de Gourmont (1858–1915) was a French Symbolist writer who favored better relations between France and Germany, which earned him the ire of French nationalists. The phrase "Origins are forever hidden from us" was also used by Yockey, uncited, in *Imperium*, p. 74.

[10] Pieter Geyl (1887–1966) was a Dutch historian who was well-known as a critic of Toynbee's work, and debated Toynbee on several occasions.

ganic unity, that it thus has a destiny which can be read in the accomplished lives of other members of the genus. Since it is a unity, it has the same organic development as all life-forms whatever, i.e., birth, growth, fulfillment, death. To life belongs death,[11] and to each living stage belongs its appropriate tasks and events.

Toynbee saw that he could make a niche for himself by becoming the "mouthpiece" of those who simply could not bear the idea of the downgrade of the Western Culture. The only way to deny that the West will die is to deny that it is organic, i.e., to deny that it lives. It thus becomes a mere aggregate. But this is what nineteenth-century materialism thought, so Toynbeeism is mere reaction.[12]

Toynbee wants everything both ways. He always treats a "civilization" as though it is a unity, but always specifically denies that it is an organism; thereby it has no Destiny. He speaks of civilizations "aborting," "dying," "being born," "committing suicide," etc., but his "civilizations" are not organisms. These elementary contradictions, which appear on every page, and in almost every sentence of his works, completely eliminate Toynbee's massive word-eruption from the category of philosophy,

---

[11] Of interest in assessing this work as Yockey's is the exact phrase used by Yockey in *Imperium* when discussing the supposed "pessimism" of Spengler's culture-morphology: "To Life belongs Death" (Yockey, *Imperium*, p. 49).

[12] This is the nineteenth-century idea of the "march of progress" that is still in vogue, seeing Western science and technology, and the ideologies that have arisen during the epoch of the West's decay, as exemplified in the Jacobin slogan: "liberty, equality, fraternity," or the United Nations Declaration on Human Rights, as the culmination of millennia of a supposed "world history." The present-day equivalent is, for example, the historian Francis Fukuyama, who refers to the victory of Western liberalism over the world as the "end of history": the final achievement after which nothing more need be attained politically, morally, and religiously. Toynbee was writing in the same vein, seeing the culmination of history as a "World State" where the African would come into his own as a civilization-builder, and thus the achievements of Western technics have their justification in preparing the way for the universal melting-pot.

because the "system" contradicts itself on every single fundamental point.

AVOIDING ETHICAL IMPLICATIONS

Mainly Toynbee wants to avoid the ethical implications of the Spenglerian philosophy, and these he avoids by simple affirmation (and later, naturally, denial) of "the free will" of the Western Culture (or "society" in Toynbee's jargon). Spengler showed us the exact point in our historical development at which we now stand. He developed his thesis before the First World War, and at that time foretold the broad outlines of our coming development in all branches of our Cultural life—in religion, philosophy, science, the arts, education, law, society, economics, war, politics, and technology. Spengler's principal work was published in 1917, and in the forty years since then, the Spenglerian thesis has been empirically proved beyond any possibility of empirical refutation. It is silly in the twentieth century (as Toynbee does) to try to raise once again the old Gothic problem of free will versus necessity. We have long since ceased to see any conflict—with Goethe, with Spengler, we see that we are free *to do the necessary*. In prospect, we are free. In retrospect, we see that we did what we had to do. *Free will* is the *form* of all our actions, and *necessity is the content*.

TOYNBEE LOGIC—EVERYTHING BOTH WAYS!

Toynbee has everything both ways—denying "historical laws," he speaks of "regular patterns." He says the West is disintegrating, and is perhaps dead (*sic*), but it need not disintegrate further, if it follows his advice. Although he affirms "free will," all his proposals for the future avoid the imperative mood, and present his personal ideas as *historically necessary*. A typical Toynbee formula is: ". . . the writer of the present article may as well put his cards on the table at once. He believes that where there is life there is hope, and that, with God's help, man is master of his own destiny, at least to some extent in some respects." This sort of talk can hardly be called philosophy, and is hardly even bold enough for a high-school graduation speech. On the very next page, after throwing Destiny out, he hales it back in:

"In this old-fashioned field of battles and policies, captain and kings, does history turn out to have repeated itself as it does in fields of human activity that are manifestly governed by cycles in the movement of physical nature? . . . The present writer inclines to this view."

His logic is as purely personal and eclectic as "his philosophy." "Why am I a historian, not a philosopher or a physicist? For the same reason that I drink tea and coffee without sugar. Both habits were formed at a tender age by following a lead from my mother. I am a historian because my mother was one before me . . ." One would look in vain for any such mother-passages in Burckhardt, Buckle, Gibbon, Mommsen, Lamprecht, Breysig, or Spengler. But Toynbee's mother pops up repeatedly in his writing. Might not the Freudians find a case here?

An example of Toynbee logic follows:

> There is one curious result of our immense modern scientific discoveries which is, I think, often overlooked. On the vastly changed time-scale which our astronomers and geologists have opened up to us, the beginning of the Christian era is an extremely recent date; on a time-scale in which nineteen hundred years are no more than the twinkling of an eye, the beginning of the Christian era is only yesterday. It is only on the old-fashioned time-scale, on which the creation of the world and the beginning of life on the planet were reckoned to have taken place not more than six thousand years ago, that a span of nineteen hundred years seems a long period of time and the beginning of the Christian era therefore seems a far-off event. In fact it is a very recent event—perhaps the most recent significant event in history . . .

Any student of elementary logic can easily demonstrate the meaninglessness of this comparison of physical time with organic time. They are completely incommensurable. This is no mere slip on Toynbee's part, arising perhaps from fatigue after writing millions of words, or from the necessity of meeting a deadline (for Toynbee must be numbered among the journalists, and is obviously paid by the word). Again and again, he recurs to this puerile error: ". . . the last three or four thousand years . . . are periods of such infinitesimal brevity that it would be impossible to show them, drawn to scale, on any chart of the whole history of this planet . . ."

TOYNBEE, THE HISTORICAL GEO-POLITICIAN

Toynbee's historical judgments are on a logical par with the foregoing, but they expose his ethical-political values. He is boundlessly enthusiastic for Venice, Holland, and Switzerland, and says they arose as "responses" to the "challenges" of the sea and the mountains. Just how the sea challenges the coast more in one place than in another is unexplained. And if mountains challenge mankind to produce "a high level of social achievement," we should expect to find Switzerlands scattered throughout the Hindu Kush, the Atlas, the Himalayas, *et al.* Toynbee delights in talking about "little bits and pieces like Holland and England," and says England is only a "bow-shot" from "the Continent," by which he means Asia. His distaste for anything leads him to deny its existence. Thus, because he is "against war," he calls war old-fashioned, although nothing could be more modern than the preparations for the coming Third World War. His detestation of Western Imperialism and for the application of war to policy leads him into nonsensical inversions of fact, and denials of the entire content of human history. For instance, he says that "civilizations" grow when they do *not* expand geographically, and when they do *not* make war. But consistency would be too much to expect from Toynbee, and certain wars receive his approval; e.g., the English attack on the Boers in 1900 arose because of Boer nationalism, and "the statesmen of the British Empire were driven to make use of their overwhelming military superiority because the national ambitions of the two backward independent miniature states made their preservation inconsistent with any other solution; and, indeed, at the cost of a small local war, it proved possible subsequently to pursue a constructive policy within the Empire, which gave satisfaction to Dutch nationalism." All very nice, but Toynbee applies this only to England. *German* annexations are always "brutal militarism." The Opium

War, which England waged against China to preserve the English opium monopoly there, was an "international crime," *but* later the English were "ashamed," and this redeemed the "crime" (they kept the monopoly, despite the "shame")! "I well remember," says Toynbee, "this, I hope, redeeming sense of shame being communicated to me by mother when I asked her about 'the Opium War' and she told me the facts." Toynbee grieves that the Irish nationalists "go on fostering their hatred of England," but finds it essential that all Europeans find German ascendency "abhorrent."[13]

Toynbee is an enthusiast for India, for China, for Islam, and for the savages of Africa, but uniformly disapproves of everything Western except our technics. These, he says, we must at once deliver to all the colored peoples. He says, "the triumph of the White Race may be judged to have been a misfortune," because he finds the Whites are "race-conscious." Toynbee looks to Islam for leadership in the battle for "racial toleration." Intoxicated with love for Islam, he goes on to hope that Islam, with its "outstanding moral accomplishment" of "the extinction of race-consciousness," will lead us also to the extinction of the *second* "conspicuous source of danger in the world—alcohol" (*sic!*). En-

---

[13] This mentality is typical of an English puritan Whig; hypocritical moralizing was the foundation of British Imperial policy. The Anglo-Boer War was fought to secure the gold and diamond fields. The Afrikaners were vilified as "backwards" to justify English intervention. The "small local war" cost the lives of more than thirty thousand Afrikaner women and children who succumbed to starvation and typhus in British concentration camps. England felt "shame" for what was done to the Chinese, albeit to maintain the opium monopoly of the distinctly non-English dynasty of David Sassoon, but not to any European people such as the Afrikaner or the German. The Whig puritan derision of the Afrikaners was maintained for his "backward" Apartheid, again in the interests of industrialists such as Oppenheimer, behind the inane slogan of "human rights," which reduced South Africa to an unworkable shambles for everyone, including Oppenheimer. The Irish, too, are a "backward" affront to the liberal march of progress, but not Bantu, Xhosa, Matabele, or Mashona tribalism, *ad infinitum*.

ter Toynbee the temperance-lecturer. Mother again, perhaps?

TOYNBEE THE POLITICAL PROPAGANDIST — A SECOND FACE

We begin to see Toynbee's second face: — Toynbee the philosopher, with his Sunday supplement enthusiasm for "modern science," his journalistic nonsense about the "atomic bomb" destroying the entire human race, with his puerile logic, ill-informed in history — (he asserts for example that Adolf Hitler and Mussolini both obtained power "by force"), with his inversion of the facts, his completely arbitrary historical judgments, ridden by prejudices, disordered in all his thinking. *This Toynbee* is so patently an intellectual lightweight that he would not, even in these times, have obtained any vogue whatever were it not for his political doctrines. These doctrines have caused him to be adopted by the Washington regime and elevated above fundamental criticism. If one would attack him, one must first praise him. Thus Sorokin[14] first praises Toynbee's "brilliant mind," "majestic vision," etc., before he finishes by saying — "The author displays both ignorance and deliberate neglect."

Toynbee is essentially a political propagandist and nothing else! All the gilt of scholarship, "systematic" interpretation of history, objectivity, and the rest of it are mere show. The most effective propaganda (with a certain level of mankind) is that which is *apparently objective*. Accordingly, politicians have always been glad to have priests, philosophers, scientists, and unworldly scholars of all sorts support them morally before the public. It purifies their motives. Vulgar lust for power is dignified and disguised by these propagandists.

This is Toynbee's second, his real face. Every word he writes is in support of Zionism and the Washington regime, which two forces presently dominate the Western world. Every idea of Toynbee's is *polemical*, and not in the least objective. This is the reason why his "system" leaves every question open. When the situation indicates, he can ring the changes upon Necessity, *and*

---

[14] Pitirim Sorokin (1889–1968) was a Russian sociologist who opposed Communism, and emigrated to the United States in 1923, where he lived for the rest of his life.

when it alters, he can ring up Free Will. Civilizations are units, then they are not units, but aggregates; they have a Destiny, then they have no Destiny, but are subject to "man's free will"; civilizations die, then they need not die; Toynbee is a Christian, then he is not a Christian; Russia has a Western ideology, then it has a non-Western ideology; Russia is an aggressor, then Russia is the victim of aggression from the West, etc., etc. It is all there. You can find whatever you want, wrapped in heavy layers of wooly words.

Where Washington vacillates, Toynbee vacillates; where Washington is firm, he is unshakeable. He can furnish, at short notice, a convenient historical moral foundation for *any* policy it may adopt. He has already created, in his *Study of History,* a library of material to justify all the firm, long-range policies of Zionism, the Washington regime, and the United Nations. Thus, he unceasingly belabors Western nationalism, Western imperialism, Western racial pride, and Western accomplishments. Just as unceasingly, he praises and justifies the colored revolt against White world-supremacy. The Washington regime implements the "Point Four" program,[15] to arm and industrialize the colored races against the white Western world, and Toynbee rallies around saying: "It is immoral for us to have more than our backward brothers." The cultural monument of the Pyramids merely distresses Toynbee—he only thinks of the "forced human labor" which erected these monuments. He cries when he thinks that the White masters of today are despoiling the colored slaves, "as cold-bloodedly as we rob our bees of their honey." Just what fact-situation he has in mind here is not clear. The White Race definitely occupies an inferior position in the world today. But if Toynbee wants to learn about despoiling, he ought to be turned loose in Egypt, where the Arabs would lose no time in separating him from his last sixpence, and send him running to the British Consul for aid. Toynbee weeps, like Roosevelt, about "the underprivileged majority" of the human race, but at last report he is living comfortably in his villa, enjoying every

---

[15] The same program of President Truman's that was referenced in "Brotherhood."

luxury that the detested Western Civilization can give him, even though, if he were to practice his doctrine instead of merely mouthing it, there are countless worthy colored families in London's vast proletariat to whom he could consign all his worldly goods, as he wants the White Race to do on the world-scale. Toynbee is just a posthumous abolitionist, and he is weeping over the slaves even after they have installed themselves in the master's seat!

He is opposed to White "race-consciousness," but he glows with pleasure to see colored faces in his audience of students. Colored "race-consciousness" is not bad, and Saint Arnold feels it himself, even though his skin is unfortunately white. "Islam remains," he says, "with a mighty spiritual mission still to carry out." The African Negroes, he says, "have a pure and lofty conception of the nature of God and of God's relation to man. They might be able to give mankind a fresh start." The presence of the atomic bomb generates the thought in Toynbee that the extreme catastrophe is that we might succeed in exterminating the African Negros.

TOYNBEE, THE WORLD MARXIST

Toynbee is a Marxist, on the world-scale. The resentment-feeling that Marx directed against the upper stratum in each country, Toynbee applies to the Western Culture collectively. Marx worked for the proletariat; Toynbee, like Zionism, works for the savage, the barbarian, the fellah. To keep his line back to Marx quite straight, he calls the colored races "the outer proletariat." This is a meaningless phrase, like all Toynbee jargon, but there is a very special reason for this one! Zionism is Marxist. It claims to have the true Marxist line, and deliberately continues the Marxist language. Like Marx, Toynbee lives comfortably, without working, despite his sympathy with the "toiling masses of Asia"; like Marx, he belongs to the stratum he detests, pointing to a neurotic origin for his doctrines; like Marx he wraps his hatred and resentment in strong *moral* indignation—*listen*: ". . . the unequal distribution of this world's goods between a privileged minority and an underprivileged majority has been transformed from an unavoidable evil into an intolerable injustice by the latest technological inventions of Western man"; and "In a society that has discovered the 'know-how' of Amalthea's cornucopia, the always ugly inequality in the distribution of this world's goods, in ceasing to be a practical necessity, had become a *moral enormity.*" Like Marx, Toynbee wants a "classless society," and wants to "abolish war." "We have to abolish War and Class—and abolish them now—under pain, if we flinch or fail, of seeing them win a victory over man which, this time, would be conclusive and definite." So speaks Toynbee!

THE LATEST TOYNBEE LINE

Toynbee presently hammers home two general ideas, both fundamental to Zionist policy: (1) Europe must never again be independent; and (2) the colored races must dominate the world.

On the first point, Toynbee is for once clear. He agrees with Adolf Hitler that the only kind of Europe which can survive as a power in the world would be a Europe guided by his policy, but Toynbee then states with precise clarity that "it would be better for there to be no Europe whatever." The welfare of the two hundred fifty million Europeans whom he is thus condemning to financial servitude and colonial status does not concern him. Nor can there be any sort of united independent Europe whatsoever, for, says Toynbee, "eventually the Germans would become the mistress of Europe" and they would then "ply the whip" and "dig in the spurs," whatever that means. He concludes: "This German crux would appear to be an insurmountable obstacle to the construction of a European 'Third Great Power.'"

Analysis shows this outlook to be simply *anti-German.* Toynbee thinks that it is better for all Europe to be held in fee by Russia and Washington-Zionism than for Europe to be independent. And this, because there are Germans there! It would not in the least distress Toynbee to be called anti-German to his face, because this is an "approved" *anti*—it is not immoral to be anti-German; no one loses caste by being anti-

German. But what if someone called Toynbee *anti-Semitic*?[16] He would deny the charge with several million words!

Toynbee's Zionistic-pathological anti-Germanism leads him into laughable absurdity. For example, he wishes to strip Germany of the geographical description it has always had as "the heart of Europe." Instead, he writes, "Western Europe is the heart of Europe," as though the center of an area could be its western part! When he writes about Germany, this sublime scholar sounds like a vile pamphlet by Ben Hecht or Peter Viereck.[17]

But the rise of the colored races is his *favorite* topic. We must even merge with them, in every way, and here it is no question of Freedom, but of Necessity. It is going to happen, says Toynbee, and we must help it along. When we merge with them, on every plane, it will mean, of course, our extinction, for in the resulting amalgam, Europe will cease to be the center of the world, and "the center-point of human affairs" will probably be "in the

---

[16] Ironically, several years later, Toynbee was called "anti-Semitic" for stating that the Jews belonged to a "fossil" civilization, which seems close to Spengler's concept of a "fellaheen" people: those who have passed through the Culture-cycles and become stagnant and historically passé. See Yair Sheleg, "This is How We Ruined Toynbee's Theory," *Haaretz*, January 24, 2007. Toynbee had become a victim of his own internationalism, and did not understand that expecting the Jews to give up their racial exclusivity, as they demand of everyone else, would be seen as "anti-Semitic." He had tried to project the mentality of nineteenth-century English Whig-liberalism onto the Jews and ascribe to Judaism and Israel a world-mission of that type.

[17] Ben Hecht (1894–1964) was a Jewish-American writer who was an ardent Zionist activist, and who wrote about the plight of Europe's Jews during the Second World War and about the birth of Israel, praising the Zionist Irgun terrorist group which fought the British. Peter Viereck (1916–2006) was a writer and historian who opposed both Communism and fascism, in sharp contrast to his father, George Sylvester Viereck, who was also a writer and who worked as a propagandist for the Third Reich, for which he was imprisoned during the war in the US. George Sylvester Viereck was acquainted with Yockey's collaborator, H. Keith Thompson.

neighbourhood of Babylon, on the ancient portage across the isthmus between the Continent (to Toynbee, Asia is THE CONTINENT) and its peninsulas (*sic*) of Arabia and Africa. The centre might even travel farther into the interior of THE CONTINENT to some locus between China and Russia (the two historic tamers of the Eurasian Nomads), and that would indicate a site in the neighbourhood of Babur's Farghana,[18] in the familiar Transoxanian meeting-place and debating ground of the religions and philosophies of India, China, Iran, Syria, Israel,[19] and Greece." Toynbee makes it quite obvious, despite the fog of words, that he is trying to designate Palestine, now called Israel, but one must not look to Toynbee for the short, straight word.

Carried away, he believes this Zionist dream is reality, and he cries, "From the beginning, mankind has been partitioned; in our day we have at last become united." On the next page, he says partition would be a better word for the present union of the world, so we have complete union and permanent partition, all at once. The reader will find whatever he wants in Toynbee!

We are now watching "the awakening of the peasants of the world," and the propagandist for Zionism, glorying in it, shakes his fist at us, like a good Marxist: ". . . though to-day there are still some fifteen hundred million not yet awakened peasants—about three-quarters of the living generation of mankind—in India, China, Indo-China, Indonesia, Dar-al-Islam, and Eastern Europe, their awakening is now only a matter of time, and, when it has been accomplished, *numbers will begin to tell.*" Toynbee, like a good propagandist, treats it as self-evident that in a looming contest between colored and white, every white man will naturally be on the side of the colored races, and he fits this perversion out with a historical-teleological rationale: "the whole purpose of the Western Culture from the beginning has been to do something not simply for ourselves but for mankind as a whole." Once again, Toynbee says mankind is "united," and he goes on—"The Western handiwork that has made this union possible has not been carried out with open eyes, like David's

[18] Present-day Uzbekistan.
[19] Israel does not actually appear in the original text.

unselfish labours for the benefit of Solomon; it has been performed in heedless ignorance of its purpose, like the labours of the animalculae that build a coral reef up from the bottom of the sea till at length an atoll rises above the waves." Our magnificent Western Culture was nothing but an accompaniment to Western technics, and these mighty technics are mere "handiwork"; our proud and gigantic Western ancestors were "animalculae," and the "purpose" of the whole majestic evolution was to give physical comfort to the negroes of the Congo, the coolies of the Yangtse, and the fellaheen of India! In the nineteenth century, the materialists assumed that the entirety of world history had taken place only to arrive at the Western Culture, that we, somehow, were the *purpose* of the others having lived. Toynbee now inverts it—history is to go backward! Instead of the dead Cultures having lived for our sake, it is our Western Culture which has only lived, and is only living still, for the sake of the historical waste-products of the dead Cultures, the primitives, the savages, the barbarians, the fellaheen of the entire world.

Toynbee leaves no doubt either about the necessity for the extinction of Western Civilization, nor about the desirability of it. The "technological scaffolding" will at last "fall away" and mankind "will be united at last," on "the bedrock of religion." Consequently, the fusion of our religion with theirs must occur. It is only our Western outlook which is narrow. All the colored peoples have a world-horizon, and by amalgamating our religion with theirs, the foundation will have been laid for the World-State, which is the dream of the Zionists and the toynbees, with its "center of human affairs" in Israel. Here he gives himself away again—if mankind is to be religious and nothing else, why will there be a "center of human affairs" at all? One can make his soul worship God in one place as well as in another. Or is Toynbee really thinking of politics after all? Every policy is always radiated from a capital, which strives to make itself the "center of human affairs."[20]

---

[20] Despite Toynbee falling afoul of the Zionists a few years later, the internationalist plan that is being ascribed to him here is indeed the ideal of a greater Zionism. In 1962 David Ben-Gurion, founding

In the essay, "The Dwarfing of Europe,"[21] Toynbee records with deep satisfaction, "the Dwarfing of Europe is an unmistakably accomplished fact," and "the Marshall Plan gives Western Europe at least the solace of seeing her dead supremacy given Christian burial." "Europe's [tradition] will no longer decide Europe's destiny. Her future lies on the knees of the giants who now overshadow her." Toynbee tells us this!

Our descendants will not even have the European concept, for the All-Knowing says, "the history of the Chinese, Hindus, Japanese, and Moslems is going to become part of our Western history in a future world which will be neither Western nor non-Western but will inherit all the cultures which we Westerners have now brewed together in a single crucible. Our descendants are not simply going to be Western, like ourselves. They are going to be heirs of Confucius and Lao-Tse, of Buddha and Deu-

---

Prime Minister of Israel, told *Look Magazine*:

> The image of the world in 1987 as traced in my imagination: The Cold War will be a thing of the past. Internal pressure of the constantly growing intelligentsia in Russia for more freedom and the pressure of the masses for raising their living standards may lead to a gradual democratization of the Soviet Union. On the other hand, the increasing influence of the workers and farmers, and the rising political importance of men of science, may transform the United States into a welfare state with a planned economy.
>
> Western and Eastern Europe will become a federation of autonomous states having a Socialist and democratic regime. With the exception of the USSR as a federated Eurasian state, all other continents will become united in a world alliance, at whose disposal will be an international police force. All armies will be abolished, and there will be no more wars.
>
> In Jerusalem, the United Nations (a truly United Nations) will build a Shrine of the Prophets to serve the federated union of all continents; this will be the seat of the Supreme Court of Mankind, to settle all controversies among the federated continents, as prophesied by Isaiah. (*Look*, January 16, 1962.)

[21] Toynbee, *Civilization on Trial*, pp. 150–63.

tero-Isaiah, Elijah, Elisha, Moses, Peter and Paul, Shankara and Ramanuja, of Ibn Khaldun, Lenin, Gandhi, Sun Yat-sen, and Mazzini." But our descendants will have nothing Spanish, English, or German in their heritage. Culturally, in Toynbee's Zionist dream-world, there will only be colored people.

The toynbee sermon of the moment—still well wrapped in theologico-historico-journalistic wool—is on the theme of "peaceful co-existence." By sheer coincidence, this happens to be a policy of Zionism and the Washington regime. As the Korean War showed, the Zionists want no victory over the Russian bloc. Fighting Europe, they demanded "unconditional surrender," and "total annihilation" of the opponent. Against Red China they fought "not for victory, but for a just truce."[22] Arrived at the frontier of the Chinese-Russian power, the Zionists became the prey of moral scruples—they found they had no "moral right" to cross the frontier. At the German frontier in 1944, they had no such qualms.

What Toynbee's Mother Didn't Tell Him

Russia presents a different problem to the Zionists and toynbees than Europe did. Europe is decided; Russia is vacillating; Europe is clear, united, definite in its will and its aim, as in its spiritual and physical need; Russia is unclear, unstable, unsure of its aims, without any physical needs, with uncertain spiritual needs. *The Zionists have by no means given up hope of integrating Russia into their world-system.* The idea is impossible, but it is the only policy the Zionists have. They are no empire-builders, but the sons of fish-peddlers and coin-clippers, who suddenly find themselves, by virtue of the political vacuum in America, in control of a gigantic irresponsible machine capable of immense destruction. Their present policy is as bankrupt and schizophrenic as their sudden ascent to world-power is accidental and transitory. The mighty evolution of Western Culture is not to be suddenly nullified by a gang of rootless fellaheen, however sly, however stupid their dupes.

Among the Zionists, as in all political groups, there are fac-

---

[22] In the Korean War.

tions. They have their Whigs, who counsel of the uncertainties of wars, of the superiority of negotiations over ultimatums. They have their elders, who remind them that, after all, Europe-Germany is the main enemy, and of what value would be a military victory over Russia if an aroused Germany emerged from the war, with its mighty heart beating again, striking terror into the rulers in Washington—"Ach habe moira"! Toynbee belongs to this school, but not so firmly that tomorrow he cannot join the Tory-war mongers, whose mouthpieces are of the ilk of Walter Winchell and Henry Luce.[23]

The Zionist Tories came, during the Second World War, to know the intoxication of directing armies from the security of their citadels, and they crave for the moment when they can order the planned concentric assault on the Russian land-mass, which is already completely surrounded by their subject military forces. For this grand assault, they are even willing to organize a mercenary army of German dupes, under American-French-English generals, all subject to the high Zionist command in the provisional world-capital of Washington. The mission of this German army will be to supply the casualties, a necessary part of any proper war.

The "peaceful co-existence" policy of Toynbee, Washington, and Zionism simply advocates a long-term non-aggression pact between the Zionist-American sphere and the Soviet Russian sphere. During this time, the Russian sphere will increase vastly in population, and Europe will decline more and more. Europe's birth-rate is at present artificially decelerated by the arbitrary linking of Europe's economy to America, with its ensuing maintenance of economic chaos in Europe, unemployment among men, and full employment of women, whose mother-potential is thus nullified.

During the proposed long-term non-aggression period, the Washington regime will continue its Point Four program of arm-

---

[23] Walter Winchell (1897–1972) was a Jewish-American journalist, and Henry Luce (1898–1967) was an American magazine magnate, both of whom agitated in favor of American intervention against Germany in the Second World War.

ing and industrializing the colored races, thus wiping out the sole advantage, the industrial-military technical, that the White Race has in its coming struggle for bare survival. After, say, twenty-five years of such a development, the colored races will so outnumber and in every sense so outweigh the White Race, that the White Race must fall beneath the colored yoke, and Toynbee's dream of "united humanity" will become a reality—with Chinese soldiers looting Europe and European prisoner-slaves[24] toiling in Toynbee's "familiar Trans-oxanian[25] meeting place and debating ground of the religions of China, India . . . and Israel . . ."

The "co-existence" program would have to rest on Russian willingness to allow Zionist penetration, in the propaganda and financial sense at least, of the Russian sphere.[26] Thus, even as the Russian-dominated world increases enormously in numbers and striking power, the possibility will still be there that all this power will be subject—as in America—to Zionist leadership. And, as the term of the non-aggression period draws to a close—so unfolds this dream—Zionists in Russia will stretch out their hands to the Zionists in America, and together they can proclaim the practical abolition of Russian and American Sovereignty, the absolute rule of the "United Nations,"[27] the coming of the Messiah, the fulfillment of the Cov-

---

[24] The present development of the so-called "New Silk Road" or "One Belt, One Road" will bring China physically into the heart of Europe. So far from being feared by the US-based globalist cabals, it is being promoted. See K. R. Bolton, "The Silk Road to Globalisation," *Geopolitica*, October 26, 2017.

[25] Transoxania is Central Asia, comprising present-day Uzbekistan, Tajikistan, southern Kyrgyzstan, and southwest Kazakhstan.

[26] This almost came to fruition in the aftermath of Stalin's death (murder?) in 1953, when Lavrenti Beria, chief of the NKVD, briefly assumed power and announced his intention of opening Russia up to the American cabals. He was promptly overthrown by a military coup. See K. R. Bolton, *Stalin: The Enduring Legacy* (London: Black House Publishing, 2012), pp. 147–48.

[27] Far from being an assumption by Yockey, this was the policy offered by the "Washington regime" in the aftermath of the Second

enant and of the prophecy of Moses, and the establishment of the capital of the world ("center of human affairs") in Palestine-Israel ("familiar Trans-oxanian meeting place," etc.).

Toynbee with his wide vision in Zionist affairs, can see the merits of both Whigs and Tories![28] He is, of course, fundamentally opposed to war, but that is a generality, and all he needs to do is to turn a page, sharpen a new pencil, and he can easily support a specific war. Thus he put his seal of approval on the Boer War, and, thus also he approved mightily the Second World War against Europe-Germany. He will not commit treason to Zion by putting his party above the higher cause. His writings have paved the way for a *volte face* on the question of war, if it becomes necessary. Repeatedly he has stated categorically that one more war will destroy all humanity (he hopes the African Negritos are spared), but he has covered everything by writing: ". . . even if the Second World War proves not to have been the last, we shall survive the rest of this batch of world wars as we survived the first two bouts, and shall eventually win our way out into the calmer waters." The worst condemnation he finds for the Zionist Tories is to call them "old-fashioned."[29]

There stands Arnold Toynbee, the "historian," the "philosopher," the "theologian" ("I . . . am a Christian" "I . . . am not a Christian"), the "scholar," the journalist, the propagandist *par excellence* for the great mass of one-buttock intellectuals who need something on which to chew their verbal cud. He detests

---

World War, and was called the "Baruch Plan." This would have turned the United Nations Organization into a World Government, buttressed by nuclear weaponry: all nuclear programs were to be placed under a United Nations authority. It is notable that the proposals were named after Bernard M. Baruch, who was the leading Zionist political and financial wire-puller in the US, and lauded as America's "senior statesman." Stalin rejected the plan without ado. See K. R. Bolton, *Stalin*, pp. 125–39.

[28] Today we might refer to them as "globalists" and "neocons" respectively.

[29] Albeit, sufficient to fall afoul of them a few years later, and be called an "anti-Semite."

our Western history, our Culture, our heritage, our accomplishment, our vestigial remnants of wealth and splendor. He wants our destruction by forcible assimilation into the mass of the colored races, and rejects, with the journalistic catch-word "totalitarian," any self-defense on our part, any attempt to preserve our race, our individuality, or our culture.

"Man is master of his own destiny," writes Toynbee. But he also writes, "Europe's [tradition] will no longer decide Europe's destiny." Only the colored races have free will, and our will to mastery is thus vain, while theirs is pure and sanctified. We must submit to their will, says Toynbee. Over the formless and hideous amalgam will wave the happy blue-and-white banner of Israel and the "United Nations," and a monument will be erected to Toynbee in his cherished "Trans-oxanian meeting-place." This monument will bear the Toynbee Slogan of the Age: *"Hang on and Pray."* But, by then, there will be no White Race to "Hang on," and prayers will be in vain!

The principal flaw in this dream is that it is a *mere dream*. Was it Lincoln who said something about fooling all of the people all of the time? The Zionist Tories are bemused, drunk with military wine, but the Zionist Whigs and the toynbees are intoxicated with their own billions of words of clever propaganda. Empires are founded, not by slyness, but by force. In the coming tests, Zionism will find that it lacks the force to inaugurate its schizophrenic World-Kingdom.

Against Toynbee's mountains of words, which seek to prove the inevitability and the desirability of Europe's complete destruction in permanent partition between Zionism and Russia, we say quite simply this:

> *The future belongs to Europe, the home-soil of the Western Culture, to its Colonies, its Christendom, and to its White Race; and not to Zionism, nor to the black-yellow-brown masses which it seeks to mobilize against us.*

Let History decide.

X. Y. Z.

A Warning to America: An Estimate of China, A Warning to the West

1959

Editors' Note

One of the last essays Yockey wrote, in August 1959, was on China and the world situation.[1] The original manuscript was never published.[2] Douglas T. Kaye, publisher of the lively Yockeyan journal *TRUD* as well as *Yockey: Four Essays* during the 1970s, found the manuscript among the files of the long-running and relatively successful, Yockeyan-influenced newspaper *Common Sense*, during the process of the latter's closure.

While *Common Sense* existed during the Cold War era and reflected many of the often-puerile concerns of the American Right, during the 1970s new columnists, influenced by Yockey and Spengler, in particular "Fred Farrell," assumed primacy over the direction of the paper.

Common Sense then took a distinctly pro-Russia line, seeing the Soviet bloc since the triumph of Stalin over Trotsky as the primary obstacle to World Zionism and plutocracy, and New York as the real headquarters of "Bolshevism." This was at a time when the CIA was promoting an anti-Soviet Left throughout the world, via the Congress for Cultural Freedom.

Most of the rest of the American Right, with the exceptions of *TRUD* and the National Renaissance Party, and later *Instaura-*

---

[1] Douglas T. Kaye in private correspondence with Kerry Bolton, February 15, 2015.

[2] Ibid. Kaye held the original, and made a copy available to the Christian Identity publisher James K. Warner, then proprietor of Sons of Liberty, who circulated a limited "botched copy" of the text. Warner stated that he no longer had any use for Yockey because the latter had "turned Communist," undoubtedly a reference to Yockey's realism concerning the Soviet bloc.

tion, regarded the conflict between Zionism and the Soviet bloc as a cunning plan engineered by Jews who controlled both sides of the "Cold War" to fool the Gentile world. The unconventional line of Farrell and his colleagues caused dispute within *Common Sense*'s own board, which included old-line anti-Semitic conservatives such as Lieutenant General P. A. del Valle of the US Marine Corps.

Yockey stated that there was "an unconditional belief of China's invincibility [that] has never been mentioned by the China specialists at Foggy Bottom."[3] Yockey contrasts the great deal that is known about the Greek and Roman civilizations with the little that had been studied at the time about the impress of the landscape on the Culture-People-Nation-Race of China. To understand the temperament and destiny of China, like any other, it is necessary to understand the landscape. Much of what Spengler wrote in *The Decline of the West* deals with landscape, and the forming of a Culture-soul, reflected in a race's art, music, literature, architecture, religion, technics, state-forms, and so forth.

At the time Yockey was writing, China's landscape was predictable. The floods, which required massive human collective effort to rectify, were the type of challenge that shapes a civilization, as the Sumerian was shaped by the Euphrates, and the Egyptian by the Nile.

The Chinese landscape, however, so far from being "practically changeless," has since become increasingly volatile, and this will impact the way in which China proceeds in the coming decades. If the Chinese learnt in Yockey's time of the way in which the landscape had shaped the history of prior civilizations, then today they are learning how their now-changing landscape will affect their future and their relationship with their neighbors.[4] Yockey refers to the Himalayan headwaters which irrigate much of Asia being controlled by China. China indeed still has power over the water resources of the region,

---

[3] A nickname for the US State Department.

[4] K. R. Bolton, *The Geopolitics of the Indo-Pacific* (London: Black House Publishing, 2013).

which are more vital than oil. This is a problem that has only begun to be addressed by some geopolitical analysts in recent years, this writer among them.[5]

One primary factor that has not changed is the Chinese belief in their country as the Middle Kingdom, from whence power emanates out in every direction to the world, what Yockey calls "mystical universalism." This has been synthesized in a dialectical manner with the raw power for which Mao longed. Indeed, Mao assumed the power of a God-King. Yockey states here that Confucianism, or what he calls "mystical universalism," was "still very much alive" even during Mao's reign.

Today, Confucianism is being revived as a part of the Chinese educational curriculum—not to return China to its traditions, but to maintain social discipline amidst the Western-imparted modernization that has proceeded apace since Yockey's time, recreating China as a technological Middle Kingdom, an Axis Mundi extending its empire in every direction via what is now being touted by the West's oligarchic "inner traitors" as the "New Silk Road."[6]

While little was known of Mao during Yockey's time—although he had attained heroic proportions not only in China, but among the Western intelligentsia and news media as well[7]—we now know that he was a craven coward and narcissist every bit as decadent as the depraved emperors during the epochs of China's dynastic end-cycles,[8] and devoid of heroic virtues.[9]

---

[5] K. R. Bolton, "Water Wars: Rivalry Over Water Resources," *World Affairs*, vol. 14, no. 1, 2010. See also "Rivalry over water resources as a potential cause of conflict in Asia," *Journal of Social, Political & Economic Studies*, vol. 35, no. 1, Spring 2010.

[6] K. R. Bolton, "The Silk Road to Globalisation," *Geopolitica*, October 26, 2017.

[7] For example, see Edgar Snow, *Red Star Over China* (London: Victor Gollancz, 1937).

[8] For China's recurrent dynastic cycles of rise and fall, see K. R. Bolton, *The Decline and Fall of Civilisations* (London: Black House Press, 2017), pp. 260–69.

[9] K. R. Bolton, *The Psychotic Left* (London: Black House Publishing, 2013), pp. 124–37. See also Jung Chang and Jon Halliday, *Mao: The*

There is also more to Chiang Kai-shek than being a corrupt fool and stooge of the Americans, and that this is the manner by which Chiang is usually portrayed by the "establishment" media and academia should give rise to questions. Chiang was acutely aware of the decadent and corrupt tendencies in China and recognized that Western liberalism was the contemporary means by which China was being recolonized and rotted. In somewhat Spenglerian terms, he saw luxury as well as extreme poverty as physically and morally debilitating. A balance was sought with a new ideal. He envisioned adapting foreign ideas rather than being dominated by them; a conscious repudiation of what Yockey called Culture-distortion and Culture-retardation, and saw the danger of the Chinese becoming "slaves of foreign theories"—Western liberalism no less than Marxism.[10]

About a decade after Yockey had written this essay, Richard Nixon and Henry Kissinger had opened China up to Western capitalism, and David Rockefeller came back from a visit to China to describe Maoism in glowing terms:

> One is impressed immediately by the sense of national harmony. From the loud patriotic music at the border onward, there is very real and pervasive dedication to Chairman Mao and Maoist principles. Whatever the price of the Chinese Revolution, it has obviously succeeded not only in producing more efficient and dedicated administration, but also in fostering high morale and community of purpose. General economic and social progress is no less impressive . . .[11]

The rapidity with which China was opened up to Western capital and markets—and vice versa—has resulted in a Chinese

---

Unknown Story (London: Jonathan Cape, 2005), passim.

[10] K. R. Bolton, *The Decline and Fall of Civilisations*, op. cit., pp. 270–78.

[11] David Rockefeller, "From a China Traveller," *The New York Times*, August 10, 1973; www.nytimes.com/1973/08/10/archives/from-a-china-traveler.html.

consumer mentality proceeding at excessive speed. While China continues to be heralded as the economic powerhouse of the world, and proceeds with its world-domineering ambitions not via Mao's threats of an expansive population or its willingness to sacrifice a third of the Chinese population in a nuclear war, but rather with economic expansion—China is over-producing.

China is scattered with "ghost cities" devoid of residents, not because people have left but because nobody has filled them; some factories are idle, while others produce steel and cement to build new residential and office tower blocks that will not be used, and peasants are uprooted to make way for them. Debt is mountainous. While it is owed to state institutions, the debt is nonetheless based on credit created through orthodox finance. Default is prolonged, but inevitable.[12]

The great danger to the world from China is no longer in the form of one billion fanatical Maoists, but rather that the capitalist economies have so entangled themselves with China's economic expansion that the former's implosion will cause the world economic structure to collapse, and China will then indeed resort to drastic actions in Asia, such as through its control of the headwaters of the region's entire water system.

China's rulers continue to see China as the center of the world, as they have for millennia, whether under the "mandate of heaven" or in the name of "dialectical materialism," or today as the aspiring new leaders of globalization, based on the aim of surpassing the United States as the world's number one economy. The "inner traitors" of the West are not bothered whether their profits continue via American or Chinese global hegemony. Yockey alludes to Mao's China as aspiring to be a leader—or *the* leader—"in the coming scheme to 'unify the peoples.'"

However, the stable climatic conditions, which Yockey saw as being of prime importance, and China's "homogeneous social tradition and organization" that seemed to give it strength while still maintaining a façade, are eroding at an accelerating pace; it

---

[12] See Dinny McMahon, *China's Great Wall of Debt: Shadow Banks, Ghost Cities, Massive Loans and the End of the Chinese Miracle* (London: Little, Brown, 2018).

is the price of out-of-control economic growth. The "inner traitors" of the West are pleased to deal with this colossus, but it is one with feet of clay.

Even during Mao's lifetime, China began succumbing to the economic model of the Late West, with the moral rot that comes with it, and the dictatorship of the Communist Party has not succeeded in maintaining the moral Party discipline that Mao attempted to preserve with the deaths of perhaps eighty million Chinese during the first quarter-century of his regime. The "inner traitors" still see China as a vast market of both consumers and workers; and its Communist Party leadership see it the same way. A moral and economic collapse will throw China back to the wretchedness from which it stagnated for centuries, which will also wreak havoc on those Western states that have hitched their economic wagons to a star that will eventually fall.

The Chinese have entered the *Zeitgeist* of the Late West by accepting the economics of this epoch. And like the Late Westerner, the Chinese now see money as power; Spengler saw it as the harbinger of decay.

INTRODUCTION
by Douglas T. Kaye

In May 1972, the bi-weekly newspaper *Common Sense* (originally *Think*) published at Union, New Jersey, printed its final issue, as gleefully reported by the *New York Times* on June 16, 1972. Founded by Condé McGinley in 1946 as "The Nation's Anti-Communist Newspaper," the tabloid had a remarkable success throughout the turbulent late 1940s and early 1950s, when Communist activities within the United States were at their most virulent.

After McGinley's death in 1963, faltering efforts were made to keep the enterprise solvent and relevant, to no avail. Events were moving quickly beyond Cold War histrionics, subversion scenarios, and even the conservative campaign against fluoridated water. In 1972 reasonable persons no longer became excited over how many Reds were in Hollywood or who was responsible for purloining America's atomic bomb secrets.

McGinley's longtime personal secretary, confidante, and deathbed nurse became heiress to daily operations by approval of a four-person board. She honestly proclaimed lack of adequate editorial skills, and after years of fending off the mailing-list grubbing and profit-seeking advances of diverse "patriotic" and "Right-wing" defectives, finally, in a classic case of burnout desperation, threw it all overboard and sought repose within the confines of the heretical Catholic sect at St. Jovite, Quebec.

During the lengthy sorting-out process at the newspaper's office prior to the migration to Quebec, and the sale of the headquarters building at a huge loss, many files and other extremely valuable materials were hastily reviewed and either given to interested parties or summarily discarded.

The Yockey "China Estimate" draft manuscript dated 1959 turned up by surprise, nested in several folders of articles by others that, for whatever reason, were never published.

Yockey was on the lam in Europe and other places at the time, and had been since 1952, when the US State Department refused to renew his passport. He gained entry to and traveled guardedly throughout Europe and the United States, always a step ahead of Big Brother and the Ministry of Truth. He moved from pillar to post, from safe house to flophouse, aided and sheltered by friends and political co-workers.

> "[A man] whose doublings and turnings are such as
> would trouble a right good hound to trace him."

Circulating mysteriously throughout the world, he wrote as logistics allowed.

Every indication points to assistance from his close collaborators Frederick LeBlanc-Weiss and H. Keith Thompson. The original manuscript segments were produced in part by a Royal typewriter (with its distinctive upper-case "R") and partially by an early IBM film ribbon "Executive" model. The typed pages from the IBM (a very expensive machine at the time) were most likely produced at one of Thompson's offices in New York City. Other pages were certainly from Yockey's Royal "Arrow" portable machine, which he always had in tow when traveling.

The manuscript is entirely in English, but *duplicate* parts are in German. The resulting pastiche contained numerous redundancies and disjointed ramblings, including grandstanding paragraphs about physics, which never appeared in any works authored exclusively by Yockey. This extraneous material was surely from the pen of Frederick LeBlanc-Weiss, for it was his literary trademark (as a Sorbonne graduate with courses in physics) to insert these gems into anything he planned to finance, which is entirely evident in this case.

Drafts in both English and German denoted a plan, already partially carried out, to introduce Yockey's output to a German readership, as was Yockey's *Der Feind Europas* (*The Enemy of Europe*), which was published in 1953 in the German language. The translation was faulty and the publication surreptitious, for at the time Yockey's writings, and Yockey himself, were banned by the West German government. *Der Feind Europas* has since been republished as retroversion in English, and is currently available. It is considered the third volume to *Imperium.*

In his masterwork, *Imperium* (1948), Yockey touches only briefly on the subject of China and the Chinese. Brief mention is made of the tension between the European and Chinese populations in the American West during the nineteenth and twentieth centuries, and the resultant "mutual persecution, hatred, riots, and bloody excesses."[13] Additionally, from *Imperium*: "In California, every accretion of economic strength, every public display of collective energy on the part of the Chinese called forth new outbreaks of anti-Chinese activities among the Americans."[14] Passing mention is made of the Boxer Rebellion: "Chinese ports were attacked . . ."[15] In *Imperium*'s Foreword, there is reference to "[t]he Western Culture . . . suffering from disease, and the prolongation of this disease is the prolonging of Chinese conditions in [post-Second World War] Europe,"[16] which naturally alluded to astoundingly base conditions of human exist-

---

[13] Yockey, *Imperium*, p. 380.
[14] Ibid., p. 416.
[15] Ibid., p. 491.
[16] Ibid., p. xlvi.

ence in both places. There were a few other scattered references to Chinese history and politics on pages 251, 312–13, 432–33, and a very brief comment on the Opium War found on page 427. Additionally, *Imperium*'s index contains no entry for either Mao Tse-tung (old spelling) or Chiang Kai-shek.

❖ ❖ ❖

In Yockey's brilliant 1952 essay on the Prague treason trial of Rudolf Slansky, *et al.*, he takes George C. Marshall, cited as a "nincompoop" in a later essay,[17] to task for acting "consciously and openly as a Russian agent in undermining the Chiang [Kai-shek] regime in China and delivering quietly to Russian vassaldom a quarter of the world's population."

One also sees this contradictory twisting along the path in the appearance of Yockey's final essay, "An Estimate of the World Situation," retitled "The World in Flames," written on New Year's Day in 1960 and published posthumously on February 1, 1961, a joint effort of LeBlanc-Weiss and Thompson, and issued under the imprint of LeBlanc Publications, Parkesburg, Pennsylvania.

The Introduction to "The World in Flames" essay contains the usual excursions into the world of Spengler and physics, and while the essay was assuredly written by Yockey, it seems to have been tampered with. China is said to have been "given to Russia" (in 1949) . . . as if Russia, then severely wounded, and four years after losing nine percent of her population and most of her infrastructure, was in any way capable of exerting control over the endless expanse of China and its huge, unwieldy population. Nor was Stalin eager to hand over Russian aid to Mao, whom he routinely referred to as a "margarine Communist."

In the same essay, a bad evaluation is also made of the Korean War, in which it was stated, "the Zionists [through America] fought against the Chinese armies they had created . . . and these armies used the very equipment which Marshall had delivered to them, sufficient to equip sixty divisions . . ." America created no Chinese armies, at least not directly. The equipment sufficient

---

[17] "The World in Flames."

for equipping "sixty divisions" was initially delivered to Chiang but then hastily sold on the international black market or simply abandoned, as the leaders of "Free China" scurried off their sinking ship and paddled furiously to Taiwan.

> There are millions of Chinamen. Many of them living on very short rations in the *interior* and as much interested in Chiang Kai-shek as they are in the White Sox and the Phillies. . . . A *lot* of China is *not* pro-Chiang Kai-shek. A lot of China is *not for* that gang of foreign investors.
>
> —Ezra Pound, radio broadcast of October 2, 1941, "Last Ditch Democracy"

In the Second World War, four-star General Joseph Stilwell (1883–1946) commanded the China-Burma Theater and had responsibility for all Lend-Lease (US taxpayers' aid) sent to "stabilize" China. Simply put, this largesse in the amount of $380,584,000 (an enormous amount at that time, about five billion in current value) was handed to Chiang Kai-shek and his corrupt minions—the so-called Yoke Forces—so that America wouldn't "lose China." Every last dollar of this handout disappeared down Chinese Nationalist rat-holes. "Vinegar Joe" Stilwell, the soldiers' soldier, known for his no-nonsense command and often caustic opinions, tried to prevent such massive waste but was always overruled by Washington and eventually recalled from his command in October 1944. He was ceaselessly smeared by *conservative* operatives in the US who either directly or indirectly siphoned off Chiang's dirty money, all for the greater glory of God, family, and country.

Yet another strange note: Yockey had joined the staff of Senator Joseph McCarthy in early 1952 and wrote a speech for the Senator (never delivered), "America's Two Ways of Waging War," hitting the "go-easy" policy of the Truman-Acheson duo in conducting the US "police action" (war) in Korea, which he referred to as a "Chinese war." This was not at variance with the prevailing promotions of nearly all the conservative and patriotic agitprop themes enveloping America at the time.

Obviously there came a reversal of opinion between 1952 and 1959 regarding China and Chiang Kai-shek's value as statesman. What happened?

In 1951, Yockey was also very much within the orbit of the Reverend Gerald L. K. Smith and those second-tier executives who operated what was then the largest, most well-heeled "anti-Communist" organization in America, the good Reverend's Christian Nationalist Crusade. Yockey even delivered speeches at several of their meetings in St. Louis.

Smith was poster boy for the fossilized conservatives who regularly scooped from the endless supply of dollars so freely distributed by Chiang and his wife, Madame Chiang—supplied by Chiang's wealthy and infinitely corrupt Chinese and OSS-CIA backers. Much of this largesse flowed into southern California, Washington, DC, and New York City, where the tom-tom beat for "Free China" never ceased, viz.: "Those State Department commies made Uncle Sam lose China." Free China?—how free? And, "we" lost China—was it "ours" to begin with?

Such activities were all covered under the umbrella phrase, "China Lobby," and were energetically promoted by an odd collection of characters known as "China hands." As the 1950s moved along, Yockey veered away from the ever-huckstering Smith and his cuckolded conservatives, for he had obviously gained a totally fresh perspective on the China situation.

Yockey's assessment of Chinese prowess written in 1959 doesn't easily square with his early 1950s musings and the later, posthumously published in 1961 document that was revised by others. Life is filled with mysteries, and very few of them are easily unwound. Allow this "China Essay" to stand as is, and draw your own conclusions.

Yockey the prophet—a mind projecting the long view, one not suited to the mutterings and bellicosities of a typical "Right wing" meeting.

Yockey the realist—he eerily predicted the Vietnam War in just so many words. And, he very accurately described the invisible spiritual movement, the underpinnings of fanaticism and abiding loyalty shown by virtually all Chinese for their awakening Dragon, a spiritual-organic force that was comprehensible to only a handful in the West.

Paragraphs about the Twin Giants are of course passé. Yockey did not survive to see the Globalists cleverly decoupled from their Grand Soviet Scheme, which they had violently foisted on the citadel of Old Russia in 1917 and then directed by remote control from New York City. The Russians, returning to the pure wellsprings of their ethnic, cultural, and religious traditions, simply reinvented themselves and thus emerged as a massive and ungovernable headache for the hated Trotskyites and other parasitic outsiders.

So much easier to bring about Culture-distortion and revamped Bolshevism to America, drum up never-ending defense spending and "anti-terrorism" police operations, and launch endless youth-killing punitive wars in the Middle East and elsewhere.

But—*China* . . . what to do about *China*?

Little could Yockey have foreseen the earth-shaking consequences of Richard Nixon's and Henry Kissinger's trip to China in February 1972 and the subsequent high-speed reversal of US trade policy toward the billion-fold work-and-brain beehive which now gives every indication of outstripping America in science, engineering, quality of goods, and rapaciousness of competitive spirit.

But I'll venture a guess that, somehow, he *knew* it was coming.

A WARNING TO AMERICA:
AN ESTIMATE OF CHINA, A WARNING TO THE WEST

"I recognize only two nations, the Occident and the Orient."

—Napoleon[18]

"East is East and West is West and never the twain shall meet."

—Kipling[19]

It is 1959. In this hour of decision the fundamental problem of American existence must be addressed.

It makes a great difference whether Americans accept their lives as an element within a far wider life-course that transcends hundreds of years and thousands of years, or whether, in their conceit, they think of themselves as something rounded off, self-contained. Americans have completely failed to perceive their true position within the Higher History of mankind. From its little part-world America has misjudged its importance and direction. Thus, the firmament of the United States is treated as a fixed pole, a unique patch on the sphere's surface, chosen for no better reason than because biological entities live on it. Great histories of millennial duration and mighty far-away cultures like the Chinese are made to revolve around this pole in all modesty. Is it not self-evident that the existence of Washington is of far greater importance than Lo-Yang?[20]

It is catastrophic to found a world-history on this basis. If this were the right modus of historical evaluation, then the Chinese historian is entitled to frame a world-history in which America's War of Independence, War of Secession, and Europe's entire history are passed over in silence as insignificant.

America prefers myths to history. So, too, the case of ancient

---

[18] Yockey also uses this quotation as an epigraph to the "Cultural Vitalism" chapter of *Imperium*, p. 245.

[19] From Rudyard Kipling's poem, "The Ballad of East and West."

[20] Lo-Yang is a city in the Henan province of China.

Greece, where men read Homer but never thought of excavating Troy. By contrast, whoever travels in China assiduously pursues old traces (*Kutsi*) and the untranslatable Tao, the basic principle of Chinese existence which derives all its meaning from deep historical feeling.

That this actually is the case, the Chinese have learned to their greatest sorrow. It took Mao Tse-tung to arouse his nation and show six hundred eighty million Chinese how utterly ridiculous and dangerous it is to treat the whole of European and American histories as mere appendix-matter to China's well-ordered and well-proved six-thousand-year history.

The most appropriate designation of the current American scheme of history, in which great cultures are made to follow orbits around the presumed center of world happenings, is the Ptolemaic system of history in contrast to the Copernican discovery in the historical sphere.

If America is to survive it must speedily change that mentality to a Copernican system which no longer permits a privileged position for American culture *vis-à-vis* that of other cultures in general and the Chinese culture in particular. In world-politics an incredible total of intellect and power has been squandered in false directions. It was not realized that in the present global struggle, neither the Soviets nor the West will have the slightest chance to win, the moment those neutral, discounted nations existing on the globe become aware of their own power and use it for their own benefit instead of yielding it to one or the other of two Giants as a gift in the struggle for world-hegemony.

Numerically strongest among these neutrals are of course the one billion, two hundred million Asians. And, within these, six hundred eighty million Chinese undoubtedly have the best chance to become the undisputed leaders of those nations which have found that liberty and bread grow on one and the same tree.

It is decisive for America's fate whether it properly comprehends the world-changing events in Eurasia in general and those in China in particular.

On the following pages is shown what actually causes the Nation-Race-People-Society of China to revolt against the West, how far this revolution has progressed, and what ultimately will be its results with respect to its impact on the cultural and political structure of the entire world.

If Kung-Fu-Tse[21] demanded millennia ago from every individual "the adjustment of one's own heart" as the prime condition for understanding the world, so it is hoped that the American people have the heart to put themselves for a moment in the shoes of a Chinese and then attempt to picture how they would act *vis-à-vis* the outside world. Such a rigorous self-scrutiny is not easy. The background of Asian thinking is a *concrete and static infinity*, not a *dynamic* one, the infinity of Space and Time which is particularly Western. Medieval Churchmen and their educated faithful understood the Asian mind-form, as do the rocket-men of today.

The outer power of American adventurism is soon to appear on the flank of the Chinese Landmass, the Indo-Chinese Peninsula. The groundwork has been prepared for this adventure. Where the French land armies have failed in 1954, the American air armada is poised. The proposed purpose of this intrusion is twofold: to halt the spread of "Communism" and to bring the Asian masses blessings of the "American Way of Life."

On May 15, 1884, there appeared in the *Revue des deux Mondes*[22] the following article by Tschen Ki-Tong: "After a ten-year long sojourn in Europa, and after profound studies of the cultural institutions and philosophies of the West, I still to this day ask myself in vain which principle vested in any European or American institution is worthy to be called democratic or liberal."

Tschen Ki-Tong found ridiculous the specifically Western notion that selection for high political office should be determined by the "will of the majority" as expressed by the ballot box, that the destiny of a nation should be dependent upon the caprice and thoughtlessness of a majority which is moved by forces and opinions having nothing to do with the nation in its organic

---

[21] Confucius.

[22] A French news magazine that has been in print since 1829.

form. Ballot box democracy is more of an Anglo-Saxon aberration than a universal Western doctrine. To illustrate, the French Revolution was inspired in the main by English ideas. A thorough analysis of this phenomenon may be found in Spengler's *Decline of the West*.

Tschen continues:

> If one were to propose the selection of the members of the French Academy of Sciences by the same majority system as exercised now in the selection of the Western state-governing élite, one would find oneself exposed to monstrous and contemptuous laughter. Yet I ask: is it not much more portentous to select the shapers of political fate by the voice of the mob than to let a majority of morons judge over the composition of a scientific body? Is there today in Europe the slightest chance that the knowledge, ability, and nobility of character alone, regardless of any other advantageous relationship, can seat a man on the throne? In China—yes, in Europa—never!

> "When the master governs, the people are hardly aware that he exists."
>
> —Tao Te Ching

The grand flow for exercising the observance and perseverance of this invisible spiritual movement was the controlled activity of innumerable small and local organisms, and that instrument was the Han-Lin Academy, founded one hundred twenty-four years before Christ.[23] This unique state-controlled organization lasted until 1905.[24] Only two hundred (and later two hundred thirty-two) of the proven Masters of the Confucian Way of Reason and Way of Right were invited twenty-one cen-

---

[23] In fact, the Han-Lin Academy was founded in the eighth century AD. Yockey may be thinking of the Imperial University, which was founded approximately at the time he states and fulfilled the function he describes.

[24] The Quing Dynasty collapsed late in 1911.

turies ago by Emperor Wu-Ti[25] to his palace and from thereon acted as the sole control-body over the nomination of everyone in whom was vested state authority, including the Emperor himself. The first members were selected by the Emperor, and onward until 1905, members of this illustrious body were the sole judges over the admission of each new candidate. Every three years, only one of two million Chinese had the good fortune to be selected on the basis or outstanding spiritual-organic capability. Like wildfire the name of each new member spread throughout the giant land, even to the most lonely peasant hamlet.

So tremendous was public esteem of this institution that not even foreign invaders like the Manchu[26] dared molest a single member of the truly sovereign Han-Lin Academy. Nowhere in the world has there ever existed such an efficient political and life-encompassing ethical control-body. Yet, its pervasive control was exercised in such a tactful way, mainly through clan association, that the average citizen hardly felt any state intervention at all. Thus, a state method was achieved and upheld by the most personal and organic of social forms—family and clan.

Because members of this censoring and ethical body had their roots in all strata of the population, China was the only state in the world where city-dweller and peasant cannot be recognized. The spiritual force of long ages of tradition and élite rule succeeded in implanting a national conscience, unfettered by economic or other artificial means. The Mao Tse-tung victory should surprise nobody, for this peasant's son acquired during his career as a librarian of Peking University a thorough knowledge of his fatherland's history, and a superior knowledge of the teaching of China's thinkers. None of his closest collaborators is a proletarian, but rather a litterateur in the sense of the former members of the Han-Lin.

---

[25] Emperor Wu-Ti (157–87 BC) was the seventh emperor of the Han dynasty, who greatly expanded Chinese territory through conquest and reorganized the government by centralizing it and adopting Confucian methods.

[26] The people native to Manchuria.

As soon as any question of national importance arises, it is first opened to debate throughout the lower political bodies. However, when the Politburo, with Mao at the helm, reaches a final decision after weighing the arguments of the lower instances, its decision becomes absolute, the law which everybody must respect and observe to the letter. *Ultima Ratio Regum.*[27]

Chinese Communism, in contrast to that of ukase-producing, ever-suspicious doctrinaires in the Kremlin, resembles more a monastic institution held together by rigid discipline. For the benefit of his Russian brethren, Mao still declares himself a Marxist. But, with the passing of every day, more about Mao's deep and purely national feeling that allows him and his advisors to interpret and judge the recommendations of the lower echelons is aired in innumerable assemblies. In Russia, two million Communists dictate law for two hundred million Russians.

Since times immemorial the Chinese despised any orthodox thinking and made every exaggerated Logic and Casuistic a laughing-stock, not only for the few wise and learned men, but for the entire population. For millennia the Chinese Way of Life always had a down-to-earth, practical purpose, and this practical adaptability to any combination of natural and human events surpassed that of every other nation. To this day the Chinese have never lost for one moment their truly unique sense of Reality. And to repeat, because all his reforms and his entire tactic remained so much closer to Reality, it was possible for Mao and his staff to gain victory over Chiang Kai-shek and the unlimited power of Chiang's backers, the military machine of the USA.

He did away with mortal enemies just as he did away with the third intruder, the Russians. Mao laughs at "blind bigots" in the Kremlin, at those non-Russian doctrinaires who seized for themselves the role of apostles for spreading the "purity" and infallibility of Marx and Lenin.[28]

And here it cannot be emphasized enough that Mao's boasting in Moscow of being the genuine task-master in the Marx-

---

[27] Latin: "the final argument of kings," meaning war.

[28] See Mao's essay, "On Khrushchev's Phoney Communism," *Peking Review*, July 17, 1964.

Lenin camp is motivated by a most clever anti-Russian master plan: keep the doctrinaires in the Kremlin split, not only amongst themselves, but also from the entire world-Communist bloc. Almost daily the Chinese administration deems it opportune to spread articles in pamphlets throughout the giant land about Kremlin barbarians who are unable to "shed their Byzantine skins"—who still believe in the "unerring truth" of their holy book, *Das Kapital,* who supplant the original exploration and spiritual mastering of Reality by various methods of distorted citations and interpretation. The sharp and quick-sighted Chinese absorbs in delight this polemic against Moscow with its distracted distortion of Reality in the name of orthodoxy.

America has no idea of the intensity of Mao's spiritual offensive against Moscow within China's borders. It may shock many when they read the following excerpt of a letter by Mao addressed to the Department of Theoretical Physics in Peking, a polemic dealing with the symbolic difficulty of modern mathematics. He began by demonstrating Faraday's[29] metaphysical resemblance to Newton, whose forces-at-a-distance point to a mystical background. And he concluded his dissertation with the following quotation of a speech by Lenin, characterized by Mao as one of the most stupid statements emanating from the mouth of a world-celebrity.

Lenin: "There is no doubt that the concept of infinite Space as understood by even our Soviet culture is a Symbol of the first order. However marvelous from the point of view of common human intellect, the transformation of the unweighable ether into weighable material, however strange the electron's lack of any electro-magnetic mass, however unusual the restriction of the mechanical laws of motion to but one real or natural phenomena and their subordination to the deeper laws of electromagnetic phenomena . . ." . . . and so on.

And then Mao remarked: "Never was greater nonsense uttered by a great man." Again, from one of Mao's anti-Soviet pamphlets: "There is no doubt, however reason may contend it,

---

[29] Michael Faraday (1791–1867) was an English scientist who pioneered the study of electromagnetism.

that Spatial Extension is capable of infinite variety." Certainly it operated differently between a Chinese savant and a Kremlinist. Every physicist, Greek, Russian, Chinese, has dissected "Nature" into ultimate elements, so why have they not reached the same conclusion? Because all defensively believed with naïveté, not in the least the Kremlinists, that the others shared in common the same world-idea.

In the same pamphlet Mao criticized the Soviet philosophical interpretation of the Quantum Theory, which despite innumerable experimental proofs to the contrary, would never lead those doctrinaires away from their simple materialistic views that prevailed in the natural sciences of XIX century Europe. And then he continues: "The acerbity of the criticism of blind Soviet *apparatchiks* shows that we contend not with science, but with a confession of an almost casuistic faith in a stubborn adherence to a creed that will never relinquish the claim to absolute and final infallibility."

From these lectures by Mao we learn the fact that this simple son of a Chinese peasant, an autodidact *par excellence*, kept well abreast of events and reexamined all sides of historical endeavor, which specialists in the West, not to mention America's statesmen, believed could be safely left unexplored. Thus he must be well aware of the new vistas in terms of world and human development that emanated not only from the expansion of technical science, but also from the revolutionary discoveries in applied and even theoretical physics in general, and especially in the most difficult field of quantum mechanics.

Only his profound knowledge can explain why Mao taught his nation that in order to survive, they had to master the same combination of natural and technical science, initially for military purposes, as the West had done so successfully. He convinced the executive élite of his people that only the penetration of science into the more remote parts of Nature would enable China's engineers to use the forces of Nature, which in former years had scarcely been known. And here, penetration of Chinese science, especially into the thermonuclear field, was much easier because it was not burdened by the naïve materialistic thinking that prevailed in the West as late as the first decade of this century. Which one of the West's guiding minds can boast such a commanding array of knowledge in many fields, and, additionally, apply this knowledge to pursue a great world-political mission?

That Mao is so far the winner is undeniable. That his knowledge about progress in natural science has now made him skeptical *vis-à-vis* those thinkers who a century ago introduced dialectical materialism cannot be negated. Almost daily one reads about Mao's stance against those whose concepts of matter and reality can no longer be adapted to the results of the refined experimental technique of today.

That unfolding events are on Mao's side when he brings about the fusion of inner being with outer reality throughout the huge mass of his followers is quite obvious. Modern transportation and communication methods made it possible for Mao to penetrate the Middle Kingdom Nation-Race-People-State by spiritual and moral reforms with incredible speed, directly into the last corner of the Chinese Landmass.

As to the *social dynamic*, it cannot be emphasized enough that Mao's subjugation of the human being, which made the West, and especially the Russians, tremble with fearful anticipation, occurred at the same time when the political significance of modern science, and especially modern physics, made popular by the explosion of the Hiroshima bomb, surged to every corner of the map.

In Russia, the forces which turned Lenin's mill-wheels came from springs beyond his experience. He mobilized the religious fervor of the peasant masses for worldly, *anti*-religious purposes. Mao's task was different. Even before the time of Confucius, until about 1850, the Chinese had honestly believed in the possibility of establishing a peaceful social order on Earth, a contained people striving to adapt themselves as best they could to the here and now.

The Opium War awakened them, and their Utopian dream came to an end.

At this time, the most respected official and scholar, Feng Kuei-Fen (1809–1874), proclaimed: "We have only one thing to learn from the barbarians and that is: strong ships and effective guns. At first the Chinese may take the foreigners as their teachers and models. Then they may come to the same level. Finally they may move ahead and surpass them."

Between 1857–1860, the intruders France and England extended the position that they had won in the Opium War. And in 1860 the end of China became a fact when eleven more ports were opened to the barbarians and the Yangtze River was yielded as a route of commerce to the West. From that point, until 1945, the ruthless exploitation of China never let up for a single moment.

Yet the majority of leading Chinese men inclined toward the opinion that, while it was necessary to learn the technical skills of the West, the Confucian substance must be retained. In 1867 the scholar Wo-ten, for instance, wrote to the Emperor that "the attitude of men was more important than technology, that one could not bring about a rise of a nation by means of mathematics," that furthermore, "the West had not introduced anything new, but had merely developed early Chinese beginnings in the field of natural science which the Chinese had intentionally neglected as being unimportant."

"We, the Chinese people, have now stood up."

—Mao, 1949[30]

The Chinese learned to their despair a lesson like no other people in the annals of modern history. That Mao's revolution succeeded should not come as a surprise, for all he did was open the books of China's historical events from 1850–1945. He reminded the people of the shameful climax when Chinese batteries lay defenseless under Japanese fire because money for shells had long since found its way into numerous open pockets according to the magic recipe of China's enlightened friends of the Washington régime.

---

[30] From a speech made to open the First Plenary Session of the Chinese People's Political Consultative Conference on September 21, 1949.

To what political ends will the spiritual and material revolution of the Chinese people lead?

The right answer to this question should be of greatest concern. There is not one nation, not even a combination of racially related nations or peoples, that can match the indestructible ethnological form of six hundred eighty million Chinese. There is not one large national human unit on this Earth that is more intensely held together by the unity of physical origin than the Sons of the Middle. In no other nation does the felt harmony of a common Destiny find itself more intensely and uniformly expressed than in this segment of the Asian Race that populates the vast lands between the Pamir Mountains and the Chinese Sea.

In what other people can we now find a stronger sense of a bellicose world-mission than the strictly secular desire to extend their Middle Kingdom everywhere? They are assured by their leaders that they have the obligation, the strength, to bring order to the present chaos, when formerly the average Chinese simply refused to emerge from his family sphere, and turned away from slogans, ideas, or movements of any kind. The political lethargy of the masses had been replaced by a will-to-power, thanks to the cruel fleecing of the Chinese coolie from the beginning of the Opium War until 1945, and to the inability of American geniuses with their heads full of humanitarian cant and ledger-book ethics to comprehend or even recognize events of historical importance.

It cannot be emphasized enough that this miracle, this spiritual metamorphosis, could never have been achieved without the deep humiliation the Chinese people endured at the hands of the West and Japanese during the past one hundred years, the "Century of Humiliation."[31] Which other nation is now more

---

[31] This term was first coined by Chinese nationalists in 1915 in response to demands against Chinese sovereignty that were made by Japan during the First World War, and to which President Yuan Shikai acquiesced.

Although Mao declared the Century to be over with the formation of the People's Republic of China, the Chinese government has continued to invoke the end of this period in relation to its achievements,

convinced of its historical and moral right to enforce a change of present conditions, to change this world in which they feel condemned to play the role of pariah?

No other nation can match the versatility and adaptability of the Chinese people, qualities that enable them to cope with any surprises, should they experience momentary setbacks in the planned enforcement of their will.

The Chinese of today are afraid of nobody, least of all the Russians or Americans.

Is there any other population that knows better than the Chinese how to live happily in unimaginable poverty, to forget troubles and anxiety, and to master the art of life under the most adverse conditions? Is there a nation that will die more serenely if necessary and with more philosophical tranquility? And lastly, which other people could ever perform a similar transformation and complete assimilation of human material of any and every provenance into the bodily and spiritual identity of its own, than the Chinese did over two thousand years ago, ergo, what became of the conquering Manchu and Mongol?

> "Weapons are an important factor in war, but not the decisive one. It is man and not the material that counts."
>
> —Mao

If there was ever an aggregate of men that felt itself united, it is the Chinese Nation-Race-People-Society-Culture, whose present leadership has been molded by twenty years of guerrilla fighting in thousands of nameless battles by small heroic units, often against the well-equipped Japanese and Chiang units, with practically bare hands and existing often for years on end, having no personal contact with headquarters.

Can we perhaps attribute the same qualifications to the leaders of the eighty million true Russians and the other one hundred twenty millions of disparate peoples which comprise the Soviet Union? Or, can we attribute the same qualifications to the

---

such as during the 2008 Summer Olympics held in Beijing.

leaders of two hundred million people that fight each other to the death in television-dominated, melting-pot America?

Wishful thinkers will tell you that Mao cannot emerge victorious with the transformation of the Chinese nation into a first-class world power. Above all, they forget that despite radically different ideological differences, the new Communist governing élite resemble in many ways the Han-Lin élite which governed China successfully for two thousand years. China now possesses a matchless combination of ideological, administrative, and political *authority*, and above all, ethical leadership by a rigorous selection from the stratum of those who passed with honor through twenty long years of war.

Portentous experts in Chinese affairs are deceived by the pleasant politeness of their intimate Chinese friends, who never reveal to the Westerner the abysmal hatred and revenge-imperative that has been stored in the soul of every Chinese against the White man who sinned against the precious and highly esteemed cultural heritage. And this holds true for the relationship between White and Chinese anywhere, even in the United States.

"The future belongs to those with the longest memory."

—Nietzsche

The Chinese have the best memory among the human species. His written language alone proves this. A Chinese wanting to read newspapers or books must know two thousand to four thousand root characters by heart. That this presupposes extraordinary capability of mental training and concentration is obvious. For over two thousand years this systematic mental training was exercised by generation after generation, to this day. *Thus, a Chinese never forgets,* least of all that what happened in his homeland during the Age of Humiliation was at the hand of the White and Japanese intruder. And even if he was born in America and enjoyed the luxury of a carefree American career, the destiny of China will absorb his innermost feeling. He may abhor the prospect of returning to China to live as one of Mao's subjects, but if Mao prevails, enthusiasm for his fatherland and beloved ancestors will be boundless.

The greatest hope for Mao's failure was placed on China's "rebellious intellectuals." News analysts and Press prophets will again be wrong. Above all, Mao, in contrast to the cunning barbarian Stalin, had from the very beginning a deep respect for the intellect. And this respect was reciprocated by the entire Chinese nation. The example of Mao's heroic resistance against the Japanese fanned into flames a contagious enthusiasm throughout the land. And so complete was his victory in 1949 that, again in contrast to Lenin, China was not wracked and bled dry by the horrors of a protracted civil war. These facts had slowly but surely gained for Mao the sympathy and often the admiration of the majority of the intellectuals.

The intellectuals realize that without total mobilization of the Chinese masses under a totalitarian and specifically Chinese ideology, the struggle for all or nothing would be a hopeless one. Again and again, Mao, in addresses to the intelligentsia, pointed out that once Technological Revolution had achieved its goal, China would no longer be exposed to atomic blackmail. "Who will even try to contest our largest possible role in the final state of world-unification which has to come whether anybody likes it or not?" So spoke Mao to the troublesome intellectuals.

China's chance to be among the leaders, if not *the* leader, in the coming scheme to "unify the peoples" is hardly based on the uncompromising belief of the Utopist. We cannot close our eyes to the fact that the vast majority of the Chinese people have a uniformized judgment concerning the correctness of Mao's ideas about China's future-obligated role in world affairs, for who can match China's homogeneous social tradition and organization which, in its main structure, was taken over by Mao? Who can match the ethnological unit of six hundred eighty million Chinese in an immense land that enjoys standard climatic conditions without which no world power could ever exist for any length of time?

Remembering the experience in modern physics, so well known to Mao, there must always be in statesmanship a fundamental rapport between deliberation and decision. On innumerable occasions, Mao pointed out to the criticizing intelligentsia, and to the entire nation, that in practical life-decisions it is never possible to go through all the arguments, pro or con. Only one possible decision can be reached, and to that end, cutting off further discussion becomes a *necessity*.

The mightiest source from which China's present leaders draw and then radiate their phenomenal strength in the unconditional belief of China's invincibility has never been mentioned by the China specialists at Foggy Bottom. This is hardly surprising. For exactly as the poor sum total which historians have assembled for the law and economics of Egypt, India, and China (in contrast to the immense work done on Greek and Roman law), the history of the countryside and landscape, in which man's known history has been staged for six thousand years, is a complete blank to the West.

And yet, man has painfully wrestled himself from the history of the *Landscape*. He will hold to it by myriad ties, for without them, human life, soul, thought, and fate are inconceivable.

Innumerable publications teach the Chinese people about the history of their countryside, the Inner Landscape in which the Chinese Nation-Race-People-State has its roots and its home, a home that has formed the essential uniform characteristics of body and soul of untold millions. They also learn that this uniformity of race-characteristics was greatly enhanced because the whole of China enjoys a practically changeless climate despite the endless expanse of the land.

They are taught how every year the soil of the blessed Middle Kingdom is fertilized "from heaven" when dry north winds deposit immense quantities of loess[32] which in some regions reaches a depth of twenty-five feet. In contrast, they learn how American dust storms carry away topsoil from fields, and how the desert slowly creeps further to the north of the Rio Grande and how the groundwater tables recede across the US Southwest.

They learn that in the course of successive Egyptian, Classical, Arabian, and Western Cultures, a climatic change developed

[32] A type of fertile topsoil made up of wind-blown dust.

around the Mediterranean and Black seas which resulted in relentless struggle against the ever-advancing desert. On maps the Chinese are shown how in Hannibal's time the Sahara lay very far to the south of deserted Carthage, and that today it already penetrates into northern Spain, Italy, and as far as the southern Urals. And again, on maps, they are shown how four thousand years earlier China was densely populated when nomads changed the racial characteristics of Egypt, Babylonia, and especially Europe. The obvious conclusion is then reached that all they must do is bide their time which has to come, whether the red-haired barbarian of the West approves or not.

To a people who think in such terms a thousand-year span is nothing.

From Spengler we learn that when Alexander the Great appeared on the Indus River, the piety of three great Cultures, Chinese, Indian, and Classical, had long been molded into non-historical forms: a broad Taoism, Buddhism, and Stoicism. But what we did not learn was that the idea of a ruler whose writ should run throughout the whole historical realm, whose destiny would be that of all mankind, was always a fundamental part of Confucian thinking. "For the ruler of the Middle there is no foreign land" (Kung Yang).[33] "Heaven speaks not, for it causes its thought to be promulgated by a man . . . his errors affect the whole Cosmos and bring about cataclysm in Nature" (Tung Chun-Shu).[34] Such mystic universalism was completely alien to the other two state-forms: Indian and Classical, both so dear to Alexander. Yet in China this mystical universalism *is still very much alive.*

Now, after Confucianism—Maoism!

And how the world buzzes with horrified excitement!

Maoism has proceeded in a decade to force upon six hundred eighty million Chinese, as example and model for all, a way of

---

[33] The *Kung-yang Commentary* is a text on the Confucian *Annals of Lu* which has been dated to the third or fourth century. Yockey got this quotation from Spengler, *The Decline of the West*, vol. II, p. 373.

[34] Tung Chun-Shu (179–104 BC) was a scholar who is credited with having helped to establish Confucianism as the official ideology of the Han Dynasty. The quotation is again from Spengler, ibid.

life which had formerly existed only in limited communities, such as monastic orders: *the total collectivization and absolute subjugation of the human being.*

Maoism proudly declares that in world history it is not technique but man, the masses of people—six hundred eighty million Chinese people—who shall determine the *fate* of mankind.

Maoism incites millions of listeners by announcing that the basic problem of the future is *that of world population.* What will become of the Earth when it is inhabited by *twenty billion* persons, and what chance has China to impose its will upon these billions?

How will these billions be sustained, where will they be sustained, where will they live? Can they possibly be governed by any other system than Maoism? And the answer is of course an emphatic no, because Maoism, with its particularly Chinese feeling, alone gives historical thought its characteristically wide and unbounded horizon which has been guided by Chinese thinking over millennia, a Maoism that to this day has preserved the militant spirit of The Long March,[35] the militancy of the entire nation, that Spartan time-of-ordeal spirit, of share-and-share-alike, that great sense of comradeship in thousands of battles against the Japanese and the satrap Chiang Kai-shek.

> "We Whites will have to abandon our tacit assumption of permanent dominance over Asia, while Asiatics will have to forgo their dreams of emigration to White lands and the penetration of Africa and Latin America."
>
> —Prof. Lothrop Stoddard, 1921

Maoism laughs at America's threat to bomb China's atomic installations, and then declares it a good thing, not a bad thing.

---

[35] Pursued by the nationalist Kuomintang, the Chinese Communist Red Army undertook a retreat for a year from October 1934 to 1935, crossing nearly six thousand miles and some of the most difficult terrain in China. It became a defining historical moment for the fledgling Communists.

"It has not harmed a single hair of China. On the contrary, it has aroused the whole Party and people to unite in setting up millions of little backyard shops where we will manufacture bomb parts—small parts, medium parts, big parts, such as we did in times of our backyard steel furnaces. Try and find these million-and-one spots.

"You poor stupid devils! You advertised to the entire world your atomic achievements when in 1945 you dropped the Hiroshima bomb, and gave away a weapon that could have assured you of world hegemony a few years later, had you kept your achievements secret. We so far have tested only a few small bombs, and are satisfied with the results. You keep guessing what's going on within our tunnel factories.

"As to the delivery of our bombs on you: they are within a three hundred fifty-mile distance from our northern, western, and southern frontiers, not to speak of Japan, prime targets to put the whole of Asia, nay, the whole world, aflame. For years our launching installations covering this distance and beyond are well tunneled-in. So you better think twice before carrying out threats."

Ever since the war with Japan, China became aware of the vital importance to keep its corridors to the Burma and Bengal coastlines open. Any threat from the flank, the Siamese Peninsula, China cannot permit to anybody, just as America could never permit the Chinese to occupy Mexico. Any Western adventurism within this peninsula means indirectly an attack on China.

Long ago the Chinese appraised their vulnerability to nuclear war and their capacity to retaliate. And, unlike the 1936–1939 Spanish curtain-raiser to the War Against Europe, the use of military-technical power is useless. Hence, the present Chinese concentration of assistance to guerrilla fighters along the six thousand-mile frontiers to the north, west, and south.

And how to stop the rapid onslaught of millions of Chinese foot soldiers in all directions, each one ready to calmly sacrifice his life for the beloved Middle Kingdom? Shall we attempt to put an atomic curtain over six thousand miles of mountainous front, studded with Earth's largest glaciers beyond the Arctic? There is not one major river system in Asia whose headwaters are not found along the mountain ranges of China's borders: Mekong, Yellow, Yangtze, Salween, Brahmaputra, Ganges, Indus. Any tampering by atomic bombardiers with these snow- and ice-capped frontiers would have catastrophic effects not only in China, but in every land bordering China.

The Chinese have also carefully appraised something else, the scene of a deadlocked atomic arms race in the West, and the European feeling that an American bomb intended for China is a nail in the coffin of Europe's hopes. West Germany, not Russia, is China's main trading partner.

The Chinese are elated that the Twin Giants feel that what they do now forces the most fundamental decision—the choice, namely, of giving more emphasis to offense or an immensely costly defense system in the thermonuclear arms race. And they further register with contentment that both Giants rapidly conclude that in order to save their present economic equilibrium, both need a span of at least two decades when the strategic environment would be suitably tranquil, forcing both powers to resist the temptation to disrupt it, even when a much less costly mirage than guided missiles should appear.

Mao concludes that it is quite unlikely one of the Twin Giants would risk the disruption that would set in immediately if thermonuclear bombs were dropped on China.

As to the European theater, Mao smiles with delight that all of Europe is tired of being asked by America to revere the "American Way of Life" as repository of superior wisdom, the dollar-engine that is entitled to intervene here, there, and everywhere with arms and GIs to ensure the inferior thoughts of two hundred fifty million Europeans not prevail.

And, with delight, Mao views the rapidly growing atomic potential of France and her planned creation of a French-German political-military bloc of one hundred ten million men. Plans for proposed atomic installations in Pierrelatte, the approximate size of missile stations in La Haute Provence, the as-yet secret facility in Guyana, and the testing ground to the east of Queensland in the Pacific are circulated throughout China with the comment, "US armchair strategists hope that two Giants will gang together against us and that Russia will obediently jump into the fray for

America, for the America that is seven thousand miles away from the intended war theater."

Does any sane American have the wish-thought of an Asian fighting another Asian for the purpose of converting Asia to the detested "American Way of Life"?

The tragic fact that millions of defectives advocate a bombs-and-hellfire-on-China policy shows only complete failure to comprehend an event that would inevitably be the direct result of such a mad act: World War Three, with all its terrible and fatal consequences.

FINIS

The World in Flames:
An Estimate of the World Situation

1960

Editors' Note

Yockey's final work was published posthumously in 1961, the year following his death, by his primary American backers, Frederick Weiss and H. Keith Thompson, under the imprint of Weiss' Le Blanc Publishers and typeset by Thompson. The essay was written in collaboration with Thompson, who suggested the title.[1] This essay provides the basis for a *Realpolitik* that remains relevant to an estimate of the present world situation.

The World in Flames

In October 1946, in a quiet garden in Wiesbaden, an unknown person, whose writings and actions are only valued by his enemies, and that negatively, composed a short monograph entitled "The Possibilities of Germany,"[2] and this Estimate can best begin by a short citation from that unpublished work: "Eventually—not before fifteen years, not more than thirty—the Anglo-Saxon-Jewish combine and the Russian Empire will wage the third of the series of World Wars."

1960 was the first year in which the world political situation was ripe for a great war. But the exact moment of its outbreak is known to no one at this time, not even to any clairvoyant. It may take place this year, or any year after this, the last possible time being about 1975.

I

---

[1] Keith Stimely, Interview with H. Keith Thompson on Francis Parker Yockey.

[2] Yockey was in Wiesbaden in October, 1946 and is likely referring to one of his own lost writings.

A brief comparison is in order with the situation of 1946. In that year, America-Jewry controlled, in a political if not military sense, the entire Western Hemisphere, all of Western Europe except a part of Germany, all of Africa, all the Near East, the Middle East, and the Far East. This all amounted to nine-tenths of the surface of the Earth and more than three-quarters of the Earth's population.

Since then, this preponderance of power *vis-à-vis* Russia has dwindled to a point where the Washington regime at this moment has no preponderance of power *vis-à-vis* Russia but stands in an inferior power-position.

The basic reason for the diminution of power is spiritual-organic. Power will never stay in the hands of him who does not want power and has no plan for its use. Desire for revenge, desire to "stop Hitler," desire to destroy Europe, desire to kill eighty million Germans by the Morgenthau Plan—all these are not will-to-power. Will-to-power means inherently the will to do something positive with that power, not the will to prevent something.

The more superficial and direct reason for the diminution of power was political incapacity on the part of the Zionists, or Washington regime as it is here interchangeably called. This incapacity manifested itself first in total incomprehension of the Russian soul, leading to the belief that this wild, chaotic spirituality had surrendered itself permanently to the guidance of a small group of Jewish intellectuals.

A person who believes that the seizing of the apparatus of power—government, army, police, press, education—guarantees the continuance of power is a political non-entity. Yet the whole Washington regime believes this. In philosophy they are materialists and thus cannot ever understand that visible facts are only the manifestation of invisible spiritual movements.

To the extent that a people is materialistic in its religion and philosophy, it is non-revolutionary, but the Russians are completely non-materialistic, being completely dominated by feelings, and acting always from their feelings. Thus it was that the Russians, even without disturbing the Bolshevik governmental structure or ideology, effected a complete revolution and deprived the Jewish leadership of all power. The Jew in contemporary Russia is allowed to be a Jew, if he is first and foremost a Russian. In other words he is not allowed to be a Jew, and is being exterminated without physical violence.

Since the Washington regime believed in the "friendliness"—i.e., Jewish domination—of Russia, it gave China to Russia, as it had already given part of Germany and part of Japan. One cannot call this treason on the part of the nincompoop Marshall who accomplished the actual transfer of China from the Washington regime to the Russian sphere, for he was sent by the Washington regime on this very mission, and when he died, years later, was called by the Zionist press the greatest soldier, etc., etc. Legally speaking, it makes no sense to say the entire government of a country is committing treason, for it is they who define the enemy. In a spiritual sense, of course, the Washington regime are traitors to the United States and its people, but they have so defined the relationships that those who are loyal to the United States in a spiritual and political sense are regarded as traitors in a legal sense.

India was surrendered in 1947 and lost to the control of the Washington regime. Together with China it accounts for about forty percent of the world's population.

Since then, Egypt has been lost and half the Arab world, through the creation of the foolish, unnecessary Jewish State in Palestine.

Cuba and Venezuela have been lost, with only financial bridgeheads retained, and all the Latin American possessions of the Washington regime, from Nicaragua to Argentina, are growing restive.

Because it retained the fiction of the independence of the European lands, the Washington regime has imperiled its grip on France, by allowing De Gaulle to set himself up as a leader.

In Korea, the Zionists fought against the Chinese armies they had created, through the Great General Marshall, and these armies used the very equipment which Marshall had delivered to them, sufficient to equip sixty divisions. Not only did they lose the war, but they demonstrated to the entire world that the United States infantry is inferior, and that the Zionist empire is, in the Chinese phrase, a paper tiger.

On the positive side, there is little to record. The Zionists conquered Spain without a war and have occupied it with their troops. They have completely incorporated England and occupied it once more with troops.

Of all that they possessed in 1946, there remain only the greater part of Latin America (now precariously held), all Europe except part of Germany, and the greater part of the Mediterranean littoral (also precariously held). Japan has been lost, but Australia, without military value, is still held. The Philippines are still precariously held.

What the Washington regime has lost, Russia has gained, either by extension of its influence directly or by increasing the neutral area. The extension of neutrality is of immediate benefit to Russia, exactly as it is of immediate loss to America-Jewry. This is so because of the concentric shape of the geographical theater of the political struggle. Russia occupies an inner circle, and America-Jewry an outer circle. The neutralization of India, Japan, Egypt, *et al.* represent breaks in the outer circle, and weakening of the Jewish-American economic-political structure.

This is so also for a moral reason. Jewry always claims to speak for, and to represent, all humanity, with the exception of one unit, which is thus automatically the enemy of humanity. In a war of attrition, it is a positive detriment to be labelled by most of the world's press as the enemy of humanity, even though in a short war it makes no difference. Therefore, the more the Jewish-American control over the press of the countries of the world is weakened, the better is Russia's moral-political position.

II

It is instructive to compare the Second and Third World Wars in their aspect of the quantitative relationships of the combatants. In the Second World War, on the one side (Germany, Italy, Japan, Hungary, Finland, Rumania, and Bulgaria) were two hundred twenty-five million people, with an area of less than one million square miles at the beginning of the conflict. On the other side were approximately one billion people and approximately fifty million square miles. In addition the so-called neutrals (with unimportant exceptions) were enrolled in the economic service of the Jewish-American-Russian coalition, since the coalition possessed a monopoly of their trade.

In the distribution of 1960, the quantitative aspect looms thus: on the one side of the Jewish-American leadership is a population of four hundred million and an area of approximately thirty million miles. (These figures include all North and South America, all Western Europe, and more than half of Africa, together with Australia and environs.) On the other side of the Russian-Chinese coalition is a population of eight hundred million and an area of approximately fifteen million square miles. (This includes Russia, China, and the Russian-held areas of Europe.)

These quantitative estimates are generous to the American-Jewish front, for much of what is given is questionable, from the standpoint of military value of the population and accessibility of the territory. Thus it is quite clear that none of the armies in Jewish-American occupied Europe will have great military value, since the essence of the armies, i.e., morale, will be absent. Furthermore, the entire population of Latin America is at best available only for economic service; there is no expectation that in the Third, any more than in the First or Second World Wars, this population can be used as cannon-fodder. And if the movement for Latin American independence spreads, almost a third part of the figures, both for population and land area given above must be stricken. If the Arab revolt spreads further, it may cut off much of Africa from Zionist control.

On the moral side, the two wars are quite different. In the Second World War, Germany and Japan were both nationalist. Only secondarily, and in a propaganda way, did they claim to represent any principle which was of universal validity. Thus they offered no great persuasion to the population in enemy countries or neutral countries to sympathize. The Jewish-American-Russian-English etc. etc. coalition, however, used no nationalist feelings except as propaganda against Germany. Their whole war cry was a universal one: Freedom, Happiness, Justice; a birthday-party every day for every person in the world.

In the Third World War two universals are offered by the

contestants: on the one side the joys of Capitalism, on the other the perfect happiness of Communism. Germany, Italy, and Japan all got out of the League of Nations when it was clear that it was entirely dominated by the enemy. Russia stayed in the United Nations all through a long period when the thing was entirely Jewish-American and has persevered to the point where the thing can be sometimes useful to them even though they do not have the major control.

Thus, while the United Nations was at war against Russia's ally in Korea, a Russian was the head of the Security Council, the organ charged with the prosecution of the war.

A national, or particular, principle against a universal principle is at a crushing disadvantage in a World War. But this time, the Zionists face another Universal, and one with which half of their very own people are secretly, half-openly, or openly in sympathy. In a war between Capitalism and Communism, the Jewish people finds itself physically on the one side, but spiritually on the other. Their minds are divided from their pocketbooks. This weakens leadership corps of America-Jewry, for this corps is entirely Jewish. The Jewish-American entity is Jewish as respects its head, American as respects its body.

In view of the complete lack of spirituality, intellect, political awareness, and moral courage in the American population, the possibility of an American revolt against Jewish domination has been entirely omitted. Such a thing is only a possibility after America-Jewry suffers a thorough military defeat, and even then only if it is followed by large-scale economic disasters.

III

The regimes of Washington and Moscow together make up a Concert of Bolshevism, just as the Culture-States of the West made up the Concert of Europe of the eighteenth century. Moscow and Washington share all basic values and recognize it mutually. No matter how strong their political rivalry, they make "cultural" agreements whereby each may export its brand of culture to the other. Thus Washington sends the clown Bob Hope to Russia, and Moscow sends the cacophony expert Shostakovich to North America, causing the intellectuals to gush with admiration. The American cinema is not anti-Russian, regardless of preparations for the Third World War. Compare this with the preparations for the Second World War, when this same cinema created many thousands of hate-Germany films, which it is still turning out.

Bolshevism means, as simple historical fact, destruction of the West and of the remnants of its Culture. *The Communist Manifesto* sets forth a program to accomplish this on the economic-social side. In the ten demands that it makes, only nine are possible, and all these have been realized in the United States, but not one of them has been realized in Russia. The barbarian nature of the Russians is itself Bolshevism, but Marxian Communism is purely an export article in Russia, while in the United States, it is an accomplished fact.

The reality of this Concert is shown especially by the Policy of America-Jewry toward Germany. Much as it needs a German Army, it will not create a real German Army, but only a mass of helpless rifle-battalions to be slaughtered by Russia without a chance of winning. Both Russia and America-Jewry have failed to get the best performance from their German captives who make the rockets for them. Russia overworks its German rocket-men, and America-Jewry has so thoroughly denationalized, brain-washed, and Americanized its German rocket-men that they are no longer German and have thus lost the source of their technical superiority, i.e., their German inwardness. This is the final explanation why the German rockets made in Russia are better than the German rockets made in the USA.

Most of the cinema in North America treats Russia and Russians as interesting and admirable, human and good. The cinema's purpose in the general scheme of propaganda is to control the *emotional* attitudes of the population. Control of the intellectual attitudes is the work of the press, and here Russia is treated negatively. Why this duality? Every ruling regime gives perforce in its propaganda a picture of itself, and the Washington Zionist regime itself suffers from this quality. Russia is not a total enemy but a *rival*. The Korean War, 1950–1953, expressed the limited hostility of the Washington regime toward Russia and its official war-aim was not "victory" or "unconditional surrender," but "a just truce."

When the Germans in Russia make some new technical advance, Eisenhower congratulates the Moscow regime. Roosevelt never congratulated Hitler on such occasions. The Russian flag is flown in the United States on all festive, "international" occasions. Never did the German flag appear, nor does it today. The fundamental ineradicable Jewish hatred of Germany appears in the fact that even the Germany they control directly is not permitted to sit among the United Nations, on a par with the other puppets. The spate of anti-German films in the theatres and on television continues unabated. The anti-Russian films are few indeed.

One conclusion emerges, of military-political significance: *in the Third World War, the Washington regime will list Germany among its enemies.* Already the radio propagandists say "Russia and Red Germany." The intention here is, not only that the German rifle battalions be slaughtered by the Russian advance, but that the way be opened for the bombardment of Germany again, this time with more destructive bombs.

The Concert of Bolshevism is a reality only because of the attitude of the Washington regime. Russia does not disturb it, since it works to their ends—it gave them China, neutralized India and Japan. But they do not take it seriously, any more than they regard the United Nations as a serious thing.

IV

We now come to the military aspect of the Third World War. It is perfectly clear that the Washington regime has put its entire faith in "strategic bombardment." They plan to deliver the explosives to their targets by ballistic missiles, guided missiles, submarines, and airplanes, land-based and carrier-based. This faith in bombardment is just that: it is *faith,* but not rational. Faith has certain advantages, but not in the realm of technics. Belief that I will discover a new weapon will, or at least may, lead me to that discovery, but belief that this weapon will destroy my enemy all by itself will not increase the power of the weapon.

Black magic would be better in this case, for it works directly on the morale of the enemy, whereas the faith in the weapon merely *assumes* that if his cities are destroyed, he will be disheartened.

Russia is a porous target, and rockets are effective only against dense targets. The Jewish-American citadel is far denser than the Russian citadel and is thus vulnerable to rockets to a far greater degree. America-Jewry would be better off if rockets did not exist. In that case its citadel would be inviolate, and it could never sustain a military disaster of the greatest magnitude, for its armies would be at the antipodes, and their victory or defeat would be of minor consequence. Thus the basic Jewish-American military doctrine is one which cannot possibly give it victory. But this same military doctrine, if adopted by the enemy, could give victory to the enemy.

Russian morale is tough, because of the barbarian nature of the soldier-material, and not because of good leadership, organization, or indoctrination. The Jewish-American morale is poor, the soldier material is utterly worthless in itself. This population has no political awareness, no significant military tradition, no military instinct, no military ambition, no moral strength, and no respect for or belief in anything whatever. This youth is characterized by the Beatnik, the American form of the Nihilist. He believes in nothing and respects nothing because there is nothing within his range of vision worthy of respect or inspiring belief. The Beatnik is not an insignificant entity: he is the ruling type in the American youth. He represents the fashion, all other youth feel inwardly inferior to him, as non-fashionable elements always do toward the fashion-corps.

Russian barbarians cannot be demoralized by rockets. The Beatnik can, because he has no morale to start with, no inner participation. The Russian population is young, and it is rural, mostly in fact, the rest in spirit. The American population is old, and it is megalopolitan, mostly in fact, the rest in spirit. Speaking in general, only rural people are good fighters, not city-people, especially if the fighting is severe.

Rockets are merely artillery, and thus can never conquer. It is true that the doctrine arose in military circles during 1914–1918 that "artillery conquers the ground; the infantry occupies it." But this is mere stupidity, on a level with the military leadership and conduct of that war. Only infantry can conquer.

From this fact comes the Russian military doctrine. It derives from Clausewitz and is valid for all wars between powers based on the same continent. That doctrine is that *the aim of war is the destruction of the enemy's armies by decisive blows*. The Russian military sees in the Jewish-American bombardment of German cities in the Second World War mere stupidity, and here they are correct. But this same Russian military has not yet fully grasped the fact that the Clausewitz doctrine on The Aim of the War is not valid for intercontinental warfare. As far as the Jewish-American puppet armies in Europe go, the doctrine is correct. For Russian victory in Europe, these puppet armies must be rounded up, as they inevitably will be. But there still remains the Jewish-American citadel. How is Russia, without massive means of sea-transport as it is, to destroy the Jewish-American armies? It is simply not possible. Does this mean therefore that Russia cannot win?

It is clear that both contestants in the Concert of Bolshevism have a ruling military ideation according to which they cannot possibly win.

America-Jewry, which believes in rockets, can win only with infantry.

Russia, which believes in infantry, can win only with rockets.

So much for their similarity; now for the difference. Although the ruling doctrine in Russian military circles is an infantry-oriented one (as it should be), nevertheless the Russian military has equipped itself with good German rockets, better than the German rockets of America-Jewry.

But the military of America-Jewry, though it talks out of one side of its mouth about "balanced forces," has not equipped itself with good infantry, for the simple reason that it cannot, entirely lacking any human material which could be shaped into good infantry. The Jewish-American naval forces now have the doctrine that they are mere artillery auxiliaries. The submarines exist to throw rockets; the carriers exist in order to carry airplanes to throw rockets; the cruisers exist to—yes, why do they exist? Away with them, to the mothball closet! The naval battle at sea, the meaning of the fleet, is not contemplated. Protection of commerce is forgotten, since overseas commerce will almost all be cut off in the Third World War.

The Russian forces are prepared to fight with infantry, with artillery, with armor, with air forces, with missiles, ballistic and guided, thrown from land and from submarines. The American-Jewish forces are prepared to fight only with rockets.

Since the rocket is the only Jewish-American weapon, it is understandable that they do not want to abolish atomic weapons, nor to agree to stop their further testing and developing. By the same token it is understandable that the Russians sincerely want to render illegal the only weapon which America-Jewry can use against them.

But here only the Russian position is rational. The American-Jewish position would make sense if (1) it could win with rockets, and (2) it had superiority in rockets. But neither condition is present. It would be better to get out of the competition before the war than to lose the war, but politicians in general do not think that way.

The dispute rages in Russian military circles on whether American rocket manufacturing, storing, and launching facilities should have top target priority, or whether that should be given to American cities. Those who think nationalistically, organically, patriotically, humanly, would attack the rocket facilities first; those who think in terms of cold reason, regardless of domestic damage and losses, would attack the great cities as the prior targets.

V

Now, it has been said that America-Jewry can win only with infantry, and that Russia can win only with rockets. These propositions must be fully explained.

First, the meaning of the concept to win. Immediately the political and military planes separate themselves out. Politically, the concept of winning means the conclusion of peace on terms satisfactory to one's self. Militarily it means that the enemy asks for peace.

This does not contradict Clausewitz in his statement that the military aim of war is the destruction of the enemy's armies. It merely widens the concept of military victory to cover the case, which arises now for the first time in world-history, in which a war is fought between two powers whose armies can have no contact with one another.

This assumes that in the first phase of the war the Jewish-American forces in Europe and their local auxiliaries will be entirely destroyed or expelled from Europe, including England of course. A minor series of operations will follow, hardly to be called a phase of the war, i.e., the finishing of the complete domination of Asia by Russian or Chinese arms. This will include the occupation of Hong Kong and Singapore, the neutralization of Pakistan, the occupation of Persia, the conquest of Turkey, and the delivering of the Jewish-American puppet formations in the Near East to the United Arab movement. A small-scale war may also be necessary to clean out completely the Jewish-American bases in North Africa. Japan will be neutral or allied to Russia.

But after this phase, the issue of victory remains undecided. The Jewish-American regime will not surrender, since the very existence of Jewry is at stake, and the whole United States and its population is there to secure the existence of Jewry.

So here is a war between continents whose armed forces have no contact, nor can they have any contact. Russia has no possibility of delivering a large army to the North American continent. Nor is it possible for America-Jewry to deliver a large army to the Eurasiatic continent, first because it has no such army, nor can it raise it in the numbers and quality necessary, and second, because it is impossible to mount an invasion of Eurasia from the North American continent.

Thus the only "contact" the hostile armies can have with one another is in the limited form of an intercontinental artillery duel. By these means, it is possible for neither contestant to destroy the armies of the other, since these will be widely deployed, offering no target. The only real target for intercontinental ballistic missiles is a large city. Here the United States offers a plethora of targets, and Russia few.

What is the effect of Jewish-American bombardment of Russian cities? And what is the effect vice versa? The Russian is a peasant, whether or not he tills the soil. He is not city-oriented, even when he lives in the city. When the city is destroyed, little is destroyed, so he feels. The American, and *a fortiori* the Jew, is a megalopolitan, whether or not he lives in Megalopolis. When the city is destroyed, all is destroyed, so he feels. He who reads may draw his own conclusion at this point.

Next is the question of bombardment at intercontinental range by guided missiles. Since their precise degree of accuracy is a secret-secret-secret-secret matter, only common sense is available. Common sense teaches first that at thousands of miles distance no rocket can be guided to, say, a factory, or within destructive range of it, and second, that against every weapon, even superior weapons, defenses, even if not complete and perfect, are always worked out. It would appear that guided missiles will be simply an auxiliary to the basic artillery, namely ballistic missiles, and will thus not be decisive.[3]

Next is the question of bombardment by bomb-carrying aircraft. After the first phase of the war, the heaviest Jewish-American aircraft will have to take off on their bombing missions thousands of miles from their targets in Russia and Germany. These targets will be Russian rocket factories, stockpiles, and launching facilities, as far as they know where these are located. On this point there is no doubt whatever that Russian counter-espionage is many times as effective as that of America-Jewry. There is also little doubt that Jewish-American espionage in Russia labors under almost invincible handicaps. Thus, these aircraft will not be too well supplied with targets and will not be decisive.

What was said above about bombardment at intercontinental

[3] This, and the following paragraphs about nuclear war, are a fair assessment of the problems facing nuclear strategists at the beginning of the 1960s. Yockey was correct that nuclear-tipped missiles were not very accurate at the time. However, by the 1970s, both the US and the USSR developed and fielded large numbers of Intercontinental Ballistic Missiles which were accurate enough to destroy military targets; this altered the nature of nuclear strategy considerably, with the emphasis shifting from civilian to strategic targets.

range by ballistic and guided missiles applies equally well to bombardment at continental ranges by the same type of missiles, launched from ships of all types. And what was said about land-based bombing aircraft applies still, even though with less force, to bombing aircraft based on aircraft-carrying ships. These have a shorter distance to travel, but since they cannot destroy something whose location is unknown to them, such airplanes are no more dangerous than Jewish-American espionage makes them.

On the point of bombardment by aircraft, Russia is thus better situated by virtue of the superiority of its espionage, and the relative inferiority of the counter-espionage of America-Jewry. But the fact that they have few if any aircraft carriers means that their aircraft must fly thousands of miles before reaching the target.

We come back to the city as the target. If bombardment of cities is not decisive, no other form of bombardment will be decisive. But it is quite clear that only in the case of America-Jewry can bombardment of cities even possibly be sufficient for a decision to ask for peace.

If this happens, an interesting new possibility opens up. In November 1918 Germany surrendered to the English-led coalition, consisting of England, France, Italy, Japan, China, India, Portugal, USA, etc. But *after the surrender*, England continued the blockade, a war-measure after the war. Since the war was over, this could not be called a means of destroying the enemy's armed forces. It was solely a means of killing civilians, and in this blockade, continued until July 1919, a million people died of starvation in Germany.

Now England was a civilized power, yet it continued war after surrender of its enemy. There is thus the distinct possibility that barbarian Russia, signatory to no treaty to mitigate the harshness of war, would continue to bombard the USA after a surrender, in order finally to eliminate it as a potential world-power, by complete destruction of its industrial potential (which is almost entirely in cities). That which the Jewish-American-English-French forces did in Germany *after* the Second World War—destruction of industrial plants, and irrational plundering of natural resources in order to destroy them—could be equally well done by Russia after the Third World War: further destruction of cities, perhaps occupation (large armies might no longer be necessary) to destroy industry systematically, on the pattern used by American-Jewish forces in Europe 1945–1950. If there were no occupation, the forest areas could be destroyed by systematic bombardment, converting most of the North American Continent into desert.

VI

The foregoing has assumed that Russia and China would be able completely to occupy the Eurasiatic continent. How far is this assumption justified?

At present the Russian Army is in a class by itself, being the only large army in existence which is fully equipped with the best weapons and of good fighting quality. The Chinese army is large, not fully equipped, not equal to the Russian in moral qualities. The Jewish-American army is quite inferior in size to both its enemies, extremely well equipped, but of poor fighting quality. The German army is small, entirely without equipment, entirely without morale. The Turkish army is small, well equipped, and of good moral quality. The Italian and French armies are both small, ill-equipped, and without morale. The English army is small, well equipped, and without morale. The Spanish army is small, not well equipped, but of good morale.

In a war between a coalition and a single power, the single power will win if other conditions are equal. A coalition must outweigh a single power. The coalition forces against Russia in Europe, however, are vastly outweighed by Russia in addition to their decisive handicap of being quite lacking in fighting morale.

The only army in the coalition of the Jewish-American forces in Europe which can be expected to fight well is the Spanish. The terrain in Spain also favors a defender. If De Gaulle is able to consolidate his regime, he may neutralize France, and, as already seen, neutrality works for Russia. Not only France would be affected by such a development. *Neutrality is the wish of all the peoples of Europe,* and this force will definitely reach the political plane if it's given the encouragement of an example.

While it is possible that the Jewish-American forces might be able more or less to stabilize a front in France, in Spain, or in Turkey, this possibility is abstract at this moment, for the armies are neither in existence nor in a position which could stop a Russian invasion in force.

Thus, the assumption that the first phase of the Third World War will develop as outlined above is one justified by the conditions of 1960.

No estimate would be complete which leaves two great political developments out of account, both of recent years. The first is the Arab Revolt, led by a great and vigorous man, Gamal Abdel Nasser. The second is the formation of nationalist, neutralist regimes by such brilliant statesmen as Marshal Josip Broz Tito of Yugoslavia, Nehru of India, Field Marshal Ayub Khan of Pakistan, General Ibrahim Abboud of the Sudan, Sékou Touré of Guinea, Sukarno of Indonesia, Nkrumah of Ghana, and others. These personalities embody an Idea; none are out for money or publicity. They live simply, work for, and live for their ideas. One such man, in a position of leadership, is a world-historical force. All lead weak political units and cannot by themselves fight either of the great world-powers. But all want independence for their people; Nasser, for example, for some three hundred million Moslems. Each is a symbol to great human masses. Their significance, in each case, in this Estimate, is that they diminish the Jewish-American power without augmenting the Russian-Chinese power. By their Palestine policy, the Zionists may even succeed in driving the Arab world to fight for Russia.[4]

Eventually, responsible leadership for a restive mass of some one hundred eighty million Latin Americans will evolve. Already the seeds of revolt against Jewish-American economic domination have been sown. Witness Cuba.

The growing tide of neutralism in the world is due to the political incapacity of the leadership corps of America-Jewry. If this

---

[4] In correspondence with the editors, Thomas Francis, who saw Yockey's original typescript, claims that this paragraph on Third World leaders was added by H. Keith Thompson.

tide rises in Europe, America-Jewry would be defeated before the war. De Gaulle is not a great man, but if he is able to gain French independence, he will immediately find himself the spiritual leader of all Europe, pygmy though he is. De Gaulle is a cretin, but people will follow even a cretin if he embodies their deepest, most natural, instinctive feelings. De Gaulle's driving force is a vanity of super-dimensional extent. Even Churchill, the embodiment of the Idea of Vanity itself, was still content to be a Zionist executive with a front position, a big office, and a resounding title. But De Gaulle wants more: he wants to be equal to the masters who created him and blew him up like a rubber balloon. Because of the spiritual force upon which he has accidentally alighted—the universal European desire for neutrality—he may even succeed. An idiot might save Europe. History has seen things as strange.

VII

An unusual point among the historically-unique relationships of the Third World War is that while neither side can win—in the classical military meaning—neither can lose, in the classical military meaning of that word. The armies of America-Jewry cannot destroy the armies of Russia, and the armies of Russia cannot destroy the armies of America-Jewry on the North American continent. Into the middle of an Age of Annihilation Wars comes now a war in which political and military annihilation is mutually impossible to the contestants.

But in a political sense, victory is still possible. Victory means, in the Third World War, not annihilation of the opponent, but conclusion of peace on one's own terms. Speaking thus of political victory, it is clear that America-Jewry—under the conditions of 1960—must lose, and Russia must win.

Russia holds the initiative, it has the moral force, it has the arsenal. America-Jewry has no moral force, completely inadequate military forces, and has moreover a military doctrine (or, perhaps, an anti-military doctrine?) according to which it does not need any military force except artillery.

This Russian preeminence is not at all owing to Russian cleverness but solely to its opponent's stupidity. To cite once more the unpublished "Possibilities of Germany" from the year 1946: "In every respect but one, Russia is superior to the enemy. Technically, America-Jewry is better prepared. The only way Russia can overcome its handicap in this respect is through German brains. In a word, Russia needs Germany." Since 1946, Russia has obediently armed itself with such rockets as Germans have made for it, and this has been its main cleverness.

It was not Russian cleverness which drove out Chiang from China, but the Jewish-American agent Marshall. Russia did not neutralize India—the Anglo-American troops there were withdrawn by order from Washington. Russia did not occupy Eastern Germany—America-Jewry gave it to Russia. Russia did not take the Suez Canal—Nasser did it. Russia did not liberate Cuba—Cubans did that. Russia is not making trouble in France for America-Jewry—that is being done by De Gaulle, and the Communist Party there has opposed him to the utmost. The Russian Communist Party in the Western European countries harms the Russian interests, and merely serves as scapegoat, bogey, and whipping boy for the Washington regime.

Russian "successes"—except for its German-made rockets—are all the gift of the Washington regime. Jewish-American political stupidity is invincible. But the power-gifts which the Washington regime has made to Russia are not explicable entirely by simple stupidity, simple incapacity. There is the further factor at work that the Zionist Washington regime is on both sides of most power-questions in the world. Its sole firm stand is its fundamental anti-German position: Germany must be destroyed, its young men must be slaughtered. In Algeria, Washington is on both sides: it is with the French Government, as its "ally": it is with the rebels by virtue of its world-program of "freedom" for everybody. In Egypt, the Washington regime told Palestine, England, and France to attack, and when Russia rose, it told them to stop. It was, within a week, anti-Nasser and pro-Nasser. It occupied Lebanon, then evacuated. It held back Chiang when, from his island, he would have attacked China, with whom the Washington regime was then at war. It defended South Korea, but helped the Chinese maintain their supply line to the front.

During the Chinese War in Korea, it made war and negotiated peace at the same time, for years. In Cuba it forbade exportation of arms to the loyal Batista and thus helped Fidel Castro; now it is committed to the overthrow of Castro.

It is a psychological riddle, decipherable only thus: the Zionists have two minds, which function independently. As Zionists, they are committed to the destruction of the Western Civilization, and in this they sympathize with Russia, with China, with Japan, with the Arabs, and as such they anathematize Germany, which is the mind and heart of the Western Civilization. As custodians of the United States, they must half-heartedly remain at least the technical and political domination of that Civilization even while destroying its soul and its meaning. In a word, they are working simultaneously for and against the Western Civilization. Quite obviously they are thus doing more damage than conferring benefit! If a commander of a fortress sympathizes with the enemy, but yet insists in defending the fortress rather than surrendering it, he has surely found the highest formula of destruction.

Thus the newspaper tag of "East versus West" is meaningless. It is East versus East, with the West supplying the lives and treasure for destruction.

If Russia represents the Principle of Stupidity, then Zionism represents the Principle of Malice. Of course neither of the two is without the leading characteristic of the other, but stupidity reigns in Moscow, and Malice in Washington.

The orchestra is in the pit, the spectators gape uncomprehending, the curtains rustle with expectation. The play is entitled *Where Ignorant Armies Clash by Night*. Stupidity is in the lead, supported by Malice. The producer is Destruction, and the company is called *The Forces of Darkness*.

It is already the predetermined curtain-time. Will the drama commence on time?

The Suicide Note

June 16 or 17, 1960

Editors' Note

Following his arrest, Yockey feared being left in a vegetative condition by the state's psychiatric system. He also feared that he would be "forced to reveal" "knowledge about people he loved," according to a cellmate.[1] This fear was more than paranoia. His cleverness in having fooled a psychiatrist in 1943 to get a discharge from the Army came back to haunt him in 1960, although this was only one factor in the state's determination to railroad Yockey into a mental institution, and certainly not the crucial factor.

As stated throughout the FBI files on Yockey, their primary interest was in questioning him about his worldwide political activities and contacts. In particular, the FBI cryptically alluded in the press to Yockey's capture being a major security issue, but its character remains unknown.

This was a time when the state was using psychiatric institutions against political dissidents, and it must suffice here to only mention the notable example of General Edwin Walker. But Yockey would not have been able to summon the public support and outrage that resulted in Walker's prompt release. It was also the time of the CIA's MK-ULTRA program, which saw the widespread use of LSD, electrodes, and other torture methods in which many individuals were zombified. Yockey's answer to this predicament was suicide.

An FBI teletype dated June 17, 1960 from San Francisco advised J. Edgar Hoover that Yockey had been found dead in his jail cell. Yockey's cellmate had tried to awaken him when the coffee wagon was being taken around the cells[2] at 7:25 AM.[3] The

---

[1] Dave Braaten, "Man of Many Names: Nazi Prophet?," *New York Post*, June 19, 1960; FBI file no. 105-8229 – A.

[2] FBI teletype, San Francisco to J. Edgar Hoover, June 17, 1960; file no. 105-8229 – 3.

FBI office advised that Yockey had left a note in pencil which was found in a fold of the blanket under his head.[4]

How Yockey obtained cyanide remains a mystery. However, an unknown person contacted the FBI on June 30, claiming that she had overheard someone stating he knew the individual who had given Yockey a potassium cyanide pill when Yockey was in court. The woman was of unknown reliability, and FBI agent A. Rosen commented that such information often comes "through Ouija boards or other sources which are obviously not reliable."[5]

Yockey had been given a complete body search after his arrest, and all of his belongings had been searched as well. He was transferred from the Oakland Police Department's jail to San Francisco on June 8, and was brought from the County Jail for hearings at the Commissioner's Office on eight occasions, during which he was interviewed by media, family, "and miscellaneous persons."[6]

Yockey had prepared two copies of a will, and had given them to an inmate at the Oakland City Jail, asking that a copy be given to "any lawyer," and the other to his brother-in-law, Lieutenant Commander William Coyne. The inmate had left the copies under a mattress at the jail, and had forgotten them. However, when the inmate was moved to another jail, the remaining contents were removed and destroyed—presumably including the will.

It is clear that Yockey was accorded no respect or dignity while in custody, despite the charges being mere passport fraud. Bail was set at a preposterous $50,000, and the authorities made a ludicrous claim that he might bomb synagogues because he was an "anti-Semite." Yockey was taunted with the certainty that he would be confined to a lunatic asylum, which would have denied him the trial during which he had entertained

---

[3] A. Rosen, FBI memorandum, June 25, 1960, 105-8229 – 3.

[4] Yockey's suicide note, FBI teletype, San Francisco to J. Edgar Hoover, June 17, 1960; file no. 105-8229 – 3. p. 2.

[5] A. Rosen, FBI memorandum, July 1, 1960; file no. 105-8229 – 3.

[6] A. Rosen, FBI memorandum, June 25, 1960, p. 2, file no. 105-8229 – 3.

thoughts of publicizing his views.

The prison authorities had been fully appraised of Yockey's intention to commit suicide if he could not escape, the information having been furnished on June 13, after statements from two prison inmates with whom Yockey was planning an escape. James Eagan, Deputy US Marshall; Captain Frank Heugle of the San Francisco City Jail; Daniel Quinlin, Captain of Inspectors of the San Francisco Police Department; and Lieutenant Donald Scott of the General Works Detail in the San Francisco Police Department were advised of Yockey's intentions by FBI Special Agent Willard Ruch. That same day, Special Agent Wayne Welch had also advised Assistant US Attorney William Clancy, Jr.[7] Hence, the authorities were fully aware that Yockey intended to either escape or kill himself. The authorities did nothing to thwart him. Yockey would be railroaded into an asylum, would commit suicide, or would be shot in the course of his escape. Did an obliging federal agent slip the cyanide pill to Yockey at the Commissioner's court? The FBI was most adamant that the Yockey matter should not be allowed to proceed, and FBI memoranda show that there was much aggravation that after Yockey's death, the case was being pursued by the US State Department.

On being told of her brother's death, Vinette Coyne murmured, "He felt that he was not going to get a fair trial . . . and he was right. Now—all that talent and brilliance—*gone*."[8]

The day before Yockey's reported suicide, Assistant US Attorney Clancy commented that "on the evening of June 16, 1960, that he had come into the possession of a 'super-secret' file regarding YOCKEY, which was 'dynamite.'" The FBI was intending to send two agents to speak with Clancy regarding this file on the afternoon of June 17.[9] What this "dynamite" in a "super-secret" file was has never been revealed. Yockey died that very night. What was such dynamite that had not already been pursued by the FBI over the course of nearly a decade? Clancy stat-

---

[7] FBI report, July 7, p. 50, file no. 105-8229 - 3.

[8] Willis Carto, "ADL Closes its File on Yockey, Creative Genius Driven to Suicide," *Right*, no. 99, August 1960, p. 2

[9] FBI office memorandum, June 19, 1960, file no. SF105-1769.

ed that the Yockey case was one of "national security" which they would continue pursuing, and that others might be involved.[10] Nothing further is known.

THE SUICIDE NOTE

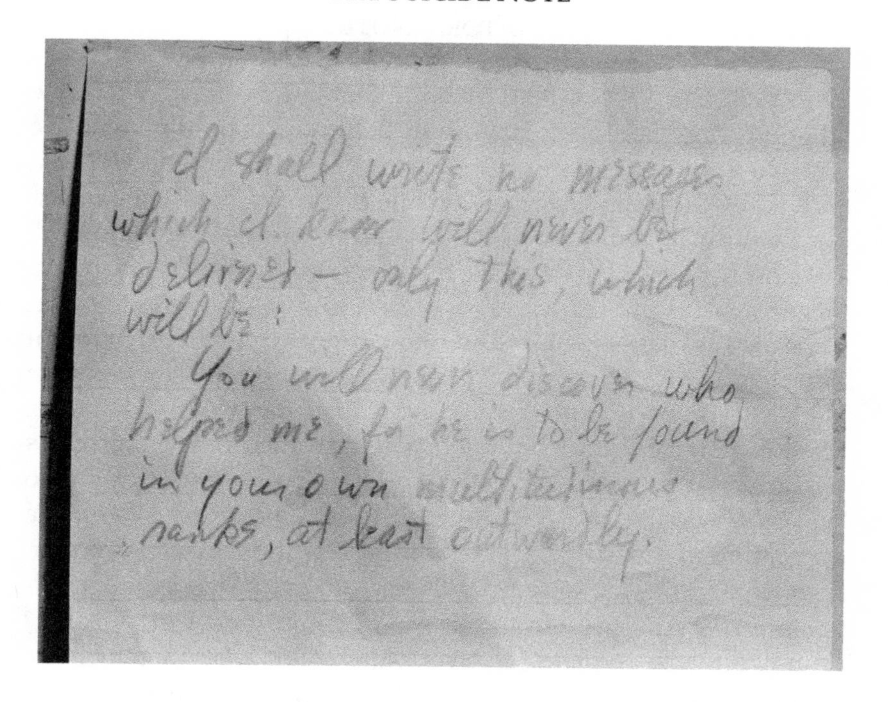

I shall write no messages which I know will never be delivered – only this, which will be:
You will never discover who helped me, for he is to be found in your own multitudinous ranks, at least outwardly.

I shall write no messages which I know will never be delivered—only this, which will be:

You will never discover who helped me, for he is to be found in your multitudinous ranks, at least outwardly.

---

[10] "Yockey's Death Hints Spy Work," *San Francisco Examiner*, June 19, 1960; file no. SF105-1769.

FRAGMENTS

1952–1960

EDITORS' NOTE

In 1952, the FBI obtained material that had been left at a home where Yockey had been staying in Baltimore. These items were the two-volume edition of *Imperium*, two issues of *Frontfighter*, and "The American Destiny." (While it is clear that "The American Destiny" is the same as the essay that was published in 1955 as "The Destiny of America," the version the FBI obtained differs from the published version in some respects, given that some of the passages cited in their report appear in different form in the *NRP Bulletin*. It is possible that the FBI's versions are Yockey's original text, which was then rewritten by James Madole. They are thus included here.) To these were added, as possibly being "pertinent to the investigation," "America's Two Ways of Waging War," "The Masculine Choice of a Wife" (a translation of an essay by Hans Blüher,[1] with numerous annotations by Yockey), "America's Two Political Factions," "Handbook of Imperialism," and "Europe's Honour and Kurt Meyer"[2] (also printed as an article in two issues of *Frontfighter* which are no longer extant). A stamp on the file states that the material was destroyed on May 18, 1960. All that is presently known to remain of several of the items, "Europe's Honour and Kurt Meyer," "Handbook of Imperialism," and "Spengler and the West-

---

[1] Hans Blüher (1888–1955) was a philosopher associated with the German *Wandervogel* youth movement who wrote on masculinity, sexuality, and eroticism, and about the concept of all-male initiatory Orders, or *Männerbunde*. According to Kevin Coogan, Yockey's Flemish girlfriend Elsa Dewette reported that Yockey appreciated Blüher's work, *The Role of the Erotic in Male Societies,* so much so that he translated the entire second volume into English for her.

[2] "Francis Parker Yockey, was; Edigio Boschi," Canada, Security Matter—X, FBI Office Memorandum, December 23, 1952 (Baltimore, 105-643).

ern Imperium" are the synopses and quotes contained in the FBI reports.

It is possible that "Europe's Honour and Kurt Meyer" and "Handbook of Imperialism" will one day surface, as has the other material cited: "The American Destiny," "America's Two Political Factions," and *The Proclamation of London*, but the chance of there being a surviving copy of the 62-page manuscript "Spengler and the Western Imperium" seems unlikely. In another report, the FBI also mentions another, earlier manuscript, "Why the Americans Did Not Go to Berlin."

Why did Yockey choose Kurt Meyer to laud as a symbol, and a question, of Europe's honor? Meyer was a heavily decorated Waffen-SS general, and had been the commander of the SS Division Hitlerjugend, which had fought in Poland, Russia, the Balkans, France, and elsewhere. The kind of fighting he saw is vividly described in his autobiography, such as in this scene from the Russian Front:

> . . . Our steps slowed down. We came to a standstill. We dared not go further. Steel helmets were held as if in prayer. Not one word desecrated this place. Even the birds were silent. The naked bodies of a brutally butchered company of German soldiers were before us. Their hands were fastened with wire. Widely staring eyes gazed at us. The officers of this company had met an end that was perhaps even more cruel. They lay a couple of meters away from their comrades. We found their bodies torn to pieces and trampled underfoot.[3]

Meyer had been awarded the Knight's Cross of the Iron Cross with Oak Leaves and Swords. After the war, he was accused of having committed war crimes in Russia and France. He was tried by a Canadian military court of his peers (twelve generals) for ordering the shooting of Canadian prisoners in Normandy. He was found guilty of three of five charges. He did not seek clemency and defended the integrity of his men. He was sen-

---

[3] Kurt Meyer, *Grenadier* (Pennsylvania: Stackpole Books, 2005), p. 74.

tenced to death, but the Canadian military had a crisis of conscience. Major-General Christopher Vokes, under whose authority the trial was held, stated that he too had ordered the shooting of prisoners (albeit overruled by his superior officer), and commented that "there isn't a general or colonel on the Allied side that I know of who hasn't said, 'Well, this time we don't want any prisoners.'" Thus, Meyer's sentence was commuted to life imprisonment. Meyer was released in 1954, several years prior to Yockey writing this essay.

We might hypothesize that Meyer's significance for Yockey was that when he was transferred from Canadian to German imprisonment in 1951—that is, shortly prior to the writing of this article—Meyer commented to the press that nationalism was past its time, and that "a United Europe is now the only answer."[4] On his release, Meyer became a leading member of HIAG,[5] the Waffen-SS veterans' association formed in 1951. It seems plausible that Meyer, as both an advocate of European unity and a leader of the twenty thousand-strong HIAG, would have been among Yockey's contacts with German veterans.

In regard to the lengthy essay "Spengler and the Western Imperium," which is described in the FBI synopsis as "a commentary on 'Prussianism and Socialism,'" this is a reference to Oswald Spengler's 1919 essay of the same name. Although not as well-known as Spengler's *Decline of the West, Man and Technics,* and *The Hour of Decision,* "Prussianism and Socialism"[6] is a very significant explication of Spengler's worldview. In it, Spengler examines Marxism and other forms of class war-based socialism as emanating from the English materialist nineteenth-century *Zeitgeist,* rather than as transcending capitalism.

In other words, Marx was a man of his time and place. Speng-

---

[4] Patrick Brode, *Casual Slaughters and Accidental Judgements: Canadian War Crimes Prosecutions, 1944–1948* (Toronto: University of Toronto Press, 1997), p. 210.

[5] *Hilfsgemeinschaft auf Gegenseitigkeit der Angehörigen der ehemaligen Waffen-SS* ("Mutual Aid Association of Former Waffen-SS Members").

[6] See K. R. Bolton, ed., *Oswald Spengler: Prussian Socialism and Other Essays.*

ler alludes to these matters in *The Decline of the West* and *The Hour of Decision*, but "Prussianism and Socialism" is dedicated to examining these questions in detail. Marxism and other types of socialism sought to expropriate capitalism, not to replace it. This was the product of English materialism, in which can also be included Darwinian and the Manchester School of Free Trade. England was representative of the materialist *Zeitgeist*, and Germany/Prussia was representative of the new *Zeitgeist* of a socialism that would transcend capitalism not merely in an economic sense, but more significantly in spiritual and ethical ways. "Prussian socialism" was based on duty, state, and class collaboration in an organic society. Private property was a reflection of a deeper spiritual meaning, and not just a reflection of the forces of production. The entrepreneur, as well as the menial laborer, had a duty to the state which represented the will of the *Volk*. Hence, Spengler opposed the anonymous and rootless economics of international finance and the stock exchange. Property must be personal, reflect the personality of the owner, and be subject to duty.

It seems that the full extent to which "Prussianism and Socialism" contributed to Yockey's thinking has not yet been realized, although it should be evident it was as influential on Yockey's thought as was *The Hour of Decision* and *The Decline of the West*. It is from this essay that Yockey came to embrace the concept of what he renamed "ethical socialism," and it is here in Spengler's essay that one sees a term that was frequently used by Yockey: the *Michel* strata of Europe, the bourgeois inner traitors upon which Yockey vented much contempt.

FROM FBI REPORT DATED JANUARY 27, 1953

Yockey served as a United States Review Attorney in Germany and created an unfavorable impression by interceding on behalf of a German war criminal who had been sentenced to death.

Yockey had written a pamphlet entitled "Why the Americans Did Not Go to Berlin" which proposed to expose the Jewish-Communistic influences that were directing American military policy.

From FBI Report Dated July 20, 1953

Summary of Subject's Writings

The following material had been left in [blacked out] home by Yockey at the time Yockey and [blacked out] left in the spring of 1952. [blacked out] was formerly married to [blacked out] This material was obtained from [blacked out] on December 17, 1952 by SA[7] Donald M. Holland.

It is noted that Ulick Varange is Yockey's pen name.

1. *Imperium*

[The first item was an extensive summary of *Imperium*.]

2. Two Editions of the Pamphlet *Frontfighter* Which Contains Articles by Ulick Varange

a. *Frontfighter* No. 20, January, 1952 issue. This publication is published by the BCM Westropa Press, London, W. C. This article consists of six pages in this issue and is entitled, "Europe's Honour and Kurt Meyer."

Contained on page three.

> If the word honour seems strange to Western ears today, that is in itself no sign that our Western honour is dead, that it was hanged along with the victims of American 'war crime' atrocities. No—neither Jew nor American can deprive Europe of its honour—only Europe can do that.

The author states that General Kurt Meyer of Germany, who is still in jail, should be released from jail and that he, Meyer, has served Europe well. The author believes that by occupation forces, America is ruining Europe.

Contained on page seven.

> Let no European think he can bridge this bottomless pit

[7] Special Agent.

and cooperate with American Bolshevism to 'save' Europe, for such an idea has no meaning.

Varange believes that the Americans are profiteering on the Germans today and taking advantage of the Germans because the Americans were victors in World War II.

b. *Frontfighter* No. 21, February, 1952 issue. Continuing from the last issue of "Europe's Honour and Kurt Meyer," by Ulick Varange. This conclusion consists of six pages.

The author claims that the only way for honour of the Germans is to refuse to cooperate with the Americans.
Found on page three.

The Jew with his perverted sense of honour allows himself to cringe and bow today in the hope of revenge tomorrow.

Written on page three.

The Japanese honour code lists as dead the soldier captured by the enemy. The family is notified and the funeral duly celebrated.

On page four.

China and India are landscape words—they describe no State, no Nation, no People. They embody no Mission, no Idea. They have no prestige, no meaning, and no honour is attached to them.

Found on page five.

Hindus, Chinamen, Sikhs, Moslems, Negroes, these can be mobilized by any dynamic power whatever to fight against the enemy of its choosing.

The author believes that if Europe cooperates with the United States, that the population would be utterly dispersed over the world and Europe would end up as slaves, but if Kurt Meyer refuses to cooperate with Eisenhower, Europe will keep its honour and therewith the promise of reconquering once again on a permanent basis.

3. "The American Destiny" by Ulick Varange

Dedicated to the "White American dead of the Second World War who died in vain in a cause not their own." This manuscript consists of nineteen pages.

The author states the early Americans, after a terrific struggle, made this nation great by continuing with their European culture. However, America today has been taken over by the Jews.

Found on page seven.

> It was a political master-stroke on the part of the Jew to bring out the movement known as Zionism.

The author states that the Jews did not help this country with any of our early wars during our struggle for freedom because there were no Jews in this country, but today they have taken over America. He believes that the Jews today receive special privileges in the Army, in colleges, and control the police and big business. The Jews, after the 1932 election, moved into the Democratic Party and into Washington and have been there ever since.

It is noted on page ten.

> In 1933 there descended on Washington a swarm of Jews headed by Baruch, Rosenman, Frankfurter, and Morgenthau.

Varange states that the Jews today run the government, the newspapers, and influence our entire lives.

Found on page eleven.

> The truth is that the Jew is spiritually worn out. He can no longer change. He can no longer develop. He can produce nothing in the sphere of thought or research. He lives sole-

ly with the idea of revenge on the nations of the white European-American race.

The Jew went about his aim of destroying the hated Western nations, not by massing fleets and armies of Jews, but by working within each nation.

Noted on page thirteen.

In 1933 when the Jew captured America, he immediately extended diplomatic recognition to Soviet Russia, and an Ambassador, Litvinov-Finkelstein, was sent to Washington to congratulate his successful kin.

1933 was the year of fate for the Jew. In that year, while he gained America, he lost Europe.

Found on page fifteen.

While white prestige in the world melts away, while the living standard of the white peoples moves steadily downward, the Jew is planning great new power combinations.

He (meaning the Jews) wants a war at his time and on his terms, on an issue he chooses, in theatres he will decide—a war that he plans for America to lose.

The author believes that America will lose World War III and that someday the Jewish flag will fly over the United States.

4. "America's Two Political Factions" [reproduced in this volume]

5. "Handbook of Imperialism"

Which consists of three pages, the front page and two pages of "Morphology of Imperialism." The name of the author was not shown.

The author of this articles gives examples of types of imperialism and then gives examples of decadence and compares imperialism and decadence. The author concludes by questions. Why does a culture last only a thousand years or a man live to approximately seventy years of age? Why can't they last longer?

6. "Europe's Honour and Kurt Meyer" [summarized above]

7. "Spengler and the Western Imperium"

A commentary on "Prussianism and Socialism" consisting of sixty-two pages, name of author not shown.

The German reader has much better reading than the American. In order for a people to improve themselves, they must improve their culture. Spengler saw correctly the German Revolution of 1918 and the future of Germany. The author believes that the West is slowly declining in its civilization.

After the First World War, Japan, Russia, and the United States were the victors. England, France, and Germany lost the war. A power cannot be made great unless it can stand alone. America is very weak politically and tends to lose everything politically that they gain militarily.

The coming of World War I and II was realized by all political thinkers. Russia emerged from World War II as the greatest power in the world. America in defeat of Japan was an aid to Russia.

The United States is preparing for World War III and is trying to get a European Army to fight for them. Any nation which welcomes foreign troops is dead. Europe has been great in the past and the author believes it will be again someday. Europe has many inner enemies, the worst enemy being capitalism.

The outer enemies of Europe are America and the coloured revolution against the world supremacy of Europe. The other enemy is Russia.

Europe paid for America's victory with seven million battle deaths. America needs Europe to start World War III. In America and Russia people are used to thinking of large distances as being near due to the size of the countries, but in Europe, due to the small size of their country, people think in terms of small distances. Both Europe and the United States are trying to gain an advantage. The only thing to save Europe from both Russia and the United States is for the United States to get out of Europe.

8. "Proclamation of London of the European Liberation Front" [reproduced in this volume]

FROM FBI REPORT DATED JULY 7, 1960

EDITORS' NOTE:

After Yockey was arrested while travelling in 1960, the FBI examined and summarized the contents of his luggage in their final report. Among his effects were several that were described by the FBI as "obscene"—in other words, pornographic. Their authorship is unknown, although since they were typewritten manuscripts, it seems likely that they were written by Yockey himself. The FBI's laboratory examined them and concluded in their report that they had not been produced on an Olivetti typewriter, which was what Yockey's political writings that were in the FBI's possession were produced on. No copies of any of these manuscripts are known to exist today, and since the ones in the FBI's possession were destroyed, most likely they will never come to light. It has been speculated that Yockey was writing and selling pornography under pseudonyms as a way of making ends meet, but we may never know for certain. (Although according to the reports, the FBI investigated and could find no published writings under the name John Priapus, which was the name on one of the manuscripts.) There was one published pornographic booklet in Yockey's suitcase, *Arduous Figure Training at Bondhaven*, which has survived, and while it has been speculated that Yockey was its author, this has not been proven. Some non-pornographic materials of unknown authorship were also described. Given that these manuscripts were originals, it seems at least possible that Yockey was their author. Thus, for the sake of completion, this is what was listed in the FBI's report (excerpted from a larger list of items):

6. An original and one carbon copy of a two-page typewritten philosophical essay regarding the "Principle of Polarity," which is described in the text of the essay as a system which "will solve . . . any problem this side of the Absolute." The identity of the author was not shown.

9. A 62-page paper-bound booklet captioned "Arduous Figure Training at Bondhaven," published by the Nutrix Company, 38 Montgomery Street, Jersey City, New Jersey. This booklet appeared to be practically new, the author was unidentified, and the cover bore a stamped figure "$8.," indicating the possible cost of the booklet. The date of the publication was not listed. The text of the booklet contained numerous sketches of partially clad females and the booklet was of a masochist or sadistic nature.

10. A three-page typewritten obscene document written on one sheet of paper captioned "John's Wife." The author was unidentified.

11. An 18-page typewritten obscene document written on white paper, bound with staples, captioned "Strange Iris." Author unidentified. One photograph of a nude female, apparently cut from a magazine, was attached to one page of the document.

12. A 48-page typewritten obscene document captioned "The Misfortunes of Yvonne," by John Priapus, written on white paper bound with staples and Scotch tape. Stapled to various pages of the document were eleven photographs of nude or semi-nude females, all but one of which appeared to have been cut from magazines. The name John Priapus is probably a pen name inasmuch as the Greek god of procreation was Priapos.

30. Folder captioned, "Fragments," which contains the following:

(a) Page and a half article entitled, "The Thirty-two Foot Face." The reverse side bears abbreviations of cities beginning with "NY10" and ending "Bos 3."

(b) One page of notes beginning, "Chekhov's Unfortunate Widow."

(c) Four pages of an article concerning a "superannuated kingdom" called "Islapays."

(d) Nine-page article entitled, "How to Lose an Empire."

32. Two pages entitled, "Thoughts," concerning the cinema as an art form.

33. Folder captioned, "Gedanken," containing the following material:

(b) Duplicate copies of a one-page article captioned, "Gedanken," beginning, "Where there is one."

(c) One page entitled, "Gedanken," beginning, "One Aspect of Feminism."

(d) One page containing a chart beginning, "understanding . . ." The reverse side of the page begins with, "Everything that exists does so as a pole of a polarized entity."

(e) One page beginning, "Notes for Espinty," attached to which are two pages; the first page begins, "From Latin America against . . .," and the second begins with, "Concentration."

(f) Four pages of an outline entitled, "The Driving Forces."

(g) Two-page article, dated February 1959, relating to the "American Organism."

(h) One-page article entitled, "The Polarity of Psyche."

(i) Two-page article entitled, "The Structure of the Psyche."

(j) One-page article entitled, "The Limits of Polarity."

(k) Two-page article entitled, "Landscape."

(l) Eight-page article relating to the third world war and World Wars I and II.

(m) Five-page article entitled "Thoughts," concerning man, time, etc.

(n) One page beginning, "Things can only be experienced," and the reverse side contains the note, "Every polarized entity."

(o) Eleven pages of material entitled, "Thoughts on Polarity Relating to the Calculus of Polarities." Also are included thoughts regarding gambling, cancer, psychiatry of taste, and metaphysics in relation to the plans of polarity.

DER WEG, FEBRUARY 1952

EDITORS' NOTE:

In Volume 6, Number 2 of *Der Weg – El Sendero*, dated February 1952, in the column "Das Weltgeschehen" (World Affairs), compiled by Erwin Neubert and "finished on 20 January 1952" as it reads, the following excerpt from an unknown issue of *Frontfighter* was published on pages 147–48 (translated from the German):

ITALY

The voice of the European Liberation Front in Britain writes:

> The most miserable, infamous, and detested coward of Europa today is Alcide De Gasperi. This poor subhuman creature neither possesses the grandiose villainy of a Churchill, nor Franklin D. Roosevelt's brazen slyness. He is a dead-end man. One cannot expect anything from the successors of the Badoglio coup,[8] and even less from De Gasperi. In the First World War, the "Italian" De Gasperi fought against Italy in the ranks of the Austro-Hungarian Army. Since 1945 he has been on top, as the worshipper of a self-created social justice characterized by the worst social conditions in Europe, with three million unemployed. Since 1945, De Gasperi, the "apostle of political freedom," has arrested, persecuted, and murdered without trial the surviving leaders of Fascism. Since 1945, the "anti-Communist" De Gasperi permits the unrestricted rebellion of the Communist Party of Italy and created those social conditions necessary for its triumph. Since 1945, De Gasperi, the Catholic, openly promotes the reestablishment of the Masonic lodges.

---

[8] Pietro Badoglio (1871–1956) was an Italian General who was made Prime Minister of Italy following the removal of Benito Mussolini from office in July 1943, overseeing the signing of an armistice with the Allies and Italy's declaration of war on Germany. He remained Prime Minister until June 1944.

FRONTFIGHTER

1950–52

EDITORS' NOTE

Frontfighter was the monthly newsletter of the European Liberation Front, covering both its activities and ideology. Although Peter J. Huxley-Blythe, later to achieve note as author of *The East Came West* and as an advocate of Czarist "Russian liberation" movements, was listed as the first editor until his recall to naval duties in 1951, Anthony Gannon states that he was primarily responsible for *Frontfighter*. Starting with issue number 11, L. F. Simmons, a motor mechanic, was listed as editor.[1]

Frontfighter was by-lined "The Voice of the European Liberation Front," and published by Westropa Press in London. *Frontfighter*'s circulation reached five hundred, including—and perhaps mostly going to—supporters outside Britain, running from late 1949 until August 1954. *Frontfighter* was printed on a rotary duplicator which was "worked to death" by Len Simmons and his wife, or by Gannon and his wife, at one or the other of their homes.[2]

Each issue was produced on a typewriter and then mimeographed onto A4 sheets. They included no graphics outside of the logo of the European Liberation Front in the masthead. Copies of only six issues are presently known to exist by the editors, and are reproduced here. See also the fragments of other issues of *Frontfighter* that are preserved in FBI reports or were found in *Der Weg*, all of which are in the "Fragments" chapter.

FRONTFIGHTER
"The Voice of the European Liberation Front"
No. 4, August 1950

---

[1] *Frontfighter*, No. 11, April 1951.

[2] Letter from Anthony Gannon to Keith Stimely, November 24, 1981.

Editor: P. J. Huxley-Blythe

ATTENTION!

Gothic Ripples as of July 15, no. 66, and *Free Britain* as of July 25, no. 69, contain a loathsome attack and smear-campaign directed against the *Front* and the author of the book *Imperium*, Ulick Varange. I am, therefore, placing this issue of *Frontfighter* at the disposal of the Front-leader, A. Gannon, and of Ulick Varange. They will deal with the smears and with the smearers. I am proud to state that I have played a leading role in the uncovering of this low, lying attack. The smear-campaign opened in a letter to me from Arnold Leese. He gave me the poisoned-ivy, and I threw it back in his face. Any other evil-intentioned character writing to me will get the business as well. Lying attacks made on any one member of the *Front* is an attack on the entire *Front*. That is our order-code.

P. J. Huxley-Blythe

**THERE'S NO FOOL LIKE AN OLD FOOL
OR ENGLAND'S WALTER WINCHELL**

Arnold Leese is an old heel. He should be knitting socks instead of spending his senility in lying about and smearing men whose boots he isn't fit to black, and smearing organizations in which he would not be accepted as an office janitor. My attention has been drawn to a low, malicious, blackguardly, lying attack on Varange and the *Front* made by this character-assassin, this would-be hatchet-man of the Jews—Arnold Leese in his bulletin *Ripples*. A similar smear, this time in the form of an alleged "Book Commentary," appears in the Leese sub-sheet *Free Britain* under the name of one Gittens. I will deal with Leese first.—Arnold Leese poses as an honest-to-God, truth-loving, straightforward Aryan. When that gallant, old American fighter, Judge Armstrong,[3] issued a great anti-Jewish book, Leese felt com-

[3] Judge George Washington Armstrong (1886-1976) author of, *inter*

pelled to refuse to handle it because it contained some alleged inaccuracies. This holy-joe, this truth-worshipper, this Leese is a liar, a hypocrite, a poison-penman. He writes to me saying that he accepts the *Front* as sincerely anti-Jewish and that he cannot accuse us of pulling-our-punches against the Jew; and then he writes to my Editor saying that the *Front* is part of the Jew-Plan. He writes to me saying that there will be no fratricidal strife between the *Front* and him; and then he smears the Front with lying accusations in the *Ripples*. He advised people to join an obscure group named the "National Workers Movement" led by an unknown character—A. F. X. Baron. Then Leese writes to me and says that Baron will get nowhere! [illegible] rely on the word of an arnold leese?—Leese accuses the *Front* of Lysenkism—the pseudo-scientific thesis of the Soviet environmental biologist Lysenko. This Lysenko is a materialist like Leese. He does not believe in the human soul. Leese must have picked this one with a pin. The *Front* rejects materialism *in toto*—lysenkoist and leesist. It believes in the supremacy of the spirit. When we talk about environment we refer to spiritual environment. For example, the spiritual ghetto which the Jew carries everywhere with him and which makes Jews even in Eskimoland. We categorically state that the Jew is unassimilable *totally* in European populations. We state that like Blacks and Asiatics the Jew is a *total culture alien*. We state that very many Gentile traitors with fair-hair, blue-eyes, and long-heads who have been subjected to a Jew environment, spiritually, *behave exactly like Jews*. For all practical purposes, and we are *realists* always, these ex-Gentile lackeys must be considered as Jews. That is what we term *horizontal race – total race!* Who will deny that the Jews could never have reached their present supremacy without the willing aid of millions of Gentile traitors? These people are in many cases more Jewish than the Jews. All the fair-hair, blue-eyes, and long-heads on God's earth did not halt this wretched conversion to Jewism—proof-positive of the supreme deciding factor of the spirit over non-deterministic material factors. All are Jews to the

---

alia, The Rothschild Money Trust (1940), *Zionist Wall Street* (1949), and *The Zionists* (1950).

Front who behave as Jews, whether they be winchellists like Leese or baruchists like Churchill.—Leese has never read Spengler or *Imperium* in his life. If he had all the time in this world Leese could not make the high mental grade required. Spengler stated in his *Hour of Decision* that he hoped that the National (Nazi) German Revolution of 1933 would make the grade. The Jews have said that had Spengler lived that he would have been tried with the other Nazi heroes at Nuremberg as a "War Criminal." The Prussian character which Spengler cherished was the backbone of Nazi discipline. The Jews rightly regard Prussianism and Nazism as identical in spirit and inspiration—service, honor, hierarchy, discipline, and authority. Imperium *is dedicated to the hero of the Second World War—Adolf Hitler*. Leese and his ilk should stick to works containing words of not more than one syllable—that way they will not overtax their microscopic brains.—The *Liberation Front* has no connection whatsoever with Mrs. Alice von Pflügl, nor has Mrs. von Pflügl ever had any connection with the *Front* in the past. The *Liberation Front* has no connection whatsoever with Mr. Guy Chesham, he is not a member of the *Front*, nor has he ever been connected with the *Front* in any way. We do not believe the lies spread about Mr. Chesham by Leese, but any statements made by Mr. Chesham are his own, personal views and they have no bearing upon the *Front*, nor do they represent the views of the *Front* in any way whatsoever. Mr. Chesham is a free-agent.—Who does Leese think he is? He is a very old man. This flea-bitten, nasty old buzzard did not know what a Jew was until he was heading on for 50 years of age. He is not quick to see the obvious, you will admit. I was fighting Jews at the age of 18 years. I have dedicated my life to this fight—not my retirement like Leese. Leese was a veterinarian. Obviously he gets his horses and men all gummed-up. He was a complete political failure before the War, and he is still a failure. Why should anybody follow Arnold Leese? Then Leese writes to me and says that Baron will get nowhere. [illegibile] rely on the word of an arnold leese? I find it very hard to take the other winchell—Anthony Gittens (The Git)—seriously at all. Like Leese, his master, Gittens could not read either *Imperium* or Spengler. I remember having a conversation with this poor fellow in a railway tea-room. I tried to talk to him about real things and, in particular, about Spengler. He tried to pretend to me that he had read Spengler then. Every word he spoke proved that to be a lie. Being a kind-hearted fellow, I did not try to show-him-up, but he knew that I knew that he had never read Spengler in his entire life. Hitting political-babes is not in my line, so I will say only one thing more about the Git: Leese told me in a letter that he enables the Git to live. If the Git gets off the lease-line, Leese may stop him living. That is all anybody needs to know about Anthony Gittens. That big-hearted fellow Leese: he provides, and he talks. Similarly, Leese told me that A. F. X. Baron had one use—he was the legal guarantor for the Britons. That makes Baron the libel fall-guy: brave man Leese! H. H. Beamish must have been turning over in his grave these many years, tortured with the thoughts of what Big-Hearted Arnold is doing with the Trust.—Finally, if any person wishes to injure me or the *Front,* he should get in touch with the Board of Jewish Deputies or Arnold Leese; he will find every facility provided for there—hatchets and poison-pens. We can't please everyone and aren't trying to do so. These people in Britain who are against the *Front* are not in the European-Gentile-White-Fascist world; those who are with the *Front* are in that World. It is as simple as that. We do not pick fights with one-time Fascists, but we can win them—*every time!*

Anthony Gannon
British Frontleader

VARANGE SPEAKS!

[Reproduced as Chapter 9 in this volume.]

SPECIAL NOTE

Recently the Frontleader had an exchange of correspondence with Arnold Leese. He completely demolished the pathetic Leese objections to the idea of a European State. He challenged Leese to produce *real* evidence to support his wish-dreams. Leese failed. We invite him to publish that correspondence for the information of his few followers.—The *Liberation Front* is supported by famous fighters all over the world—Arcand of Canada; Åberg of Sweden; Binet, Bardèche, and Dagen of France; Amaudruz of Switzerland; Patrizi, Stasi, and Gatti of Italy; Colmant of Belgium; Dos Santos of Portugal; Pirow of Africa; G. L. K. Smith of USA, *et semini.*[4] German names are omitted for security reasons.

March with the Front!

FRONTFIGHTER

Voice of the European Liberation Front in Great Britain

Editor:
P.J. Huxley-Blythe

Price: 2d.
12 Issues 3/- post

Published by BCM/Westropa Press,
London, W.C.1.

Number 7. NOVEMBER 1950-XXVIII

THE STRASBOURG FARCE is now ignored by all serious, thinking people, for the reality that the so-called "European representatives" are only agents of the Jewish-White House-Wall St. clique is widespread.

These Inner Traitors believe that by their Jew-adoration prattling they will be able to climb on the bandwagon of the New Age. They are foredoomed to failure. Blinded by the sign of super-materialism, and refusing to acknowledge the existence of the Spirit of the Age condemns such epithets as "democracy"; demands the eradication of the International Jewish Money Power; and commands the erection of the *organic state*. they are without any *future* political potentiality at all.

---

[4] In the Catholic liturgy, it is said that God promised the Kingdom of Heaven to Abraham *et semini eius* (to Abraham and his seed). It is therefore likely that by using the words here, the author is humorously classifying these men in the same category.

Europe turned its back for all time on the Party Politician, who brought about ruin and desolation, and condoned the desecration of her holy soil by the mongols of Moscow.

Through the years of agony following upon the Jewish War of Hate, Europe looked for a standard that would once again free it from the alien yoke of extra-European domination, and recapture the greatness of the Fascist Revolutions of 1922 and 1933. Europe has not yearned in vain, for out of the ruins there came the *Idea* of *Imperium!*

This *Idea* is the logical conclusion of the *New Order* envisaged and worked for by Hitler and Mussolini. Fittingly, the organizational expression of the *Idea* of *Imperium*—the *European Liberation Front*—instinctively adopted the symbol of the *New Order*—the *Sword* of *Liberation!* The mantle of the *Heroes* has fallen upon our shoulders, and it is the mantle of invincibility.

Let the Jackals of Strasbourg strut their little hour. Their slogans and exhortations will freeze upon their palsied lips even as they are uttered. Only the final rigidity of Death awaits them. Strasbourg will provide only planned future would-be JUSA colonization. The *future* belongs to the *European Imperium* alone. Thus, it is the clear duty of every White man and woman to join the ranks of the Front: to fight with us, and to win with us.

EUROPE AWAKE!
FRONT HAIL!

P. J. Huxley-Blythe

The spirit of Mussolini lives on in Italy today enshrined in the dynamic and heroic activity of the new champions of the Italian destiny—the Movimento Sociale Italiano.[5] This is the organiza-

---

[5] The Movimento Sociale Italiano (MSI), or Italian Social Movement, was founded in 1946 by former Fascists and attempted to continue some elements of the Fascist program into the post-war era. It occasionally garnered significant public support. In 1995, the MSI was converted into the Alleanza Nazionale (National Alliance) by its final leader, Gianfranco Fini. In 2009, it was in turn merged into the Il Popolo della Libertà (The People of Freedom) party, which was led

tion which the American administration in Italy, headed by the judas-like de gasperi, is now seeking to illegalize.

Over the past two years the growth of the MSI has been tremendous. It publishes no less than a score of first-rate weekly papers, a "daily," and several monthly magazines of high quality. Its organization covers the length and breadth of Italy, the Italian colonies overseas, and embraces the large Italian communities existing in all European lands and South and North America. In the face of every form of persecution, murder, and imprisonment, the MSI has secured the election of its Deputies to the "National" Chamber. Its policies are endorsed by ninety-eight percent of all Italian university students. Its tens of thousands of demonstrators throng the squares of Italy. Marching shoulder to shoulder they sing again the songs of Italy's great era. Not for them the judeo-african cacophony of their jitterbug occupiers.

However, the success of the MSI has not escaped the attention of the Washington Regime. Down the lightning-conductor, known as the Marshall Plan, flashed the directive: Outlaw the MSI! True to form, the de gasperis have hastened to obey. Thus, it is that a Bill to outlaw the MSI has been approved by the "Italian Cabinet" (American Administration), and will shortly be presented to the Deputies for "approval." Under the so-called democratic Constitution of the "Italian Republic," such a decision as that being taken by the "Cabinet" is the rightful prerogative of the Magistracy alone. Because the Magistracy is openly on the side of the MSI, the de gasperis have usurped the function of the Magistracy; the characteristic hypocrisy of Democracy knows no bottom.

What is the underlying implication of this latest Washington-insisted persecution? It is nothing less than this: By every means within its power the Washington Regime is determined to prevent the revival of Fascism, even whilst it countenances and condones the existence of Communist parties everywhere. By this latest action, Washington underlines the undeniable truth of our accusation that: The Washington Regime *and* the Moscow

---

by then-Prime Minister Silvio Berlusconi.

Regime are essentially identical in purpose and inspiration, and that purpose and inspiration is one hundred percent *Jewish!*

Nevertheless, in spite of repression-campaigns organized by the de gasperis the MSI will not go down. There are no badoglios in the MSI camp. None to unlock the fortress gate for the Enemy. The overwhelming majority of the Italian people played no part in that earlier infamy, and they realize now, more than ever, what they lost when Mussolini was murdered by dollarized Communists. Twenty-three years of social progress and economic justice were liquidated at one stroke on that ill-fated 28th of April, 1945. Since that day, by carefully created economic conditions, the enforced absence of the Fascist Party, and the enormous subsidization of the Communist Party, coupled with the inept and corrupt de gasperi administration, the Italian people have been drinking deep of the wine of bitterness and remorse. The advent of the MSI changed all that, and the Italian people rediscovered that spirit which the Duce had first kindled in 1922. Will they again stand by in stunned silence whilst the new badoglios again strike the murderer's blow? With the voice of millions the MSI answers: NO!

Let our Italian comrades know that in this their time of crisis, we of the *Front* are solidly with them. Our faith in their loyalty to the principles of the Duce is complete, and we have no doubt that they will prove in every way capable of meeting the new menace to the Italian people even if this means for many of the leaders the making of the supreme sacrifice! The *Spirit* of *Mussolini* hovers over the Italian scene again. The stern, unsmiling features of their murdered Duce beckons to *Young Italy*. He will not beckon in vain! *The MSI is keeping faith!*

SALUTO ROMANO!
FRONT HAIL!

A. GANNON
British Frontleader

Are you doing all you can to help the Front? Will you send us a regular monthly contribution to help us expand and intensify our public campaign? Can you introduce a new reader to our circulation list? Are you prepared to organize a group of activists in your part of Britain? Can you address public meetings? Let us hear from *you!* Address as follows: *Finance,* Gilbert Hardman; *Circulation,* Pat Simmons; *Editorial,* P. J. Huxley-Blythe; *Organization,* L. F. Simmons; *Propaganda,* Thos. Davies; *London enquiries,* J. Stanley. Mail all matter to: BCM/Westropa Press, London W. C. 1. Cheques and Postal Orders to be made out to: Westropa Press, and crossed. *Will we be able to thank you?*

Front public meetings have gone on since last April on the market-squares of the principal towns in the North and North Midlands areas of England. These meetings have proved highly successful, and only the coming of severe winter weather has, temporarily, brought them to an end. We are now looking for suitable halls in which to continue our campaign throughout the winter months.

Thos. Davies
Director of Propaganda

Our differences with Arnold Leese are well known to our readers, and nothing is altered in that respect at all. However, in spite of all that has gone before, we place on record our complete sympathy and solidarity with him in his impending prosecution on a charge of criminal libel against the chief of police. Furthermore, we agree with every word spoken by Leese on the question of paying Fines imposed by the Enemy, instead of electing to go to gaol. We do not doubt that in this instance Leese will conduct himself like a man and like a Fascist.

A. Gannon

The Mosley group will have to get along without its Organizing Secretary, L. F. Flockhart, who has been sentenced to two years' imprisonment after conviction on a charge involving sexual assault upon a youth. What next, O Lord?

Messages of support have been received during the past month from Ray K. Rudman, the *Boernasie* of South Africa, also from O. E. Kellerman of the *Universal Civic Association*, also of South Africa.

Maurice Bardèche, the brilliant and courageous author of *Nuremberg ou la Terre Promise*, was recently expelled from the "British" Zone of Deutschland, after giving a lecture advocating the unity of the French and German people against Bolshevism. This was too much for the "anti-Communists" in the "British" Zone this year.

You must read *Imperium* by Ulick Varange, obtainable from this address at 12/6 per set of 2 volumes post free. No complete understanding of the current situation is possible without the aid of this great book. *Imperium* demolishes Marxism, Darwinism, Freudianism, Democracy. *Imperium* tells you how the present chaos came about, and what steps must be taken to restore the dignity and independence of Europe. Forceful, brilliant, prophetic, scholarly, and, above all, uncompromising in its assault upon the International Jew. Write for free resume of comment on this Book by famous thinkers and fighters. *It is a must for your bookshelf!* Also write for your copy of the soul-stirring, fighting *Proclamation of London of the European Liberation Front*, containing the dynamic *Program* of the *Front*; Priced at 1/- post free.

MARCH WITH THE FRONT!

FRONTFIGHTER

Voice of the EUROPEAN LIBERATION FRONT in Great Britain

Editor:
P.J.Huxley-Blythe

Price: 2d.
12 Issues 3/- P.F.

Published by BCM Westropa Press,
London, W.C.1.

Number 10. FEB/MARCH 1951-XXIX E.F.

"Senator" Attlee hands over the British Navy to Wall Street

by his latest move in accepting an American admiral as Supreme Naval Commander of the fleet of the Atlantic "power."

For centuries the White Ensign has been the outward sign of European sea-power. Wherever it flew it indicated White rule, order, and the world-mission of Europe. It remained for Attlee to formally end this state of affairs—for, in fact, five- and six-pointed stars have been becoming ever more plain on the White Ensign for the last ten years. What the German Army was to Europe on the land, so was the British Navy at Sea. Truly, is Europe now stripped of its last vestige of sovereignty over its own armed forces, and, thus, for the moment, ends the proud history of European armed might—for the "bottom of the barrel" has now been scraped.

The German military and political leaders have either been foully murdered, imprisoned, and tortured, or consigned to the lowest levels of human existence. Men of genius and honor rot in the Jewish prisons of Spandau, Landsberg, and Nuremberg. The threat of execution has hovered over the heads of many of them for more than six years, and still does so. Their families and loved ones have been humiliated and tortured by a body of Jewish hirelings, posing as an occupation authority. No crime has been too low to commit for these creatures. Women and children, the aged, and the wounded have all constituted a fair target for their foulness. Jewish hate demands that millions of Gentiles be tortured and murdered to satisfy its age-old blood-lust. When will the people of Europe rise from their chloroformed stupor and end this carnival of bestiality? Smashing the jackal-regimes of Europe, and sweeping away forever this filthy, insane Jewish terror-machine. It must come soon! Open the gates while there is yet time, for if this is long delayed, the taking back will prove to be one of the bloodiest periods in the long history of Europe. Let the Jews and their curs take note: We shall take back our own!

And now for the moment I must say au revoir to *Frontfighter*. As an active member of the Royal Fleet Reserve I have been recalled to duty. But I shall continue to fight and spread the message of the coming Fascist European Imperium, to denounce its enemies, the Jewish Bolshevisms of Washington and Moscow, and to remain a loyal member of the *Front*. So I say: God speed Europe's rebirth!

Front Hail
P. J. Huxley-Blythe

"FÜHRER" IN SEARCH OF A FOLLOWING!!!
by A. GANNON

Occasions for laughter are rare indeed in England these days. However, this week saw such an occasion. Let me heartily recommend to all wearied by Socialist starvation, nauseated by Jewish corruption, and enraged by popular complacency—the funniest thing yet; it is the organ of the Mosley circus, *Union*, number 58, dated March 10th.

Most of the entire front page of this hilarious sheet is devoted to the news "Mosley Moves to Ireland." The negative suggestion is almost unbelievable. Like a man who feels it apt to hang a card around his neck bearing the legend "I am not a thief." *Union* feels obliged to state, and more than once, that this move is no "retreat," that Mosley's reasons are "entirely convincing" and "welcome" (start looking around for another job, Raven Thomson!). Shining forth like Truth from the proverbial bushel are verities like this: "As far as members of the Movement in this country are concerned the change will make no difference whatsoever, as their Leader will be *perfectly free* to spend as much or more time in this country, as he has spent in British headquarters during the past year or so" (a time less than that referred to is not demonstratable). Other priceless pieces are: "*We* shall lose nothing from this move, from which Europe as a whole will gain so much," and "in fact all members will recognize that this is the only possible answer to a pettyfogging tyrannical Government . . ." To run-away from your alleged enemies is the "only possible answer," that is for a molsey. Then follows what amounts to a gigantic insult to the intelligence, entirely presumed, we admit, of all readers of *Union*, and, in particular, to performers in the Mosley Circus. Here it is: "Anyone who seriously wishes to devote himself to the Union of Europe is compelled to seek another base . . ." If this statement means anything it means that all members of the Mosley Circus must immediately leave England and settle elsewhere, presumably in Eire, otherwise they will be doing nothing of any use to Europe. The irreducible minimum of people living in England still attaching any importance to Mosley are, self-evidently, not bright, but if they cannot see through the hollow mockery of this classic mosleyism, then they are, indeed, quite institutional in their mosley-fixation. Of course, except for the unimportant item of personal wealth, all Mosleyites have an opportunity equal to that of Sir Oswald to leave the "Island Prison" and to seek in Eire, sustained by thick steaks and succulent bacon rashers, a better means of serving Europe. Long ago, as a very young member of the pre-war BUF, I used to join in singing a popular parody of "Onward Christian Soldiers" which went something like this: Onward Conscript Army marching as to war, Isaac Hore-Belisha[6] leads you from the rear. A further variation on the same theme may now suggest itself to Mosley adherents.

Side by side with Raven Thomson's adieu to the "Leader" is a framed statement by the "Leader" himself. Written in his typical wordy, pompous, post-War style, the "Leader" takes no less than five paragraphs to get over the message that he doesn't relish the idea of prison-life just for the privilege of addressing a few ticket-holders behind locked doors twice a year, or maybe even once. He wants to "break locks" or something else equally vague—a sort of frustrated Will-to-Burglary.

What are the real facts behind the Mosley run-out? They are (1) Mosley's complete failure to attract any measurable following in Britain. (2) Mosley's inability to hold his initial body of supporters. (3) Mosley's rejection as the Leader of Europe by all major European Fascist movements. (4) Mosley's cowardice in the face of minor difficulties within Britain and his deliberate

---

[6] Isaac Hore-Belisha (1893–1957) was a British Jew who was Minister for War in Neville Chamberlain's government between 1937 and 1940. He called for Britain to prepare itself for war against Germany, and is regarded as one of the politicians most responsible for Britain's declaration of war in September 1939.

abstention from addressing genuine public meetings.

To cover up his own utter defeat, and spiritual-isolation, Mosley has employed a simple technique of deception, to his residual followers within Britain he has pretended that his main support lay on the Mainland of Europe, and in doing this, banked upon their lack of intelligence of current Fascist developments on the Mainland. Alternatively, Mosley has informed his tiny band that the present lack of support by the people of Britain is of no consequence, and that their chance will come when a major economic depression hits Britain. This depression has been arriving almost weekly for the past two years; like the charlatans of religion Mosley promises a Victory in the Hereafter if only the ashes of the present will be sucked with faith. That such a transparent deception should still succeed with Mosley's few supporters is the greatest proof of their general political ignorance. Of course, his paid lackeys are under no real illusion as to the failure of the "Leader," but they prefer their present occupations to the prospects of a reversion to their former callings as laundry-van drivers, laborers, junior clerks, and stair-sweepers; for them Mosley represents social-security—that and nothing more.

On the Mainland Mosley has told a slightly different story to account for his failure within Britain, for at various times representatives of the European movements have visited Britain to see at first-hand the decaying political mushroom which is Union Movement. Unlike Mosley's humble few, these men have been shrewd, experienced political organizers. In spite of their obvious difficulties, language and unfamiliarity with the British locale, they have soon perceived the truth of the situation. To these representatives of genuine political organisms, mosley has lyingly asserted that the Labour administration has persecuted him and prevented his access to large public meeting halls and open-air sites. The truth is, that Mosley has made no attempt to engage any large hall for the purpose of holding a mass-meeting. Many such halls throughout Britain have been, and still are readily available to him. When they have been suggested to him by past officers of the movement, he has refused them all, for reasons which were entirely unconvincing and hollow. His failure to address large open-air rallies is equally of his own doing. In the three years of Union Movement's existence, mosley has addressed only one genuine public meeting, for his few comic-opera appearances before small audiences of ticket-holders, in tiny halls behind locked doors are in no sense public meetings. Within eighteen months of its establishment, Union Movement had lost eight-tenths of its effectivess as a result of Mosley's cowardice and lack of purpose. None of these facts have, in the end, escaped the genuine European movements of the Mainland, and they now know mosley for what he is: a strutting, pompous poseur—a matinee-idol grown old and fat, rejected by the gallery, but still trying to keep up face. Such is Oswald Mosley—the micawber[7] of British politics, the "Leader" without a following!

Perhaps the most worthless attempt to deceive made by Mosley, was his suggestion of a voting scheme for a European Assembly, whereby any European could be elected by any group of Europeans to the Assembly, even if they were resident in a different country to that of the candidate. What this suggestion meant really was that as no British electors could be found who would vote for Mosley under any circumstances, perhaps some ill-informed group of people somewhere in Europe would vote for him, in the mistaken belief that he had something in common with Hitler and Mussolini. This attempt to deceive has failed like the others, but if there is anywhere in Europe one man who is still unconvinced of the charlatanism of Mosley, let that man read the Mosley sheet *Union*. There he will find the Enemy terminology used in toto, references to "Gestapo tactics," cheap sneers at Hitler and Mussolini, who are alleged to have held narrow views and to have failed, whereas Mosley's mind is broad and he has succeeded. Decriers of Fascism are welcomed into Union Movement with open-arms, and criticism of the role of Jewish Washington, Churchill, Truman, and of the Jewish Na-

---

[7] A reference to the character of Wilkins Micawber in Charles Dickens' novel *David Copperfield*. Micawber is a dogged optimist who constantly reiterates his confidence that "something will turn up" to resolve whatever problems are at hand.

tion is verboten. The classic example of this journalistic diarrhea was an attempt to prove that it is the Jews who are the Fascists, and not Union Movement, which abhors the word and can only bear to print it in inverted commas, as an unjustifiable adjective when applied to them. By such thomschian[8] logic it will emerge that as the Jews are the Fascists—then Union Movement is the Jew. We will not disagree with the latter proposition.

The final Mosley lie is revealed by his own miserable newssheet. That is, that he is leaving Britain because his entry to, movement within, and exit from Britain is somehow restricted by the Labour regime. For two years Mosley has been free to leave Britain as he wished and to return at will, and *Union is at pains to assure the readers that this situation is unchanged! So why is Mosley running away?* When mosley received his passport two years ago it proved that the Jews and their creatures had no fear of him, and were prepared to let him indulge his *will-to-tour* and *will-to-comfort.* One of Mosley's super-political uses of this freedom was to lunch with that famous hostess of Kosher society, the three-quarters Jewess Mrs. R. Fellowes (Sinder-von Lowenthal), upon her yacht. Any day now we may hear of a resumption of Mosley's former synagogue-opening activities, as in the days when he referred to the followers of the Duce as "ice-cream men in blackshirts." Farewell, Sir Oswald—*and good riddance!*

❖ ❖ ❖

With this issue of *Frontfighter* we say *au revoir* to P. J. Huxley-Blythe as Editor. We are losing an Editor, but not a comrade. He will be succeeded by the Director of Organization, L. F. Simmons. February and March issues have been combined to enable publication of the April and consecutive issues on time.

ALL WITHIN THE FRONT—
NONE OUTSIDE THE FRONT—
NONE AGAINST THE FRONT

[8] Perhaps a reference to Alexander Raven Thomson (1899–1955), who is mentioned elsewhere in the article. Thomson was the chief ideologue of Mosley's British Union of Fascists and post-war Union Movement.

FRONTFIGHTER

Voice of the EUROPEAN LIBERATION FRONT in Great Britain

Editor:
L.F. Simmons

Price: 2d.
12 Issues 3/- P.F.

Published by BCM/Westropa Press,
London, W.C.1.

Number 11 APRIL 1951-XXIX E.F.

MUSSOLINI THE IMMORTAL!

This issue of *Frontfighter* is dedicated to the memory of Benito Mussolini—European Hero and Martyr. It is just six years since the Duce was foully murdered—April 28, 1945—by the agents of the Kremlin. But the march which led to the Piazza Venezia did not end in the Piazzale Loeto!

When the history of the twentieth century is written it will emerge that the idea which dominated the political life of that Century was Mussolini's *Dottrino de Fascismo*. Before the mantle of martyrdom descended upon the shoulders of the Duce, the Idea of Fascism had reached the ends of the Earth. The final actualization of this Idea will be completed in the second-half of this Century. Let no man doubt this: The events of 1945 may only be viewed as a temporary set-back, for the growth of the Fascist European Imperium is, like all *real* things, organic. As a plant attacked by parasites becomes stunted and retarded before the life-force conquers and destroys the invaders, so has Europe, under the plague of the Jewish Bolshevisms of Moscow and Washington, become frustrated and distorted. But the roots of the European Civilization grow deep and wide. Soon will come the counter-offensive, the destruction of the Jewish pestilence, and the full flowering of the European Imperium.

The tragedy of Benito Mussolini, and of his comrade Adolf Hitler, was the usual one which befalls all men of genius and destiny—that of being born ahead of contemporary political thought and action. What was true of Napoleon Bonaparte was equally true of Mussolini and Hitler. To them fell the task of striking the death-blows at the bleated mass of putrefaction which is the Jewish Mammon System; the blows from which we shall see it does not recover.

On the horizon, summoned by Destiny, appears the Shining State of the Future—the hierarchical, monolithic, heroic Fascist European Imperium, conceived by the brilliant Mussolini, and nourished by the blood and sacrifice of the Duce and Führer and the countless legionnaires of Europe. Over our ranks waves the symbol of the New Order—the Sword-banner. Our eyes are fixed resolutely on the Jewish, extra-European, enemy horde. *We shall not fail!*

ARGENTINE ENIGMA???

This item does *not* relate to the winding-up of the newspaper *La Prensa* of Buenos Aires, by the Argentine Government. It *does* relate to the disgraceful persecution of Emilio Gutiérrez Herrero, Secretary-General of the *Union Civica Nacionalista*, of Argentina, by the Argentine Government. Our relations with the UCN are of the best, based as they are on the solid ground of a common ideology and a practical, comradely solidarity of action.

It has long been believed by European Fascists that the Argentine Government was a quasi-Fascist regime: it was hoped that it would become a *real* Fascist state. It is true that the greatest reason for this belief was a negative reason, turning on the point that all the *wrong* interests of the world appeared to be attacking General Perón and his Government. Lesser reasons, on the positive side, were General Perón's constructive attitude to the Spanish Government, and his immigration policy towards German and Italian exiles. However, for a long time now certain disquieting developments have been apparent. One of these, and the most important, by far, has been the attitude of the Argentine Government in regard to the Jewish World Pest. That reliable organ of Jewish opinion, the *Jewish Chronicle* of London, has on several occasions referred to the existence of Jewish organizations in Argentina which are "pledged" to the support of the Perónista regime: the same source has also reported General Perón as stating that he will not permit any organized anti-Jewish activity in Argentina. Other official stupidities include the pronouncements that the Perónista party is based on the same aspirations as the "British" Labour Party, which is enough in itself to make any European Fascist vomit. A lot more could be said in similar vein. Someone should inform General Perón, for his country's good, and his own, of what happens to those who get into bed with the Jews—they are usually found suffocated! Jewry knows only one law of conduct in regard to Gentiles—that of a blood-sucking vampire. Let General Perón believe he is "using" the Jews. He will learn the hard way, from which there is no recovery.

In marked contrast to the mediocre conduct of the Perónista party is that of the UCN and the courageous Emilio Gutiérrez Herrero. At whatever cost to himself, this man and his loyal comrades have attacked the triple, satanic creations of Jewry: Masonry, Communism, and Finance-Capitalism. For so doing, Gutiérrez Herrero has undergone police persecution, detention, and now exile from his beloved Argentina. All this at the hands of a regime which was thought to be becoming one-of-us.

With the greatest deliberation, we of the *Front* stand shoulder-to-shoulder with Gutiérrez Herrero and the *Union Civica Nacionalista*. Our aims are the same—*our enemies are the same!*

A. Gannon
Frontleader

DOCTRINE OF FASCISM

The considered statements of really great men are timeless. The following quotations have been extracted from the *Doctrine of Fascism* by Benito Mussolini, and from the appendix to that work:

"Fascism sees in the world not only those superficial material aspects in which man appears as an individual, standing by himself, self-centered, subject to natural law which instinctively urges him toward a life of selfish momentary pleasure; it sees not only the individual but the nation and the country; individuals and generations bound together by a moral law with common traditions and a mission which, suppressing the instinct for life closed in a brief circle of pleasure, builds up a higher life, founded on duty, a life free from limitations of time and space, in which the individual, by self-sacrifice, the renunciation of self-interest, by death itself, can achieve that purely spiritual existence in which his value as a man exists."

"Never before have the peoples thirsted for authority, direction, order, as they do now. If each age has its doctrine, then innumerable symptoms indicate that the doctrine of our age is the Fascist. That it is vital is shown by the fact that it has aroused a faith; that this faith has conquered souls is shown by the fact that Fascism can point to its fallen heroes and its martyrs."

"Today I hold that Fascism as an idea, a doctrine, a realization, is universal: It is Italian in its particular institutions, but it is universal in the spirit, nor could it be otherwise. The spirit is universal by reason of its nature. Therefore anyone may foresee a Fascist Europe drawing inspiration for her institutions from the doctrine and practice of Fascism; Europe, in other words, giving a Fascist turn to the solution of problems which beset a modern State, the Twentieth Century State which is very different from the States existing before 1789, and the States formed immediately after. Today Fascism fulfills universal requirements, Fascism solves the threefold problem of relations between State and individual, between State and associations, between associations and organized associations."

". . . Democratic regimes may be described as those under which the people are, from time to time, deluded into the belief that they exercise sovereignty, while all the time real sovereignty resides in and is exercised by other and sometimes irresponsible and secret forces. Democracy is a kingless regime infested by many kings who are sometimes more exclusive, tyrannical, and destructive than one, even if he be a tyrant."

"I believe that . . . if a people wish to live they should develop a will-to-power, otherwise they vegetate, live miserably, and become prey to a stronger people, in whom this will-to-power is developed to a higher degree."

BELIEVE — OBEY — FIGHT!

THE LIE OF THE SIX MILLION

Surely the greatest lie churned out by the Jewish propaganda factories is the allegation that National-Socialist Germany exterminated six million Jews. The very immensity of this lie was calculated to ensure its belief by the gullible masses. It has been slavishly repeated by all sections of the Yellow Press, whether allegedly socialist or avowedly capitalist, for more than six years. The idea behind the Big Lie was to arouse popular hatred against the German Nation, thus facilitating the murder of the German leaders for alleged crimes against humanity by the Jewish terror-machine, and the starvation and humiliation of the entire German people.

On numerous occasions the truth has come out, and the Big Lie has been revealed in all its hollowness. Of course, these instances have been ignored by the Yellow Press, which hopes that the Big Lie can still be exploited for a few more years. In the course of the last month our attention has been drawn to two more significant statements bearing upon this issue. The first is extracted from *The Broom* of San Diego, Cal., USA, dated January 17, 1949, and reads:

> *Aufbau,* a Jewish weekly published in the German language in New York City, finally admits in its *Anti-Anti* column, written by Kurt Heller, December 24, that the whole story about Hitler killing six million Jews is pure fabrication.

The second is quoted in the *Cross and the Flag,* St. Louis, Mo., USA, January 1951, and has been extracted from Lyr Clark Van Hyning's journal *Women's Voice,* of USA. It reads:

> In 1948 there were in the world 15,600,000 to 18,700,000 Jews; according to Hanson W. Baldwin, who is a leading authority on matters relating to population.
>
> In 1938 there were in the world 15,688,259 Jews. These figures are from the *World Almanac,* which figures were given to said publication by the American Jewish Commit-

tee and the Jewish Statistical Bureau of the Synagogues of America.

Where are those 6,000,000 Jews who were murdered by Hitler? . . .

EUROPA NAZIONE

The first issue of this new Italian journal contains a review of the book *Imperium*, by Ulick Varange, written by Italy's greatest living authoritarian philosopher, Julius Evola. *You must read* Imperium! Order *your* copy (2 vols.) *today*, price 12/6d., post free from BCM/Westropa Press, London, W. C. 1. Ask for free resume of comment on this Book by famous Europeans.

FRONTFIGHTER
"The Voice of the European Liberation Front in Great Britain"
Number 13, June 1951-XXIX E. F.

Editor: L. F. Simmons

GREAT ELECTION RESULTS IN EUROPE

We of the European Liberation Front are greatly heartened to learn of the successes of the MSI in Italy and the SRP in Germany.

It is understandable that the Italians and Germans, who have tried the Leadership principle and also the decadent Democratic Party system, should once again turn their backs on the old way of life and the Party squabbles. For these people know the vital realities of life and on *no* account will they give them up.

The results of the Italian and German elections gives us of the Front a real target to emulate. Now that the struggle in this country is in full swing, we shall not fail them. Never again must we twentieth-century thinkers fall into the trap of the Yesterday thinkers and go to war with our European brothers.

With the final success of the MSI, SRP, and the ELF against

the inner traitors, the life and defense of the European Culture is assured. With such great results in so little time after the terror that was unleashed against Europe, and with the success of the ELF in this country, we know that the inevitable must soon take place. That which was written only yesterday in the *Proclamation of London*, we know tomorrow will be reality.

L. F. Simmons.

POLICY TOWARD THE ISLAND

[Reproduced as Chapter 16, "The Death of England," in this volume.]

ARE *YOU* DOING ENOUGH!

Throughout the coming summer months the *Front* will engage itself in an intensive propaganda campaign of outdoor public meetings, covering the principal towns of the North, North-West, North-East, and North Midlands of England.

A similar campaign last summer produced markedly successful results, and from the strong-points established then, we are now expanding and consolidating.

The first public meeting of 1951 was held on northern redoubt—Preston Market Square—on Sunday, June 3rd. As usual on this site, a great and enthusiastic crowd assembled to hear the Director of Organization, L. F. Simmons, the Frontleader, A. Gannon, and myself deliver the message and the challenge of the *Front* to International Jewish Finance and International Jewish Communism. This sturdy town of Preston is going to prove to be a "Lower Saxony"[9] for the *Front*. The Reds dare not speak there. The Tories are despised. The Socialists are rejected. We do not have to deal with hecklers or Trouble-raisers at Preston—the Prestonians deal with this pest themselves. Since June 3rd, a schedule of bi-monthly meetings has been arranged for Preston,

---

[9] Before and during the Third Reich, Lower Saxony was a center of staunch support for the NSDAP.

and our other open-air venues. By the end of the current year, we hope to be in a position to enter candidates for the Preston municipal elections.

It is also encouraging to note that our sales of *Frontfighter* have continued to rise with each month of publication. The letters of appreciation and congratulations which we receive from our readers, all over the world, are a constant inspiration to us all. Nevertheless, we feel that many of our readers and supporters could do more in the way of concrete, practical support than they are at present doing. Since we commenced publication of *Frontfighter*, the cost of duplicating paper has risen three hundred percent, and stencils have undergone a further sharp increase. To meet the steadily increasing demand for *Frontfighter* we installed new duplicating equipment, and we feel sure our readers will understand the expense of such a step under present conditions. As a slight measure of economy, we have altered the format of *Frontfighter* and left the price of this item unchanged at 2d. However, the newly increased cost of mailing will have to be borne by our readers, and, thus, from this Issue onwards the charge for 12 issues of *Frontfighter* will be increased to 3/6.

Our message is not addressed to the fifty-percenters, the do-noughts, or the pleasure-mad escapists. We believe that our readers and supporters are serious-minded, determined people, who realize that the task we have undertaken is immense, dangerous, and calls for a spirit of sacrifice. Thus, we call upon you to increase your efforts in our support; to gain for us even more new readers; to give us some of the money—however little—you spend weekly on routine pleasure, smoking, cinemas, sport, etc. This money will be made to *fight!* The *Front* employs no professional hangers-on. All its staff are unpaid, voluntary workers.

Will *you* help us? Send your donations, names of new readers to me: c/o BCM/Westropa Press, London, W. C. 1.

Thos. Davies
Director of Propaganda.

FRONTFIGHTER

Voice of the EUROPEAN LIBERATION FRONT in Great Britain

Editor:

L.F. Simmons

12 Issues
5/6 P.F.
Subscription of n of
Honour 10/8

Published by BCM/Westropa Press
London, W.C.1.

Number 23 APRIL 1952-XXX E.F.

ANNIVERSARY OF THE HEROES

It is just seven years since the passing of the Duce and the Führer and seven years in which the vindication of their policies has been complete.

The physical death of Mussolini and Hitler has not diminished their dynamic presence. Greater even in death than their pygmy-like would-be murderers are in life, their spiritual leadership lives on in the new Fascist movements of the present, reaching now far beyond the old national boundaries of the German Reich and the Italian Empire to embrace all Europe and the outposts of Europeans overseas.

Today, many who were opposed to Hitler and Mussolini in their lifetime, owing to the distortion of the truth and the mass-production of lies, now see through the mountain of perfidy and recognize the greatness of their mission.

In every Western land at this moment new Fascist movements are operating, and in Germany, Italy, and Austria these are of great strength, and are already on the eve of victory. To the future which will be as great as the momentarily interrupted past we give eternal salutes—HEIL HITLER! VIVA IL DUCE!

L. F. Simmons

WHAT THE FRONT IS FIGHTING FOR!

POINT 5:
CLEANSING OF THE SOUL OF EUROPE FROM THE ETHICAL SYPHILIS

OF HOLLYWOOD & THE MARXIST BOLSHEVISM OF MOSCOW

Who has never at times looked upon what passes for the youth of Britain, France, and the other administrative areas of Washington Occupied Europe, and not despaired of the Future? Did we not know in our hearts that this is *not* the Youth of Europe we should, indeed, feel incurably saddened. Nevertheless, this pathological and retarded stratum is too serious to be ignored. Hag-ridden with Sex, shaking and twitching to the mechanistic, afro-israeli cacophony of bebop, reefer-doped and alcohol-stewed, this motley group of long-haired males and short-haired females requires—and will receive—a major operation. In this group God has been replaced by Lust, the Priest by the Psycho-analyst, the Hero and Heroine by the promiscuous Lounge-Lizard and the glittering Harlot. For all of these things Jewish Hollywood is responsible. This doctrine of decadence and degeneration has been preached without pause since Hollywood began. Its objective has been the seduction of the youth from the stern, selfless, patriotic tasks which constitute the duty of each generation.

More readily understood, and therefore not as dangerous, is the virus of Jewish Bolshevism. Here the destruction of religion, patriotism, tradition, has been open and blatant and has aroused a strong reaction. Very few people in any European land fail to recognize the essential negation of Bolshevism, and short of European occupation by the Red Army it has no possibility of establishing itself openly on any governmental level. What is not so well understood is the *fact* that Bolshevism is the technical spearhead of the Jew-organized Colored Revolution—the revolution of asiatics and negroes to destroy the West. Against the demoralization of Jewish Hollywood and the barbarism of Jewish Bolshevism we oppose the unconquerable spirit of white, Christian Europe!

AMERICA'S TWO POLITICAL FACTIONS, PART 2

[Reproduced in Chapter 18, "America's Two Political Factions," in this volume.]

Europe vs. Israel

Herbert Kuehne
Rio de Janeiro, Brasil

In a time like the present, in which cant and hypocrisy allied with decadence and incompetence are stultifying a world which God planned better, it is worthwhile to seek out an honest viewpoint.

In the *Noite*, a widely read evening paper of Rio de Janeiro, there appeared in the final edition of January 10th, 1952, an AFP dispatch from Jerusalem, which ought to be brought to the attention of every European.

The dispatch, freely but faithfully translated, reads as follows:

We Will Destroy Any Envoy & Destroy Any German Goods

> Jerusalem, January 10th (AFP) The spokesman of a group of former members of Irgun Zwi Leumi and the Stern Gang[10] (hitherto non-political movements) declared today to a journalist of *France-Presse* that "any diplomatic representative or plenipotentiary for trade negotiations of Eastern or Western Germany, who sets foot on the soil of Israel will be treated as a war criminal, condemned, and stuck like a pig."
>
> The spokesman added: "We have no connection with any political party, but we shall never endure any connection between Israel and Germany, and if need be we shall resort to terror.
>
> "Every German product that may come into Israel will be seized and destroyed, even [if] it is already in the course of trade. We most earnestly warn all Israelitic firms not to enter into any commercial relations with West or East Germany."

---

[10] Irgun and the Stern Gang were Zionist terrorist groups which sought to evict the British and repress the Arabs through assassinations and bombings in the years prior to Israel's independence in 1948.

It is lamentable that the so-called leaders of occupied Germany cannot muster up even a fraction of the attitude which characterizes the leading men of the operetta State of Israel. The whole situation becomes most interesting when one remembers that present-day Germany counts great numbers of Jews in its highest places. Is the unvarnished Israeli threat also against these, or are only non-Jews included?

This Jewish attitude neither surprises nor frightens us. We are grateful for its frankness—but how can Messrs. Heuss and Adenauer now be consoled? Perhaps they will notice the practical implications which lie hidden in this Jewish emotional outburst?

The "German" (?) Foreign Office can prescribe a holiday in Israel for its used-up diplomats, or for those gentlemen approaching the age of retirement. This will result in a great saving for the Reich, and will in no way injure the interests of Germany, for on the one hand the "German" Foreign Office does not dare to pursue a German policy, and on the other hand there are no politicians at the helm who would even know how to pursue such a policy!

FROM *THE PROCLAMATION OF LONDON*

[Two paragraphs reprinted verbatim from "The Proclamation of London" chapter in this volume, the first starting with "The message of Hollywood is the total significance of the isolated individual . . ." and the second with "This condition of degeneration . . ."]

In Memoriam — Francis P. Yockey

H. Keith Thompson

1960

Editors' Note

This poetic eulogy to Yockey was written by H. Keith Thompson who, besides Frederick Weiss, was Yockey's closest American colleague. This is probably the first time the eulogy has ever been published. It is reproduced from what is also most likely the only copy, which was provided courtesy of Mrs. Elisabeth Carto from the literary estate of her late husband, Willis A. Carto, as no copy appears in the H. Keith Thompson papers held at Stanford University, nor in the Keith Stimely collection held at the University of Oregon.

We knew him well, as few men knew
His nobility of purpose and his fiery determination
To set aright a world of rapidly diminishing values;
These tasks to him mattered,
Not the bourgeois struggle for comfort and convenience,
Nor the magnet of conformity to the petty edicts
Of a suicide-bent Society.
When the history of this century is written,
There will be chroniclers who will remember
The contributions of Francis Yockey—
Of Ulick Varange and *Imperium*.
The European Liberation Front will remember,
An embattled continent will remember,
And honor his sacrifice.

H. K. T. 1960

ABOUT THE CONTRIBUTORS

FRANCIS PARKER YOCKEY (1917–1960) was born in Chicago to an upper-middle class family of Irish and German descent. Yockey gave a touch of genius (his IQ was measured at 170) to everything in which he was involved. His destiny would probably have been as a concert pianist, but that was aborted by a car accident as a youth. Given Yockey's Catholic upbringing and education, his outlook was probably shaped at an early age by counter-Enlightenment ideas. At college he was writing Spenglerian essays, and his ideas were already maturely formed. He had also become a notable presence in the Rightist and America First movements. A brilliant student, he attended Georgetown University's School of Foreign Service, De Paul Law School, and Notre Dame Law School, receiving his degree in law *cum laude* in 1941.

Despite his known association with such notorious figures as William Pelley of the Silver Shirt Legion and Father Charles Coughlin, Yockey entered the Army but promptly sought an honorable discharge by feigning mental illness, which was to backfire on him two decades later. He was next employed as assistant district attorney for Wayne County (Detroit). In 1946, eager to get to Europe to seek out what remained of the European resistance, he joined the Allied war crimes tribunal in Wiesbaden, where he promptly found himself out of favor with his superiors, and returned to the United States.

A perpetual traveler, Yockey went to Britain in mid-1947 where he made initial contact with followers of the British Fascist leader Sir Oswald Mosley, who were planning Mosley's return to politics. He then went to Ireland, where at Brittas Bay he secluded himself for months to write *Imperium*, his *magnum opus*. Although Yockey modestly insisted that he was merely following Spengler, his conception of "cultural vitalism" added a new dimension to historiographical thought, seeking out the organic historical laws that have resulted in the rise and fall of a succession of civilizations, which he believed would lead to the fulfilment of the destiny of Western Civilization as an organic unity, liberated from the "inner traitor" and the "outer enemy."

With his manuscript, he returned to England with the hope that Oswald Mosley would publish *Imperium* under his own name as the leader of a movement for European unity. The offer was rebuffed because of ideological differences between the two. Yockey, having joined Mosley's Union Movement and served in the overseas liaison office, left the movement, along with some key members such as Guy Chesham and Antony Gannon, taking with them about 150 members—that is, about 10% of the membership—to form the European Liberation Front in 1948. Although there was acrimony between the supporters of Yockey and Mosley, Sir Oswald himself never seems to have uttered anything but favorable words about Yockey when asked, despite wide ideological differences.

Imperium was published in two volumes in 1948. In 1949 *The Proclamation of London of the European Liberation Front* was published as a synopsis (backdated to 1948 because it was meant to be an answer to *The Communist Manifesto* on its 100th anniversary). The activities of the European Liberation Front were more dynamic than is often supposed. Outdoor speaking was a regular event. A newsletter, *Frontfighter*, was published.

Favorable reactions to *Imperium* were forthcoming from notable individuals such as Captain Basil Liddell Hart, the military historian; Major General J. F. C. Fuller, the tank strategy expert and Mosley's pre-war military adviser; German veteran leader Major General Otto Remer; German air ace Hans Rudel; the German émigrés centered around *Der Weg* in Argentina; former South African cabinet minister Oswald Pirow; and the pre-war Canadian Fascist leader Adrien Arcand. Conversely, diehard anti-Semites such as Arnold Leese of the pre-war Imperial Fascist League and The Britons Society, regarded as anathema Yockey's Spenglerian definition of "race" and his heretical view that the USSR had freed itself from Jewish control.

Yockey continued to seek contacts throughout the world. In the US he found mentors in German World War I veteran Frederick Weiss, founder of LeBlanc Publications, and H. Keith Thompson, who had maintained contact with German military and political notables before and after World War II. Attempting to forge links with Gerald L. K. Smith—who had been Governor Huey Long's aide in Depression-era Louisiana, and who was now heading the Christian Nationalist Crusade with comparatively large resources—proved futile, despite the enthusiastic applause Yockey received from audiences at two Smith rallies. The failure was symptomatic of the inability of much of the Right in Europe and the US to adapt to new post-war realities.

Traveling between the US and Europe at will, like a Scarlet Pimpernel, on multiple passports, a step ahead of Military Intelligence, the State Department, the CIA, the FBI, and Interpol, Yockey worked for the American Red Cross in Germany; addressed a neo-Fascist rally in Naples in 1951, organized by Princess Maria Pignatelli, a war heroine of the Italian Social Republic; stayed with Arcand in Canada the same year, and even travelled through the Soviet bloc and to Cuba at the height of the Cold War, for reasons that remain conjectural, but which were of particular concern for the US regime.

Also in 1951, the Czechoslovak Soviet regime embarked on purging "Zionists" (sic) from their ranks and the "Prague treason trial," at which it is believed Yockey was present, was the title of one of Yockey's most controversial essays among the Right. In 1953 Yockey was in Egypt writing anti-Zionist material for the newly formed Ministry of National Guidance of the Nasser regime. The following year he was in the US, in his second marriage, playing piano at a cocktail bar and teaching piano in California. In 1955 he was back in Germany under the name of Edward Max Price, then as Franz Yorck, working for two of Germany's leading magazines, *Quick* and *Weltbild*. During 1954 to 1956 Yockey traveled around Western Europe, but was completely off the FBI radar during 1955 to 1958, possibly living in the Soviet bloc. The FBI was making bizarre guesses as to Yockey's whereabouts and identity, wondering whether he was the underground segregationist "The Patriot," who was causing trouble in the South, or the journalist Don Bell.

Yockey's luck ran out in June of 1960. A luggage mix-up at

Fort Worth Airport, Texas, had resulted in a search to identify the owner. Multiple passports were found. Yockey was arrested at the Oakland, California home of an enigmatic Jewish acquaintance, Alex Scharf, the precise circumstances of Yockey's relationship with Scharf remaining a mystery. After a dash to escape, during which an FBI agent was injured, Yockey was arraigned before US Commissioner Joseph Karesh, a some-time rabbi, who set Yockey's bail at $50,000 at the request of the State Department. With the prospect of a mental examination looming, his foremost concern was that information on friends and colleagues would be extracted from him and that psychiatric "treatment" would reduce him to a vegetative state.

Yockey took his life with a cyanide pill during the night of June 16–17, 1960. That evening Assistant US Attorney Willian Clancy had commented that he had come into possession of a "super-secret file" on Yockey, which was "dynamite." The nature of that file, and the means by which Yockey obtained the cyanide pill, remain unknown. Yockey's enduring legacy remains with his writings: *Imperium, Proclamation of London, The Enemy of Europe*, and his many essays.

KERRY BOLTON (b. 1956) has certifications in theology, historical theology, social work, and psychology. He is widely published in scholarly and specialist journals, such as *India Quarterly; Journal of Social, Political, & Economic Studies; International Journal of Social Economics*, and others. He has also been a contributing writer for *Foreign Policy Journal* and *New Dawn*. His published books include *Artists of the Right; More Artists of the Right; Revolution from Above; The Parihaka Cult; The Psychotic Left; Stalin: The Enduring Legacy; Babel Inc.; The Decline & Fall of Civilisations; The Banking Swindle; Opposing the Money Lenders; The Occult & Subversive Movements; Geopolitics of the Indo-Pacific; Perón & Perónism; Russia & the Fight against Globalisation; Yockey: A Fascist Odyssey*; and *Zionism, Islam & the West*. He has also annotated and edited a selection of Oswald Spengler's essays entitled *Prussian Socialism & Other Essays*. Bolton is a Fellow of several learned societies.

John Morgan (b. 1973) was raised in New York State and graduated with a degree in literature from the University of Michigan. He was one of the founders of Integral Tradition Publishing in 2006, and was also a founder of its successor, Arktos Media, in 2010, where he served as Editor-in-Chief until 2016. He was Book Editor at Counter-Currents Publishing from 2016–2019. He has written for *Counter-Currents*, *New Dawn*, and other publications.

Charles Harold Keith Thompson, Jr. (1922–2002), more familiarly known as H. Keith Thompson, was born in Orange, New Jersey. While serving in the US Navy and later the Marine Corps, he became sympathetic to both National Socialism and Communism. For the remainder of his life he was a prominent organizer, activist, and donor on the Right, both in America and internationally, and was a close confidante and supporter of Yockey.

Frederick Charles Ferdinand Weiss (1885–1968) was, along with H. Keith Thompson, Yockey's primary collaborator in America. Born in Germany, Weiss emigrated to the US in 1909 but returned in 1914 to serve in the German army during the First World War. Although he lived in the US for the remainder of his life, Weiss never became a naturalized citizen. Weiss, like Yockey, was a dedicated Spenglerian who viewed America as "the enemy of Europe." Weiss collaborated with Yockey and Thompson on joint literary projects that were published by Weiss' Le Blanc Publications under the authorship of "X. Y. Z." Their style and ideas were so similar it is difficult to determine who authored which texts.

Douglas T. Kaye was the founder of the satirical Yockeyite periodical *TRUD*, which ran from 1968 until 1972 and published a serialized translation of part of Yockey's *The Enemy of Europe*. Kaye also founded Nordland Press, which published Yockey's *The Proclamation of London* and *Four Essays*. A close friend of Yockey's mentor Frederick Weiss and his wife Maria, Kaye was the custodian of many anecdotes about Yockey as well as Yockey's "China Estimate," which thanks to him is published in this volume.

John Anthony Gannon was Yockey's closest colleague in Britain, and a co-founder of the European Liberation Front (ELF). Gannon had previously been a prominent speaker of Mosley's British Union of Fascists (BUF), leading to his detention during the Second World War, and met Yockey at the founding of the post-war Union Movement (UM), which he later resigned from to co-found the ELF. He left England for South America in 1954 and had no further contact with Yockey.

Peter Huxley-Blythe (1925–2013) was a naval officer who served throughout the Second World War. Huxley-Blythe had joined the British Union of Fascists in 1935 and soon became a BUF speaker in the north of England. He was later a speaker for the Union Movement as well. Having become disillusioned with Mosley, he left the UM in 1949 and joined the European Liberation Front. He is named as the editor of *Frontfigher* until the tenth issue, when he was recalled to the Royal Fleet Reserve in early 1951. Huxley-Blythe eventually turned against Yockey, regarding him as pro-Soviet. He became involved in White Russian émigré intrigues and made a name for himself as the author of *The East Comes West* (1964), a book about the forcible repatriation by the British Army of anti-Soviet Russians back to the USSR at the end of the war. In 2005, Huxley-Blythe wrote a glowing reappraisal of Yockey for *The Barnes Review*.

Len F. Simmons, Director of Organisation for the European Liberation Front and an editor of *Frontfighter*, was a motor mechanic by trade.

Thomas Davies was Director of Propaganda for the European Liberation Front.

Herbert Kuehne was a Brazil-based contributor to *Frontfighter*.

INDEX

Numbers in bold refer to a whole chapter or section devoted to a particular topic.

T

CPSIA information can be obtained
at www.ICGtesting.com
Printed in the USA
LVHW091312220720
661281LV00002B/345